macOS® Ventura™

by Guy Hart-Davis
International Man of macOS

macOS® Ventura™ For Dummies®

Published by: **John Wiley & Sons, Inc.**, 111 River Street, Hoboken, NJ 07030-5774, www.wiley.com

Copyright © 2023 by John Wiley & Sons, Inc., Hoboken, New Jersey

Published simultaneously in Canada

macOS® Ventura™

A Wiley Brand

Contents at a Glance

Table of Contents

Introduction

L ooks like you've made three good choices: a Mac, macOS Ventura (aka macOS version 13), and this book. If you're brand-new to the Mac, you're all set to start enjoying computing with the finest operating system on the planet. If you've been using your Mac and macOS for a while, you're ready to start enjoying using them even more. Sure, this book is a computer book, but it's not one of those dull doorsteps; it's one that makes discovering the ins and outs of macOS Ventura easy and even fun.

About This Book

macOS Ventura For Dummies is the latest revision of the best-selling book by legendary Mac maven Bob "Dr. Mac" LeVitus, technology columnist at the *Houston Chronicle.* The book has been completely updated for macOS Ventura to cover all the exciting new features — such as Stage Manager, Passkeys, and the capability to unsend messages — and everything else that has changed. This edition combines all the old, familiar features of dozens of previous editions with the very latest information on Macs and on macOS Ventura.

Why write a *For Dummies* book about macOS Ventura? Well, Ventura is a big, somewhat-complicated personal-computer operating system. So *macOS Ventura For Dummies,* a not-so-big, not-too-complicated book, shows you what Ventura is all about without boring you to tears or poking you with sharp objects.

But why *For Dummies?* Well, that's the series name, and Wiley, the publisher, is understandably keen on using it. But remember, *dummy* is just a word. I don't think you're a dummy at all — quite the opposite, given your smart move in choosing this book!

The book is chock-full of information and advice, explaining everything you need to know about macOS Ventura in language you can understand — along with time-saving tips, tricks, techniques, and step-by-step instructions, all served up in generous quantities.

Another rule we *For Dummies* authors must follow is that our books can't exceed a certain number of pages. (Brevity is the soul of wit and all that.) So although I wish I could have included some things that didn't fit, I feel confident that you'll find what you need to know about using macOS Ventura in this book.

Still, a few things bear further looking into, such as these:

>> **Information about many of the apps (applications or programs) that come with macOS Ventura:** An installation of macOS Ventura includes nearly 60 apps, mostly located in the Applications and Utilities folders. I'd love to walk you through each one of them, but that would have required a book a whole lot bigger, heavier, and more expensive than this one.

This book briefs you on the handful of bundled applications essential to using macOS Ventura — Calendar, Contacts, Messages, Mail, Safari, Siri, TextEdit, and the like — as well as several important utilities (such as Activity Monitor, Disk Utility, and Migration Assistant) you may need to know how to use someday.

>> **Information about Microsoft Office, Apple lifestyle and productivity apps (iMovie, Numbers, Pages, GarageBand, and so on), Adobe Photoshop, Quicken, and other third-party applications:** Okay, if all the gory details of all the bundled (read: *free)* macOS Ventura applications don't fit here, you'll understand why digging into third-party applications that cost extra was out of the question.

>> **Information about programming for the Mac:** This book is about *using* macOS Ventura, not writing code for it. Dozens of books, most of which are double the size and triple the density of this one, cover programming on the Mac.

Within this book, you may note that some web addresses break across two lines of text. If you're reading this book in print and want to visit one of these web pages, simply key in the web address exactly as it's noted in the text, as though the line break doesn't exist. If you're reading it as an e-book, you've got it easy: Just click the web address to be taken directly to the web page.

Foolish Assumptions

Although I know what happens when you make assumptions, I've made a few anyway.

First, I assume that you, gentle reader, know nothing about using macOS — beyond knowing what a Mac is, that you want to use macOS, that you want to understand macOS without having to digest an incomprehensible technical manual, and that you made the right choice by selecting this particular book. So I do my best to explain each new concept in full and loving detail.

Oh, I also assume that you can read. If you can't, ignore this paragraph.

Icons Used in This Book

Little pictures (icons) appear to the side of text throughout this book. Consider these icons to be miniature road signs, telling you a little something extra about the topic at hand. Here's what the icons look like and what they mean.

TIP

Look for Tip icons to find the juiciest morsels: shortcuts, tips, and undocumented secrets about Ventura. Try them all; impress your friends!

REMEMBER

When you see this icon, it means that this particular morsel is something you may want to memorize (or at least write on your shirt cuff).

TECHNICAL STUFF

Put on your propeller-beanie hat and pocket protector; these parts include the truly geeky stuff. They're certainly not required reading, but they'll help you grasp the background, get the bigger picture, or both.

WARNING

Read these notes very carefully. Warning icons flag important cautionary information. The author and publisher won't be responsible if your Mac explodes or spews flaming parts because you ignored a Warning icon. Just kidding. Macs don't explode or spew these days.

NEW

Well, now, what could this icon possibly be about? Named by famous editorial consultant Mr. Obvious, this icon highlights things new and different in macOS Ventura.

Beyond the Book

In addition to what you're reading right now, this book comes with a free access-anywhere cheat sheet that provides handy shortcuts for use with macOS Ventura, offers recommendations for backing up your Mac to avoid losing data, and more.

To get this cheat sheet, simply go to www.dummies.com and type **macOS Ventura For Dummies Cheat Sheet** in the Search box.

Where to Go from Here

The first few chapters of this book explain the basic things you need to understand to operate your Mac effectively. If you're new to Macs and macOS Ventura, start there.

Although macOS Ventura looks slightly different from previous versions, it works the same as always (for the most part). The first part of the book presents concepts so basic that if you've been using a Mac for long, you may think you know it all — and okay, you might know some (or most) of it. But remember that not-so-old-timers need a solid foundation too. Here's my advice: Skim the stuff you already know, and you'll get to the better stuff sooner.

Enough of the introduction. Go on and enjoy the book!

1

macOS Basics

IN THIS PART . . .

Master the basics, including how to turn on your Mac.

Make the dock work harder for you.

Get a gentle introduction to Finder and its desktop.

Find everything you need to know about Ventura's windows, icons, and menus (oh my)!

Get all the bad puns and wisecracks you've come to expect.

Discover a plethora of Finder tips and tricks to make life with macOS even easier (and more fulfilling).

Wrangle System Settings to make your Mac easier to use.

Chapter **1**

macOS Ventura 101 (Prerequisites: None)

ongratulate yourself on choosing macOS version 13, generally known as Ventura. Now congratulate yourself again for making your Mac even easier to use, with hundreds of tweaks to help you do more work in less time, and even easier on the eye.

This chapter starts at the very beginning and talks about macOS in mostly abstract terms; then it moves on to explain what you need to know to use macOS Ventura successfully. A number of features described here haven't changed in years, so if you've been using macOS for a while, much of the information in this chapter may seem hauntingly familiar.

But if you decide to skip this chapter because you think you have all the new stuff figured out, you'll miss at least a couple of things that Apple didn't bother to tell you.

Tantalized? Let's rock.

Okay, What Does macOS Do?

The operating system (that is, the *OS* part of *macOS)* is what makes your Mac a Mac. Without it, your Mac is nothing but a pile of silicon and circuits — no smarter than a toaster.

"So what does an operating system do?" you ask. Good question. The simple answer is that an OS controls the basic and most important functions of your computer. In the case of macOS and your Mac, the operating system

>> Manages memory

>> Controls how windows, icons, and menus work

>> Keeps track of files

>> Manages networking and security

>> Does housekeeping (but only its own — not yours)

Other forms of software, such as word processors and web browsers, rely on the OS to create and maintain the environment in which they work their magic. When you create a memo, for example, the word processor provides the tools for you to type and format the information and save it in a file. In the background, the OS is the muscle for the word processor, performing the following crucial functions:

>> Providing the mechanism for drawing and moving the onscreen window in which you write the memo

>> Keeping track of the file when you save it

>> Helping the word processor create drop-down menus and dialogs for you to interact with

>> Communicating with other programs

>> And much, much more (stuff that only geeks could care about)

So, armed with a little background in operating systems, take a gander at the next section before you do anything else with your Mac.

One last thing: macOS Ventura comes with nearly 60 applications in its Applications and Utilities folders. Although I'd love to tell you all about each and every one, I have only so many pages at my disposal.

A Safety Net for the Absolute Beginner (or Any User)

The following sections deal with the stuff that macOS Help doesn't cover — or doesn't cover in nearly enough detail. If you're a first-time Mac user, please, *please* read this section of the book carefully; it could save your life. Okay, okay, perhaps that's overly dramatic — but reading this section could save your Mac, your sanity, or both. Even if you're an experienced Mac user, you may want to read this section. Chances are you'll see at least a few things you've forgotten that will come in handy now that you've been reminded of them.

Turning the dang thing on

Okay. This is the big moment: turning on your Mac!

Apple, in its infinite wisdom, has manufactured Macs with power buttons on every conceivable surface: on the front, side, and back of the computer itself, and even on the keyboard and monitor.

So if you don't know how to turn on your Mac, don't feel bad; just look in the manual or booklet that came with your Mac. It's at least one thing that the documentation *always* covers.

You don't have that little booklet? Most MacBook models have the power button in the upper-right corner of the keyboard, most iMac models have the button at the back of the screen, the Mac mini and the "trash can" Mac Pro have it at the back of the enclosure, and the big Mac Pro boxes have it on the front. The power button usually looks like the little circle thingy you see in the margin — but on some Mac models, the power button doubles as the Touch ID button for identifying you via your fingerprint and doesn't show the icon.

TIP

Launch the Books app, click the Search field at the top of the sidebar on the left, and type the name of your Mac plus the word *Essentials* — for example, "MacBook Air Essentials" or "iMac Essentials." In the Suggestions section, click the right result, and grab the free Essentials ebook with your Mac's name, by Apple. At around 150 pages each, these booklets aren't in any way comprehensive, but they do include some vital information, including where to find the power button on your particular Mac.

What you should see on start-up

When you finally do turn on your Mac, you set in motion a sophisticated and complex series of events that culminates in the loading of macOS and the appearance of the macOS desktop. After a small bit of whirring, buzzing, and flashing (meaning that the OS is loading), macOS first tests all the Mac's hardware — slots, ports, disks, random access memory (RAM), and so on. If everything passes, you'll see a tasteful whitish Apple logo in the middle of your screen, as shown in Figure 1-1.

FIGURE 1-1:
This is what you'll
see if everything
is fine and dandy
when you turn on
your Mac.

Here are the things that you might see when you power up your Mac:

>> **Login screen:** Depending on your settings, you might or might not see the macOS login screen. Here, you choose your user account, enter your password, and press Return (or click the little right-arrow-in-a-circle in the password field), and away you go.

If you don't want to type your password every time you start or restart your Mac (or even if you do), check out Chapter 20 for the scoop on how to turn the login screen on or off.

You should turn off the login screen only if you can guarantee you'll be the only one touching the machine. With the login screen disabled, your Mac and everything in it is completely available to anyone who turns it on, which is usually *not* a good thing. So I don't recommend turning off the login screen on a MacBook. And even desktop Mac users should think twice before turning it off.

Either way, the desktop soon materializes before your eyes. If you haven't customized, configured, or tinkered with your desktop, it should look pretty much like Figure 1-2. Now is a good time to take a moment for positive thoughts about the person who convinced you that you wanted a Mac. That person was right!

>> **Blue/black/gray screen of death:** If any of your hardware fails when it's tested, you may see a blue, black, or gray screen.

The fact that something went wrong is no reflection on your prowess as a Mac user. Something is broken, and your Mac may need repairs. If this is happening to you right now, check out Chapter 23 to try to get your Mac well again.

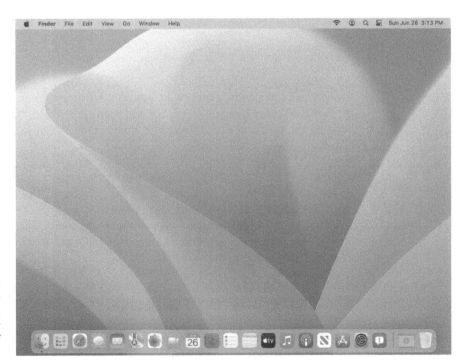

FIGURE 1-2:
The desktop after a brand-spanking-new installation of macOS Ventura.

If your computer is under warranty, set up a Genius Bar appointment at your nearest Apple Store or dial 1-800-SOS-APPL, and a customer-service person can tell you what to do. Before you do anything, though, skip ahead to Chapter 23. It's entirely possible that one of the suggestions there will get you back on track without your having to spend even a moment on hold.

>> **Prohibitory sign or flashing question mark in a folder:** Most users eventually encounter the prohibitory sign or flashing question mark in a folder (as shown in the margin). These icons mean that your Mac can't find a start-up disk, hard drive, USB thumb drive, or network server containing a valid Mac operating system. See Chapter 23 for ways to ease your Mac's ills.

>> **Kernel panic:** You may occasionally see a block of text in several languages, including English, as shown in Figure 1-3. This means that your Mac has experienced a *kernel panic,* the most severe type of system crash. If you restart your Mac and see either message again, look in Chapter 23 for a myriad of possible cures for all kinds of ailments, including this one.

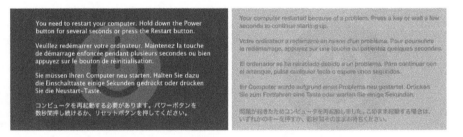

FIGURE 1-3:
If you're seeing something like this, things are definitely not fine and dandy.

How do you know which version of macOS your computer has? Just click the menu at the left end of the menu bar and then click About This Mac. A window pops up on your screen, as shown in Figure 1-4. The version you're running appears on the macOS line.

If you're curious or just want to impress your friends, you might want to know that version 12 was Monterey; version 11 was Big Sur; version 10.15 was Catalina; 10.14 was Mojave; 10.13 was High Sierra; 10.12 was Sierra; 10.11 was El Capitan; 10.10 was Yosemite; 10.9 was Mavericks; 10.8 was Mountain Lion; 10.7 was Lion; 10.6 was Snow Leopard; 10.5 was Leopard; 10.4 was Tiger; 10.3 was Panther; 10.2 was Jaguar; 10.1 was Puma; and 10.0 was Cheetah.

Shutting down properly

Turning off the power without shutting down your Mac properly is one of the worst things you can do to your poor Mac. Shutting down your Mac improperly can really screw up your hard or solid-state drive, scramble the contents of your most important files, or both.

Mac mini

Chip Apple M1
Memory 8 GB
Serial Number C07F1NJQT6NV
macOS Ventura 13.0

More Info...

™ and © 1983–2022 Apple Inc.
All Rights Reserved

FIGURE 1-4:
See which version of macOS you're running.

ETERNALLY YOURS . . . *NOW*

macOS is designed so that you never have to shut it down. You can configure it to sleep after a specified period of inactivity. (See Chapter 20 for more info on the Energy Saver and Battery System Settings panes.) If you do so, your Mac will consume very little electricity when it's sleeping and will usually be ready to use (when you press any key or click the mouse) in a few seconds. On the other hand, if you're not going to be using your Mac for a few days, you might want to shut it down anyway.

Note: If you leave your Mac on constantly, and you're gone when a lightning storm or rolling blackout hits, your Mac might get hit by a power surge or worse. So be sure you have adequate protection — say, a decent surge protector designed for computers — if you decide to leave your Mac on and unattended for long periods. See the section "A few things you should definitely not do with your Mac," elsewhere in this chapter, for more info on lightning and your Mac.

One last thing: If you have a MacBook, and it will be enclosed in a bag or briefcase for more than a few hours, turn it off. Otherwise, it could overheat — even in Sleep mode.

If a thunderstorm is rumbling nearby, or you're unfortunate enough to have rolling blackouts where you live, you may really want to shut down your Mac and unplug it from the wall. (See the next section, which briefly discusses lightning and your Mac.) If you have a MacBook, you can just disconnect it from its charging cable and continue using it if you like.

To turn off your Mac, always use the Shut Down command from the (Apple) menu and then click the Shut Down button in the Are You Sure You Want to Shut Down Your Computer Now? dialog.

When the Shut Down button (or any button, for that matter) is highlighted, you can activate it by pressing the Return key rather than clicking it.

The Are You Sure You Want to Shut Down Your Computer Now? dialog sports a check-box option: Reopen Windows When Logging Back In. If you select this check box, your Mac will start back up with the same windows (and applications) that were open when you shut down (or restarted). This can be a real time-saver, but you can clear the check box and disable this option if that's not what you want.

Most Mac users have been forced to shut down improperly more than once without anything horrible happening, of course — but don't be lulled into a false sense of security. Break the rules one time too many (or under the wrong circumstances), and your most important files could be toast. The *only* time you should turn off your Mac without shutting down properly is when your screen is completely frozen or when your system crashed due to a kernel panic and you've already tried everything else. (See Chapter 23 for a list of those "everything elses.") A stubborn crash doesn't happen often — and less often under macOS than ever before — but when it does, forcing your Mac to turn off and then back on might be the only solution.

A few things you should definitely not do with your Mac

This section covers the bad stuff that can happen to your computer if you do the wrong things with it. If something bad has already happened to you, see Chapter 23.

> » **Don't unplug your desktop Mac when it's turned on.** Very bad things can happen, such as having your OS break. See the preceding section to learn about shutting down your system properly.
>
> Note that this warning doesn't apply to MacBooks as long as their battery is at least partially charged. As long as there's enough juice in the battery to power

your MacBook, you can connect and disconnect its power adapter to your heart's content.

» **Don't use your Mac when lightning is near.** Here's a simple life equation for you: Mac + lightning = dead Mac. 'Nuff said. Oh, and don't place much faith in inexpensive surge protectors. A good jolt of lightning will fry the surge protector and everything plugged into it, including computers, modems, printers, and hubs. Some surge protectors can withstand some lightning strikes, but those warriors aren't the cheapies that you buy at your local computer emporium. Unplugging your Mac from the wall during electrical storms is safer and less expensive. (Don't forget to unplug your external routers, network hubs, printers, and other hardware that plugs into the wall as well; lightning can fry them too.)

For MacBooks, disconnect the power adapter and other cables connected to grid-powered electrical equipment, because whatever those cables are connected to could fry — and fry your MacBook right along with it. After you do that, you can use your MacBook during a storm if you care to. You can have your iPhone or your AirPods connected to your MacBook for charging, as long as it's off the grid.

» **Don't jostle, bump, shake, kick, throw, dribble, or punt your Mac, especially while it's running.** Older Macs contain a hard drive that spins at 5,200 revolutions per minute (rpm) or more. A jolt to a hard drive while it's reading or writing a file can cause the head to crash into the disk, which can render many — or all — files on it unrecoverable. Ouch!

TIP

Don't think you're exempt if your Mac uses a solid-state drive with no moving parts. A good bump to your Mac could damage other components. Treat your Mac like it's a carton of eggs, and you'll never be sorry.

» **Don't forget to back up your data!** If the files on your hard drive mean anything to you, you must back up. Not maybe. *Must.* Even if your most important file is your last saved game of Bejeweled, you still need to back up your files. Fortunately, macOS includes an awesome backup utility called Time Machine. (Unfortunately, you need an external hard drive to take advantage of it.) Please read Chapter 21 now, and find out how to back up before something horrible happens to your valuable data!

WARNING

Definitely do not use household window cleaners or paper towels on your screen. Either one can harm it. Instead, use a soft clean cloth (preferably microfiber), and if you're going to use a liquid or spray, make sure it's specifically designed not to harm computer displays. Finally, only spray the cleaner onto a *cloth;* never spray anything directly onto the screen.

Point-and-click 101

Are you new to the Mac? Just figuring out how to move the mouse around? Now is a good time to go over some fundamental stuff that you need to know for just about everything you'll be doing on the Mac. Spend a few minutes reading this section, and soon you'll be clicking, double-clicking, pressing, and pointing all over the place. If you think you have the whole mousing thing pretty much figured out, feel free to skip this section.

Still with me? Good. Now for some basic terminology:

>> **Point:** Before you can click or press anything, you have to *point* to it. Place your hand on your mouse, and move it so that the pointer arrow is over the object you want — such as on top of an icon or a button.

  If you're using a trackpad, slide your finger lightly across the pad until the pointer arrow is over the object you want.

>> **Click:** Also called *single click*. Use your index finger to push the mouse button (or the left mouse button if your mouse has more than one) all the way down and then let go so that the button (usually) produces a satisfying clicking sound. (If you have one of the optical Apple mice, you push the whole thing down to click.) Use a single click to highlight an icon, press a button, or activate a check box or window.

  In other words, first you point and then you click — *point and click,* in computer lingo.

  If you're using a trackpad, press down on it to click. You can also configure the trackpad so that you can tap to click; see Chapter 6.

>> **Double click:** *Click twice* in rapid succession. With a little practice, you can perfect this technique in no time. Use a double click to open a folder or to launch a file or application.

  Trackpad users: Press down on the pad two times in rapid succession. If you've enabled Tap to Click, you can double-tap to double-click.

>> **Secondary click:** Hold down the Control key while clicking (also called *Control-clicking* or *right-clicking).*

  Trackpad users can either hold down the Control key while pressing down on the trackpad with one finger or tap the trackpad with two fingers without holding down the Control key.

  If tapping your trackpad with two fingers didn't bring up a little menu, check your Trackpad pane in System Settings (see Chapter 6).

  Control-clicking displays a *contextual* menu (also known as a *shortcut menu).* In fact, if you're blessed with a two-or-more-button mouse, you can right-click and avoid having to hold down the Control key. If it doesn't work, you can enable this feature in the Mouse pane in System Settings.

>> **Drag:** *Dragging* something usually means you have to click it first and hold down the mouse or trackpad button. Then you move the mouse on your desk or mouse pad (or your finger on the trackpad) so that the pointer and whatever you select moves across the screen. The combination of holding down the button and dragging the mouse is usually referred to as *clicking and dragging.*

>> **Wiggle (or jiggle):** This welcome improvement is awesome when you lose track of the pointer on your screen. Just wiggle your mouse back and forth (or jiggle your finger back and forth on the trackpad) for a few seconds, and the pointer will magically get much bigger, making it easier to see on the screen. When you stop wiggling or jiggling, the pointer returns to its normal size.

>> **Choose an item from a menu:** To get to macOS menu commands, you must first open a menu and then choose the option you want. Click the menu name to open the menu, and then click the command you want. When the menu is open, you can also type the first letter or letters of the item to select it, and then press the spacebar or Return to execute the command.

TIP

You can also use the menus a different way. Point at the name of the menu you want with your pointer and then press the mouse button to open the menu. Keep holding down the mouse button and drag downward until you select the command you want. When the command is highlighted, let go of the mouse button to execute the command.

Go ahead and give it a try!

REMEMBER

The terms given in the preceding list apply to all Macs — both MacBooks and Mac desktop systems. If you use a trackpad with your Mac, you'll want to add a few more terms — such as *tap, swipe, rotate, pinch,* and *spread* — to your lexicon. You can read all about them in Chapters 2 and 11.

Getting Help

One of the best features of macOS is the excellent built-in help. When you have a question about how to do something, Help is the first place you should visit (after this book, of course).

Clicking the Help menu reveals the Search field at the top of the menu and the macOS Help item. Choosing macOS Help opens the window shown in Figure 1-5.

Table of Contents icon

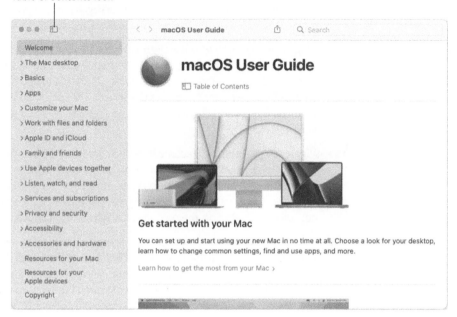

macOS User Guide

Table of Contents

Get started with your Mac

You can set up and start using your new Mac in no time at all. Choose a look for your desktop, learn how to change common settings, find and use apps, and more.

Learn how to get the most from your Mac >

FIGURE 1-5:
Mac Help is nothing if not helpful.

TIP

Press Shift+⌘+? to open Help for the current app.

You can browse Help by clicking a topic in the table of contents and then clicking a subtopic. If you don't see the table of contents, click the Table of Contents icon, labeled in Figure 1-5.

To search Mac Help, simply type a word or phrase in either Search field — the one in the Help menu itself or the one near the top of the Help window on the right side — and then press Return. In a few seconds, your Mac provides one or more articles to read, which (theoretically) are related to your question. As long as your Mac is connected to the Internet, search results include articles from the Apple online support database.

REMEMBER

Although you don't have to be connected to the Internet to use Mac Help, you do need an Internet connection to get the most out of it. (Chapter 13 can help you set up an Internet connection, if you don't have one.) That's because macOS installs only certain help articles on your hard drive. If you ask a question that those articles don't answer, Mac Help connects to the Apple website and downloads the answer (assuming that you have an active Internet connection). These answers appear when you click Show All near the bottom of some article lists. Click one of these entries, and Help Viewer retrieves the text over the Internet. This is some-times inconvenient but also quite smart, because Apple can update the Help system at any time without requiring any action from you.

Furthermore, after you ask a question and Mac Help has grabbed the answer from the Apple website, the answer remains on your hard drive forever. If you ask for it again — even at a later date — your computer won't have to download it from the Apple website again.

If you see a See More Results on the Web link, you can click it to launch Safari and perform a web search for the phrase you typed.

Mac Help also has a cool feature that literally points you to the commands you need. Try this:

1. **In the Help menu's Search field, type a word or phrase.**

2. **Select any item that has a menu icon to its left (such as the items with** *side* **in their names in Figure 1-6).**

   An arrow appears, pointing at that command in the appropriate menu.

Finally, don't forget that most apps have their own Help systems, so if you want general help with your Mac, you need to first click the Finder icon in the Dock, click the desktop, or use the app-switching shortcut, ⌘+Tab, to activate Finder. Only then can you choose Mac Help from Finder's Help menu.

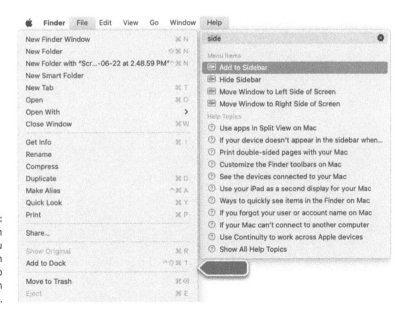

FIGURE 1-6:
If you choose an item in the Menu Items section, an arrow points to that item in context.

IN THIS CHAPTER

» **Understanding Finder**

» **Checking out the parts of a window**

» **Opening a dialog with your Mac**

» **Resizing, moving, and closing windows**

» **Getting comfortable with menu basics**

Chapter **2**

Desktop and Windows and Menus (Oh My!)

This chapter introduces important features of macOS, starting with the first things you see when you log in: Finder and its desktop. After a quick look around the desktop, you dig into two of its most useful features: windows and menus.

Windows are (and have always been) an integral part of using your Mac. In fact, Macs had windows before Microsoft Windows was invented.

Windows in Finder show you the contents of different storage containers, such as the hard drive, an optical drive, a flash (thumb) drive, a network drive, a disk image, or a folder. Windows in apps do many things. The point is that windows are part of what makes your Mac a Mac; knowing how they work — and how to use them — is essential.

Menus are another quintessential part of the Mac experience. The latter part of this chapter starts you out with a few menu basics. As needed, I direct you to other parts of the book for greater detail. So relax, and don't worry. By the end of this chapter, you'll be ready to work with windows and menus in any app that uses them (and most apps, games excluded, do).

Touring Finder and Its Desktop

Finder is the app that creates the desktop, keeps track of your files and folders, and is always running. Just about everything you do on your Mac begins and ends with Finder. It's where you manage files, store documents, launch apps, and much more. If you ever expect to master your Mac, the first step is to master Finder and the desktop.

Finder is the center of your macOS experience, so before I go any further, here's a quick description of its most prominent features:

>> **Desktop:** The *desktop* is the area behind the windows and the Dock. In macOS Ventura, the default desktop picture is a colorful abstract graphic.

The desktop also may contain an icon for your Mac's start-up disk.

TIP

If you don't see a disk icon on the desktop, never fear — you learn how to enable this behavior in Chapter 4.

The desktop isn't a window, yet it acts like one. Like a folder or disk window, the desktop can contain icons. But unlike most windows, which require a bit of navigation to get to, the desktop is always there behind any open windows, making it a great place for icons you use a lot, such as oft-used folders, apps, or documents.

TECHNICAL STUFF

Some folks use the terms *desktop* and *Finder* interchangeably to refer to the total Mac environment you see after you log in — the icons, windows, menus, and all that other cool stuff. Just to make things confusing, the background you see on your screen — the picture behind your hard drive icon and your open windows — is *also* called the desktop sometimes, although Apple is now trying to get people to call it *wallpaper*. This book refers to the app you use when the desktop is showing as *Finder*, whereas *desktop* means the picture background behind your windows and the Dock, which you can use as a storage place for icons if you like.

Don't panic. The desktop metaphor used by macOS will become crystal clear in upcoming pages and chapters.

>> **Dock:** The Dock is Finder's main navigation shortcut tool. It makes getting to frequently used items easy, even when you have a screen full of windows. Plus it's extremely customizable, as you find out in Chapter 3.

>> **Icons:** Icons are the little pictures you see in folder and disk windows and on your desktop. Icons represent the things you work with on your Mac, such as apps, documents, folders, utilities, and more.

>> **Windows:** Opening most items (by double-clicking their icons) makes a window appear. Windows in Finder show you the contents of disk drives and

folders; windows in apps usually show the contents of documents. In the sections that follow, you can find the full scoop on macOS windows.

» **Menus:** Menus let you choose to do things, such as create new folders; duplicate files; and cut, copy, or paste text. You learn menu basics later in this chapter in the "Menu Basics" section; you find details about working with menus for specific tasks throughout this book.

Whereas this chapter offers a basic introduction to Finder and desktop, Chapter 8 explains in detail how to navigate and manage your files in Finder. But before you start using Finder, it helps to know the basics of working with windows and menus; if these Mac features are new to you, read this entire chapter now and pay special attention to Chapter 8 later.

Anatomy of a Window

Windows are ubiquitous parts of using a Mac. When you open a folder, you see a window. When you write a letter, the document that you're working on appears in a window. When you browse the Internet, web pages appear in a window . . . and so on.

For the most part, windows are windows from app to app. You'll probably notice that some apps (Adobe Photoshop or Microsoft Word, for example) take liberties with windows by adding features such as custom toolbars or textual information (such as the zoom percentage or file size) around the edges of the document window and on toolbars.

Don't let it bug you; that extra fluff is just window dressing (pun intended). Maintaining the window metaphor, many information windows display different kinds of information in different *panes,* or discrete sections within the window.

When you finish this chapter, which focuses exclusively on Finder windows, you'll know how to use most windows in most apps. And so, without further ado, the following list gives you a look at the main features of a typical Finder window (as shown in Figure 2-1). Later sections of this chapter discuss these features in greater detail.

TIP

If your windows don't look exactly like Figure 2-1, don't be concerned. You can make your windows look and feel any way you like. As the upcoming "Working with Windows" section explains, moving and resizing windows are easy tasks.

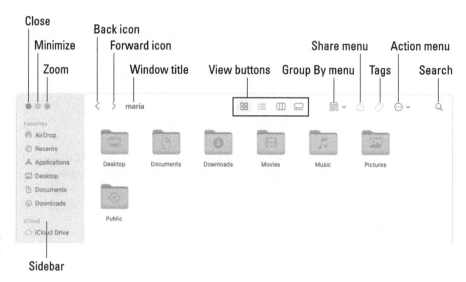

Close
Minimize
Zoom
Back icon
Forward icon
Window title
View buttons
Group By menu
Tags
Share menu
Action menu
Search

Favorites
AirDrop
Recents
Applications
Desktop
Documents
Downloads
iCloud
iCloud Drive

Desktop
Documents
Downloads
Movies
Music
Pictures
Public

FIGURE 2-1:
A typical Finder
window in macOS
Ventura.

Sidebar

Meanwhile, here's what you see on the toolbar:

>> **Close, Minimize, and Zoom buttons:** Shut 'em, shrink 'em, and grow 'em.

>> **View icons:** Choose among four exciting views of your window: Icon, List, Column, and Gallery. Find out more about views in Chapter 4.

>> **Group By menu:** Click this little doohickey to group this window's icons by Name, Kind, Application, Date Last Opened, Date Added, Date Modified, Date Created, Size, or Tags. Or by None, which is the default.

>> **Action menu:** This icon opens a pop-up menu of commands you can apply to currently selected items in the Finder window or on the desktop. It's nearly the same list of commands you'll find in the contextual (shortcut) menu when you right-click or Control-click that item or items.

TIP

Note that some menu icons and items in these menus aren't available (appear dimmed) until you select one or more icons in the Finder window. If nothing happens when you click a toolbar icon, click a file or folder icon to select it and try again.

>> **Window title:** Shows the name of the window (*maria* in Figure 2-1).

TIP

⌘-click (or Control-click) the window title to see a pop-up menu with the complete path to this folder. (Try it now.) This tip applies to most windows you'll encounter, not just Finder windows. So ⌘- or Control-click a window's title (a right click or two-fingered tap on a trackpad will work too), and you'll (usually) see the path to its enclosing folder on your disk, though some third-party apps don't follow this convention.

TIP

To see the path from your Mac's hard or solid-state drive to the active window, choose View ➪ Show Path Bar. The path will appear at the bottom of all Finder windows until you choose View ➪ Hide Path Bar.

>> **Share menu:** Another icon that opens a menu. Click it to share selected files or folders via Mail, Messages, AirDrop, or Notes. Or click Edit Actions to add other commands to your Share menu, such as Add (the selected item) to Photos or Reminders.

>> **Tags menu:** Yet another menu; click it to assign a tag to the selected files or folders.

>> **Search:** Click the magnifying-glass icon and then type a string of characters in the field that appears. The Spotlight search feature digs into your system to find items that match by filename or document contents (yes, it will find words within most documents).

>> **Scroll bars:** Use the scroll bars for moving around a window. macOS hides the scroll bars when it thinks you don't need them.

>> **Sidebar:** Frequently used items live here, giving you quick access to them. You can customize the Sidebar with the items you need.

>> **Forward and Back icons:** These icons take you to the next or previous folder, respectively, displayed in this particular window. The first time you open a window, neither icon is active, because there's no next or previous folder to display yet.

As you navigate from folder to folder, these icons remember your bread-crumb trail so you can quickly traverse backward or forward, window by window. You can also navigate backward or forward from the keyboard by using the shortcuts ⌘+[for Back and ⌘+] for Forward.

REMEMBER

The Forward and Back icons remember only the other folders you've visited in *that* tab. If you've set a Finder setting so that folders always open in a new window — or if you forced a folder to open in a new window, which we'll get to shortly — the Forward and Back icons won't work.

Top o' the window to ya!

Take a gander at the top of a window — any window. You see three buttons in the top-left corner and the name of the window to the right of the Back and Forward icons. The three buttons (called *gumdrop buttons* by some folks because they look like, well, gumdrops) are officially known as Close, Minimize, and Zoom, and their colors (red, yellow, and green, respectively) are designed to pop off the screen.

Here's what they do:

>> **Close (red):** Click this button to close the window.

>> **Minimize (yellow):** Click this button to minimize the window. Clicking Minimize shrinks the window to an icon on the right side of the Dock.

TIP

See the section about minimizing windows into app icons in Chapter 3 if a document icon doesn't appear in your Dock when you minimize the document's window.

To view the window again, click the Dock icon for the window that you minimized. If the window happens to be a QuickTime movie, the movie audio continues to play, and a tiny still image from the video appears as its icon in the Dock. (I discuss the Dock in detail in Chapter 3.)

>> **Zoom (green):** Click a window's green Zoom button, and the window expands to cover the whole screen, including the menu bar.

TIP

If you prefer the old behavior, where a window zoomed to the largest size it could but didn't cover the full screen, hold down the Option key when you click the green button.

To shrink the window back to its previous dimensions, slide the pointer up to the very top of the screen, wait for the menu bar to appear, and then click the green Zoom button.

Another way to escape from a full-screen window, at least in Finder, is to press the Esc key on your keyboard. Sadly, this trick doesn't work with all apps, though it's quite useful in apps that support it (most Apple apps and many others) as well as in Finder.

Split View is semi-hidden beneath the green Zoom button. To see Split View in action, either click and hold the green button for a moment or *hover* the pointer over the Zoom button for a moment (without clicking).

Either way, a pop-up menu with three (or more) options appears: select Enter Full Screen, Tile Window to Left of Screen, or Tile Window to Right of Screen. And if you hold down the Option key and hover the pointer over the green Zoom button, the menu displays the options Zoom, Move Window to Left Side of Screen, and Move Window to Right Side of Screen.

NEW

You may see additional options to move the window to a different device (such as an iPad) via Sidecar if a suitable device is close enough to your Mac (see Chapter 24).

After you move a window to the left or right half of the screen, the other half displays miniature versions of all open windows. Hover the pointer over a miniature window to see its name; click a miniature window and it fills that half of the screen. This behavior is called *tiling*.

If you want to move a window to the left side or right side of the screen without putting another app window in the unoccupied half, hold down the Option key as you move the pointer over the green gumdrop, and then click the Move Window to Left Side of Screen command or the Move Window to Right Side of Screen command, as appropriate.

To work in Split View, click either window to activate it and do what you have to do. To activate the other window, click it. To exit Split View, do one of the following:

- Press Esc.
- Move the pointer to the top of the screen; when the buttons (for both windows) reappear, click any button.
- Quit either app.

A scroll new world

Yet another way to see more of what's in a window or pane is to scroll through it. Scroll bars appear at the bottom and right sides of any window or pane that contains more stuff — icons, text, pixels, or whatever — than you can see in the window. Figure 2-2, for example, shows two instances of the same window: Dragging the scroll box, also called the "thumb," on the right side of the smaller window would reveal the icons above and below the six (whole) icons that are currently visible. Dragging the scroll box on the bottom of the smaller window would reveal items to the left and right of the six that are currently visible.

Simply click and drag a scroll box to move it up or down or side to side.

If your scroll bars don't look exactly like the ones in Figure 2-2 or work as described in the following list, don't worry. These are System Settings you can configure to your heart's desire, as you discover in Chapter 6.

Here are some ways you can scroll in a window:

>> **Click a scroll box and drag.** The content of the window scrolls proportionally to how far you drag the scroll box.

>> **Click in the scroll bar but don't click the scroll box.** The window scrolls either one page up (if you click above the scroll box) or down (if you click below the scroll box). You can change a setting in the Appearance pane in System Settings to cause the window to scroll proportionally to where you click.

Scroll box (gray)

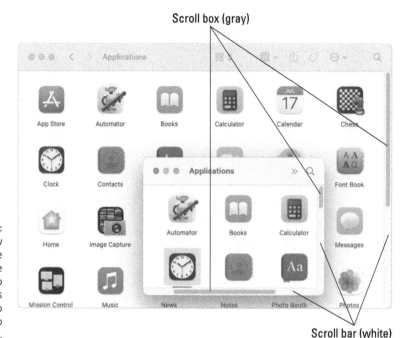

FIGURE 2-2:
The same window
twice. Use the
scroll bars in the
front window to
see the icons
above, below, to
the left, or to
the right.

Scroll bar (white)

TIP

The Page Up and Page Down keys on your keyboard function the same way as clicking the vertical scroll bar in Finder and many apps. These keys don't work in every app, though, so don't become too dependent on them. Also, if you purchased a mouse, a trackball, or another pointing device that has a scroll wheel, you can scroll vertically in the active (front) window with the scroll wheel or press and hold down the Shift key to scroll horizontally. Alas, this horizontal scrolling-with-the-Shift-key works in Finder windows but not in all apps. It works in the Apple TextEdit app, for example, but not in Microsoft Word.

>> **Use the keyboard.** In Finder, first click an icon in the window and then use the arrow keys to move up, down, left, or right. Using an arrow key selects the next icon in the direction it indicates — and automatically scrolls the window, if necessary. In other apps, you might or might not be able to use the keyboard to scroll. To find out, try it.

>> **Use a two-finger swipe (on a trackpad).** If you have a MacBook, or you use a Magic Trackpad or Magic Mouse with your desktop Mac, just move the arrow pointer over the window and then swipe the trackpad or Magic Mouse with two fingers to scroll.

(Hyper)active windows

To work within a window, you must make the window active. The *active* window is always the frontmost window, and *inactive* windows always appear behind the active window. You might not see an inactive window if it's behind a bigger window, active or not. If a window is minimized, you'll see it only as a button on the Dock.

Only one window can be active at a time. To make a window active, click it anywhere — in the middle, on the title bar, or on a scroll bar. It doesn't matter where; just click anywhere to activate it.

The exceptions are the Close, Minimize, and Zoom buttons on inactive windows, which always do what they do, regardless of whether a window is active or inactive.

Look at Figure 2-3 for an example of an active window in front of an inactive window (the Applications window and the Utilities window, respectively).

Inactive window   Active window

FIGURE 2-3:
An active window
in front of an
inactive window.

The following is a list of the major visual cues that distinguish active from inactive windows:

>> **The active window's title bar:** By default, the Close, Minimize, and Zoom buttons are bright red, yellow, and green, respectively, and the inactive windows' buttons are light gray.

This is a nice visual cue. Colored items are active, and gray ones are inactive. Better still, if you move your mouse pointer over an inactive window's gumdrop buttons, they light up in their usual colors so you can close, minimize, or zoom an inactive window without first clicking it to making it active. Neat!

>> **The active window's toolbar:** Toolbar icons are darker and more distinctive; the inactive window's toolbar icons are light gray and more subdued.

>> **The active window's drop shadow:** Notice how the active window has a more prominent shadow? This tricks your eye into thinking the active window is in front of the inactive one.

One last thing: If you're wondering how to resize a window, just hover the pointer over a window's edge or corner or over the dividing line between two panes in the same window (such as the sidebar and the main area of Finder windows). A helpful little double-headed arrow appears as a visual cue that you can now drag the edge, corner, or dividing line to resize the window or pane.

Opening a Dialog with Your Mac

Dialogs are special windows that pop up over the active window. You generally see them when you select a menu item that ends in an ellipsis (. . .).

You may sometimes see a dialog referred to as a sheet. What's that about? Well, technically, a *sheet* is a dialog that's anchored to a particular window. Say you fire up the TextEdit app, create two new documents, and then press ⌘+S to save the second document. The Save As dialog that opens is actually a sheet that's attached to that document's window rather than a free-floating dialog. That doesn't sound too exciting, but a sheet has the advantage that it blocks only its own window rather than the whole app; in our example, you can continue working in the first document while the Save sheet blocks the second document.

Given that the difference between sheets and dialogs is largely academic, this book refers to both sheets and dialogs as *dialogs.*

Dialogs can contain a number of standard Mac controls, such as radio buttons, pop-up menus, tabs, text-entry fields, and check boxes. You see these features again and again in dialogs. Take a moment to look at each of these controls in Figure 2-4.

Tabs

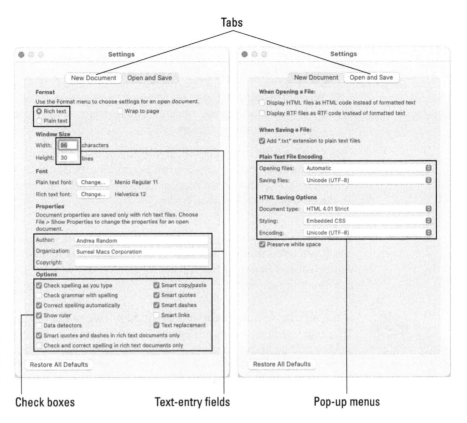

FIGURE 2-4:
This Settings window offers most of the dialog-box controls you're likely to encounter.

Check boxes   Text-entry fields   Pop-up menus

>> **Radio buttons:** *Radio buttons* are so named because, like the buttons on your car radio (if you have a very old car), only one at a time can be active. (When they're active, they appear to be pushed in, just like the old radio buttons.) Radio buttons always appear in a group of two or more; when you select one, all the others are automatically deselected. To select a radio button, click either the button part or the button's name.

>> **Tabs:** When a dialog contains more information than can fit in a single window, the info may be divided among panes denoted by tabs. In Figure 2-4, the New Document tab is selected on the left, and the Open and Save tab is selected on the right.

>> **Pop-up menus:** These menus are appropriately named because they pop up when you click them. In Figure 2-4, right, all five pop-up menus (Opening Files, Saving Files, Document Type, Styling, and Encoding) are unclicked and unpopped.

You can always recognize a pop-up menu because it appears in a slightly rounded rectangle and has a double-ended arrow symbol (or a pair of arrows, if you like) on the right.

Have you figured out yet what radio buttons, tabs, and pop-up menus have in common? *Hint:* All three enable you to make a single selection from a group of options. (Well, okay, that was more of an answer than a hint.)

>> **Text-entry fields:** In text-entry fields, you type text (including numbers) from the keyboard. In Figure 2-4, left, the Width, Height, Author, Organization, and Copyright settings are text-entry fields.

>> **Check boxes:** The last type of control that you see frequently is the check box. In a group of check boxes, you can select as many options as you like. Check boxes are selected when they contain a check mark and deselected when they're empty, as shown in Figure 2-4.

There's one other control you should become familiar with, the disclosure triangle. If you see a triangle in a dialog, try clicking it. If it's a disclosure triangle, it will reveal additional options (or its contents if it's a folder in Finder's List view, as you see in Chapter 8).

TECHNICAL STUFF

Some apps have *tri-state* check boxes (and no, we're not talking geography here). These special check boxes are empty when nothing in the group is selected, sport a check mark when everything in the group is selected, and sport a minus sign (–) when some items in the group are selected and some are not.

Working with Windows

In the following sections, you take a closer look at windows themselves: how you move them, size them, and use them. And although Ventura windows are similar to windows you've used in other versions of macOS (and even Windows), you may just discover a new wrinkle or two.

Opening and closing windows

To start peering into windows on your Mac, first you need to know how to open and close them. When you're working in Finder, you can choose the following commands from the File menu. Note that you'll probably find similar commands on the File menu of apps other than Finder.

TIP

You'll use many of these commands frequently, so take a minute to memorize their keyboard shortcuts. If you're not sure how keyboard shortcuts work, check out "Using keyboard-shortcut commands" later in this chapter.

- >> **New Finder Window (⌘+N):** Opens a new Finder window. In other apps, ⌘+N might open a new document, project, or whatever that app helps you create.

- >> **Open (⌘+O):** Opens the selected item, be it a file, a window, or a folder.

- >> **Close Window (⌘+W):** Closes the active window. If no windows are open or if no window is selected, the Close Window command appears dimmed and can't be chosen. Or if you prefer, you can close a window by clicking the red Close button in the top-left corner.

REMEMBER

If you hold down the Option key with the File menu open, the Close Window command changes to Close All. This useful command enables you to close all open Finder windows. But it shows up only when you press the Option key or use its keyboard shortcut (⌘+Option+W); otherwise, it remains hidden.

TIP

Note that several other commands in the File menu transmogrify when you press the Option key. It would be off topic to get into them here, but here's a tip: Press the Option key, and browse all Finder menus. At least a dozen useful commands appear only when the Option key is pressed. Press it early and often for hidden (often time-saving) commands.

Resizing windows and window panes

If you want to see more (or less) of what's in a window, just hover the pointer over any edge or corner and drag. When the pointer turns into a little double-headed arrow, click and drag to resize the window.

Display windows, like those in Finder, frequently consist of multiple panes. In a Finder window, note the thin line that divides the sidebar pane on the left from the contents pane on the right. When your mouse pointer hovers over the thin line, the pointer changes to a vertical bar with little arrows pointing out of both sides, as shown in the margin. If the pane is horizontal, the pointer morphs into a horizontal bar with arrows pointing up and down.

When you see this pointer, you can click and drag anywhere in the dividing line that separates the sidebar from the rest of the window. Doing so resizes the two panes relative to each other; one gets larger, and one gets smaller.

Moving windows

To move a window, click anywhere in a window's title bar or toolbar (except on a button, an icon, a menu, or a search field) and drag the window to wherever you want it. The window moves wherever you move the mouse, stopping dead in its tracks when you release the mouse button.

TIP

If you can't find the pointer on the screen, wiggle your finger on the trackpad or jiggle the mouse. These movements magnify the pointer to make it easier to find onscreen.

Shuffling windows

You now know the essentials of how to work with windows. But wait. There's more! The commands on the Window menu provide tools you can use to manage your windows.

Here is a brief look at each of the items on the Window menu. (And if you're unfamiliar with menus and keyboard shortcuts, you find out how they work later in this chapter.)

>> **Minimize (⌘+M):** Use this command to minimize the active Finder window to the Dock and unclutter your desktop. It's the same as clicking the yellow gumdrop button.

>> **Zoom:** This command does the same thing as the green gumdrop button. If you've forgotten what the green gumdrop does already, just turn back a few pages to the "Top o' the window to ya!" section, and read it again.

>> **Tile Window to Left Side of Screen:** Invokes Split Screen mode and moves the active window to the left half of the screen.

>> **Tile Window to Right Side of Screen:** Invokes Split Screen mode and moves the active window to the right half of the screen.

You may see additional options to move the window to a different device (such as an iPad) via Sidecar when a suitable device is close enough to your Mac (see Chapter 24).

>> **Cycle through Windows (⌘+`):** Each time you choose this command or use the keyboard shortcut for it, a different window becomes active. So if you have three windows — call 'em Window 1, Window 2, and Window 3 — and you're using Window 1, this command deactivates Window 1 and activates Window 2. If you choose it again, the command deactivates Window 2 and activates Window 3. Choose it one more time, and it deactivates Window 3 and reactivates Window 1.

The next four commands in the Window menu help you manage Finder-window tabs. If you're a fan of tabbed browsing (*à la* Safari), you'll love tabs in a Finder window.

Tabs let you view multiple folders or disks or both in a single window, with each folder or disk in its own tab, as shown in Figure 2-5. Tabbed windows are an ingenious way to cram a lot of information into a little space.

Utilities tab   Applications tab   Downloads tab

FIGURE 2-5:
Finder tabs let
you view the
contents of
several folders
merely by
clicking the
appropriate tab.

Ventura, like its last few predecessors, includes system-wide tabbed windows, which should work in almost every app that uses windows. The cool part is the app doesn't have to be updated in any way — macOS grafts tabbed windows onto almost every app that displays multiple windows.

The remaining commands in the Window menu are as follows:

>> **Show Previous Tab (Control+Shift+Tab):** Each time you choose this command or use its keyboard shortcut, the previous tab — the one to its left, unless it's the leftmost tab, in which case it wraps around to the rightmost tab — becomes active. In Figure 2-5, Utilities is the active tab. Use this command, and Downloads becomes the active tab. Use it a third time, and Applications becomes active.

>> **Show Next Tab (Control+Tab):** Same as Show Previous Tab, except in reverse. Instead of showing the previous tab (the one to the left), this command shows the next tab (the one to the right).

>> **Move Tab to New Window (no keyboard shortcut):** Does just what it says; it moves the active tab into a new window of its own.

>> **Merge All Windows (no keyboard shortcut):** Combines all open windows and tabs in one window.

TIP

You can click a tab and drag it left or right to change the order. You can also drag and drop a tab from one Finder window to another. The trick is to click directly on a tab and drag it *onto the tabs in the target window*. If you release it anywhere else, the tab will be displayed in a new window.

One more thing: In Ventura, all these commands and keyboard shortcuts appear in most apps that display windows.

» **Bring All to Front (no keyboard shortcut):** Windows from different apps can interleave. You can have (from front to back) a Finder window, a Microsoft Word window, an Adobe Photoshop window, another Microsoft Word window, and another Finder window. In this example, choosing Bring All to Front while Finder is the active app enables you to have both Finder windows move in front of those belonging to Word and Photoshop.

TIP

If you want to bring all the windows belonging to Finder (or any other app, for that matter) to the front at the same time, you can also click the appropriate Dock icon (Finder, in this case).

If you hold down the Option key when you click the Window menu, Minimize Window changes to Minimize All, and the Zoom command changes to Zoom All.

» **Other items:** The remaining items on the Window menu — if any — are the names of all currently open Finder windows. Click a window's name to bring it to the front.

Menu Basics

To check out the macOS menus, click the Finder button on the Dock to activate Finder and then look at the top of your screen. From left to right, you see the Apple menu, the Finder menu, and six other menus. To use an macOS menu, click its name to make the menu appear and then click to select a menu item. Piece of cake!

Note that menus stay down after you click their names and stay open until you select an item or click outside the menu's boundaries.

The ever-changing menu bar

REMEMBER

Before you start working with macOS menus, you really, really should know this: *Menu items can change unexpectedly.* Why? Well, the menus you see on the menu bar at the top of the screen always reflect the app that's *active* at the time. When you switch from Finder to a particular app — or from one app to another — the menus change immediately to match whatever app you switched to.

Figure 2-6 shows the menu bars for Finder and the Preview and TextEdit apps.

FIGURE 2-6:
The menu bar
changes to reflect
the active app.

 Finder   File   Edit   View   Go   Window   Help

 Preview   File   Edit   View   Go   Tools   Window   Help

 TextEdit   File   Edit   Format   View   Window   Help

An easy way to tell which app is active is to look at the application menu — it's the leftmost menu with a name, just to the right of the Apple menu. When you're in Finder, of course, the application menu reads *Finder.* But if you switch to another app (by clicking its icon on the Dock or by clicking any window associated with the app) or launch a new app, that menu changes to the name of the active app.

When you have an app open, the commands on the menu change, too — but just a little bit. What makes this cool is that you have access to some standard application menu items whether you're running Mail, Safari, or almost any other app. Most (but not all) apps have Cut, Copy, and Paste commands in their Edit menus, and Open, Save, and Print commands on their File menus. You can find much more about commands for apps in Part 3, which explains how you can use the apps that come with macOS Ventura to get things done.

Contextual (shortcut) menus: They're sooo contextual!

Contextual menus (also called *shortcut menus)* list commands that apply only to the item that is currently selected. Contextual menus might be available in windows, on icons, and in most places on the desktop.

To see whether a contextual menu is available, either hold down the Control key and click — which you can call a *Control-click* to sound cool to your Mac friends — or, for those with two or more buttons on their mice, *right-click.* Finally, MacBooks (as well as the Magic Trackpad and the Magic Mouse) let you click the trackpad using two fingers to simulate a right click or a Control click.

TIP

If this doesn't work for you, launch System Settings, and click the Trackpad icon in the Sidebar. In the Point & Click section, go to the Tap to Click line, and make sure its switch is set to on (blue). Then move up to the Secondary Click line and select the Click or Tap with Two Fingers item in the pop-up menu.

Another reason the contextual menu might not appear is that it is available only if any of its commands make sense for the item that you Control-click or right-click. That's why people call 'em *contextual!* They're specific to the current context, which is whatever is selected or Control-clicked.

Figure 2-7, left, shows the contextual menu that appears when you Control-click (or right-click) a document icon. Figure 2-7, right, shows the contextual menu you see when you Control-click the desktop.

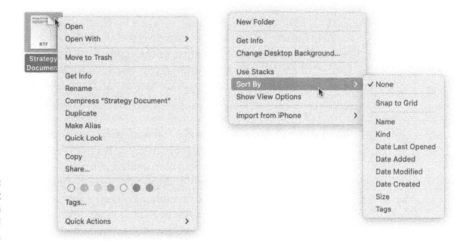

FIGURE 2-7:
Only relevant items appear on a contextual menu.

Contextual menus are also available in most apps. Open your favorite app and try Control-clicking to find out whether those menus are there. In most cases, using a contextual menu is a quick way to avoid going to the menu bar to choose a command. In some apps — such as iMovie and Music — contextual menus are the *only* way to access some commands.

To make the Finder-related contextual menus available to users who didn't have the foresight to purchase this book, Apple added the Action menu (shown in the margin) to the toolbar. As a result, people who don't know about Control-clicking or right-clicking (or have only one free hand) can access most — but not all — contextual-menu commands by clicking the Action button and displaying its context-sensitive menu of shortcuts.

Get in the habit of Control-clicking (or right-clicking or two-finger clicking) items on your screen. Before you know it, using contextual menus will become second nature to you.

REMEMBER

Recognizing disabled options

Menu items that appear in black on a menu are currently available. Menu items that aren't currently available are grayed out, to indicate that they're disabled for the time being. You can't select a disabled menu item.

In Figure 2-8, the File menu on the left is pulled down while nothing is selected in Finder; this is why many of the menu items are disabled (in gray). These items are disabled because an item (such as a window or an icon) must be selected for you to use one of these menu items. For example, the Show Original command is grayed out because it works only if the selected item is an alias. On the right side of Figure 2-8, I selected a document before I pulled down the menu; note that many of the formerly disabled commands are enabled when an icon is selected. (The Show Original command is still grayed out because the selected icon is not an alias.)

FIGURE 2-8:
File menu with nothing selected (left) and with a document icon selected (right); the disabled items appear grayed out.

Finally, note that items that end in an ellipsis (. . .), such as the Tags command in Figure 2-8, will open a dialog with additional options.

Navigating submenus

Some menu items have more menus attached to them, and these are called *submenus,* which are menus that are subordinate to a menu item. If a menu has a > arrow to the right of its name, it has a submenu.

To use a submenu, click a menu name once (to drop the menu down) and then slide your pointer down to any item with a > arrow. When the item is highlighted, move your pointer to the right just slightly. The submenu should pop out of the original menu's item, as shown in Figure 2-9.

FIGURE 2-9:
The Apple menu's
Recent Items
selection, with its
submenu
popped out.

Under the Apple menu tree

On the far-left side of the menu bar sits a little , which displays a menu when clicked. No matter what app is active, the menu is always available in the top-left corner of your menu bar.

TIP

The menu bar is always available, even with apps that hide it in full-screen mode. To make it reappear, move the pointer to the top of the screen, wait a second or two, and watch the menu bar magically reappear.

From top to bottom, the menu gives you a number of options, including the following:

>> **About This Mac:** Choose this item to see what version of macOS you're running, what kind of Mac and processor (chip) you're using, how much memory your Mac has, and the Mac's serial number.

>> **System Settings:** Choose this item to open the System Settings app (which I discuss further in Chapter 6 and elsewhere).

>> **App Store:** Choose this item to launch the Mac App Store app.

>> **Recent Items:** This option lets you quickly access apps, documents, and servers you've used recently, as shown previously in Figure 2-9.

>> **Force Quit:** Use this option only in emergencies. What's an emergency? Use it when an app becomes recalcitrant or otherwise misbehaves or refuses to quit when you say Quit.

TIP

Memorize the keyboard shortcut for Force Quit (⌘+Option+Esc). Sometimes an app gets so badly hosed that you can't click anywhere and other keyboard shortcuts won't do anything at all. It doesn't happen often, nor does it happen to everyone. If it should happen to you, calmly press ⌘+Option+Esc, and the Force Quit Applications dialog (usually) appears. Click the name of the app that's acting up and then click the Force Quit button or press the Return key to make the balky app stop balking.

WARNING

The reason Force Quit should be used only in an emergency is that if you use it on an app that's working fine and have any unsaved documents, your work since the last time you saved the file will be blown away.

Or not. The Auto Save and Versions features are *still* the default for Apple's own apps. You read more about these features in Chapter 7; if the app you're using supports Auto Save features, you shouldn't lose much (if any) work regardless of when you last saved.

>> **Shut Down options:** These five commands do exactly what their names imply:

- *Sleep:* Puts your Mac into an energy-efficient state of suspended animation. See the section about Energy Saver in Chapter 20 for details on the Energy Saver pane in System Settings and sleeping.

- *Restart:* Quits all open apps and restarts your Mac. It's quite polite about this task, asking if you want to save any unsaved changes in open documents before complying.

- *Shut Down:* Turns off your Mac. Refer to Chapter 1 for details.

- *Lock Screen (⌘+Control+Q):* Locks your screen instantly, and then requires your account password to unlock it.

- *Log Out <your account name> (⌘+Shift+Q):* Quits all open apps and logs you out. Again, your Mac will be ever so polite, asking if you want to save unsaved changes in open documents before complying. When it's done, the login screen appears.

Using keyboard-shortcut commands

Most menu items, or at least the most common ones, have *keyboard shortcuts* to help you quickly navigate your Mac without having to haggle so much with the mouse. Using these key combinations activates menu items without using the mouse; to use them, you press the Command (⌘) key and then press another key (or keys) without releasing the ⌘ key. Memorize the shortcuts that you use often.

Learn how to change keyboard shortcuts and even how to create ones of your own in Chapter 6.

REMEMBER

Some people refer to the Command key as the *Apple key*. That's because on many keyboards that key has both the pretzel-like Command-key symbol (⌘) and an Apple logo (🍎) on it. To avoid confusion, this book always refers to ⌘ as the Command key.

Chapter **3**

What's Up, Dock?

T he Dock appears at the bottom of your screen by default, providing quick access to your most-used apps, documents, and folders.

TIP

Some users prefer to have the Dock located on the left or right side of the screen instead of at the bottom. You see how to relocate your Dock (and more) in the coming pages.

Folder icons on the Dock are called *stacks,* which display their contents as your choice of a fan, a grid, or a list when clicked.

Other icons on the Dock open an app or document with one click.

The Dock is your friend. It's a great place to put files, folders, and apps you use a lot so that they're always just one click away.

REMEMBER

A Dock icon is merely a pointer (also known as an *alias* or a *shortcut)* to an app, document, or folder stored on your hard drive. So, you can add and remove icons from your Dock (as you discover shortly) without affecting the actual apps, documents, and folders. Don't be shy about adding items you use often; be even less shy about removing items you don't use.

A Quick Introduction to Your Dock

Take a minute to look at the row of icons at the bottom of your display. That row, gentle reader, is the *Dock* (shown in Figure 3-1), and those individual pictures are known as *icons* (which I discuss in greater detail momentarily). Note that I chopped the Dock in Figure 3-1 into two pieces (with the left half on top) to make the icons bigger and easier to see.

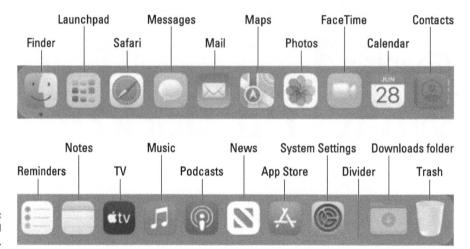

FIGURE 3-1:
The Dock and all
its default icons.

REMEMBER

Icons on the Dock and Launchpad (see Chapter 10) are odd ducks; you activate them with a single click. Just remember that most everywhere else in Finder, you click an icon to select it and double-click it to open the item it represents.

Here's the rundown on what happens when you click Dock icons:

>> If it's an **app icon,** the app opens and becomes active. If the app is already open, it becomes active, which brings all its windows to the front and displays its menu on the menu bar.

>> If it's a **document icon,** that document opens in its appropriate app, which becomes the active app. If that app is already open, it becomes the active app with this document in the front.

REMEMBER

If the item is an app or document and is already open when you click its Dock icon, the app or document becomes active.

>> If it's a **folder icon or disk icon,** a stack, fan, or grid with its contents appears so you can choose an item. If you choose Show in Finder from this menu, a Finder window opens, showing the contents of the folder or disk.

The default icons of the Dock

By default, the Dock contains icons for a number of commonly used macOS apps, and you can add icons for your own apps, files, or folders there. (The "Adding Dock icons" section later in this chapter shows you how to do that.)

But first, look at the items you find in a standard macOS Ventura Dock. If they aren't familiar to you, they certainly will be as you get to know Ventura.

I admit that I can't do justice to all the apps that come with macOS Ventura that aren't, strictly speaking, part of the operating system (OS). Alas, some of the apps in the default Dock are ones you won't be seeing much more of. But I'd hate to leave you wondering what all those icons in the Dock are, so the following list gives you a brief description of each default Dock icon (moving from left to right onscreen). If additional coverage of an item appears elsewhere in the book, the list tells you where:

>> **Finder:** The always running app that manages the desktop, files, folders, disks, and more (this chapter and Chapters 4–8)

>> **Launchpad:** A display of all your apps on a grid that looks like it belongs on an iPad or iPhone (Chapter 10)

>> **Safari:** A web browser (Chapter 13)

>> **Messages:** An app for sending and receiving text and multimedia messages as well as transferring files to and from and remotely controlling other Macs (Chapter 15)

>> **Mail:** An email app (Chapter 15)

>> **Maps:** An app that serves up maps and driving directions (Chapter 11)

>> **Photos:** An app for managing and editing photographs (Chapter 18)

>> **FaceTime:** An app for making and receiving audio and video calls (Chapter 14)

>> **Calendar:** A calendar app for managing appointments and events (Chapter 10)

>> **Contacts:** A contact-manager app (Chapter 14)

>> **Reminders:** A to-do list and reminder app (Chapter 10)

>> **Notes:** An app for making notes (Chapter 10)

>> **TV:** A video player and store (Chapter 18)

>> **Music:** An audio player and store (Chapter 17)

>> **Podcasts:** A podcast player (Chapter 18)

>> **News:** A news reader (Chapter 12)

>> **Mac App Store:** Where you access paid or free Mac apps (Chapter 20)

>> **System Settings:** An app to configure the way many aspects of your Mac work (Chapters 6, 16, and 20)

>> **Divider:** The line that separates apps on the left and documents or folders on the right (this chapter)

>> **Downloads folder:** A folder that contains files downloaded by apps such as Safari or Mail (Chapter 4)

>> **Trash:** Where you drag files and folders to delete them, or drag removable media to eject it (this chapter)

TIP

To get a quick look at the name of a Dock icon, just move (hover) your pointer over any item in the Dock. Like magic, that item's name appears above it.

It's likely that your Dock won't look *exactly* like the one shown in Figure 3-1. If you added icons to your Dock before you upgraded to Ventura, for example, you'll see those icons. If you have Apple apps such as iMovie, GarageBand, Pages, Numbers, or Keynote installed, or you get a new Mac with Ventura preinstalled, you may see their icons in your Dock. And if you've deleted one of the default icons shown in Figure 3-1 from your Dock under a previous version of macOS, it won't come back when you upgrade to Ventura.

TIP

If you don't understand what I just said or want to make your Dock look exactly like the one shown in Figure 3-1, I have good news: You find out how to do that and much more before the end of this chapter.

Also, if you see a question mark instead of an icon in the Dock, the file (app, document, or folder) it represents has been deleted.

Trash talkin'

The *Trash* is a special container where you put the items you no longer want to hang around on your hard drive(s). Got four copies of a document named *Letter to the Editor re: Bird Waste Issue* on your hard drive? Drag three of them to the Trash. Tired of tripping over old PDF and DMG files you've downloaded but no longer need? Drag them to the Trash too.

To put something in the Trash, just drag its icon onto the Trash icon in the Dock and it will move into the Trash. As with other icons, when the Trash icon is highlighted you know that you've connected with the Trash while dragging. And as with other Dock icons, the Trash icon's name appears when you move the pointer over the icon.

Two other ways to put items into the Trash are to select the items you want to dispose of and then choose File➪Move to Trash or press ⌘+Delete (⌘+Backspace on some non-Apple keyboards).

TIP

If you accidentally move something to the Trash and want it back right now, you can magically put it back where it came from in two ways.

Way #1

Choose Edit➪Undo or press ⌘+Z.

Finder usually remembers more than one action for Undo and can often undo the last *few* things you did in Finder. That's the good news. The bad news is that it redoes things in reverse order, so don't wait too long. If you perform several other file-related activities in Finder, you'll have to Undo all those actions before you can Undo your accidental Move to Trash.

In other words, as soon as you create or rename a folder, move a file from one place to another, drag a different file to the Trash, create an alias, or almost anything that affects a file or folder, choosing Edit➪Undo or pressing ⌘+Z will undo *that* action first.

You'll find that some Finder actions — most of the items on the View menu, for example — don't affect Undo. So if you drag a file to the Trash and then switch views (see Chapter 4), Undo will still un-trash the file.

Even if you do something and can't use Undo, files you drag to the Trash aren't deleted immediately. You know how the garbage in the can on the street curb sits there until the sanitation engineers come by and pick it up each Thursday? Your Mac's Trash works the same way, but without the smell. Items sit in the Trash, waiting for a sanitation engineer (you) to come along and empty it.

Way #2

So if you miss the window of opportunity to use the Undo command, don't worry. You can still retrieve the file from the Trash:

>> **To open the Trash and see what's in there,** just click its icon on the Dock. A Finder window called Trash opens, showing you the files it contains (namely, files and folders put in the Trash since the last time it was emptied).

>> **To retrieve an item that's already in the Trash,** drag it back out, either onto the desktop or back into the folder where it belongs.

Or use the secret keyboard shortcut: Select the item(s) in the Trash that you want to retrieve and press ⌘+Delete. This technique has the added benefit of magically transporting the files or folders you select from the Trash back into the folder from which they came. And, unlike Undo, the secret keyboard shortcut will work on a file or folder at any time, or at least until the next time you empty the Trash. Try it — it's sweet.

And if that doesn't work, you can Control-click or right-click a file and choose Put Back from the contextual menu. Heck, you can even click the file, click the Action button, and then click Put Back on the Action menu.

>> **To empty the Trash,** choose Finder ➪ Empty Trash or press Shift+⌘+Delete. If the Trash window is open and files are in the Trash, you see an Empty button just below its toolbar on the right. Clicking the button, of course, also empties the Trash.

You can also empty the Trash from the Dock by positioning the pointer on the Trash icon and Control-clicking or right-clicking the Trash icon. The Empty Trash menu item pops up like magic. Move the pointer over Empty Trash, and click it.

Think twice before you invoke the Empty Trash command. After you empty the Trash, the files that it contained are pretty much gone forever, or at least gone from your hard drive. There is no Undo for Empty Trash. My advice is: Before you get too bold, read Chapter 21, and back up your hard drive at least once (several times is better). After you get proficient at backups, chances improve greatly that even though the files are technically gone forever from your hard drive, you can get them back if you really want to (from your backups).

The Trash icon shows you when it has files waiting for you there; as in real life, Trash that contains files or folders looks like it's full of crumpled paper (see Figure 3-2). Conversely, when your Trash is empty, the Trash icon looks . . . well, empty.

FIGURE 3-2: The Options submenu for an app icon (News) on the Dock.

Finally, although you can't open a file that's in the Trash, you can select it and use Quick Look (shortcut: spacebar or ⌘+Y) to see its contents before you decide to use Empty Trash and permanently delete it.

And that's pretty much all there is to know about the Trash.

Opening app menus on the Dock

Clicking an app icon on the Dock launches that app — or, if the app is already open, switches you to that app and brings forward all open windows in that app.

But some app icons on the Dock — such as Calendar, Safari, and Music — also hide menus containing some handy commands. (Folder icons in the Dock have a different but no less handy menu, as you'll see in a moment.)

You can make menus for apps on the Dock appear in two ways:

>> Press and continue to hold down the mouse button.

>> Control-click or right-click.

TIP

If you use a trackpad or a Magic Mouse, a two-finger tap should do the trick. (If it doesn't do the trick, check out the Mouse and Trackpad System Settings sections in Chapter 6.)

Do any of the preceding, and you'll see a menu for that Dock icon, as shown in Figure 3-2 for the News icon.

The Options submenu offers three choices:

>> **Keep in (or Remove from) Dock:** Adds the app's icon to the Dock (or removes it from the Dock), waiting until after you quit the app if it's running. The little dot below the icon means the app is running.

>> **Open at Login:** Launches this app automatically every time you log in to this user account. This is handy for apps you want to keep running all the time, such as Mail or Safari.

>> **Show in Finder:** Opens the enclosing folder (in this instance, that would be the Applications folder) and selects the app's icon.

The other options in the menu follow:

>> **Show Recents (if available):** Displays recently used windows for this app if there are any.

>> **Open/Quit:** Opens the app, or quits the app if it's already open.

So there you have it: the default contextual menu for apps, which is what you'll see for most apps when they aren't open.

One last thing: When you Control-click or right-click the Dock icon for an app that's currently running, you may see different menus, like the ones shown in Figure 3-3 (clockwise from top left: Safari, Preview, System Settings, TextEdit, and Music).

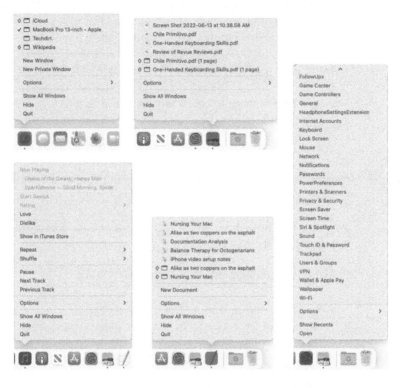

FIGURE 3-3:
Press and hold down or Control-click or right-click an open app's Dock icon, and menus such as these appear.

As you can see, some open apps provide useful app-specific commands or options.

TIP

Music has one of the best Dock menus, letting you control your music from the Dock with options such as Play/Pause, Next or Previous Track, Repeat, and Shuffle.

Other apps, including Preview and Safari in Figure 3-3, offer you a list of open windows with a check mark to indicate the active window or diamonds (as shown) to indicate windows minimized to the Dock.

Finally, the items above the list of open windows for TextEdit are recently used documents.

Reading Dock icon body language

As you use the Dock or when you're just doing regular stuff on your Mac, the Dock icons like to communicate with you. They can't talk, so they have a few moves and symbols that indicate things you might want to know. Table 3-1 should make those moves and symbols crystal clear.

TABLE 3-1

What Dock Icons Are Telling You

Icon Movement or Symbol	What It Means
The icon moves up and out of its place in the Dock for a moment.	You clicked a Dock icon, and it's letting you know that you activated it.
The icon does a little bouncy dance while that app is open but isn't *active* (that is, the app's menu bar isn't showing, and it isn't the frontmost app).	The app desires your attention; give its icon a click to find out what it wants.
A dot appears below its Dock icon.	This app is open.
An icon that isn't ordinarily in the Dock magically appears.	You see a temporary Dock icon for every app that's currently open until you quit that app. The icon appears because you've opened something or something has opened itself automatically. When you quit, its icon magically disappears.

Opening files from the Dock

REMEMBER

One useful function of the Dock is that you can use it to open an app quickly and easily. The following tips explain several handy ways to open what you need from the Dock:

>> **You can drag a document icon onto an app's Dock icon.** If the app knows how to handle that type of document, its Dock icon is highlighted, and the document opens in that app. If the app can't handle that particular type of document, the Dock icon isn't highlighted, and you can't drop the document onto it.

TIP

If the app can't handle a document, try opening the document this way: Select the document icon and choose File ⇨ Open With, or Control-click or right-click the document icon and use the Open With menu to choose the app you want to open the document with. And if you hold down the Option key, the Open With command changes to Always Open With, which enables you to change the default app that opens this document permanently.

>> **You can find the original icon of any item you see in the Dock by choosing Show in Finder from its Dock menu.** This trick opens a Finder window to the folder that contains the item's actual icon and thoughtfully selects that icon for you.

Customizing Your Dock

The Dock is a convenient way to get at oft-used icons. By default, the Dock comes stocked with icons that Apple thinks you'll need most frequently (refer to Figure 3-1), but you can customize it to contain any icons that you choose, as you discover in the following sections. You also find out how to resize the Dock to fit your new set of icons and how to choose settings for the Dock.

Adding Dock icons

REMEMBER

You can customize your Dock with favorite apps, a document you update daily, or maybe a folder containing your favorite recipes. Use the Dock for anything you need quick access to.

Adding an app, file, or folder to the Dock is as easy as 1-2-3:

1. **Open a Finder window that contains an app, a document file, or a folder you use frequently.**

TIP

You can also drag an icon — including a hard drive icon — from the desktop or any Finder window.

2. **Click the item you want to add to the Dock.**

As shown in Figure 3-4, I chose the TextEdit app. (It's highlighted.)

3. **Drag the icon out of the Finder window and onto the Dock.**

The icons to the left and right of the new icon magically part to make room for it. Note that the Dock icon isn't the actual item. That item remains wherever it was — in a window or on the desktop. The icon you see in the Dock is a shortcut that opens the item. I briefly mentioned aliases (known as *shortcuts* in the Windows world) earlier, but the icon on the Dock is actually an alias of the icon you dragged onto the Dock.

Furthermore, when you remove an icon from the Dock, as you find out how to do in a moment, you aren't removing the actual app, document, or folder. You're removing *only its shortcut* from the Dock.

TextEdit

TextEdit

TextEdit

FIGURE 3-4:
Adding an icon to
the Dock is as
easy as 1-2-3. Just
drag the icon
onto the Dock.

TextEdit

Folder, disk, document, and URL icons must sit on the right side of the divider line in the Dock; app icons must sit on the left side of it.

TIP

As long as you follow the rule, you can add several items to either side of the divider line at the same time by selecting them all and dragging the group to that side of the Dock. You can delete only one icon at a time from the Dock, however.

Adding a URL to the Dock works slightly differently. Here's a quick way to add a URL to the Dock:

1. **Open Safari, and go to the page you want to add to the Dock.**

2. **Click in the address bar to display the full URL, together with a small icon to its left that looks like a wireframe globe.**

3. **Drag that icon to the right side of the dividing line in the Dock.**

4. **Release the mouse button when the icon is right where you want it in the Dock.**

   The icons in the Dock slide over and make room, and the URL appears as a Dock icon that looks like Earth. From now on, you can click that URL icon to open that page in Safari.

TIP

If you open an item whose icon that normally doesn't appear in the Dock, and you want to keep its temporary icon in the Dock permanently, you have two ways to tell it to stick around after you quit the app:

» Control-click (or click and hold down) and choose Options ⇨ Keep in Dock from the menu that pops up.

» Drag the icon (for an app that's currently open) off and then back to the Dock (or to a different position in the Dock) without letting go of the mouse button.

Removing an icon from the Dock

Removing an item from the Dock is as easy as 1-2-3 but without the 3:

1. **Drag its icon off the Dock and a fair way onto the desktop.**

2. **When the Remove bubble appears, release the mouse button.**

3. **There is no Step 3.**

You can also choose Remove from Dock from the item's Dock menu to get it out of your Dock, but this way is way more fun.

REMEMBER

You can't remove the icon of an app that's currently running from the Dock by dragging it. Either wait until you quit the app or Control-click (or click and hold down) and deselect Options ⇨ Keep in Dock.

Also note that by moving an icon off the Dock, you aren't moving, deleting, or copying the item itself; you're just removing its icon from the Dock. The item is unchanged.

Resizing the Dock

If the default size of the Dock bugs you, you can make the Dock smaller and save yourself a lot of screen real estate. This space comes in especially handy when you add your own stuff to the Dock.

To shrink or enlarge the Dock (and its icons) without opening the System Settings window, follow these steps:

1. **Make the Sizer appear by moving your pointer over the divider line that you find between apps and documents near the right side of the Dock.**

2. **Drag the Sizer down to make the Dock smaller, holding down the mouse button until you find the size you like.**

   The more you drag this control down, the smaller the Dock gets.

3. **To enlarge the Dock again, just drag the Sizer back up.**

   Bam! Big Dock! You can enlarge the Dock until it fills your screen from side to side.

What should you put on your Dock?

Put things on the Dock that you need quick access to and that you use often, or add items that aren't quickly available from menus or a Finder window's sidebar. If you like using the Dock better than the Finder window's sidebar (for example), add your Documents, Movies, Pictures, Music, or even your Home folder or hard drive to the Dock.

Consider adding these items to your Dock:

>> **A word-processing app:** Most people use word-processing software more than any other apps. Just drag the icon for yours to the left side of the Dock, and you're good to go.

   If you don't have a word processor such as Microsoft Word or Apple Pages already, give TextEdit a try. It's in the Applications folder, and it's more powerful than you might expect from a freebie.

>> **A project folder:** You know — the folder that contains all the documents for your thesis, or all the notes for the biggest project you have at work, or your massive recipe collection . . . whatever. If you add that folder to the Dock, you can access it more quickly than if you have to open several folders to find it.

>> **A special utility or app:** You may want to add your go-to Internet apps you use (such as Skype, Spotify, and Twitter), your favorite graphics apps (such as Adobe Photoshop or Photoshop Elements), or the game you play every afternoon when you think the boss isn't watching.

>> **Your favorite URLs:** Save links to sites that you visit every day — the ones you use in your job, your favorite Mac news sites, or your personalized page from an Internet service provider (ISP). Sure, you can make one of these pages your browser's start page or bookmark it, but the Dock lets you add one or more additional URLs. (Refer to the "Adding Dock icons" section earlier in this chapter for details.)

   You can add several URL icons to the Dock, but bear in mind that the Dock and its icons shrink to accommodate added icons, which makes them harder to see. Perhaps the best idea — if you want easy access to several URLs — is to create a folder full of URLs and put that folder on the Dock. Then you can just press and hold your pointer on the folder (or Control-click the folder) to pop up a menu with all your URLs.

Even though you can make the Dock smaller, you're still limited to one row of icons. The smaller you make the Dock, the larger the crowd of icons you can amass. You have to determine for yourself what's best for you: having lots of icons available in the Dock (even though they might be difficult to see because they're so tiny) or having less clutter but fewer icons on your Dock. If you go for lots of icons, you may want to turn on Magnification, which we get to in just a moment.

TIP

After you figure out which apps you use and don't use, it's a good idea to relieve overcrowding by removing the ones you never (or rarely) use from the Dock. You can run them from Launchpad easily enough — it just takes two clicks instead of one.

Configuring your Dock settings

You can change a few things about the Dock to make it look and behave just the way you want it to. This section first covers global settings that apply to the Dock itself. After that, it explains some settings that apply only to folder and disk icons in the Dock.

Global Dock settings

To change global Dock settings, choose System Settings and then click the Desktop & Dock icon in the left pane of the System Settings window. The Desktop & Dock pane appears (see Figure 3-5).

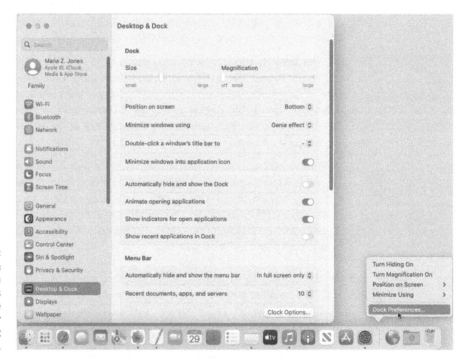

FIGURE 3-5:
The Desktop & Dock pane in System Settings (left) and the Dock resizer shortcut menu (right).

TIP

You can open the Desktop & Dock pane in System Settings also by Control-clicking or right-clicking the Dock resizer and choosing Dock Preferences from the shortcut menu.

Now you can adjust your Dock with the following settings:

>> **Size:** Note the slider bar here. Move this slider to the right (larger) or left (smaller) to adjust the size of the Dock in your Finder. As you move the slider, watch the Dock change size. (Now, *there's* a fun way to spend a Saturday afternoon!)

As you add items to the Dock, the icons — and the Dock itself — shrink to accommodate the new ones.

>> **Magnification:** This slider controls how big icons grow when you pass the pointer over them — handy when you've stuffed the Dock with so many icons it's hard to tell which is which. Or you can drag this slider to the Off position to turn off magnification entirely.

>> **Position on Screen:** In this pop-up menu, choose Left, Bottom, or Right to control which side the Dock appears on. Bottom is the default, but you may find Left or Right works better for your Mac's screen size and the apps you use most.

>> **Minimize Windows Using:** In this pop-up menu, choose the animation to play when you click a window's Minimize (yellow by default) button. The Genie Effect is the default, but the Scale Effect seems a bit faster to me.

>> **Double-Click a Window's Title Bar to Minimize (or Zoom):** In this pop-up menu, choose Minimize to minimize the window or Zoom to zoom it. Alternatively, select the – item (if you're reading this aloud, pronounce that dash as a noncommittal grunt) to have nothing happen when you double-click the title bar.

Double-clicking to minimize achieves the same result as clicking the (usually) yellow Minimize button in a window's upper-left corner. The difference is that the Minimize button is a tiny target and way over on the upper-left side of the window, whereas the title is a much easier target.

>> **Minimize Windows into Application Icon:** If you set this switch to On, you won't see a separate Dock icon for each window you minimize; instead the minimized window zips away to the app's icon on the Dock, and you restore it by Control-clicking or right-clicking the app's icon and then clicking the window name on the pop-up menu. If this switch is set to Off, each window you minimize gets its own personal icon on the right side of your Dock, and you need only click the icon to restore the window.

>> **Automatically Hide and Show the Dock:** Don't like the Dock? Maybe you want to free the screen real estate on your monitor? Then set the Automatically Hide and Show the Dock switch to On; after that, the Dock displays itself only when you move the pointer to the side of the screen where the Dock would ordinarily appear.

TIP

If the Dock isn't visible, set the Automatically Hide and Show the Dock switch to Off to bring back the Dock. Choose ⌘ ⇨ Dock ⇨ Turn Hiding On (or use its keyboard shortcut, ⌘+Option+D).

The keyboard shortcut ⌘+Option+D is a toggle, so it reverses the state of this option each time you use it.

≫ **Animate Opening Applications:** macOS animates (bounces) Dock icons when you click them to open an item. If you don't like the animation, set this switch to Off, and the bouncing ceases evermore.

≫ **Show Indicators for Open Applications:** Set this switch to On if you want each open app to display a little black indicator dot below its icon on the Dock, like the Finder icon in Figure 3-1. This app is open, whereas the others — the ones without black dots — are not. If you set this switch to Off, none of your Dock icons will ever display an indicator dot.

≫ **Show Recent Applications in Dock:** This setting automatically adds icons for apps that you've used recently but that aren't kept in the Dock. They then appear in a special Recent Applications section of the Dock between your app icons on the left and the folder and Trash icons on the right, as shown in Figure 3-6.

Notice the dividing lines, which represent the left and right edges of the Recent Applications section.

FIGURE 3-6:
The Recent Applications section of the Dock shows the three apps used most recently for which the left side of the Dock doesn't contain icons.

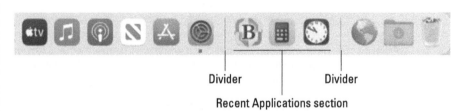

Folder and disk Dock icon menu preferences

If you click a folder or disk icon in the Dock, its contents are displayed in a fan, grid, or list menu, as shown in Figure 3-7.

If you Control-click or right-click a folder or disk icon in the Dock, its contextual menu appears, as shown in Figure 3-8.

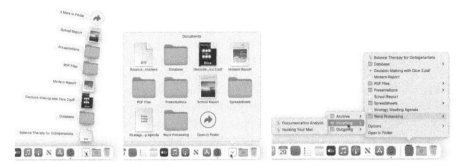

FIGURE 3-7:
My Documents
folder's Dock
menu as a fan,
list, and grid.

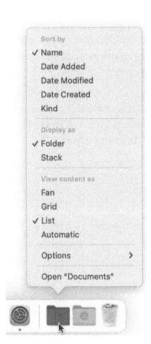

FIGURE 3-8:
The contextual
menu for my
Documents
folder.

Here are the choices on the contextual menu:

» **Sort By** determines the order in which items in the folder or drive appear when you click its Dock icon.

» **Display As** determines what the Dock icon for a folder or drive looks like. If you choose Stack, the icon takes on the appearance of the last item moved into the folder or drive. If you choose Folder, the Dock icon looks like a folder.

» **View Contents As** lets you choose Fan, Grid, or List as the menu type for the folder or drive.

TIP

The default is Automatic, which is to say that the Dock tries to choose the menu type for you. I much prefer choosing the menu type that best suits a particular folder or drive. I like list menus best, especially for folders or drives with a lot of subfolders. As you can see in Figure 3-7, the list menu is the only one that lets you see and access folders inside folders (and subfolders inside other subfolders). For folders with images, I like the grid menu because it displays easily discernible icons for the folder or drive's contents. The fan menu is fantastic (ha!) when the folder or drive contains only a few items.

» **The Options submenu** contains the following items:

- *Remove from Dock* removes the icon from the Dock.

- *Show in Finder* opens the window containing the item and selects the item. So, for example, in Figure 3-8, my Home (or iCloud) folder would open, and the Documents folder inside it would be selected.

The Dock is your friend. Now that you know how it works, make it work the way you want it to. Put those apps and folders you use most in the Dock, and you'll save yourself a significant amount of time and effort.

Chapter **4**

Getting to Know Finder and Its Desktop

O n your Mac, Finder is your starting point — the centerpiece of your Mac experience, if you will — and it's always available. In Finder windows or the desktop, you can double-click your way to your favorite app, your documents, or your folders. So in this chapter, I show you how to get the most from Finder and its desktop.

By the way, Finder has so many features that I divided them into two chapters: this one and Chapter 5, in which you discover additional desktop and Finder features to save you time and effort.

I suggest reading (or at least skimming) this chapter first. That's not just because this is Chapter 4 and 4 comes before 5. Rather, this chapter covers basic Finder and desktop features you need to grok before the features in Chapter 5 will make sense.

Introducing Finder and Its Minions: The Desktop and Icons

Finder is a special app unlike any other. Its most significant difference from other apps is that it launches automatically when you log in, is always running in the background, and doesn't include a Quit command. Put another way, Finder is omnipresent.

The desktop is a special part of Finder unlike any other.

Finally, icons and windows are the units of currency used by Finder and the desktop.

Before I dig into what Finder does and what the desktop is, here's a quick overview of some of the icons you're likely to encounter as you get to know Finder and the desktop.

Introducing the desktop

The *desktop* is the backdrop for Finder — everything you see behind the Dock and any open windows. The desktop is always available and is where you can usually find your hard drive icon(s).

TIP

If your desktop doesn't display hard drive icons and you wish it did, stay tuned.

Explaining Finder and its desktop will be a whole lot easier with a picture for reference, so take a gander at Figure 4-1, which is a glorious depiction of a typical macOS Finder window and desktop.

If you're not familiar with Finder and its desktop, here are a few tips that will come in handy as you become familiar with the icons that hang out there:

>> **Icons on the desktop behave the same as icons in a window.** You move them and copy them just as you would icons in a window. The only difference is that icons on the desktop aren't in a window. Because they're on the desktop, they're more convenient to use.

>> **The first icon you need to get to know is the icon for your start-up disk (a hard drive or solid-state drive [SSD]).** You used to be able to find it in the top-right corner of the desktop, as shown in Figure 4-1. Your Mac's start-up disk probably has the name Macintosh HD unless you've renamed it.

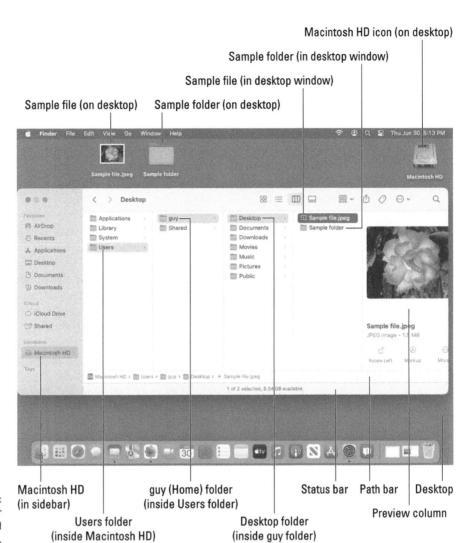

Sample file (on desktop) Sample folder (on desktop)

Sample file (in desktop window)

Sample folder (in desktop window)

Macintosh HD icon (on desktop)

FIGURE 4-1:
A typical Finder
window and
desktop.

Macintosh HD
(in sidebar)

Users folder
(inside Macintosh HD)

guy (Home) folder
(inside Users folder)

Desktop folder
(inside guy folder)

Status bar   Path bar   Desktop

Preview column

Ventura doesn't display the start-up disk's icon on the desktop by default. So if you don't see your start-up (boot) disk's icon on the desktop but would like to, select the Hard Drives check box on the General tab of Finder Settings, as described in "Configuring Finder settings" later in this chapter.

>> **Other disc or hard drive icons appear on the desktop by default.** When you insert a CD or DVD, or connect an external hard drive or a thumb drive, the disc or drive icon *does* appear on the desktop near the top-right corner. This feature *is* enabled by default; if yours isn't enabled, just open Finder Settings and select its check box, as described later in the chapter.

>> **You can move an item to the desktop to make it easier to find.** Simply click any icon in any window, and without releasing the mouse button, drag it out of the window and onto the desktop. Then release the mouse button. This action moves the file from wherever it was to the desktop. Now you can drag the icon elsewhere on the desktop if necessary.

If you drag an item from an external volume to any location on your start-up disk (including the desktop), the item is copied, not moved. Put another way, the item is moved if it's on the same disk or volume, and copied if it's on another disk or volume.

TECHNICAL STUFF

Volume is the generic term for any storage container — a hard drive, SSD, CD, DVD, disk image, or remote disk — that appears in the sidebar's Locations section.

TIP

At the bottom of the Finder window in Figure 4-1 are two optional bars. The lower of the two is called the *status bar*; it tells you how many items are in each window and, if any are selected, how many of the total you've selected, as well as how much space is available on the hard drive containing this window. And just above the status bar is the *path bar*, which shows the path from the top level of your hard drive to the selected file (which is Sample file.jpeg in Figure 4-1). You can show or hide the status bar by choosing View⇨ Hide/Show Status Bar and show or hide the path bar by choosing View⇨ Hide/Show Path Bar. Finally, when the toolbar is hidden (see the next section, "Bellying up to the toolbar"), the status bar moves to the top of the window. The path bar remains at the bottom of the window no matter what.

Bellying up to the toolbar

In addition to the sidebar (introduced in Chapter 2) and some good old-fashioned double-clicking, the macOS Finder window offers additional navigation aids on the toolbar — namely, the Back and Forward icons, as well as the extra-helpful View icons. You can find other handy features on the Go menu, discussed a little later in this chapter.

In case you didn't know, the toolbar (see Figure 4-2) is the area at the top of all Finder windows, which (among other things) displays the window's name. On the toolbar, you'll find icons that enable you to navigate quickly and act on selected icons. To activate a toolbar icon, click it.

FIGURE 4-2:
A Finder window's default toolbar.

You say you don't want to see the toolbar at the top of the window? Okay! Just choose View⇨ Hide Toolbar or press its keyboard shortcut (⌘+Option+T), and it's gone. Want it back? Choose View⇨ Show Toolbar or press ⌘+Option+T again.

Alas, hiding the toolbar also hides the sidebar, which is more useful. If only you could choose to hide them independently. To make matters worse, choosing View⇨ Hide Sidebar (shortcut: ⌘+Control+S) lets you hide the sidebar without hiding the toolbar. It's been like this for a long time, and for whatever reason, you *still* can't hide the toolbar while keeping the sidebar visible! Boo. Hiss.

REMEMBER

When you hide the toolbar, opening a folder spawns a *new* Finder window. The default, which is probably what you're used to, is for folders to open in place, displaying their contents in a tab in the current window.

The toolbar's default icons are shown in Figure 4-2. So if you customized your toolbar by choosing View⇨ Customize Toolbar, yours won't look exactly like Figure 4-2.

TIP

To see text labels for your toolbar icons (as shown in Figure 4-3), Control-click or right-click the toolbar and then choose Icon and Text from the contextual menu.

FIGURE 4-3:
Use the Action pop-up menu to perform common actions on selected items.

Here's the lowdown on the toolbar's default icons, from left to right:

>> **Forward and Back icons:** Clicking the Forward and Back icons displays the folders that you've viewed in this window in sequential order. These icons are a lot like those in a web browser.

Here's an example of how the Back icon works. Suppose that you're in your Home folder. You click the Favorites icon, and a split-second later, you realize that you actually need something in the Home folder. Just click the Back icon, and — *poof!* — you're back Home. As for the Forward icon, well, it moves you in the opposite direction, through folders that you've visited in this window. These icons are really handy, but for speed, use the keyboard shortcuts ⌘+[for Back and ⌘+] for Forward to zip along your folder paths.

>> **View icons:** The four View icons change the way that the window displays its contents.

You have four ways to view a window: Icon, List, Column, and Gallery. Some people like columns, some like icons, and others love lists or galleries. To each their own. Play with the four Finder views to see which one works best for you. Column view is great for navigating, whereas List view makes it simple to sort a folder's contents by creation date or size. And Gallery view is great for folders with documents because you can see the contents of many document types right in the window, as I explain shortly.

Each view also has a handy keyboard shortcut: ⌘+1 for Icon view, ⌘+2 for List view, ⌘+3 for Column view, and ⌘+4 for Gallery view. (Views are so useful that you'll find an entire section devoted to them later in this chapter.)

>> **Group By/Sort By:** Click this icon to see a pop-up menu with options for grouping this window's contents. Hold down the Option key to change the sort order within the selected group. Note that the Group By/Sort By menu works in all four views. Read more about Group By/Sort By in "What's next on the (View) menu?" later in this chapter.

>> **Share:** Click here to share the selected items with others. A pop-up menu lets you choose to share via apps such as Mail, Messages, AirDrop, and Notes.

macOS's extensible architecture lets you add other services (such as Vimeo or LinkedIn) and apps (such as Photos and Aperture) to your Share menu. To manage these extensions, choose Edit Actions from the Share pop-up menu. Alternatively, you can launch the System Settings app, click the Privacy & Security icon in the sidebar, click Extensions on the Privacy & Security screen, and then click Sharing.

>> **Add Tags:** Click this icon to assign one or more named and colored tags to selected items. You find out more about tags and tagging in "Customizing Finder Windows" later in this chapter.

TIP

>> **Action:** Click this icon to see a pop-up menu of all the context-sensitive actions you can perform on selected icons, as shown in Figure 4-3.

If you see angle brackets (>>) at the right edge of the toolbar, as in Figure 4-3, at least one toolbar item isn't visible. Click the angle brackets, and a menu displays all hidden items (Group By, Share, Add Tags, and Action in Figure 4-3). Or expand the window so that it's wide enough to display all the items on the toolbar.

>> **Search:** Click the little magnifying glass, and the Search box appears. This icon is a nifty way to search for files or folders quickly. Just type a word (or even a few letters), and in a few seconds, the window fills with a list of files that match. You can also start a search by choosing File ➪ Find (shortcut: ⌘+F). You find out all about searching in Chapter 10.

Figuring out what an icon is

What's an icon? Glad you asked. Each Finder icon represents an item or a container on your hard drive. *Containers* — hard drives, USB thumb drives, folders, CDs, DVDs, shared network volumes, and so on — can contain a virtually unlimited number of app files, document files, and folders (which can contain an unlimited number of app files, document files, and folders).

Icons on the dock and the sidebar of Finder windows aren't the same as the Finder icons I describe in this chapter; they're simply convenient pointers to actual Finder icons. Technically, Dock and sidebar icons are aliases. (If you don't know what an alias is, you're going to find out long before the thrilling conclusion of this chapter.)

Anyway, working with icons is easy:

>> Click to select.

>> Double-click to open.

>> Click and drag to move.

>> Release the mouse button to drop.

But enough talk. It's time to see what these puppies look like.

Identifying your Finder icons in the wild

Although all icons work the same way, they come in different kinds, shapes, and sizes. When you've been around the Mac for a while, you develop a sixth sense about icons and can guess what an unfamiliar icon contains just by looking at it.

Here are the major icon types:

>> **App icons** represent apps, also known as *applications* or *programs* — the software you use to accomplish tasks on your Mac. Mail, Safari, and Calendar are apps. So are Microsoft Word and Adobe Photoshop.

App icons are usually squarish so that they can look more or less regular on the Dock and on the Launchpad screen. The first row of icons in Figure 4-4 displays an assortment of app icons.

>> **Document icons** represent files created by apps. Letters created with TextEdit are documents. This chapter began life as a document created in Microsoft Word. And spreadsheet, PDF, video, image, and song files are all documents.

Document icons are often reminiscent of a piece of paper, as shown in the second row of icons in Figure 4-4.

TIP

If your document icons are generic (like the first three icons in the second row of Figure 4-4), but you prefer icons that reflect their contents (like the last three icons in the second row of Figure 4-4), open View Options or press the ⌘+J shortcut and then select the Show Icon Preview check box. (See Chapter 20 for additional details about View Options.)

FIGURE 4-4: Icons come in many shapes and designs.

>> **Folder and disk icons** represent the Mac's organizational containers. You can put icons — and the apps or documents they stand for — in folders or disks. You can put folders in disks or in other folders, but you can't put a disk inside another disk.

WARNING

Folders look like . . . well, manila folders (what a concept) and can contain just about any other file. You use folders to organize your files and apps on your hard drive. You can have as many folders as you want, so don't be afraid to create new ones. The thought behind the whole folders thing is pretty obvious: If your hard drive is a filing cabinet, folders are its drawers and folders. (Duh!) The third row of Figure 4-4 shows some typical folder icons.

And although disks behave pretty much like folders, their icons often look like disks, as shown in the last row of Figure 4-4.

>> **Alias icons** are wonderful organizational tools. See the next section, "Aliases Are Awesome!" to find out just how useful they are.

TIP

If you're looking for details about how to organize your icons in folders, move them around, delete them, and so on, hang in there. Chapter 8 is about organizing and managing files and folders.

Aliases Are Awesome!

An *alias* is a tiny file that automatically opens the file, folder, disk, or network volume that it represents. Although an alias is technically an icon, it's different from other icons; it does nothing but open a different icon when you double-click. Put another way, aliases are organizational tools that let you access a file from more than one place without creating multiple copies of the file.

An alias is very different from a duplicated file. The Preview app, for example, uses around 11 megabytes (MB) of disk space. If you were to *duplicate* Preview, you'd have two files on your hard drive requiring around 11 MB of disk space apiece.

An *alias* of Preview, on the other hand, looks just like the original Preview icon and opens Preview when you double-click it, but it uses a mere 4 kilobytes (K) of disk space — a tiny fraction of its parent icon's size. So try placing aliases of the apps and files you use most often in convenient places such as the desktop or a folder in your Home folder.

Why else are aliases so great? Well, they open any file or folder (or app) on any hard drive from anywhere else on any hard drive, which is a very good trick. But there are other reasons why aliases are awesome:

TIP

>> **Convenience:** Aliases enable you to make items appear to be in more than one place, which on many occasions is exactly what you want to do. You could keep an alias of your word-processing app on your desktop and another in your Documents folder for quick access, for example. Aliases enable you to open your word processor right away without having to navigate into the depths of your Applications folder every time you need it.

While you're at it, you might want to put an icon for your word processor in both the Dock and the sidebar to make it even easier to open your word processor without a lot of clicking.

>> **Flexibility and organization:** You can create aliases and store them anywhere in your Mac's file system to represent the same document in several folders.

>> **Integrity:** Some apps must remain in the same folder as their supporting files and folders. These apps won't function properly unless they're in the same folder as their dictionaries, thesauruses, data files (for games), templates, and so on. Thus, you can't put the actual icons for such apps on the desktop without impairing their functionality. Aliases let you access apps like those from anywhere on your hard drive. (But it's probably best to leave all your apps in the Applications folder, where they belong.)

macOS gives you all the tools you need to organize your files neatly in folders, but you're not obliged to do so. The speedy Spotlight search mechanism, along with tools such as Launchpad and Mission Control (all, not coincidentally, discussed in Chapter 9), as well as the sidebar's Recents item, let you find pretty much any file on your disk in seconds.

Creating aliases

When you create an alias, its icon looks the same as the original icon it represents, but a tiny arrow called a *badge* (shown in the margin) appears in the bottom-left corner of its icon. If you create the alias in the same folder as the original icon, the alias gets *alias* tacked onto its name for clarity. Figure 4-5 shows an alias and its *parent* icon — the icon that opens if you double-click the alias.

To create an alias for an icon, do one of the following:

>> Click the parent icon and choose File ⇨ Make Alias.

>> Click the parent icon and press ⌘+Control+A.

>> Click the parent icon, open the Action menu (on the toolbar of all Finder windows), and choose the Make Alias command.

>> Control-click or right-click the parent icon, and choose Make Alias from the contextual menu that appears.

>> Click the parent icon, press and hold down ⌘+Option, and then drag the icon to where you want the alias. Presto! An alias appears where you release the mouse button. If you drag to a different folder, the name of an alias you create this way doesn't inherit the *alias* suffix. (If you drag within a folder, the alias still gets the suffix.)

Agenda.docx   Agenda.docx alias

FIGURE 4-5: An alias (right) and its parent.

Deleting aliases

To delete an alias, simply drag it to the Trash icon on the dock. That's it! You can also Control-click it and choose Move to Trash from the contextual menu that appears (right-click or Control-click or two-finger tap), or select the icon and press ⌘+Delete.

Deleting an alias does *not* delete the parent item. If you want to delete the parent item, you have to go hunt it down and kill it yourself.

Hunting down an alias's parent

Suppose that you create an alias of a file, and later, you want to delete both the alias and its parent file, but you can't find the parent file. What do you do? Well, you can use Finder's Find function to find it. (Try saying that three times fast.) But here are faster ways to find the parent icon of an alias:

>> Select the alias icon and choose File ➪ Show Original.

>> Select the alias icon and press the keyboard shortcut ⌘+R.

>> Select the alias icon, open the Action menu on the toolbar, and choose the Show Original command.

>> Control-click (or right-click or two-fingered tap on a trackpad) the alias icon and choose Show Original from the contextual menu.

Any of these methods opens a Finder window to the folder containing the parent document, with its icon selected so you can't miss it.

The View(s) from a Window

Views are part of what makes your Mac feel like *your* Mac. Finder offers four views, so you can select the best one for any occasion. Some people like one view so much that they rarely (or never) use others. Other people memorize the keyboard short-cuts to switch views instantly without reaching for the mouse. Try 'em all, and use the one(s) you prefer.

Moving through folders fast in Column view

Column view is a darn handy way to look through a lot of folders quickly and at the same time, and it's especially useful when those folders are filled with graph-ics files. This view is my favorite way to display windows in Finder.

To switch the current window to Column view, shown in Figure 4-6, click the Column view icon on the toolbar (shown in the margin), choose View⇨As Columns in Finder, or press ⌘+3.

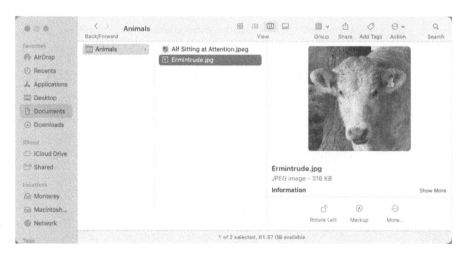

FIGURE 4-6:
A Finder window
in Column view.

Here's how I clicked around in Column view to see the list of folders and files you see in Figure 4-6:

1. When I clicked the Documents icon in the sidebar, its contents appeared in the column to the right.

2. When I clicked the folder titled Animals in this column, its contents appeared in the second column.

3. When I clicked Ermintrude.jpg in the second column, the contents of that file appeared in the third column, along with information about the file, such as its size (316 KB), and buttons for rotating the image, applying markup to it, and taking other actions.

TIP

The third column is displaying a preview — a feature that's available in all views when you choose View ➪ Show/Hide Preview. You can modify the information you see in the preview by choosing View ➪ Show Preview Options and enabling the items you want to display in the preview column.

Here are some helpful tips for poking around Column view:

>> **You can have as many columns in a Column view window as your screen can handle.** Just drag any edge or corner of the window to enlarge it so that new columns have room to open. You can also click the green Zoom (Maximize) button to make the window fill the screen. (**Hint:** To get out of full-screen mode, press Esc, or move your cursor to the top of the screen and then click the green Zoom button that appears near the top-left corner.)

TIP

If you Option-click the green Zoom button, the window expands just enough to display all columns with content in them.

>> **You can drag the column divider lines to resize the column width.** To be specific:

- If you drag a divider line left or right, the column to its left resizes.

- If you hold down the Option key when you drag a divider line, all columns resize at the same time.

- If you double-click a divider line, the column to its left expands to Right Size, which is the width of the widest item in the column plus a secret distance known only to Apple.

- If you press Option and double-click a divider line, all columns expand individually to Right Size.

- If you right- or Control-click a divider line, you see a pop-up menu with three sizing options: Right Size This Column, Right Size All Columns Individually, and Right Size All Columns Equally. You'll also see Import from iPhone or iPad if an iPhone or iPad is near (or connected to) your Mac.

>> **The preview column displays information about the highlighted item to its left, but only if that item isn't a folder or disk.** Why? Well, if the item were a folder or disk, its contents would be in this column.

For many items, the picture you see in the preview column is an enlarged view of the file's icon. You see a preview only (as in Figure 4-6) when the selected item is saved in a format that Quick Look (which you discover in Chapter 9) can interpret — which is to say most image file formats, including TIFF, JPEG, PNG, GIF, and PDF, as well as many other file formats, including Microsoft Word and Pages.

TIP

If you don't like having the preview displayed in Column view but want it to remain in all other views, choose View ⇨ Show View Options and deselect the Show Preview Column check box in the resulting dialog. You can do the same for any other view or turn the preview off in all views by choosing View ⇨ Hide Preview.

Perusing in Icon view

Icon view is a free-form view that allows you to move your icons around within a window to your heart's content. Figure 4-4, earlier in this chapter, shows Icon view.

To display a window in Icon view, click the Icon view icon on the toolbar (shown in the margin), choose View ⇨ As Icons in Finder, or press ⌘+1.

TIP

The best part of Icon view is the Icon Size slider in the bottom-right corner of the status bar, which you can drag to make the icons just the size you want. Note that the status bar and Icon Size slider move to the top of the window if the window's sidebar and toolbar are hidden.

Listless? Try viewing folders as a list

Next up is List view (shown in Figure 4-7), which displays little angle bracket to the left of each folder. These angle brackets, which were called *disclosure triangles* (and actually were triangles) in earlier macOS releases, let you see the contents of a folder without opening it. This view also allows you to select items from multiple folders at the same time and to move or copy items between folders in a single window. Finally, this view is the one in which Ventura presents Spotlight search results.

To display a window in List view, click the List view icon on the toolbar (shown in the margin), choose View ⇨ As List in Finder, or press ⌘+2.

Sorting indicator (for Name column)

Disclosure angle brackets   Column dividers   Preview

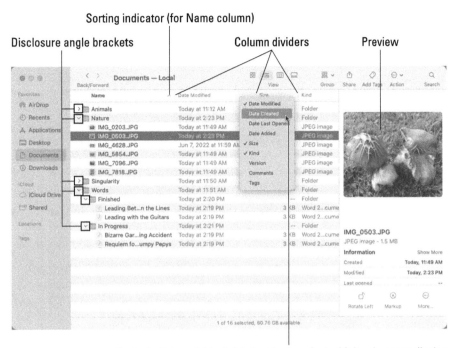

FIGURE 4-7:
A window in
List view.

Control-click or right-click in header to select which columns to display

When you're in List view, the following tips can help you breeze through your folders to find what you're looking for:

TIP

WARNING

>> **To disclose a folder's contents, click the angle bracket to its left or, if the folder is selected, press the right-arrow key.** Figure 4-7 shows the results of clicking the angle bracket to the left of the Words folder and selecting (highlighting) the Words folder and pressing the right-arrow key.

I pressed Option+→ in Figure 4-8, so all the Words folder's subfolders (the Finished folder and the In Progress folder in this case) also expanded. And if either of these subfolders (or any other subfolder in the Words folder) had subfolders, they too would have been expanded when I pressed Option+→.

To close an open folder, click the angle bracket again or select the folder and press the left-arrow key. To close all open folders in a List-view window, choose Edit ➪ Select All (or press ⌘+A) and then press Option+←.

The angle brackets don't appear if you're using groups. To see the angle brackets, choose View ➪ Use Groups or press its keyboard shortcut, ⌘+Control+0 (zero). These toggles will turn groups off if they're on or on if they're off. You could also choose None from the Group icon's pop-up menu on the toolbar.

Disclosure angle brackets and groups are an either/or situation: You have either disclosure angle brackets or groups, but not both at the same time (in the same window or tab).

>> **Click the column header to sort items in List view.** Note the little caret (^) at the right edge of the selected column (the Name column in Figure 4-7). That caret is the column's sorting indicator. If the caret points upward, as it does in Figure 4-7, the items in the corresponding column are sorted in alphabetical order; if you click the header (Name) again, the caret will flip upside down and point downward, and the items will be listed in the opposite (reverse alphabetical) order. This behavior is true for all columns in List-view windows.

>> **You can change the order in which columns appear in a window.** To do so, press and hold a column's name and then drag to the left or right until it's where you want it. Release the mouse button, and the column moves.

The exception (isn't there always an exception?) is that the Name column always appears first in List-view windows; you can move all other columns about at will. In fact, you can even hide and show columns other than Name if you like using the View Options window.

TIP

It's even easier to hide or maximize columns by Control-clicking or right-clicking any column header (as shown below the Date Modified column in Figure 4-8). Column names with check marks are displayed; column names that are unchecked are hidden.

FIGURE 4-8:
A Finder window in Gallery view.

TIP

You can fine-tune all four views and the desktop by using the View Options window. Just choose View ➪ Show View Options or press ⌘+J. The options you see apply to the active window or to the desktop. Click the Use as Defaults button to apply these options to all windows in that view (that is, Icon, List, Column, or Gallery).

» **To widen or shrink a column, hover the cursor over the dividing line between that column, and drag left or right.** When your cursor is over the dividing line in the header, it changes to a double-headed resizer, as shown in the margin.

Hangin' in the Gallery (view)

Gallery view is the latest iteration of what used to be called Cover Flow view. To display a window in Gallery view, click the Gallery view icon on the toolbar (shown in the margin), choose View ➪ As Gallery in Finder, or press ⌘+4. Figure 4-8 shows Gallery view.

Although Gallery view is useful only for folders with documents or images, it does offer at least three cool features:

» The selected item (the snappily named IMG_7818.JPG in Figure 4-9) appears in a preview at the top of the window.

» The preview column displays additional information about the selected item.

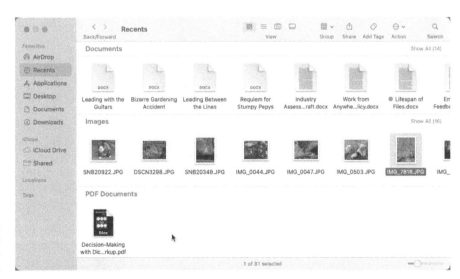

FIGURE 4-9: The items in this window are grouped by Kind.

>> You can flip through previews by clicking the images to the left or right of the current image or by pressing the left- or right-arrow key.

What's next on the (View) menu?

Finder's View menu offers several commands in addition to the four views. These commands might help you peruse your icons more easily:

>> **Use Groups** (active window only): When this command is enabled, it subdivides the items in the active window into groups, as shown in Figure 4-9. In the figure, the items in the Recents folder are grouped by Kind, which gives groups such as Documents, Images, and PDF Documents.

>> **Sort By:** This submenu offers the following options for sorting items in the active window:

- None (no shortcut)

- Snap to Grid (no shortcut)

- Name (⌘+Option+Control+1)

- Kind (⌘+Option+Control+2)

- Date Last Opened (⌘+Option+Control+3)

- Date Added (⌘+Option+Control+4)

- Date Modified (⌘+Option+Control+5)

- Date Created (no shortcut)

- Size (⌘+Option+Control+6)

- Tags (⌘+Option+Control+7)

Note that the Sort By command becomes Group By when Groups are enabled.

>> **Clean Up:** Clean Up is available only in Icon view or on the desktop when no windows are active. Choose this command to align icons to an invisible grid; use it to keep your windows and desktop neat and tidy. (If you like this invisible grid, don't forget that you can turn it on or off for the desktop and individual windows by using View Options.) If no windows are active, the command cleans up your desktop instead. (To deactivate all open windows, click anywhere on the desktop or close all open windows.)

>> **Clean Up By:** This command combines the tidiness of the Clean Up command with the organizational rigor of the Sort By command. Clean Up By sorts the icons by your choice of criteria:

- Name (⌘+Option+1)

- Kind (⌘+Option+2)

- Date Modified (⌘+Option+5)

- Date Created (no shortcut)

- Size (⌘+Option+6)

- Tags (⌘+Option+7)

Clean Up By is similar to the Sort By command, but unlike Sort By, Clean Up By is a one-time affair. After you've used it, you can once again move icons around and reorganize them any way you like.

TIP

Unlike Clean Up By, which is a one-shot command, Sort By is persistent and will continue to reorganize your icons automatically. In other words, after you've told macOS to sort the icons in a window, you can't move those icons around.

One last thing: The Clean Up and Clean Up By commands are available only for windows viewed as icons. The Sort By command is available in all four views and remains in effect if you switch to a different view or close the window. To stop Finder from arranging icons in a window, choose View ⇨ Sort By ⇨ None, or Option-click the toolbar's Group pop-up menu and choose None.

WARNING

If you take great pains to place icons carefully in specific places on your desktop, beware of the Clean Up By and Sort By commands: They'll mess up your perfectly arranged desktop icons. And alas, cleaning up your desktop still isn't something that macOS lets you undo.

Finder on the Menu

Finder's menu bar is packed with useful goodies. In the following sections, I dig into the commands that you'll find useful.

The actual Finder menu

Here are a few of the main items you can find on the Finder menu:

>> **About Finder:** Choose this command to find out which version of Finder is running on your Mac.

TIP

For Finder, the About menu item isn't particularly useful, but you'll likely find it more helpful for other apps. The About dialog for other apps usually gives information about the app's version number, which you may need for troubleshooting esoteric problems, and — for a paid app — your license or subscription number, which you may need to commandeer tech support.

» **Settings:** Use the choices here to control how Finder looks and acts. Find out the details in "Configuring Finder settings" later in this chapter.

» **Services:** One cool feature of macOS apps is the accessibility of Services. If nothing is selected in Finder, the Services menu contains only a grayed-out No Services Apply item and the Services Settings command, as shown in the top panel of Figure 4-10. When you have a Finder icon or icons selected, you can choose among several Services, as shown in the middle panel of Figure 4-10. Finally, if you have a word or words selected in an app (TextEdit is shown in the bottom panel of Figure 4-10), you have a slew of options.

As you'll have guessed, the items you see on the Services menu are context-sensitive, so what you see on yours will depend on what you have selected. If you look at the Services menu and don't find anything interesting, try selecting something else and looking again; you might be pleasantly surprised.

Finally, if you'd like to add even more services to this menu, choose the last item on the menu: Services Settings. Then you can enable dozens of useful services that aren't available by default.

» **Hide Finder (⌘ +H):** Use this command when Finder windows are open and are distracting you. Issuing the Hide Finder command makes Finder inactive (another app becomes active) and hides any open Finder windows. To make Finder visible again, choose Show All from the active app's self-named menu (if TextEdit were the active app, for example, you'd choose TextEdit ⇨ Show All) or click the Finder icon on the dock.

TIP

The advantage of hiding Finder — rather than closing or minimizing all your windows to get a clean screen — is that you don't have to open all the windows again when you're ready to get them back. Instead, just choose Show All (to see all windows in all apps) or click the Finder icon on the Dock to see all Finder windows.

» **Hide Others (Option+⌘ +H):** This command hides all windows associated with all running apps except the active app. It appears on most apps' self-named menus and is good for hiding distractions so you can focus on one thing: the unhidden app.

TIP

Another easy way to hide all open apps and windows while activating Finder is to hold down the ⌘ and Option keys and then click the Finder icon on the dock. This technique works with whatever app is active, not just Finder. So if you're surfing the web and decide that you want to see only Safari's windows onscreen, ⌘+Option-click the Safari icon on the Dock, and it will happen instantly.

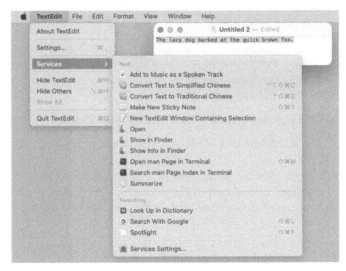

>> **Show All:** Use this command as the antidote to both of the Hide commands. Choose it, and nothing is hidden anymore.

Note that all three of these commands require at least one app to be running and not hidden (in addition to Finder). When Finder is the only app running or not hidden, these three commands are unavailable.

You can achieve much the same effect as all this hide-and-show jazz with Mission Control, which I discuss in Chapter 9. Also in Chapter 9, you learn about Stage Manager, a feature for flipping among a set of apps quickly.

TIP

Finally, if you noticed that Finder menu's Empty Trash command isn't mentioned here, that's because it gets detailed coverage in Chapter 8.

Like a road map: The current folder's pop-up menu

On every window's title bar is the name of the folder (or disk) that you're viewing in this window: the highlighted folder. You know that already. What you may not know is that the folder name offers a hidden road map to this folder from the top level. The following steps explain how it works:

1. **⌘-click, Control-click, or right-click the folder's name on the title bar.**

   A pop-up menu appears, with the current folder (Process in Figure 4-11) at the top.

2. **Select any folder in the menu, and release the mouse button to display that folder's contents.**

   As shown in Figure 4-11, the contents of the Process folder are displayed in the window. If I highlight the guy folder (as I've done in Figure 4-11) and release the mouse button, the contents of the guy folder would replace the contents of the Process folder in this window.

3. **After jumping to a new folder, click the Back button.**

   Hey, you're right back where you were before you touched that pop-up menu!

TIP

Don't forget that you can display the path bar near the bottom of the window (it's displayed in Figure 4-11) by choosing View➪ Show Path Bar. Then you can double-click any folder displayed on the path bar to open it.

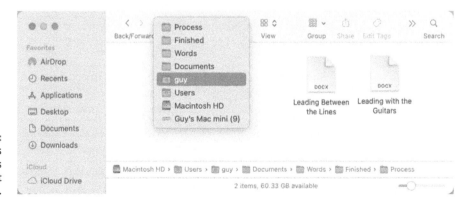

FIGURE 4-11:
Traverse folders from this convenient pop-up menu.

This pop-up-menu move works not only in Finder windows, but also on the title bar of most document windows (Word, Photoshop, and so on), showing you the path to the folder containing the document you're working on.

Go places with the Go menu

The Go menu is chock-full of shortcuts. The items on this menu take you to various places on your Mac — many of the same ones where you can go with the Finder window's toolbar — and a few other places. The following list gives you a brief look at the items on the Go menu:

>> **Back (⌘+[):** Use this menu option to return to the last open Finder window. It's equivalent to the Back button on the Finder toolbar, in case you have the toolbar hidden.

>> **Forward (⌘+]):** This command is the opposite of using the Back command, moving you forward through every folder you open. You can't go forward until you've gone back.

>> **Enclosing Folder (⌘+↑):** This command tells the Finder window to display the folder that contains (encloses) the currently selected item.

>> **Recents (Shift+⌘+F):** This command shows you all your recent document files at the same time.

TIP

After choosing Recents, you might choose View ➪ Sort By (or View ➪ Group By) to put these files in a semblance of order.

>> **Documents (⌘+Shift+O):** You'll probably use this command often because the Documents folder is a great place to save documents you create.

>> **Desktop (⌘+Shift+D):** Use this command to display the Desktop folder, which contains the same icons as the desktop you see behind open windows.

>> **Downloads (⌘+Option+L):** This command opens your Downloads folder, which is where files you download in Safari, save as attachments in Mail, or receive via AirDrop (explained shortly) are saved by default.

>> **Home (⌘+Shift+H):** Use this command to have the Finder window display your Home folder (which is named with your short name).

>> **Computer (⌘+Shift+C):** This command tells the Finder window to display the Computer level, showing your Mac's disks and the network to which the Mac is connected.

>> **AirDrop (⌘+Shift+R):** AirDrop lets you share files wirelessly with anyone around you. No setup or special settings are required. Just click the AirDrop icon in the Finder sidebar, choose this menu item, or press the keyboard

shortcut, and your Mac automatically discovers other people nearby who are using AirDrop.

AirDrop works between Macs, iPhones, iPads, and the discontinued iPod touch (RIP).

>> **Network (⌘+Shift+K):** This command displays whatever is accessible on your network in the Finder window.

>> **iCloud Drive (⌘+Shift+I):** This command opens a window that displays the contents of your iCloud drive (which you read more about in Chapter 8).

>> **Applications (⌘+Shift+A):** This command displays your Applications folder, the usual storehouse for all the apps that came with your Mac (and the most likely place to find the apps you install).

>> **Utilities (⌘+Shift+U):** This command gets you to the Utilities folder inside the Applications folder in one fell swoop. The Utilities folder is the repository of such useful items as Disk Utility (which lets you erase, format, verify, and repair disks) and Disk Copy (which you use to create and mount disk-image files).

>> **Recent Folders:** Use this submenu to go back quickly to a folder that you visited recently. Every time you open a folder, macOS creates an alias to it and stores it in the Recent Folders folder. You can open any of these aliases by choosing Go ⇨ Recent Folders. If you've been using folders that have embarrassing names, and someone is about to look over your shoulder, click Clear Menu to wipe the list.

>> **Go to Folder (⌘+Shift+G):** This command summons the Go to the Folder window. Look at your desktop. Maybe it's cluttered with lots of windows, or maybe it's empty. Either way, suppose that you're several clicks from a folder that you want to open. If you know the path from your hard drive to that folder, you can type the path to the folder in the Go to the Folder text box — separating folder names with forward slashes (/) — and then click Go to move (relatively) quickly to the folder you need.

REMEMBER

The first character you type must also be a forward slash.

This particular dialog is a tad clairvoyant in that it tries to guess which folder you mean by the first letter or two that you type after a forward slash. If the folder you seek isn't in the list of suggestions, just keep typing.

>> **Connect to Server (⌘+K):** If your Mac is connected to a network or to the Internet, use this command to reach those remote resources.

One last thing: If you're looking for the Library folder inside your Home folder, open the Go menu, hold down the Option key to display the Library item on the menu, and then click Library. macOS hides the command to discourage casual access to the Library folder.

Customizing Finder Windows

Finder is outrageously handy. It not only gives you convenient access to multiple windows, but also offers ways to tweak what you see until you get what works best for you. So whereas earlier sections in this chapter explain what Finder is and how it works, the following sections ask, "How would you like it to be?"

Adding folders to the sidebar

Adding any file or folder you like to the sidebar is easy. All you need to do is select the file or folder you want to add and then choose File⇨Add to Sidebar (or press its shortcut, ⌘+Control+T). Now you can use the item any time you like by clicking it in the sidebar of any Finder window. Better still, you can move files or folders into folders in the sidebar by dragging them to the folder's sidebar icon.

TIP

You can add folders (but not files) to the sidebar by dragging them to the sidebar.

WARNING

Be careful not to drag a folder *onto* another folder; if you do, it'll be moved inside that folder instead of being added to the sidebar. You'll see a little line above or below existing folders in the sidebar; that line shows you where this folder will appear if you release the mouse button. If a folder in the sidebar is highlighted, and you don't see the little line, releasing the mouse button won't add the folder to the sidebar, but move it into the highlighted folder.

After you've loaded up the sidebar with the items you want, you can drag them into your preferred order.

To remove an item from the sidebar, right-click or Control-click the item and choose Remove from Sidebar from the contextual menu. Or drag the item off the sidebar and release the mouse button when the little x-in-a-circle icon appears.

Configuring Finder settings

You can find Finder and Desktop settings by choosing Finder⇨Settings. In the Finder Settings window that appears, click the icons on the toolbar to display one of the four Finder Settings panes: General, Tags, Sidebar, and Advanced.

General pane

In the General pane of the Finder Settings window, you find the following options:

>> **Show These Items on the Desktop check boxes:** Select or deselect these check boxes to choose whether icons for hard drives; external disks; CDs,

DVDs, and iPods; and connected servers appear on the desktop. macOS Ventura selects the External Disks check box and the CDs, DVDs, and iPods check box by default but leaves the Hard Disks check box and the Connected Servers check box deselected. If you don't want disk icons cluttering your beautiful desktop, deselect (clear) these check boxes. When they're deselected, you can still work with hard drives, CDs, DVDs, and other types of disks. You just have to open a Finder window and select the disk or disc you want in the sidebar.

» **New Finder Windows Show:** Here, you can choose whether opening a new Finder window displays Recents, your Home folder, the Documents or Desktop folders, or any other disk or folder. Recents is the default. You may want to use your main project folder.

» **Open Folders in Tabs Instead of New Windows check box:** Selecting this check box spawns a new tab in the current window when you press ⌘ and then double-click a folder or disk.

TIP

If you don't enable this option, ⌘+double-clicking a folder or disk icon opens it in a new window.

The default behavior is for folders to open in place when you double-click (open) them, which prevents window clutter. If you want a new window or tab instead, press ⌘ before you double-click. This action forces the folder to open in a new window or tab (depending on whether the box is checked).

Tags pane

The Tags pane of the Finder Settings window is where you manage your tags, which appear on Finder's File menu, contextual menus, the sidebar, and the toolbar. You can see a file or folder's tags in Finder windows, Get Info windows and inspectors, and apps' Open and Save dialogs, and you can use them as criteria for searches and smart folders.

» To rename a tag, click its name and then type a new one.

» To change a tag's color, click the colored circle to the left of its name and then choose a different color.

» Select the boxes for tags that you want to appear in the sidebar and on the toolbar.

TIP

To see your deselected tags in the sidebar or on the toolbar, click All Tags in the Tags list in the sidebar, or click Add Tags on the toolbar and then choose Show All from the pop-up menu.

Now, here's how to use 'em. To assign tags to icons, first select the icon(s) and then follow these steps:

1. **Choose File ⇨ Tags, and click one or more of the colored dots in the Tags section of the Tags pane.**

2. **Control-click or right-click and click one or more of the colored dots in the Tags section of the shortcut menu.**

3. **Click the Tags icon on the toolbar, and choose one or more tags from the pop-up menu.**

Here are a few more handy tricks with tags:

>> **To create a custom tag on the fly:** Control-click or right-click an item, choose Tags from the contextual menu, type a label for the new tag, and then press Return.

>> **To untag an item:** Control-click or right-click the item, choose Tags from the contextual menu, choose the tag you want to remove, and then press Delete.

>> **To remove every instance of a tag from every file and folder on your disk:** Control-click or right-click the tag in the Tags pane of Finder Settings, and choose Delete Tag from the contextual menu. Don't worry — deleting a tag won't delete the items. Deleting it just removes that tag from every item.

TIP

Click the tags in your sidebar to see every file on all connected hard drives with that tag.

Sidebar pane

The Sidebar pane of the Finder Settings window lets you choose which items are displayed in the sidebar. Select the check box to display the item; deselect the check box to not display it.

Advanced pane

The Advanced pane of the Finder Settings window is just big enough to offer the following check boxes and a pop-up menu:

>> **Show All Filename Extensions check box (off by default):** Tells Finder to display the two-, three-, four-, or more-character file extensions (such as .doc in summary.doc) that make your Mac's file lists look more like those in Linux or Windows. The Finder hides file extensions from you by default, but if you want to be able to see them in Finder when you open or save files, you need to turn on this option.

>> **Show Warning Before Changing an Extension check box (on by default):** Allows you to turn off the nagging dialog that appears if you attempt to change the file extension.

>> **Show Warning Before Removing from iCloud Drive (on by default):** Does what it says, which is warn you before you remove a file or folder from your iCloud drive.

>> **Show Warning Before Emptying the Trash check box (on by default):** Allows you to turn off the nagging dialog telling you how many items are in the Trash and asking whether you really want to delete them.

>> **Remove Items from the Trash After 30 Days check box (off by default):** Does exactly what it says, which is automatically delete any item that has been in the Trash for more than 30 days. Think of this option as automatic emptying of the Trash for items that have been there 30 days or longer.

>> **Keep Folders on Top (two check boxes, both off by default):** These two options sort folders first and then files:

- *In Windows When Sorting by Name:* Enable this option to sort folders before files in all windows sorted by name.

- *On Desktop:* Enable this check box to sort folders before files on the desktop.

>> **When Performing a Search drop-down menu:** Lets you choose the default search location when you initiate a search, as described earlier in this chapter. Your choices are Search This Mac (the default), Search the Current Folder, and Use the Previous Search Scope.

Digging for Data in the Info Window

When you need more information about an item than a Finder window shows, you can open an Info window that not only gives you all the details available, but also enables you to choose which other users (if any) you want to have the privilege of using this item. (See Chapter 16 for a full discussion of sharing files and privileges.) The Info window is also where you can lock an item so that it can't be renamed or dragged to the Trash.

To open the Info window for an item, click the item and choose File ⇨ Get Info (or press ⌘+I). The Info window opens, showing several sections that you can expand or collapse by clicking their headings, such as General and More Info. Figure 4-12 shows the Info window for an image (a .jpg file named Fungi.jpg) with its various sections expanded and collapsed.

The selection of information in the Info window varies depending on the item and its file format, but you'll get the hang of the Info window in no time. The sections that you see for most icons include the following:

» **Add Tags:** Click this field to add tags to this item.

» **General:** For information of the general kind, such as

- *Kind:* What kind of file this is (app, document, disk, folder, and so on)

- *Size:* How much hard drive space the file uses

- *Where:* The path to the folder that contains this file

- *Created:* The date and time when the file was created

- *Modified:* The date and time when the file was last modified (saved)

Six other options may appear in the General section of a particular Info window. Here's the scoop on this sextet of optional options:

- *Version:* This section displays copyright information and the file's version number.

- *Shared Folder* (check box): This control designates the folder as Shared, so other users are allowed to see and use its contents. You find out all about sharing in Chapter 16.

- *Stationery Pad* (check box): This control appears only in the Info windows of document icons. If you select it, the file becomes a template. When you open a Stationery Pad document, a copy of its contents appears in a new Untitled document that you'd typically save with a descriptive name.

- *Locked* (check box): If this box is selected, you receive the following warning if you try to put the item in the Trash: *This Item Is Locked. Do You Want to Move It to the Trash Anyway?* Your options are Stop and Continue. If you choose Continue, the item goes into the Trash as usual. You can retrieve the item from the Trash like any other item by using the Put Back command or by dragging the item out of the Trash. When you empty the Trash, the item is deleted just as though it weren't locked.

- *Prevent App Nap* (check box): macOS can tell when an app is hidden behind other windows. If an app isn't doing something — playing music, downloading files, or checking your email, for example — App Nap conserves valuable battery runtime on laptops by slowing the app. As soon as you activate the app again, it shifts back to full speed instantly.

  Although App Nap can reduce CPU energy use by up to 23 percent, it may interfere with the operations of some apps. If it does, try enabling this check box.

- *Open Using Rosetta* (check box): Select this check box to use the Rosetta emulation software to run an app designed for Intel Macs on a Mac that has an Apple Silicon processor (such as an M1 or M2).

» **More Info:** This section shows when the file was created, modified, and last opened (documents only). For a photo, you also see a lot of details including the camera, focal length, light-metering mode, f-stop, and exposure time.

» **Name & Extension:** This section displays the file's full name, including its (possibly hidden) extension.

» **Comments:** In this field, you can type your own comments for Spotlight to use in searches.

  I talk about searching a little earlier in this chapter and discuss Spotlight searches in greater detail in Chapter 9.

» **Preview:** When you select a document icon, the menu offers a Preview option that you can choose to see a glimpse of what's in that document. You can also see this preview when you select a document icon in Column view; it magically appears in the rightmost column. If you select a QuickTime movie or sound, you can play your selection right there in the preview pane without launching a separate app. And when you select most pictures, you see a preview of the actual picture.

» **Sharing & Permissions:** This section shows which users have access to this icon and how much access they're allowed. (See Chapter 16 for more about access privileges.)

TIP

If you press the Option key before you pull down Finder's File menu, the Get Info command changes to Show Inspector (alternatively, press ⌘+Option+I). The Get Info Inspector window looks and acts almost exactly like the Info window, with two whopping exceptions:

» **Inspector displays info for only the currently selected icon.** If you click a different icon, Inspector instantly displays the info for the icon you clicked, so you can Get Info on lots of icons in a row by using the arrow keys or by pressing Tab or Shift+Tab. Try this feature; it's cool.

» **Cumulative info is displayed if multiple icons are selected.** In other words, if more than one icon is selected, Inspector displays the total size of all the selected files or folders, or both.

Chapter 5

Delving Even Deeper into Ventura's Desktop and Finder

I n this chapter, you discover cool features you may not be familiar with — such as Stacks and Quick Actions — as well as features you (should) already know and love, such as Quick Look and the Preview pane. Along the way, I also point out a handful of useful interface features that make Finder better.

And now, without further ado, you're ready to dive into the power and magic of Stacks on your desktop.

Cleaning Up Your Desktop Automatically with Stacks

Putting icons on the desktop can be a great way of giving yourself access to key files. The problem is that your desktop may end up looking like Figure 5-1 — or worse.

Good news: Your Mac's Stacks feature lets you streamline your desktop in moments. Click the desktop to make it active, and you can organize it with Stacks in three ways:

» Choose View ⇨ Use Stacks.

» Use the keyboard shortcut ⌘+Control+0 (that's a zero).

» Control-click or right-click anywhere on the desktop and then choose Use Stacks from the contextual menu.

REMEMBER

The Use Stacks command is available only when the desktop is active.

When you choose Use Stacks, your desktop transforms instantly from the mess shown in Figure 5-1 to the six nicely organized stacks shown in the left part of Figure 5-2. Folders on the desktop aren't affected by Stacks; all other icons on the desktop are organized automatically into stacks (Documents, Images, PDF Documents, Music, Presentations, and Spreadsheets in the example).

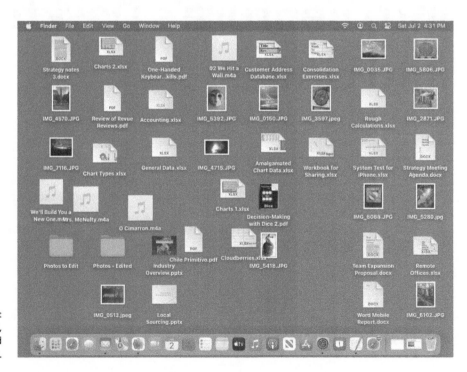

FIGURE 5-1:
A messy, disorganized desktop.

Click a stack to see its contents, as shown in the right part of Figure 5-2 for the Images stack.

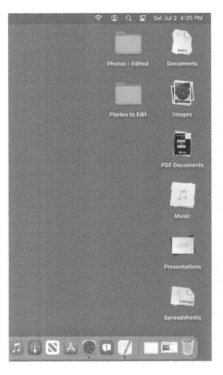

FIGURE 5-2:
Stacks (left) create order out of chaos. Click a stack (Images, right) to see its contents.

Note that the expanded stack (Images, directly below the Documents stack icon in the top-right corner) now displays a down-facing caret, indicating that the stack is expanded. Click the stack again to close it. Finally, note that stacks ignore your disk icons (if any).

Choosing Use Stacks is just the start of things. When you're using Stacks, you can group items by choosing View ⇨ Group Stacks By, which offers the following choices:

- » None (no keyboard shortcut)
- » Kind (Control+⌘+2)
- » Date Last Opened (Control+⌘+3)
- » Date Added (Control+⌘+4)
- » Date Modified (Control+⌘+5)
- » Date Created (no keyboard shortcut)
- » Tags (Control+⌘+7)

The stacks in Figure 5-2 are grouped by Kind, but it may be easier to find what you're looking for if you use one of the other options. If you know when you added, modified, or last opened the file, for example, you can choose one of the date-based options, such as Date Created, which is shown in Figure 5-3.

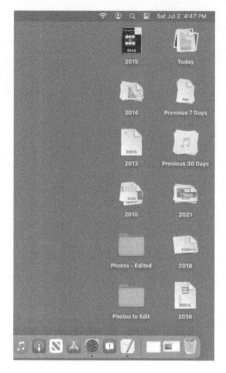

FIGURE 5-3:
Grouping stacks by Date Created gives you a different perspective from grouping them by Kind.

TIP

You can also Control-click or right-click and choose Group Stacks By. The contextual menu offers all the same commands except None.

Finally, if you're not already using Tags (discussed in Chapter 4) to organize your files, Stacks may be just the incentive you need to start.

Quick Actions: Now Playing All Over Ventura

Quick Actions are mini-apps that let you perform certain tasks without launching a full-scale application. You'll find them in the Preview pane of Finder windows, in Quick Look windows, and in contextual menus. They're super-useful and can save you the time and effort of opening a program to perform a simple task, such as adding circles and arrows to an image (and much more), trimming video, and rotating pictures.

Getting the most out of Markup

 In Ventura, the Markup icon (shown in the margin) and the Rotate icon (see Figure 5-4) are available in Quick Look windows and the Preview pane of Finder windows, and the commands are on Finder's contextual menu (Control-click or right-click).

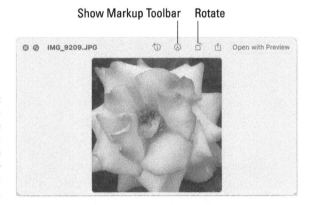

Show Markup Toolbar   Rotate

FIGURE 5-4:
Click the Markup icon to see the Markup toolbar; click the Rotate icon to rotate your image in 90° increments.

TIP

When you click the Rotate icon, the default is to rotate your document counter-clockwise by 90°. If you'd rather rotate clockwise, press Option before you click.

When you have an image selected and you click the Markup icon in a Quick Look overlay, in a Preview pane in a Finder window, or on a Finder contextual menu, an overlay appears, displaying the image below the Markup toolbar, as shown in Figure 5-5.

And here's how the tools work:

>> **Sketch:** Sketch a shape with a single stroke. Here's the cool part: If your drawing is recognized as a standard shape, such as a circle, a rectangle, or an arrow, it's replaced by a perfectly drawn rendition of the shape. If you don't like it perfect, you can use what you drew instead by choosing it from the palette that appears after you use the tool.

>> **Shapes:** Click a shape to place it on the image and then drag the shape where you want. To resize a shape, use its blue handles. If the shape has green handles, you can use them to alter the shape.

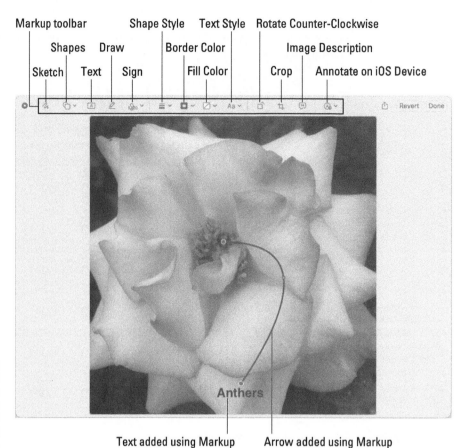

Markup toolbar   Shape Style   Text Style   Rotate Counter-Clockwise
Shapes   Draw   Border Color   Image Description
Sketch   Text   Sign   Fill Color   Crop   Annotate on iOS Device

Revert   Done

Anthers

FIGURE 5-5:
The Markup toolbar above an image to which I added text and an arrow by using Markup.

Text added using Markup   Arrow added using Markup

You can also zoom in or out and highlight specific shapes by using the pair of tools at the bottom of the Shapes drop-down menu (and shown in Figure 5-6):

- *Highlight:* Click this button to display the highlight and then drag the highlight where you want. To resize it, use the blue handles.

- *Loupe:* Click this button to display the loupe and then drag the loupe over the area you want to magnify. To increase or decrease the magnification level, drag the green handle clockwise or counterclockwise; to increase or decrease the size of the loupe, drag the blue handle in or out. To magnify an area further, you can create additional loupes and stack them, using the yellow guides that appear to align them.

>> **Text:** Type your text and then drag the text box where you want.

>> **Draw:** Use your finger to draw a shape with a single stroke. Press more firmly on the trackpad to draw thicker, heavier lines. Note that this tool is available only on computers with a Force Touch trackpad.

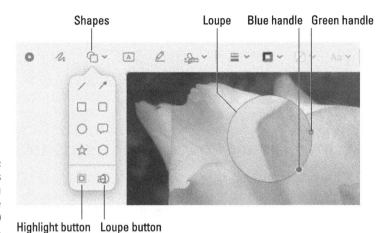

Shapes   Loupe   Blue handle   Green handle

FIGURE 5-6:
The Shapes
drop-down menu
(left) and the
loupe (right)
in action.

Highlight button   Loupe button

>> **Sign:** If signatures are listed, click one and drag it where you want. To resize it, use the blue handles.

To create a signature:

- *Using your trackpad:* Click the Sign tool, click Create Signature (if shown), and then click Trackpad. Click the Click Here to Begin prompt, sign your name on the trackpad by using your finger, and then press any key to indicate that you've finished. If the signature is good, click Done; otherwise, click Clear, and try again. If your trackpad supports it, press your finger more firmly on the trackpad to sign with a heavier, darker line.

- *Using a camera:* Click the Sign tool, click Create Signature (if shown), and then click Camera (Mac camera) or iPhone or iPad (camera). Hold your signature (on white paper) facing the camera so that your signature is level with the blue line in the window. When your signature appears in the window, click Done. If you don't like the results, click Clear, and try again.

>> **Shape Style:** Change the thickness and type of lines used in a shape or add a shadow to a shape.

>> **Border Color:** Change the color of a shape's border.

>> **Fill Color:** Change the color of a shape's fill.

>> **Text Style:** Change the font type, style, and color.

>> **Rotate Counter-Clockwise:** Rotate the item 90° counterclockwise.

>> **Crop:** Click to display crop handles at the corners of the image, plus a textual Crop button at the right end of the toolbar. Drag the handles to select the area you want to keep, and then click the Crop button.

» **Image Description:** Click this button to open the Image Description dialog, type a description of the image, and then click Done.

» **Annotate on iOS Device:** Click this button to open the image on your iPhone or iPad so that you can work on it there.

Trimming video without launching an app

Although QuickTime Player has allowed you to trim videos for years, you have to launch it and usually wait a few seconds for the video to appear. The Quick Actions feature includes a faster, easier way to trim your videos without launching Quick-Time Player (or another app).

 When a video file is selected, you'll find the Trim icon (shown in the margin) available in Quick Look windows, in Finder preview panes, and on the contextual menu (Control-click or right-click a video and choose Quick Actions⇨ Trim).

Click the Trim icon, and a filmstrip appears below the video, with handles for setting the beginning and end of the video, as shown in Figure 5-7.

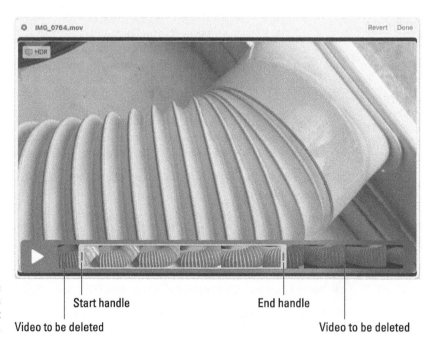

FIGURE 5-7:
Drag the handles
to set the start
and end points.

Start handle

End handle

Video to be deleted

Video to be deleted

Drag the left handle to where you want the video to begin and then drag the right handle to where you want the video to end. Click Done, and you're done. You've trimmed excess footage from your video without launching an app.

Doing Things Quicker with Finder Quick Actions

You've already seen three Quick Actions: Rotate, Markup, and Trim. This section shows you one more, the Create PDF Quick Action, which creates PDFs. This section also tells you about creating your own Quick Actions with the Automator app.

Creating PDFs without launching an app

In most applications, you can create a PDF from the Print sheet (see Chapter 19). But wouldn't it be nice if you could create PDFs without launching an application and choosing Print?

In Ventura, you can do this, though only for image files (such as JPEG, TIFF, and PNG files), not for files such as Microsoft Word documents or Microsoft Excel workbooks. Just use the Create PDF Quick Action, which you'll find in Quick Look windows, in the Preview pane of Finder windows, and on the contextual menu (Control-click or right-click).

You can tell whether the file can be converted because the Create PDF command or icon appears only when suitable files are selected, as shown in Figure 5-8.

TIP

If the Create PDF Quick Action icon doesn't appear in the Preview pane when you select an image or images, try clicking the More icon (three dots in a circle) because the Create PDF Quick Action occasionally hides on the More menu.

Here's a cool feature. If you select multiple image files and run the Create PDF Quick Action, the result is a multipage PDF file with one image on each page — a kind of virtual contact sheet. Neat!

Creating custom Finder Quick Actions

The Markup, Rotate, Trim, and Create PDF Quick Actions are useful and welcome additions to Finder, but wouldn't you love to be able to create your own Quick Actions to appear in Quick Look windows, in the Preview pane of Finder windows, and on the contextual menu (Control-click or right- click)?

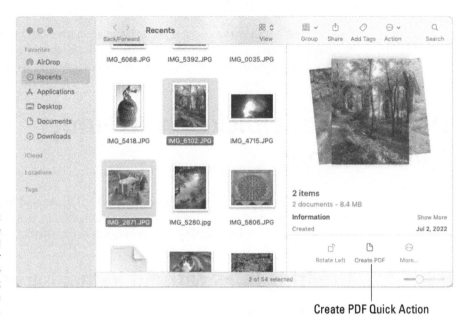

Create PDF Quick Action

You'll be happy to know that you can, and doing so is relatively easy when you use Automator, which comes with Ventura. That's all I have to say here. Near the end of Chapter 20, you'll find a nice tutorial on building Quick Actions with Automator.

Shooting Screen Stills and Movies

If you've used a Mac for long, you probably know that you can quickly grab a picture of what's on your screen by using the Screen Capture utility:

>> **Capture the whole screen.** Press ⌘+Shift+3.

>> **Capture part of the screen.** Press ⌘+Shift+4. The pointer changes to a crosshair icon. Move the crosshair where you want to start capturing, click, and then drag diagonally to the opposite corner. When you release the mouse button, Screen Capture grabs the selected area.

>> **Capture a window.** Press ⌘+Shift+4. The pointer changes to a crosshair icon. Press the spacebar, and the crosshair vanishes, replaced by a camera icon. Move this icon over the window you want to capture, so that macOS highlights the window, and then click. This method works for a menu too; just open the menu before you press ⌘+Shift+4.

These keyboard shortcuts still work in Ventura. When you capture a screen or partial screen with them, a thumbnail of the screen shot appears in the bottom-right corner of the screen.

If you do nothing, the thumbnail disappears after about 5 seconds, and the screen shot is saved. To see additional options, Control-click or right-click the thumbnail and make a choice from the contextual menu, as shown in Figure 5-9. You can click Markup on the contextual menu to open the screen shot, for example, and start decorating it with Markup.

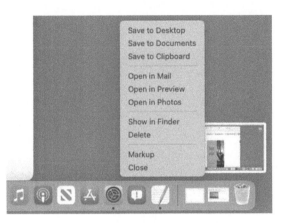

When you finish annotating, click Done to save the screen shot and annotations to the desktop, or click Revert to close the overlay without saving your annotations.

TIP

Screen Capture also lets you shoot a screen and put it straight on the Clipboard without saving it to a file. Then you can paste the screen from the Clipboard into a document. To use this trick, add the Control key to the keyboard shortcut, so you press ⌘+Shift+Control+3 for a full screen and ⌘+Shift+Control+4 for a partial screen or a window.

But one more fabulous screen-shooting shortcut provides even more control over screenshots and adds the capability to record screen movies. This magical short-cut is ⌘+Shift+5, and it's the only shortcut you really have to memorize, because its floating toolbar, shown in Figure 5-10, includes all the functionality of the ⌘+Shift+3 and ⌘+Shift+4 shortcuts — and more.

Notice the Options pop-up menu, which lets you do the following:

>> Change the destination for screen shots from the Desktop (the default) to the Documents folder, another folder, the Clipboard, the Mail app, the Messages app, the Preview app, or Other Location.

>> Set a 5- or 10-second timer for shots.

>> Turn the floating thumbnail on and off.

>> Remember the last selection you made (or not).

>> Show or hide the mouse pointer, including it in or excluding it from the screen shot.

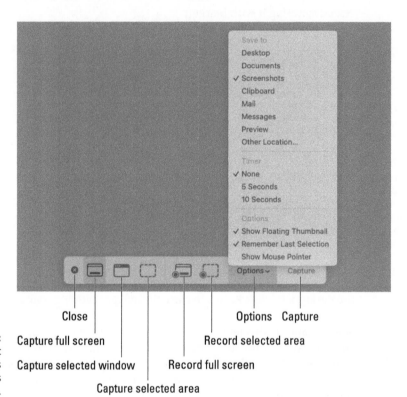

Close

Capture full screen

Capture selected window

Capture selected area

Record full screen

Record selected area

Options   Capture

 After configuring the options, you capture screen shots by clicking the Capture button. If you've chosen a movie option — Record Entire Screen or Record Selected Portion — the Capture button turns into the Record button; click it to begin recording. When you do, the Stop Recording icon (shown in the margin) appears on the menu; click it to end your recording.

Chapter **6**

Having It Your Way

E veryone works a bit differently, and everyone likes to use the Mac in their own way. In this chapter, you find out how to tweak various options so everything is just the way you like it. The first things many people like to do are set their background and screen saver to something more interesting. You can begin with that stuff, but keep in mind that you can do much more.

You can change the colors in windows, the standard font, and more if you like. macOS lets you choose how onscreen elements behave and how your keyboard, mouse, and trackpad work.

Introducing System Settings

Start by becoming familiar with System Settings, which lives in the Applications folder and appears on the menu and on the Dock.

The following steps explain how to move around the System Settings window, no matter what you're trying to tweak:

1. **Open the System Settings window, shown in Figure 6-1.**

   You can open System Settings in at least four ways:

   - Choose ⬤ ⇨ System Settings.
   - Click the System Settings icon on your Dock. If System Settings isn't running, you can go one better: Control-click or right-click the System Settings icon to display a contextual menu listing the settings categories and then click the category you want to display.
   - Click the System Settings icon in Launchpad.
   - Double-click the System Settings icon in your Applications folder. Unless you're big on the Applications folder, this method is kinda retro, but it still works fine.

2. **Click any of the icons in the sidebar of the System Settings window.**

   As usual, the sidebar in the System Settings window enables you to navigate among the app's many categories of settings. The right pane displays the settings in the category you click in the sidebar. So, for example, when you click the General icon in the sidebar, the right pane displays the General category, which (for simplicity) we'll call the General pane.

   When you finish working in System Settings, quit the app by choosing System Settings ⇨ Quit System Settings (shortcut: ⌘+Q) or clicking the red gumdrop (close) button.

   REMEMBER

   Although System Settings quits when you close its window, *many other apps DON'T quit when you close their last open window*. Worse, there's no easy way to know whether an app will or won't quit when you close its last window, so pay attention.

3. **If the pane you display contains a list of subcategories with angle brackets (>) to their right, click the subcategory you want to display.**

   Many of the categories have so many settings that they won't fit in a single pane. So instead they have a list of subcategories. You click the button for the appropriate subcategory to display its screen, which contains the settings. For example, click the Language & Region button to display the Language & Region pane (see Figure 6-2).

When you've gone one screen deeper like this, the Back arrow (<) appears to the left of the current pane's name. Click this arrow to go back to the main category pane. Or just click another category in the sidebar to zip straight to that category.

FIGURE 6-1:
The System
Settings app gives
you access to the
full range of
settings for
configuring
macOS to behave
the way
you prefer.

FIGURE 6-2:
When you
navigate to a
lower-level pane,
such as Language
& Region, click
the Back (<)
button to go back
up to the
main pane.

TIP

The sidebar shows the categories with the most frequently used categories at the top: iCloud and Apple ID, Wi-Fi, Bluetooth, Network, Notifications, and so on. If you prefer to navigate an alphabetical list, click the View menu and then click the category you want. If you need to search for the setting you want, click the Search box at the top of the sidebar and then type your search term.

Setting Wallpaper

Ventura comes with a colorful wallpaper set by default, but you'll likely want to pick your own wallpaper. You can select one of the many built-in wallpapers or use an image of your own.

To change the wallpaper, follow these steps:

1. **Control-click or right-click the desktop and then click Change Wallpaper on the contextual menu.**

The Wallpaper pane of the System Settings window appears (see Figure 6-3).

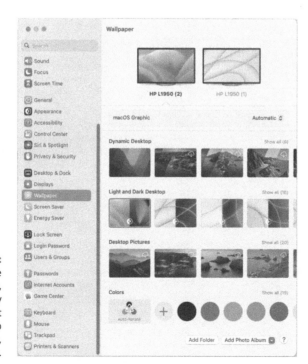

FIGURE 6-3:
From the Wallpaper pane, you can apply a different wallpaper to each display, if you like.

2. **If your Mac has multiple displays, as the example Mac does, click the display whose wallpaper you want to change.**

3. **In the Dynamic Desktop section, the Light and Dark Desktop section, or the Desktop Pictures section, click the wallpaper you want to apply.**

   Alternatively, go to the Colors section, and click a color. You can also click Add Folder at the bottom to add a folder of images or click Add Photo Album to add an album from the Photos app.

   If an icon showing a cloud with an arrow pointing down appears on a wallpaper, you can click that icon to download the wallpaper.

   You can click Show All for a category to show all the items in it.

TIP

   If you need a color other than those displayed in the Wallpaper pane, click the Add (+) button, and work in the Colors window that opens. You can use any of the five tabs across the top — Color Wheel, Color Sliders, Color Palettes, Image Palettes, and Pencils — to select a color in different ways. Alternatively, click the eyedropper icon on the Color Wheel tab and then click any color displayed on your screen to select and use that color. If you can't — or won't — settle on a single color, click Auto-Rotate in the Colors section to have macOS make the choice for you.

4. **If you chose a wallpaper from the Dynamic Desktop category or the Light and Dark Desktop category, go to the section near the top of the Wallpaper pane where the wallpaper's name appears, click the pop-up menu, and choose an option.**

   For a Dynamic Desktop wallpaper, you can choose Dynamic, Light (Still), or Dark (Still). For a Light and Dark Desktop wallpaper, you can choose Automatic, Light (Still), or Dark (Still). Automatic switches from Light to Dark around sunset and switches back to Light around sunrise.

TIP

You can quickly set an image as your wallpaper from Finder or from the Photos app. In Finder, Control-click or right-click the image and then click Set Desktop Picture on the contextual menu. In Photos, Control-click or right-click the image, click Share on the contextual menu, and then click Set Wallpaper on the Share submenu.

Configuring a Screen Saver or Just Turning Off the Display

If you like, you can set a screen saver to run on your Mac when you leave it unused for a while. A screen saver can be fun visually, but don't feel obliged to use one. Having the display simply put itself to sleep saves a little energy, and putting your Mac to sleep saves even more.

TIP

macOS comes with a bunch of built-in screen savers, but you can supplement them with third-party screen savers if you want. Be careful when downloading free screen savers, because malicious hackers sometimes use them as a vector for malware.

To set up your screen saver, follow these steps:

1. **Open System Settings and then click the Screen Saver item in the sidebar to display the Screen Saver pane (shown in Figure 6-4).**

2. **Click the screen saver you want to try, or click Random to have macOS surprise you.**

3. **Set the Show with Clock switch to On if you want the screen saver to display a clock overlay.**

4. **Click the Show Screen Saver After pop-up menu and then choose the delay: 1 Minute, 2 Minutes, 5 Minutes, 10 Minutes, 20 Minutes, 30 Minutes, 1 Hour, or Never.**

FIGURE 6-4:
If you want your Mac to use a screen saver, choose and configure it in the Screen Saver pane.

5. **If the Options button appears toward the top of the Screen Saver pane, click Options to display the Options dialog and then choose the options you want.**

   The options depend on the screen saver and what it does. Some screen savers don't have options.

6. **Click Preview to get a sneak preview of how the screen saver will look, and press Esc when you've seen enough.**

7. **When you're satisfied, close System Settings.**

What if you want your Mac to turn off the display instead of firing up a screen saver and entertaining the room? Try this quick two-step shuffle:

1. **Click the Lock Screen item in the sidebar of the System Settings app.**

   The Lock Screen pane appears.

2. **Click the Turn Display Off When Inactive pop-up menu, and choose a suitable length of time.**

   Your choices range from For 1 Minute through to For 3 Hours. On a MacBook, you can choose separate settings for running on battery power and for running on the power adapter.

Whether you set up a screen saver or just set your Mac to turn the display off, you should require a password to turn off the screen saver or turn the display back on. You do this in the Lock Screen pane: Open the Require Password After Screen Saver Begins or Display Is Turned Off pop-up menu, and choose the setting you want. Your choices range from Immediately, After 5 Seconds, and After 1 Minute all the way up to After 8 Hours. For security, go for Immediately or After 5 Seconds.

Configuring Appearance Settings

The Appearance pane in System Settings (see Figure 6-5) lets you choose between the Light and the Dark appearance, configure accent and highlight colors, adjust the size of sidebar icons, and choose how the scroll bars appear and behave. To get started, click the Appearance icon in the sidebar in System Settings.

Here's what you need to know about the color and sidebar-icon settings:

>> **Appearance:** This setting controls the overall look of macOS. Click Light to use the Light appearance all the time, click Dark to use the Dark appearance

throughout, or click Auto to make macOS go Dark at sunset and Light at sunrise.

>> **Accent Color buttons:** Set the color of buttons and other interface elements to Multicolor (the first circle) or any of eight individual colors.

To preview an accent color, click it. The check boxes, drop-down menus, and radio buttons in the Appearance pane instantly change to that accent color. Sweet!

>> **Highlight Color pop-up menu:** From here, you can choose the color that text is surrounded by when you choose it in a document or select an icon. Choose Accent Color to go with the color you chose in the Accent Color buttons; choose a specific color, such as Blue or Graphite; or click Other to open the Colors window, in which you can choose exactly the shade of Mauvey Taupe or Cerulean Cinnamon you prefer.

>> **Sidebar Icon Size pop-up menu:** Choose Small, Medium, or Large for icons in the Finder sidebar.

NEW

>> **Allow Wallpaper Tinting in Windows switch:** Set this switch to On to let the wallpaper color bleed through slightly into windows in front of the wallpaper. This option is one of those love-it-or-hate-it settings capable of starting a flame war in an empty chat room.

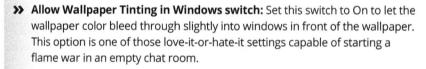
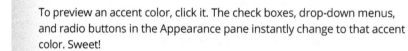

FIGURE 6-5:
Getting colorful in the Appearance pane in System Settings.

Farther down the Appearance pane are the settings for scroll bars. These settings are pretty polarizing too:

>> **Show Scroll Bars radio buttons:** These buttons let you choose when you want to see scroll bars on windows. Your choices are Automatically Based on Mouse or Trackpad, When Scrolling, or Always. I prefer Always, but you may prefer to have macOS pop up the scroll bars when it sees fit.

>> **Click in the Scroll Bar To radio buttons:** These buttons give you the option of moving your view of a window up or down by a page (the default) or to the position in the document roughly proportionate to where you clicked the scroll bar.

TIP

To give these settings a spin, open a Finder window, and place it side by side with the System Settings window, reducing the size of the window if necessary to make scroll bars appear. Select an option in the Appearance pane, observe the behavior of the scroll bars, select a different option, and observe again.

TIP

The Jump to the Spot That's Clicked option is handy for navigating long documents. Don't forget — the Page Down key does the same thing as the Jump to the Next Page option, so you lose nothing by choosing Jump to the Spot That's Clicked.

Choosing Desktop & Dock Settings

The Desktop & Dock pane in the Settings app enables you to tweak how the macOS desktop and Dock behave. You look at the Dock settings in Chapter 3, so I'll touch on them lightly here and focus on the desktop settings. To get started, open the System Settings app, click the Desktop & Dock icon in the sidebar, and then scroll down the Desktop & Dock pane until you see the Menu Bar heading.

In the Menu Bar section of the Desktop & Dock pane, you can adjust these two settings:

>> **Automatically Hide and Show the Menu Bar:** Open this pop-up menu, and choose Always, On Desktop Only, In Full Screen Only, or Never — whichever you prefer. The default setting is In Full Screen Only, but if you prefer to have the menu bar displayed even when an app is full screen, choose Never instead.

>> **Recent Items pop-up menu:** Use this menu to specify how many recent items will be remembered and displayed on your Recent Items submenu. The default setting is 10, but you can crank it up all the way to 50 if you like.

In the Windows & Apps section of the Desktop & Dock pane, you can tweak these four settings:

>> **Prefer Tabs When Opening Documents:** Your choice in this pop-up menu controls when macOS uses tabbed windows. Try all the settings — Never, In Full Screen, or Always — and stick with the one you like best.

>> **Ask to Keep Changes When Closing Documents:** macOS can save versions of your documents automatically and without any action on your part. So when you quit an app or close a document, your changes can be saved automatically. If you want to be able to close documents without having to save your changes manually, set this switch to On.

>> **Close Windows When Quitting an App:** Your Mac's default behavior is to reopen documents and windows that were open when you quit that app. When you launch the app again, all the windows and documents magically reappear right where you left them. So set this switch to On to have your apps open to a clean slate, without reopening documents or windows from the previous session.

WARNING

These last two items may not work as expected with older third-party apps. As a rule, the longer it's been since an app's last update, the more likely it is that the app will ignore these two settings.

>> **Default Web Browser:** From this pop-up menu, choose the browser you want to use as your default. Safari will be selected unless you've installed another browser, such as Google's Chrome or Mozilla Firefox.

Adjusting the Keyboard, Mouse, Trackpad, and Other Hardware

The Keyboard, Mouse, and Trackpad panes in the System Settings app provide a slew of settings for adjusting the behavior of your keyboard, mouse, and trackpad so that these devices feel just right for you. To get started, open System Settings your preferred way, and click the Keyboard icon in the sidebar.

Choosing keyboard settings

In the Keyboard pane (see Figure 6-6), you can adjust your settings in the following ways:

FIGURE 6-6:
Spend some time
choosing settings
in the Keyboard
pane to get the
most out of your
Mac's keyboard.

>> **Key Repeat Rate:** Drag this slider to set how fast a key repeats when you hold
it down. This feature comes into play when (for example) you hold down the
hyphen (–) key to make a line or the asterisk (*) key to make a divider.

>> **Delay Until Repeat:** Drag this slider to set how long you have to hold down a
key before it starts repeating.

If you have a MacBook, you also see one or more of these additional settings:

>> **Adjust Keyboard Brightness in Low Light:** Set this switch to On to let macOS
turn your MacBook's ambient keyboard lighting on and off.

>> **Turn Keyboard Backlight Off After Inactivity:** This setting (choose 5, 10, or
30 seconds, or 1 or 5 minutes from the drop-down menu) lets you determine
how long the keyboard backlighting remains on when your computer isn't
in use.

Ambient keyboard lighting is a cool feature, but it reduces run time on the
battery. Use it only when you really need it.

REMEMBER

>> **Press fn Key To** or **Press the Globe Key To:** The options on this pop-up
menu are Show Emoji & Symbols, Change Input Source, Start Dictation
(Press fn Twice or Press Globe Key Twice), and Do Nothing.

>> **Use F1, F2, etc. Keys As Standard Function Keys:** Set this switch to On if you want to make the F keys at the top of your keyboard control the active software app.

To use the special hardware features printed on each F key (display brightness, screen mirroring, sound volume, mute, and so on), you have to press the Fn (Function) key before pressing the F key. If you set this switch to Off, you have to press the Fn key if you want to use the F keys with a software app. Got it? Good.

Finally, these keys may not work if you use a third-party keyboard (one not manufactured by Apple).

>> **Keyboard Shortcuts:** Click this button to display the Keyboard Shortcuts dialog, which I discuss in the next several sections.

>> **Text Input:** Look at the Input Source line, and make sure that it shows the input source (essentially, the keyboard layout) you want, such as U.S. or Dvorak. If so, you're ready to rock. If not, click the Edit button, and work in the Input Source dialog. To add a new input source, click Add (+) in the sidebar, select the language and layout in the resulting dialog, and then click the Add button; to remove an existing input source, click it in the sidebar, and then click Remove (–). When the sidebar shows the right list of input sources, click the one you want to use and then click Done to close the Input Source dialog.

>> **Text Replacements:** Click this button to display the Text Replacements dialog, in which you can set up terms you want macOS to replace automatically for you. You might create the term *hrd* and have macOS replace it with *Human Resources Department*, for example, saving your fingertips 20-odd characters' worth of wear. Click the Done button when you finish.

TIP

Text Replacements enables you to create multiline replacement items. Just hold down Option and press Return to start a new line of text. Even easier, paste multiple lines of text from another app into the With field.

Okay, what about those keyboard shortcuts? Go ahead and click the Keyboard Shortcuts button in the Keyboard pane. The Keyboard Shortcuts dialog pops open (see Figure 6-7), showing a list of categories in the sidebar pane on the left; click the category you want, and the details appear in the right pane, as for the Mission Control category in Figure 6-7. Double-click the shortcut you want to change, and press the keys you want to use for the shortcut. A warning triangle appears if the shortcut you've pressed is already in use elsewhere.

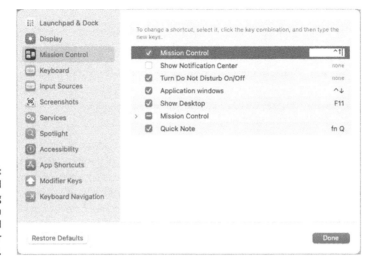

FIGURE 6-7:
The Keyboard
Shortcuts dialog
lets you futz with
keyboard
shortcuts to your
heart's content.

Here's your executive summary of what you can do in the Keyboard Shortcuts dialog:

>> **Launchpad & Dock:** Enable, disable, or change the keyboard shortcuts for turning Dock hiding on or off and for showing Launchpad.

>> **Display:** Enable, disable, or change the shortcuts for increasing and decreasing display brightness.

>> **Mission Control:** Enable, disable, or change the shortcuts for the Mission Control feature, which I explore in Chapter 9.

>> **Keyboard:** Enable, disable, or change the shortcuts for moving the focus (the part of the macOS user interface that's active) by using the keyboard. Pressing ⌘+` (the back-tick character), for example, moves the focus to the next window in the same app.

>> **Input Sources:** Enable, disable, or change the shortcuts for switching among the input sources you've set up on your Mac. If you've set up U.S., German, and Spanish input sources, for example, you can press a keyboard shortcut to select the next or previous input source.

>> **Screenshots:** Enable, disable, or change the shortcuts for shooting screens, as discussed in Chapter 5.

>> **Services:** Enable, disable, or change the shortcuts for running the services you find on the Services submenu on an app's main menu (the menu that bears the app's name, such as the TextEdit menu for the TextEdit app).

>> **Spotlight:** Enable, disable, or change the shortcuts for opening a Spotlight search overlay and for showing a Finder search window.

>> **Accessibility:** Enable, disable, or change the shortcuts for Accessibility features, such as Zoom, VoiceOver, and Invert Colors.

>> **App Shortcuts:** Enable, disable, or change the shortcuts for specific apps. There aren't many of these by default — in fact, you may find none at all — but you can add any you need by clicking the Add (+) button and working in the resulting dialog.

>> **Modifier Keys:** Choose which actions the Caps Lock, Control, Option, ⌘, and Function (fn) keys perform (see Figure 6-8). If you tend to turn on Caps Lock by mistake, for example, you might set the Caps Lock Key pop-up menu to No Action instead of Caps Lock. If your Mac has multiple keyboards connected, choose the appropriate keyboard from the Select Keyboard pop-up menu at the top before you start adjusting the key settings.

TIP

If you connect a keyboard that lacks a ⌘ key to your Mac, use the Modifier Keys category to assign ⌘-key functionality to another key, such as Caps Lock.

>> **Keyboard Navigation:** Set the Keyboard Navigation switch to On if you want to press Tab to move the focus to the next control and Shift+Tab to move the focus to the previous control.

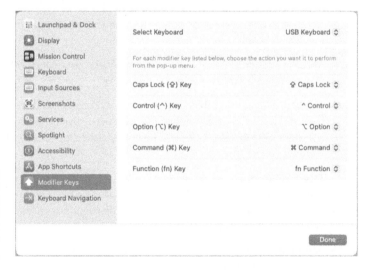

FIGURE 6-8:
The Modifier Keys category enables you to remap the modifier keys for a particular keyboard.

Tweaking your mouse

The Mouse pane of System Settings (see Figure 6-9) is where you set your mouse tracking speed, enable or disable the Natural Scrolling feature, choose how to issue secondary clicks, and set the double-click delay. Changes you make here take effect immediately, so you can see their effect easily.

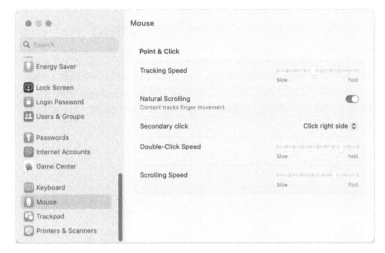

FIGURE 6-9:
The Mouse pane
in System
Settings.

If you have a MacBook or have connected an Apple Magic Trackpad to your Mac, use the Trackpad pane in System Settings to configure it. See the upcoming section "Configuring your trackpad" for details.

Here are the settings that appear in the Mouse pane when your Mac has a mouse attached:

>> **Tracking Speed slider:** Drag this slider left or right to adjust the speed at which the pointer moves onscreen as you move the mouse.

>> **Natural Scrolling:** Set this switch to On if you want content to scroll in the direction you move the scroll wheel rather than in the opposite direction (which is called *reverse scrolling*). Natural scrolling is like using an iPhone or iPad; you move your finger up the screen to scroll down, as though you're dragging the content up.

>> **Secondary Click:** Open this pop-up menu, and choose Click Right Side or Click Left Side, as needed. As you'd guess, the other side is your primary click side. So if you use the mouse with your right hand, you normally want to choose Click Right Side in the Secondary Click pop-up menu, leaving the left mouse button as the primary click.

>> **Double-Click Speed:** Drag this slider to specify how close together two clicks must be for the Mac to interpret them as a double-click, not as two separate clicks. The left end of the slider is Slow; the right end is Fast.

>> **Scrolling Speed:** This slider appears only if your mouse has a scroll ball or scroll wheel. Drag the slider to adjust the speed at which macOS scrolls the content of windows as you rotate the scroll ball or scroll wheel.

Configuring your trackpad

If you use a MacBook or a desktop Mac with a Magic Trackpad (version 1 or 2), the Trackpad pane appears in the System Settings window. This pane (see Figure 6-10) contains a laundry list of settings that enable you to bend the trackpad's behavior to your will, or at least pretty close to it.

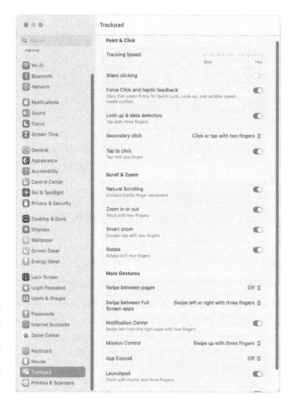

FIGURE 6-10:
The Trackpad pane in System Settings offers controls for one-finger and multifinger gestures.

TIP

If you're looking for a replacement for your mouse, consider Apple's $149 Magic Trackpad 2. This nifty wireless device can be used with any Mac or PC that has Bluetooth. It's also the biggest glass Multi-Touch trackpad yet. Yes, you can use the Magic Trackpad 2 with your MacBook, and yes, that does mean you'll have dual trackpads.

The Trackpad pane contains three tabs: Point & Click, Scroll & Zoom, and More Gestures. These are the settings you'll find in the Point & Click tab:

>> **Tracking Speed:** Drag this slider along the Slow–Fast continuum to set the speed at which the pointer moves onscreen in response to your finger sliding across the trackpad.

- » **Click:** Select the click type you prefer: Light, Medium, or Firm. This setting appears for only some trackpads.

- » **Silent Clicking:** Set this switch to On to suppress the click noise macOS plays to give you feedback when you click the trackpad.

- » **Force Click and Haptic Feedback:** Set this switch to On to use the Force Click feature, in which you click and then press the trackpad to use features such as Quick Look. Haptic Feedback is the visual and vibration feedback that lets you know you've pressed hard enough or long enough to get a response.

- » **Look Up & Data Detectors:** Set this switch to On to enable yourself to trigger the Look Up feature and data-detectors feature by tapping the trackpad with three fingers.

- » **Secondary Click:** From this pop-up menu, choose the gesture you want to use for secondary clicking (the equivalent of Control-clicking or right-clicking). Your choices are Click or Tap with Two Fingers, Click in Bottom Right Corner, Click in Bottom Left Corner, and Off.

- » **Tap to Click:** Set this switch to On to enable yourself to click by tapping the trackpad with one finger. I find using this gesture to be much easier than clicking the trackpad, but your mileage may vary.

These are the settings you'll find in the Scroll & Zoom tab in the Trackpad pane:

- » **Natural Scrolling:** Set this switch to On if you want content to scroll in the direction in which you move your finger on the trackpad rather than in the opposite direction (reverse scrolling).

- » **Zoom In or Out:** Set this switch to On if you want to be able to zoom in by placing your thumb and finger (or two fingers) close together on the trackpad and then moving them apart, and zoom out by placing your thumb and finger (or two fingers) apart on the trackpad and then moving them toward each other.

- » **Smart Zoom:** Set this switch to On to enable yourself to zoom in and out by double-tapping with two fingers.

- » **Rotate:** Set this switch to On to enable yourself to rotate an image or other rotatable item by placing two fingers on the trackpad and rotating them.

These are the settings you'll find in the More Gestures tab in the Trackpad pane:

- » **Swipe Between Pages:** From this pop-up menu, choose the gesture for swiping between pages. Your choices are Scroll Left or Right with Two Fingers, Swipe with Three Fingers, Swipe with Two or Three Fingers, and Off.

- **» Swipe Between Full Screen Apps:** From this pop-up menu, choose the gesture you want to use for navigating between full-screen apps. Your choices are Swipe Left or Right with Three Fingers, Swipe Left or Right with Four Fingers, and Off.

- **» Notification Center:** Set this switch to On if you want to be able to summon Notification Center by swiping left with two fingers from the right edge of the screen.

- **» Mission Control:** From this pop-up menu, choose the gesture you want to use to invoke the Mission Control feature, which you master in Chapter 9. Your choices are Swipe Up with Three Fingers, Swipe Up with Four Fingers, and Off.

- **» App Exposé:** From this pop-up menu, choose the gesture you want to use for App Exposé, which is part of Mission Control (again, see Chapter 9). Your choices are Swipe Down with Three Fingers, Swipe Down with Four Fingers, and Off.

- **» Launchpad:** Set this switch to On to enable yourself to display the Launchpad screen by placing your thumb and three fingers apart on the screen and pinching them together. If you can do this with four fingers on the same hand, I take my hat off to you.

- **» Show Desktop:** Set this switch to On to enable yourself to display the desktop by placing your thumb and three fingers together on the screen and then spreading them apart. (This gesture is even harder with four fingers — at least, if those fingers are on the same hand.)

Configuring Sound Settings

Out of the box, macOS comes with a preset collection of beeps and controls. From the Sound pane in System Settings, however, you can change the way your Mac plays and records sound. As you can see in Figure 6-11, the Sound Effects section appears at the top of the Sound pane. Below it is the Input & Output section, which contains the Output tab and the Input tab.

In the Sound Effects section, you can configure the following settings:

- **» Alert Sound:** Click this pop-up menu and then click the Alert sound you want. Click the Play button to the right of the pop-up menu to enjoy the sound again and again.

FIGURE 6-11:
Use the Sound
pane in System
Settings to adjust
sound effects,
sound input, and
sound output.

>> **Play Sound Effects Through:** Click this pop-up menu and then click either Selected Sound Output Device (to use whichever speakers or headphone you're using for output) or a different device you want to use for sound effects.

>> **Alert Volume:** Drag this slider to set the volume for the alert sounds.

>> **Play Sound on Startup:** Set this switch to On if you want your Mac to play its startup chime while it's booting. Usually, the start-up sound provides early reassurance that your Mac is still alive and functional.

>> **Play User Interface Sound Effects:** Set this switch to On to have your Mac play feedback sounds for actions such as dragging a file to the Trash.

>> **Play Feedback When Volume Is Changed:** Set this switch to On to have your Mac beep once for each key press when you increase or decrease volume.

In the Input & Output section, click the Output tab so that you can select the output device and set the volume:

>> **Output device:** In this (unnamed) list, click the output device for playing sounds.

>> **Output Volume:** Drag this slider to set the output volume. Couldn't be easier.

>> **Mute:** Select this check box to mute sound output.

Next, click the Input tab and then click the input device in the list that appears. The Input Volume slider controls the Input Level (how loud input from that device will be), which is displayed as a row of gray bars that go darker when active. If the dark bars reach all the way to the right side, your input volume is too loud. Ideally, no more than three fourths of the bars on the Input Level meter should be active when you're talking.

Some input sources (microphones) don't let you adjust their level in the Sound pane.

Finally, you can choose to have macOS flash the screen when an alert sound occurs, have stereo audio play back in mono, or both. To reach these options, click Accessibility in the sidebar in System Settings, click Audio in the Accessibility pane, and go to the General section of the Audio pane.

2

Getting Things Done

Understand what goes where, and why.

Save and open files.

Get the secret to finding anything, anywhere, on any disk.

Master Mission Control and run the show with Stage Manager.

Find time-saving secrets of Quick Look and Launchpad.

Go places with Maps.

Meet the many iPhone and iPad apps that are now Mac apps, too!

Chapter **7**

Opening and Saving Files

This chapter might be the most important one in this book. If you don't understand how to open and save files or how to use the file and folder system, you'll have a heck of a time finding, opening, or saving files.

TECHNICAL STUFF

Before I get started, I'll get a confusing term out of the way. Technically, macOS uses both dialogs and sheets for two-way communication with you. A *dialog,* as you know, is a window that contains controls for taking actions, such as opening a file. A *sheet* is simply a dialog that's attached to a document window's title bar and can't be moved independently from the window itself. Some apps use sheets, which prevent you only from using the active window when they appear; other apps use modal dialogs that prevent you from using any open window in the app. Apart from this difference, dialogs and sheets contain the same options. To save you from having to worry about what's a dialog and what's actually a sheet, this book uses the term *dialog* for both.

This chapter starts by showing you how to find the file or folder you need. Later in the chapter, I look at using Open dialogs and Save As dialogs within apps to find files and folders. You see these dialogs only *after* you launch an app and use that app's File menu to open or save a file. (For more on launching apps, read the parts of Chapter 4 about icons; for more on creating and opening documents, see the documentation or Help file for the app you're using.)

A Quick Primer on Finding Files

Before you even look at organizing your files, you should look at the problem that organizing files and folders can solve. Ask any longtime Mac user, and you'll hear this common lament: "Well, I saved the file, but I don't know *where* I saved it." It happens all the time, and not just to new users.

If you don't master these essential techniques, it's all too easy to become confused about where files are located on your Mac. Sure, the sidebar has an item called Recents that displays all files you've used recently, and you can use Spotlight to find almost any file in milliseconds. But if you have tens of thousands of files, it's often faster to know precisely where to find the file you desire, especially if you have files with the same name stored in different folders.

Recents (in the sidebar of Finder windows) is a fast and easy way to find a file or folder, although the sheer number of files it displays may overwhelm you, no matter how you sort or arrange them.

TIP

Recents is especially handy when you know that you either created or worked on the file recently. Just use List view sorted or grouped by Date Last Opened; the most recently used files will be at or near the top of the Recents list.

Chapter 9 is chock-full of tools and tips for finding files and folders when you misplace them. Furthermore, although you can often find files or folders by using Spotlight, you have to remember enough details about the file or its contents for Spotlight to find it.

Understanding the macOS Folder Structure

Start by looking at the folder structure of a typical macOS installation. Open a Finder window, and click the icon for your hard drive (typically called Macintosh HD, but you may have renamed it) in the sidebar.

TIP

If you don't see your start-up disk in the sidebar, choose Finder ⇨ Settings, click the Sidebar icon at the top of the window, and then select the check box for hard disks. You should see a window with the contents of your start-up disk: the Applications, Library, System, and Users folders (as shown in Figure 7-1).

FIGURE 7-1:
A bird's-eye view
of key folders on
your Mac.

In the Users folder, each user with an account on this Mac (see Chapter 16 for the skinny on users and accounts) has their own set of folders containing documents, preferences, and other information that belongs to that user and account.

TECHNICAL
STUFF

If you're the sole person who accesses your Mac, you probably have only one user. Regardless, the folder structure that macOS uses is the same whether you have one user or dozens.

In the Users folder, you find your personal Home folder (which bears your account name), along with a Shared folder, where you can put files you want to share with other users. All these files are stored in a nested folder structure that's a bit tricky to understand at first. This structure makes more sense after you spend a little time with it and figure out some basic concepts.

TIP

The structure will start to make sense much sooner if you display the path bar at the bottom of the window, as shown in Figure 7-1. (Choose View➪ Show Path Bar if yours isn't displayed.)

Examine Figure 7-1 to see how these four main folders are related. In the sections that follow, you look at each of these folders in more depth and find out more about what's nested inside each one.

Understanding nested folders

Folders within other folders are often called *nested folders.* To get a feel for the way nested folders work in macOS, check out the example of nested folders on the desktop in Figure 7-2.

You can see the following in Figure 7-2:

>> The Desktop is the top-level folder in this example; all other folders and files you see reside in the Desktop folder.

>> Folder 1 is inside the Desktop folder, which is one level deep.

>> Folder 2 is inside Folder 1, which is one level deeper than Folder 1, or two levels deep.

>> Folder 3 is inside Folder 2 and is three levels deep.

>> The two files inside Folder 3 are four levels deep.

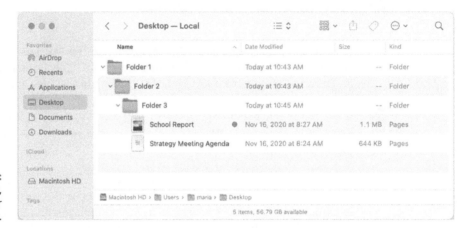

FIGURE 7-2:
Nested folders, going four levels deep.

REMEMBER

If the preceding list makes sense to you, you're golden. What's important here is that you can visualize the path to Folder 3. That is, to get to files inside Folder 3, you open Folder 1 and then open Folder 2 to be able to open Folder 3. Understanding this concept is important to understanding the relationships between files and folders. Keep reviewing this section and looking at the path bar, and eventually, everything will click.

From the top: The Computer folder

The Computer folder is the top level of the folder hierarchy. The Computer folder shows all the storage devices (hard drives, CD- or DVD-ROMs, USB flash drives, and so forth) connected to your Mac. The following steps show how you can start at the Computer folder and drill down through the folder structure:

1. **Choose Go ⇨ Computer, press ⌘+Shift+C, or click your computer's name in the sidebar's Locations section.**

   Now you're at the Computer folder. In Figure 7-3, the Computer folder is called Mac mini (look in the title bar), and it contains a drive icon (Macintosh HD) and a Network icon, from which you can access servers or other computers on your local network.

If that seems mysterious, read Chapter 16 for the scoop on sharing files (and more) with other users.

You might have more or fewer icons in your Computer folder than you see in Figure 7-1, depending on how many disks you have mounted.

If you don't find the icon for your Mac in your sidebar and want to add it, choose Finder ⇨ Settings, click the Sidebar tab at the top, and then select the check box for your computer in the Locations list.

TIP

You can change a Mac's name by opening the Sharing pane in System Settings (see Chapter 16), selecting the existing name in the Computer Name field, typing the new name, and pressing Return.

2. **Double-click the icon for the drive that holds your macOS stuff.**

   Technically, this drive is called your *boot drive*. In Figure 7-3, that drive is called Macintosh HD. Your Mac's boot drive is also probably called Macintosh HD unless you've renamed it.

3. **Check out the folders you find there.**

   You should see at least four folders on your boot drive. The next few sections walk you through what you can find in each one.

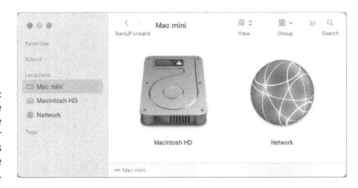

FIGURE 7-3:
Click the computer's name in the sidebar to display its drive and the Network icon.

Peeking into the Applications folder

You can access the Applications folder, located at the root level of your boot drive (the one with macOS installed on it), by clicking the Applications icon in the sidebar, by choosing it from the Go menu, or by pressing ⌘+Shift+A. In this folder, you find apps and utilities that Apple includes with macOS, as well as most (if not all) third-party apps and utilities that you've installed.

Most users of a Mac have access to all the items in the Applications folder, with the exception of managed accounts or accounts with Parental Controls, as discussed in Chapter 16.

Visiting the Library folders

The Library folder, at the root level of your macOS hard drive, is like a public library; it stores items available to everyone who logs into any account on this Mac.

There are three (or more) Library folders on your hard drive:

>> At the root level of your macOS disk (the /Library folder)

>> In the root-level System folder (the /System/Library folder)

>> In each user's Home folder (the ~/Library folder; ~ is shorthand for your Home folder — /Users/*Username*/Library)

TECHNICAL
STUFF

macOS hides your ~/Library folder from view to discourage you from making changes, because they might interfere with your Mac's running. Never fear: You'll discover the secret to making it visible if you need to in "Your personal library card" later in this chapter.

Here's the scoop on your various Library folders:

>> **/Library:** You find a bunch of folders inside the Library folder at the root level (the public Library folder). Most of them contain files that you never need to open, move, or delete.

By and large, the public Library subfolder that gets the most use is the Fonts folder, which houses many of the fonts installed on the Mac.

>> **/System/Library:** This folder is the nerve center of your Mac. You should never have to touch this particular Library folder.

WARNING

Leave the /System/Library folder alone. Don't move, remove, or rename it, or do anything within it, because doing so might prevent macOS from running.

>> **~/Library (in each user's Home folder):** This folder is where macOS stores configuration and preferences files for each user account.

Figure 7-4 illustrates the locations of these libraries.

If your Mac is set up for multiple users, only users with administrator (admin) privileges can put stuff in the public (root-level) Library folder. (For more information on admin privileges, check out Chapter 16.)

Let it be: The System folder

The System folder contains the files that macOS needs to start up and keep working.

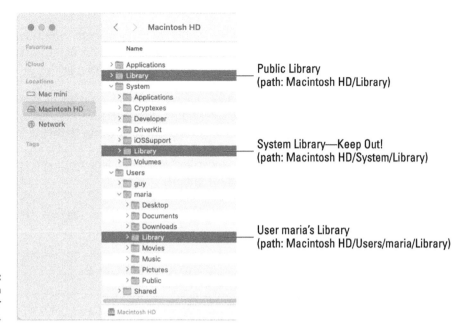

Public Library
(path: Macintosh HD/Library)

System Library—Keep Out!
(path: Macintosh HD/System/Library)

User maria's Library
(path: Macintosh HD/Users/maria/Library)

FIGURE 7-4:
A guide to which
Library folder
is which.

WARNING

Leave the System folder alone. Don't move, remove, or rename it or anything within it. It's part of the nerve center of your Mac.

So now you can forget everything outside your Home folder, because with few exceptions, that's where all *your* stuff will reside.

There's no place like Home

Your Home folder is inside the Users folder. When you log on to this Mac, the contents of your Home folder appear whenever you choose Go ⇨ Home or press the keyboard shortcut ⌘+Shift+H.

REMEMBER

Your Home folder is the most important folder for you as a user — or at least the one where you stash most of your files. Always save files to a folder or subfolder within your Home folder — preferably, in subfolders in your Home/Documents folder. The advantage of doing so is that your Home/Documents folder is easy to find, and many apps use it as the default folder for opening or saving a file.

When you open your Home folder, you see a Finder window with a little house icon and your short username in the title bar. Seeing your short username in the title bar tells you that you're in *your* Home folder. Every user has a Home folder named after their short username (as specified in the Users & Groups pane in System Settings). If you refer to Figure 7-1, you'll see that the example Home folder contains seven subfolders — Desktop, Documents, Downloads, Movies, Music, Pictures, and Public — and that the Home folder is named maria, the short name for the user account to which the Home folder belongs.

If your Mac has more than one user, you can see their Home folders in the Users folder (you can see the *guy* Home folder in Figure 7-1), but macOS prevents you from opening files from or saving files to other users' Home folders.

By default, your Home folder has several folders inside it created by macOS. The following four are the most important:

>> **Desktop:** If you put items (files, folders, apps, or aliases) on the desktop, they're actually stored in the Desktop folder.

>> **Documents:** This folder is the place to put all the documents (letters, spreadsheets, recipes, and novels) that you create.

>> **Library:** As mentioned earlier in this chapter, macOS hides this Library folder; you see how to deal with that shortly. Rest assured that even though it's hidden, this folder is still one of the most important in your Home folder, containing preferences (files containing the settings you create in System Settings and individual apps' preferences), fonts available only to you, and other stuff that you — and only you — expect to use.

>> **Public:** If others on your local area network (LAN) use file sharing to connect with your Mac, they can't see or use the files or folders in your Home folder (unless you explicitly share them), but they can share files you store in your Home folder's Public folder. (Read more about file sharing and Public folders in Chapter 16.)

You can create more folders, if you like. In fact, every folder that you *ever* create (at least every one you create on this particular hard drive or volume) *should* be within your Home folder. You find out more about creating folders and subfolders and organizing your stuff inside them later in this chapter.

TIP

Following are a couple more tidbits to keep in mind as you dig around your Home folder:

>> If you decide that you don't want an item on the desktop anymore, delete it by dragging its icon from the Desktop folder to the Trash or by dragging its icon from the desktop itself to the Trash. Both techniques yield the same effect: The file is in the Trash, where it remains until you empty the Trash. Or if you don't want it on the desktop anymore but don't want to get rid of it, you can drag it from the desktop into any other folder you like.

>> The other four folders that you should see in your Home folder are Downloads, Movies, Music, and Pictures. All these folders are empty until you (or apps such as Music, GarageBand, Photos, or iMovie, which create files inside these folders automatically the first time you launch them) put something in them.

Your personal library card

The invisible Library subfolder of your Home folder is the repository of every-thing that macOS needs to customize *your* Mac to *your* tastes. If you want to add something to a Library folder, it's usually best to add it to your Home/Library folder. You won't spend much time (if any) adding things to the Library folder or moving them around within it, and that's why macOS hides it from sight. Still, it's a good idea for you to know what's in your Home/Library.

As mentioned earlier in this chapter, the root-level (public) Library folder (refer to Figure 7-4) is used to specify preferences for all users on this Mac. *This* Library folder, however, is all about you and your stuff.

WARNING

Be cautious with all Library folders. macOS is persnickety about how the folders and files within it are organized. You can safely add items to and remove items from most public or Home/Library folders, but *leave the folders themselves alone.* If you remove or rename the wrong folder, you could render macOS inoperable. It's like the old joke about the guy who said to the doctor, "It hurts when I do that," and the doctor replies, "Then don't do that."

To find your hidden Home/Library folder, do this:

1. **Click the Go menu and then press the Option key.**

   The (formerly) invisible Library folder appears on the Go menu as long as you hold down the Option key.

2. **Click Library and then release the Option key.**

You should see many folders in the Home/Library folder; the exact number depends on the software that you install on your Mac. Many of the folders have esoteric names, such as Daemon Containers and IntelligencePlatform, but other folders have easier-to-grasp names, such as Mail, Safari, Logs, Preferences, and Printers.

TIP

If you don't want to do this dance every time you open your Home/Library folder, open your Home folder in Finder and choose View ➪ Show View Options (or press ⌘+J). Select the Show Library Folder check box near the bottom of the View Options window, and your Home Library will be visible evermore (or until you deselect the check box).

Some of the most important standard folders in the Library folder include the following:

>> **Application Support:** Some apps store their support files here; others store theirs in the main (root-level) public Library folder.

>> **Fonts:** This folder is empty until you install your own fonts here. The easiest way to install a font is to double-click its icon and let the Font Book utility handle it for you, as described in Chapter 19.

Avoid adding too many fonts for two reasons. First, the Fonts menu will become long and unwieldy. Second, and worse, installing too many fonts may make your Mac run more slowly.

>> **Preferences:** The files here hold the information about whichever things you customize in macOS or in the apps you run. Whenever you change a system or app setting, that info is saved to a file in the Preferences folder.

Don't mess with the Preferences folder! You should never need to open or use this folder unless something bad happens — say, you suspect that a particular preferences file has become *corrupted* (that is, damaged). Just forget that you know about this folder, and let it do its job. If you don't know why you're doing something to a folder (other than the Fonts folder) in your Home/Library, *don't do it.* Apple makes macOS hide the Home/Library folder to help prevent users from accidentally screwing things up.

Saving Your Document Before It's Too Late

Now that you have a feel for the macOS folder structure, it's time to get down to the important stuff — namely, how to save documents and where to save them. You can create as many documents as you want, using one app or dozens of 'em, but all could be lost if you don't save the files (or versions of the files) to a storage device such as your start-up drive, external hard drive, solid-state drive (SSD), or USB thumb drive (aka USB flash drive).

Another option is to save documents in iCloud so that you can access them on all your Apple devices all the time without syncing or doing much of anything beyond saving the file.

When you *save* a file, you're committing a copy to a drive, whether it's a drive connected directly to your Mac, one available over a LAN, a removable disc such as a

USB thumb drive or external hard or SSD, or even a drive on a cloud-based server somewhere such as iCloud.

Speaking of iCloud, you read a lot more about it — and especially the iCloud Drive feature — in Chapter 8 (after you get the hang of saving and opening files from drives or disks).

macOS's Resume feature automatically reopens all windows that were onscreen when you quit the app. So when you launch the app again, all the windows are reopened in the same positions onscreen as when you quit. Best of all, Resume seems to work with *most* (but not all) third-party apps.

Individual apps have offered Auto Save before, but it's been baked into macOS for years. Auto Save automatically saves *versions* (which you find out more about shortly) of your work as you work, when you pause, and every 5 minutes, whether you need it or not.

Versions are awesome. Every time you Save or Auto Save, a new version of the document is created. This feature is a great improvement on saving unique versions manually, which most Mac used to do by using the Save As command to save a version under a different name or by duplicating files in Finder and then renaming the duplicates. Now macOS takes over version control for you by saving versions automatically, as described in the preceding paragraph.

The big advantage is that rather than giving you a separate file on your hard drive each time you Save As or duplicate and rename a file, Versions saves all the versions in the same document. To access a previous version, choose File ⇨ Revert To ⇨ Browse All Versions or choose Enter Time Machine from the Time Machine icon on the menu bar while the document is active onscreen. (See Chapter 21 for more on Time Machine.)

WARNING

That's the good news, but there's also bad news. Although Auto Save and Versions are built right into macOS, not all third-party apps choose to take advantage of these features. So please don't get too comfortable with Auto Save and Versions until you're sure that your apps offer them. Even a decade after the debut of these features in macOS, many third-party apps continue to rely on the old-school Save and Save As commands for versioning. Furthermore, if these features aren't in a third-party app by now, don't hold your breath waiting for their appearance.

The bottom line is that if the app you're using doesn't have Auto Save and Versions, macOS takes no responsibility for saving files and saving versions of files; those jobs are up to you. Apple apps that save files — Pages, Keynote, Numbers, and Logic Pro, to name a few — use Auto Save and Versions. To keep your data safe, you may prefer to use apps that support Auto Save and Versions whenever possible.

REMEMBER

The following sections show you how to save your masterpieces. Prevent unnecessary pain in your life by developing good saving habits, so save your work (or save a version in apps that support Versions)

>> Every few minutes

>> Before you switch to another app

>> Before you print a document

>> Before you stand up

TIP

The keyboard shortcut for Save in almost every Mac app is ⌘+S, and it works with Auto Save and Versions as well as with Save and Save As. Train your finger muscles to press ⌘+S automatically every time you've made a change you wouldn't want to have to make again. Use it (the keyboard shortcut) or lose it (your unsaved work).

WARNING

If you don't heed this advice — and the app you're using crashes while switching apps, printing, or sitting idle (the three likeliest times for a crash) — you may lose everything you did since your last save or saved version. The fact that an app crash doesn't bring down the entire system or force a restart is small consolation when you've lost everything you've typed, drawn, copied, pasted, or whatever since the last time you saved.

Stepping through a basic save

This section walks you through the steps you use the first time you save a document. The process is the same whether your app supports Auto Save and Versions or not. It's only after the initial save that Auto Save and Versions come into play.

DOES IT HAVE AUTO SAVE AND VERSIONS OR NOT?

It can be hard to discern at a glance whether an app uses the Auto Save and Versions features.

The first way to discern whether an app supports Auto Save and Versions is whether the app's File menu contains the Save As command or the Duplicate command. Apps with the Save As command are old-school and mostly don't support the modern Auto Save and Versions features. Apps with the Duplicate command have usually been updated with support for Auto Save and Versions. (Interestingly, the shortcut for Duplicate and

Save As is almost always the same: ⌘+Shift+S.) If the Duplicate command appears on the File menu, you can hold down Option to display the Save As command instead.

The next way is to check whether the app has the Rename command and the Move To command on its File menu. If it doesn't, it's old-school; if it does, it's Auto Save- and Versions-savvy.

The easiest way to tell, however, is to look at the title bar of a document. If it displays a little downward caret (like a v) to the right of the document's name when you hover your cursor over it (as shown at the top of the figure here), and a pop-up window appears if you click the caret, the app supports Auto Save and Versions. (You read more about the options in the pop-up window later in this chapter.)

Click the downward caret

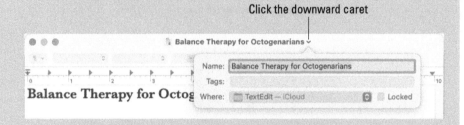

Everything I've covered so far in this chapter applies to every app that saves files, with or without Auto Save and Versions. But saving a file with Auto Save and Versions has one bonus: It creates a new version of the file that you can access with Time Machine. To obtain that kind of functionality in apps without Auto Save and Versions, you'll need to use Save As to create a new version of the file periodically if you want to be able to roll back to an earlier version.

One last thing: Using Save As to create new versions uses more disk space (possibly much more) than using Auto Save and Versions and adds files on your drive — one file for each Save As versus one file for unlimited Versions. After using Save As 11 times, you'll end up with 12 files on your drive; with Auto Save and Versions, you'd still have 11 versions, but they're all contained in a single file.

Saving a file works pretty much the same way in any app you use to create documents. This example uses the macOS text–editor app, TextEdit, but the process will be similar in Microsoft Word, Adobe Photoshop, Apple Keynote, or any other app.

TIP

To really get the hang of this process, follow along on your Mac. Click Launchpad on the Dock to display the Launchpad screen; then click the TextEdit icon to open the TextEdit app. Click the New Document button or choose File ⇨ New to create a new document, and then type a few words in the Untitled document that appears.

When you choose to save a file for the first time (choose File⇨ Save or press ⌘+S), a Save As dialog appears in front of the document that you're saving, as shown in Figure 7-5. This dialog is the *basic* Save As dialog (as opposed to the *expanded* Save As dialog, which you'll meet in a moment):

1. **In the Save As field, type a name for your file.**

   When a Save As dialog appears for the first time, the Save As field is active and displays the name of the document. The document name (usually, Untitled) is selected; when you begin typing, the name disappears and is replaced by the name you type.

2. **If the Where pop-up menu lists the location where you want to save your file, choose that location and proceed to Step 5; if not, click the disclosure button (labeled in Figure 7-4).**

   You can choose among a short list of folders and volumes listed on the basic Save As dialog's Where pop-up menu (which are the same devices and favorites you see in the sidebar of Finder windows). Or if you click the disclosure button on the right of the Save As field, the dialog expands so that you can navigate folders just as you do in Finder: by opening them to see their contents.

WARNING

If you click the Save button in Figure 7-5, your file will be saved to iCloud Drive, Apple's free online storage service (see Chapter 8). Or you can choose another location from the Where menu before you click Save and save the file elsewhere.

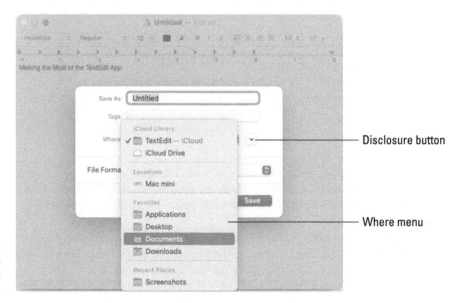

FIGURE 7-5:
A basic Save As dialog looks a lot like this example.

Disclosure button

Where menu

If you switch to expanded view (shown in Figure 7-6) by clicking the disclosure button, a standard Save As dialog appears so that you can save your file in any folder you like.

Note that the Where menu in the expanded Save As dialog in Figure 7-5 doesn't have a Favorites section; instead, it displays the path to the folder in which the file will be saved (Documents). To access Favorites in the expanded Save As dialog, you use the sidebar instead.

TIP

Switch between the basic and expanded Save As dialogs a few times by clicking the disclosure button. Make sure that you see and understand the difference between what you see on the Where menu in a basic Save As dialog and what you see on the Where menu in an expanded Save As dialog. All the steps that follow assume that you're using the expanded Save As dialog.

3. **To make it easier to find the folder in which you want to save your file, choose among views by clicking the View icon and making your choices from its drop-down menu.**

The View icon's drop-down menu, shown in Figure 7-6, allows you to choose the view that works best for you.

In Icons view, you double-click a folder to open it. List view offers disclosure brackets for folders and drives, so click the disclosure brackets of folders to see their contents. In Columns view, you click an item on the left to see its contents on the right, just as you do in a column-view Finder window.

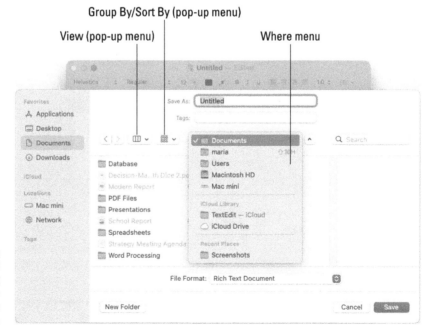

FIGURE 7-6:
An expanded Save As dialog looks similar to this one (shown in Columns view).

You can also use the Forward and Back icons or the sidebar, both available only in an expanded Save As dialog, to navigate your drive conveniently. Many of these navigation aids work just like the ones in Finder; see Chapter 4 for more details. You can enlarge the Save As dialog by dragging one of its corners or edges.

TIP

If you can't find the folder in which you want to save your document, type the folder name in the Search box, which works just like the Search box in a Finder window, as described in Chapters 4 and 8. You don't even have to press Return; the Save As dialog updates itself to show you only items that match the characters as you typed them.

4. **Choose the folder where you want to save your file from the Where pop-up menu or select in the sidebar.**

5. **If you want to create a new subfolder of the selected folder to save your file in, click the New Folder button (labeled in Figure 7-7), give the new folder a name, and then save your file in it.**

In Figure 7-7, an existing folder named Outgoing is selected. You can tell that it's selected because its name is displayed in the Where menu and highlighted below that in the first column.

REMEMBER

The selected folder is where your file will be saved.

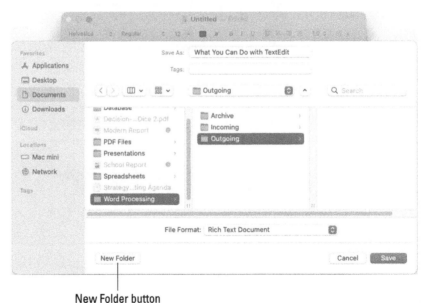

FIGURE 7-7:
Saving a file in the Outgoing folder (which is in a subfolder of the Documents folder).

New Folder button

The keyboard shortcut for New Folder is ⌘+Shift+N, regardless of whether you're in a Save As dialog or in Finder. In the example in Figure 7-7, clicking the New Folder button or pressing the keyboard shortcut would create a folder inside the Outgoing folder.

6. **In the File Format pop-up menu (which says Rich Text Document in Figure 7-7), make sure the format selected is the one you want.**

    Double-check the Where pop-up menu one last time to make sure that the correct folder is selected.

7. **Click the Save button to save the file to the active folder.**

    If you click Save, the file appears in the folder you selected. If you change your mind about saving this file, clicking Cancel dismisses the Save As dialog without saving anything anywhere. In other words, the Cancel button returns things to the way they were before you displayed the Save As dialog.

TIP

After you save a file for the first time, choosing File ⇨ Save or pressing ⌘+S won't bring up a Save As dialog. Instead, what happens next depends on whether the app supports macOS's Auto Save and Versions. If the app *doesn't* support Auto Save and Versions, Save and its shortcut (⌘+S), merely resave your document in the same location and with the same name. If you want to save a unique version with a different name, you have to choose the Save As command and save the file under a new name.

If the app *does* support Auto Save and Versions, however, the upcoming section, "Save As versus Duplicate: Different names for the same result" explains how things work.

WARNING

When you use apps that don't support Auto Save and Versions, get into the habit of pressing ⌘+S often. It can't hurt — and just might save your bacon someday.

One last thing: Figures 7-5, 7-6, and 7-7 show the Save As dialog for TextEdit as an example. In apps other than TextEdit, the Save As dialog might contain additional options, fewer options, or different options, and therefore might look slightly different. The File Format menu, for example, is a feature specific to TextEdit; it might not appear in other apps' Save As dialogs. Don't worry. The Save As dialog always *works* the same way, no matter what options it offers.

Save As versus Duplicate: Different names for the same result

The two commands File ⇨ Duplicate and File ⇨ Save As serve the same purpose and achieve the same result. The difference is that you'll find File ⇨ Duplicate in apps that support Versions and Auto Save, and File ⇨ Save As in apps that don't. They're different names for achieving the same result: saving a file that's already been saved with a different name.

If you opt for Save As: A Save As dialog appears, in which you can type a different filename in the Save As field. You can also navigate to another folder, if you like, and save the newly named version of the file there. Now you have two distinct files: the original file (which isn't open anymore) and the new file you created from it (which *is* open).

If you choose Duplicate: The app clones the file, putting the clone in a window of its own and making the clone's title bar editable so that you can change its name without even seeing a Save As dialog. (Refer to the figure in the earlier sidebar "Does it have Auto Save and Versions or not?") By default, it has the same name as the original with the word *copy* appended. Type the new name and press Return, and the app saves the duplicated file in the same folder as the original. Or if you want to save the newly renamed file in a different location, choose File ⇨ Move To, or click the little downward caret to the right of the document's name, and choose a different location from the Where menu.

Now that you understand what Save As or Duplicate are all about, here's an easier way to get the same result: Before you start, duplicate the document in Finder (choose File ⇨ Duplicate or press ⌘+D). Rename the copy, and open it. This way, when you finish making changes, you don't have to remember to choose Save As or Duplicate; you can just perform your habitual Save.

TIP

If you prefer to use Save As, just press the Option key before you click the File menu, and Duplicate magically transmogrifies into Save As. Sweet!

Versions gives you the benefits of Save As without any action on your part, but many apps still lack support for Auto Save and Versions nearly a decade after their introduction.

REMEMBER

One last thing: If the app you're using supports Versions, it creates a snapshot called a *version* automatically as you work, when you pause, every 5 minutes, and every time you choose File ⇨ Save (⌘+S). Choose File ⇨ Revert To ⇨ Browse All Versions or click the Time Machine icon in the Dock while the document is active onscreen. (See Chapter 21 for more on Time Machine.) Either way, Time Machine displays versions of the document side by side, as shown in Figure 7-8.

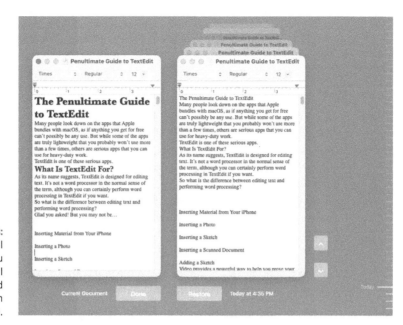

FIGURE 7-8:
Browse All
Versions lets you
compare all
versions and
revert to an
earlier version.

Open, Sez Me

You can open any item in Finder — whether it's a file or a folder — in at least six
ways. (Okay, there are at least *seven* ways, but one of them belongs to aliases,
which Chapter 4 discusses in great detail.) Anyway, here are the ways:

>> Click the icon to select it, and choose File ⇨ Open.

>> Double-click the icon.

TIP

If the icon doesn't open, you double-clicked too slowly. You can test (and
adjust) your mouse's sensitivity to double-click speed in the Mouse pane or
the Trackpad pane in System Settings, which you can access by launching the
System Settings app (from Launchpad, from the Dock, from the menu, or
even from the Applications folder) and then clicking the Mouse icon or the
Trackpad icon in the sidebar.

>> Select the icon and then press either ⌘+O or ⌘+↓.

>> Control-click or right-click the item, and choose Open from the contextual menu.

>> If the item is a document, drag it onto the Dock icon of an app that can open
that type of document. (You can also drag the item onto the app's icon
elsewhere, but usually, the Dock is the most convenient place.)

>> If the icon is a document, right-click or Control-click it, and choose an app from
the Open With submenu of the contextual menu.

You can also open any document from within an app, of course. Here's how that works:

>> **Just launch your favorite app, and choose File ⇨ Open (or press the shortcut ⌘+O, which works in most Mac apps).**

An Open dialog appears, like the one shown in Figure 7-9.

When you use an app's Open dialog, only files that the app knows how to open appear enabled (in black rather than light gray) in the file list. In effect, the app filters out the files it can't open, so you barely see them in the Open dialog. This method of selectively displaying certain items in Open dialogs is a feature of most apps. Therefore, when you're using the Preview app, its Open dialog dims all files it can't open, like the MP3 file in the Documents folder (first column) in Figure 7-9. Pretty neat, eh?

>> **In the dialog, simply navigate to the file you want to open (using the same techniques you use in a Save As dialog).**

TIP

Click a favorite folder in the sidebar, or use Spotlight (see Chapter 10) if you can't remember where the file resides.

>> **Select your file and click the Open button.**

For what it's worth, some apps allow you to select multiple files in their Open dialogs by clicking the first file and then holding down either Shift (for contiguous selections) or ⌘ (for noncontiguous selections). If you need to open several files, it's worth a try; the worst thing that could happen is that it won't work and you'll have to open the items one at a time.

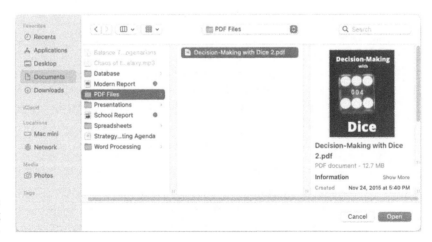

FIGURE 7-9:
The Open dialog
in Columns view.

TIP

Some apps, including Microsoft Word and Adobe Photoshop, have a Show menu or a Format menu in their Open dialogs. This menu lets you specify the type(s) of files you want to see as available in the Open dialog. When an Open dialog has such a menu, you can often open a file that appears dimmed by choosing All Documents from the menu.

With drag-and-drop

Mac drag-and-drop is usually all about dragging text and graphics from one place to another. But you can also open a document by dragging its icon onto the icon of a suitable app. If you've got a Word document on your desktop, for example, you can drag its icon onto the Microsoft Word app icon on the Dock. The app icon springs to life, and the app opens the document.

With a Quick Look

The Quick Look feature (which you meet in Chapter 10) can display the contents of many types of files. For now, know that you can use Quick Look to peek at the contents of most files in Open dialogs. Just Control-click or right-click the file and then choose Quick Look from the contextual menu, select the file and press ⌘+Y, or select the file and press the spacebar. Up pops an overlay showing the file's contents, all without launching an app.

When your Mac can't open a file

If you try to open a file, but macOS can't find an app to open that file, macOS prompts you with an alert window. Click Cancel to abort the attempt to open the file, or click the Choose Application or Search App Store button to select another application to open this file.

If you click the Choose Application button, a dialog appears (conveniently opened to your Applications folder). Apps that macOS doesn't think can be used to open the file are dimmed. For a wider choice of apps, choose All Applications (instead of Recommended Applications) from the Enable pop-up menu.

REMEMBER

You can't open every file with every app. If you try to open an MP3 (audio) file with Microsoft Excel (the spreadsheet app), for example, it just won't work; you get an error message or a screen full of gibberish. Sometimes, you just have to keep trying until you find the right app; at other times, you don't have an app that can open the file.

When in doubt, use a search engine to read about the file extension. You'll usually find out more than you need to know about what app(s) create files with that extension.

With the app of your choice

Sooner or later, you'll likely run into a file created by an app you don't use — perhaps even an app you've never heard of. macOS lets you specify the app in which you want to open a document in the future when you double-click it. More than that, you can specify that you want all documents of that type to open with the specified app. "Where is this magic bullet hidden?" you ask. Right there in the file's Info window.

Assigning a file type to an app

Suppose that you want all .jpg files that usually open in Preview to open instead in Adobe Lightroom, a heavy-duty third-party app for organizing and editing photos. Here's what to do:

1. **Click one of the files in Finder.**

2. **Choose File ⇨ Get Info (⌘ +I).**

   Or right-click, Control-click, or tap the file with two fingers and then choose Get Info from the contextual menu.

3. **In the Info window, click the disclosure arrow to disclose the Open With pane.**

4. **From the pop-up menu, choose an app that macOS believes will open this document type.**

   If you choose Lightroom, as in Figure 7-10, Lightroom will open each time you open this file (instead of the default app, Preview).

5. **(Optional) If you click the Change All button at the bottom of the Open With pane, as shown in Figure 7-10, you make Lightroom the new default app for all .jpeg files that would otherwise be opened in Preview.**

   Notice the handy alert that appears when you click the Change All button and how nicely it explains what will happen if you click Continue.

Opening a file with an app other than the default

Here's one more technique that works great when you want to open a document with a app other than its default. Just drag the file onto the app's icon or alias icon or Dock icon, and presto — the file opens in the app.

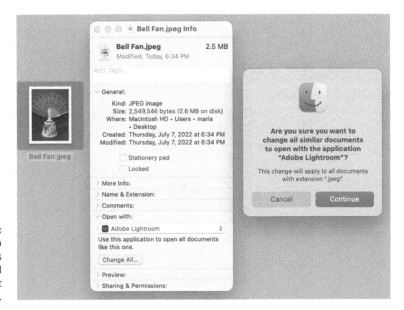

FIGURE 7-10:
Changing the app that opens this document and all others like it (that is, .jpeg files).

If you were to double-click an MP3 file, for example, the file usually would open in Music (and, by default, would be copied into your Music library). But what if you want to audition (listen to) MP3 files with QuickTime Player so that they're not automatically added to your Music library? Dragging the MP3 file onto Quick-Time Player's icon in the Applications folder or its Dock icon (if it's on the Dock) solves this conundrum quickly and easily.

WARNING

If the icon doesn't highlight, and you release the mouse button anyway, the file ends up in the same folder as the app with the icon that didn't highlight. If that happens, just choose Edit➪Undo (or press ⌘+Z), and the mislaid file magically returns to where it was before you dropped it. Just remember — don't do anything else after you drop the file, or Undo might not work. If Undo doesn't work, you must move the file back to its original location manually.

TIP

Only apps that *might* be able to open the file should highlight when you drag the file on them. That doesn't mean the document will be usable — just that the app can *open* it. Suffice it to say that macOS is usually smart enough to figure out which apps on your hard drive can open what documents — and to offer you a choice.

One last thing: If all you want to do is open a file with an app other than its default (and not change anything for the future), the techniques just described work fine, but an even easier way is to right-click the file and choose another app from the contextual menu, as shown in Figure 7-11.

FIGURE 7-11:
To open a file with an app other than its default, right-click and choose the app you desire.

TIP

You can also change the default app to open *this* file by pressing Option after you right-click the file, which causes the Open With command to magically transform into Always Open With. Alas, you can't change the default app for *all* files of this type (.jpeg in figures 7-10 and 7-11); for that task, you'll have to visit the Info window.

Chapter **8**

File and Folder Management Made Easy

Y ou'll eventually accumulate a lot of files on your disk(s): tens, hundreds, thousands, even millions of files.

In Chapter 7, you can read about Finder and opening and saving files. In this chapter, it's time to take a look at how to organize all those files so you can find them when you need them.

Organizing Your Stuff in Folders

Organizing your files is as personal as your taste in music; you develop your own style with the Mac. But these sections provide some ideas about how you might want to organize things, plus some suggestions that can make organization easier for you, regardless of how you choose to do it.

The upcoming sections look at the difference between a file and a folder, show you how to set up nested folders, and cover how some special folder features work. After you have a good handle on these things, you'll almost certainly be a savvier — and better organized — macOS user.

Working with files versus folders

To start, I'll sort out the difference between a file and a folder. This book uses the word *file* to mean a named container that holds a specific item, such as a document, an app, or an alias. If you open Microsoft Word, create a document, and save it, the document is saved in a file.

 A *folder,* by contrast, is a named container in which you can store files. You might store your Word documents in the Documents folder that macOS provides in your user account. Folders work kinda like manila folders in the real world; they can contain files or other folders, called *subfolders.* You can put any file or folder inside a folder.

Okay with that difference? Great! I'll move on.

Organizing your stuff with subfolders

To organize your stuff, you can put folders inside folders. A folder you place inside another folder is a *subfolder* or a *nested folder.* As you know, macOS sets up your user account with a default folder structure. Your Home folder (the folder that bears your short user name) contains various subfolders, including the Desktop folder, the Documents folder, and the Downloads folder.

You can create subfolders according to whatever system makes sense to you — but why reinvent the wheel? Here are some organizational topic ideas and naming examples for subfolders:

>> **By type of document:** Word Processing, Spreadsheets, Graphics

>> **By date:** Documents May–June, Documents Fall 2022

>> **By content:** Memos, Outgoing Letters, Expense Reports

>> **By project:** Project X, Project Y, Project Z

When you notice your folders swelling and starting to get messy (that is, filling with tons of files), subdivide them again by using a combination of these methods that makes sense to you. Suppose that you start by subdividing your Documents folder into multiple subfolders. Later, when those folders begin to get full, you can subdivide them even further, as shown in Figure 8-1.

Allow your folder structure to grow as you need it to grow. Don't let any single folder get so full that it's a hassle to deal with. Create new subfolders when things start to get crowded. (You see how to create folders in the next section.)

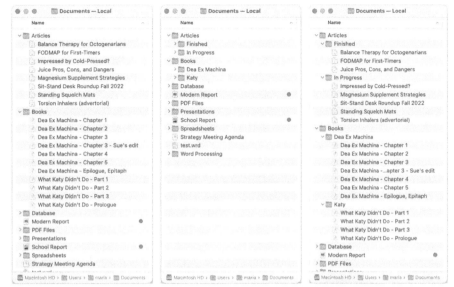

FIGURE 8-1:
Before (left) and
after (right)
organizing the
Articles folder
and Books folder
with subfolders,
shown closed
(center) and
open (right).

If you use a particular folder a great deal, drag it to the right side of your Dock, or make an alias of it and move the alias from the Documents folder to your Home folder or to your desktop (for more info on aliases, see Chapter 4) to make the folder easier to access. Or drag the folder (or its alias) to the sidebar so that it's always available, including in Open and Save As dialogs.

If you write a lot of letters, keep an alias to your Correspondence folder in your Home folder, on the Dock, on your desktop, or in the sidebar for quick access. (By the way, there's no reason why you can't have a folder appear in all four places, if you like. That's what aliases are for, right?)

TIP

If you create your own subfolders in the Documents folder, you can click that folder on the Dock to reveal them, as shown in Figure 8-2. Chapter 3 shows you how to customize the Dock.

TIP

It's even more convenient if you choose to view the Documents folder as a list, as described in Chapter 3 and shown in Figure 8-2.

Creating new folders

macOS creates your user account with a decent fistful of folders, but you're pretty much guaranteed to need more folders. Think of creating new folders the same way you'd think of labeling a manila file folder for a specific project, only quicker and easier. New folders help you keep your files organized, enabling you to reorganize them just the way you want.

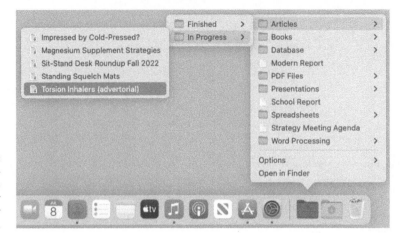

FIGURE 8-2:
It's super-
convenient to
have your
Documents folder
on the Dock.

To create a new folder, just follow these steps:

1. **Open a Finder window to the folder in which you want to create the new folder.**

   If you want to create a new folder in your Documents folder, open a Finder window showing the Documents folder. If you want to create a new folder right on the desktop, you can work directly on the desktop or open a Finder window to the Desktop folder in your user account.

2. **Choose File ⇨ New Folder (or press ⌘+Shift+N).**

   A new, untitled folder appears in the active window with its name box already highlighted, ready for you to type a new name for it.

3. **Type the name for the folder and then press Return.**

   If you accidentally click anywhere before you type a name for the folder, the name box is no longer highlighted. To highlight it again, select the icon (click it) and press Return once. Now you can type its new name.

TIP

Give your folders relevant names. Folders with nebulous titles like Stuff, Untitled, or sfdghb will make it that much harder to find a file or folder six months from now.

REMEMBER

For folders and files that you might share with users of non-Mac computers, here's the rule for maximum compatibility: Use no punctuation and no Option-key characters in the folder name. Periods, slashes, backslashes, and colons in particular can be reserved for use by other operating systems. Option-key characters are special characters that you enter using the Option key, such as ™ (Option+2), ® (Option+R), and ¢ (Option+4).

Navigating with spring-loaded folders

A *spring-loaded folder* pops open when you drag something onto it without releasing the mouse button. Spring-loaded folders work with all folder or disk icons in all views and in the sidebar, and they give you a speedy way to navigate your Mac's disks, folders, and subfolders.

Here's how spring-loaded folders work:

1. **Click the file or folder you want to move.**

   The icon highlights to indicate that it's selected.

2. **Drag the selected file or folder onto any folder or disk icon — but don't release the mouse button.**

   In a second or two, the highlighted folder or disk flashes twice and then springs open, right under the cursor. If you don't want to wait, press the spacebar to open the folder immediately.

3. **After the folder springs open, perform any of these handy operations:**

   - Continue to traverse your folder structure this way. Subfolders continue to pop open until you release the mouse button.

   - If you release the mouse button, the file or folder you've been dragging is dropped into the active folder at the time and that window remains open.

   - If you want to cancel a spring-loaded folder, drag the cursor away from the folder icon or outside the boundaries of the sprung window. The folder pops shut.

After you get used to spring-loaded folders, you'll wonder how you ever got along without them. They work in all four views, and they work with icons in the sidebar or Dock. Give 'em a try, and you'll be hooked.

TIP

If spring-loaded folders don't work, or if the springing is insanely fast or maddeningly slow, open the System Settings app, click Accessibility in the sidebar, and then click Pointer Control in the Accessibility pane. In the Mouse & Trackpad area of the Pointer Control pane, make sure that the Spring-Loading switch is set to On to enable the feature and then drag the Spring-Loading Speed slider along its Tortoise–Hare continuum to adjust the speed.

Using smart folders

A *smart folder* lets you save search criteria and have them work in the background to display the results in real time. In other words, a smart folder is updated continuously, so it displays all the files on your computer that match the search criteria set for the folder.

Figure 8-3 shows a smart folder that gathers all PNG image files with *Nature* in their name that have been opened in the past 15 days. Or you can create a smart folder that displays spreadsheet files, but only the ones bigger (or smaller) than a specified file size. Then all those files appear in one convenient smart folder.

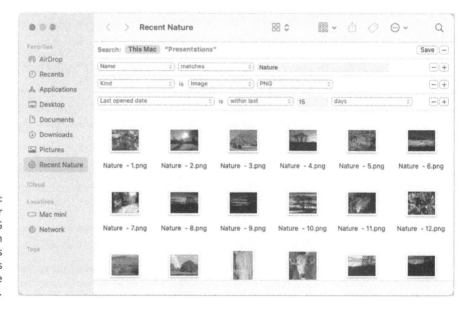

FIGURE 8-3:
A smart folder that displays PNG files opened in the past 15 days and with names that contain the word *Nature*.

The possibilities are endless. Because smart folders use alias-like technology to display items, the actual files remain in the folders in which you stored them. Smart folders don't gather the files themselves in a separate place; rather, they gather search results, leaving the originals right where you stashed them. Neat!

Also, because Spotlight (discussed in Chapter 9) is built deep into the underpinnings of the macOS file system and kernel, smart folders are updated in real time and so are always current, even after you add or delete files on your hard drive since creating the smart folder.

Smart folders are so useful that Apple provides four ways to create one. The following steps show you how:

1. **Start your smart folder by using any of the following methods:**

   - Choose File ⇨ New Smart Folder.

- Choose File ⇨ Find.

- Press ⌘+F.

- Type at least one character in the Search box of a Finder window.

If you have Recents selected in the sidebar, you can't use the last method, because Recents is a smart folder itself — one with a weird icon, but a smart folder nonetheless.

WARNING

2. **Refine the criteria for your search by clicking the + button to add a criterion or the – button to delete one.**

3. **When you're satisfied and ready to gather your criteria into a smart folder, click the Save button below the Search box.**

   A Save As dialog opens.

4. **Type a name for your smart folder in the Save As field, choose where you want to save it, and then click the Save button.**

TIP

Select the Add to Sidebar check box before clicking Save to add this smart folder to the sidebar of all Finder windows.

Smart folders are saved in the Saved Searches folder in your Library folder by default, but you can choose to save them anywhere on any drive and use them like any other folder.

If you want to change the criteria for a smart folder you created, Control-click or right-click the smart folder in the sidebar, and choose Show Search Criteria from the contextual menu.

When you finish changing the criteria, click the Save button to resave your folder. Don't worry — if you try to close a smart folder that you modify without saving your changes, macOS politely asks whether you want to save this smart folder and warns that if you don't save, the changes you made will be lost. You may be asked whether you want to replace the previous smart folder of the same name; usually, you do.

Smart folders (with the exception of the sidebar's Recents, which has its own weird little icon) display a little gear icon, making them easy to tell apart from regular folders.

Smart folders can save you a lot of time and effort, so if you haven't played with them much (or at all) yet, be sure to give 'em a try.

Shuffling Files and Folders

Sometimes, keeping files and folders organized means moving them from one place to another. At other times, you want to copy them, rename them, or compress them to send to a friend. These sections explain all those things and more.

TIP

All the techniques in the following sections work at least as well for windows that use List, Columns, or Gallery view as they do for windows that use Icon view. The figures in this section use Icon view only because it's the best view for pictures to show you what's going on. List and Columns views usually are much better for moving and copying files.

Moving files and folders

You can move files and folders around within a window to your heart's content *as long as that window is set to Icon view.* Just click and drag any icon to its new location in the window.

TIP

If the icons won't move, make sure View ⇨ Arrange By is set to None. You can't move icons around in a window displayed in List, Columns, or Gallery view. Even in Icon view, you can't move icons around in a window that's under the spell of the Arrange By command.

As you probably expect from Apple by now, you have choices for how you move one file or folder into another folder. You can use these techniques to move any item (any folder, document, alias, or app icon) into folders or onto other disks:

>> **Drag the item's icon onto a folder icon.** Drag the icon for one or more folders or files onto another folder (or disk) icon and then release the mouse button when the second folder or disk icon is highlighted. The files or folders will be inside the second folder or disk. This technique works regardless of whether the second folder is open in a separate window or tab.

REMEMBER

If you *don't* release when the second folder is highlighted, the second folder will spring open, allowing you to see its contents *before* committing to moving the item or items you're dragging into it by releasing the mouse button.

>> **Drag the item's icon into an open folder's window.** Drag one or more folders or files into the open window of a second folder (or disk), and release the mouse button when the second folder's window is highlighted.

REMEMBER

If you want to *move* an item from one *disk* to another disk, you can't use the preceding tricks, because dragging the item between disks copies the item rather than moving it. If you want to *move* a file or folder from one disk to another, hold down the ⌘ key while you drag the item from the disk it's currently on to the one you want to move it to. You'll know immediately if you've gotten this right, because you'll see the Moving Files window rather than the Copying Files window.

Selecting multiple items

Sometimes, you want to move or copy several items into a single folder. The process is pretty much the same as it is when you copy one file or folder: That is, you just drag the items' icons to where you want them and drop them there. But you need to select all the items you want before you can drag them en masse to their destination.

If you want to move all the files in a particular folder, simply choose Edit➪Select All or press ⌘+A. This command selects all the items in the active window, regardless of whether you can see them onscreen. If no window is active, choosing Select All selects every item on the desktop.

TIP

But what if you want to select only some of the files in the active window or on the desktop? Here's the most convenient method:

1. **To select more than one item in a folder, do one of the following:**

   - Click inside the folder window (without clicking any particular item), and drag the cursor while continuing to hold down the mouse (or trackpad) button. You see an outline of a box (a *selection rectangle*) around the items while you drag, and all items within or touching the box become highlighted (the six items with their names highlighted in Figure 8-4).

   - *Click one item and then hold down the Shift key while you click others.* As long as you hold down the Shift key, each new item that you click is added to the selection. To deselect an item, click it a second time while still holding down the Shift key.

   - *Click one item and then hold down the ⌘ key while you click others.* The difference between using the Shift and ⌘ keys is that the ⌘ key doesn't select everything between it and the first item selected when your window is in List, Gallery, or Columns view. In Icon view, it really doesn't make much difference.

TIP

   To deselect an item, click it while still holding down the ⌘ key.

2. **After you select the items, click one of them (clicking anywhere else deselects the items) and drag them to the location where you want to move them (or Option-drag to copy them).**

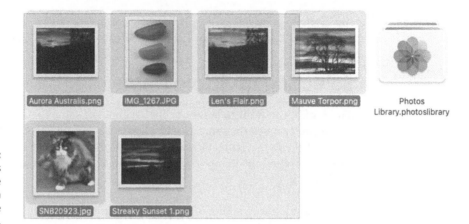

FIGURE 8-4:
The six items
touched by the
selection
rectangle become
selected.

Be careful with multiple selections, especially when you drag items to the Trash. You can easily — and accidentally — select more than one item, so watch out that you don't accidentally put the wrong item in the Trash by not paying close attention. (I dig into the Trash later in this chapter.)

WARNING

Renaming items

To rename an item, you can either click the item's name directly or click the item's icon and then press Return once to open the name for editing.

If an item is locked or busy (the app is currently open), or if you don't have the owner's permission to rename that item (see Chapter 16 for details about permissions), you can't rename it. Similarly, you should never rename macOS system items such as the Library, System, and Desktop folders.

**TECHNICAL
STUFF**

Either way, the item's name is selected and surrounded with a box, and you can type a new name. In addition, the cursor changes from a pointer to a text-editing I-beam. An I-beam cursor is the Mac's way of telling you that you can type now. At this point, if you click the I-beam cursor anywhere in the name box, you can edit the item's original name. If you don't click the I-beam cursor in the name box but just begin typing, what you type replaces the original name.

Don't change the name of a folder that contains open files, because you might screw up the saving process and possibly cause data loss.

WARNING

Renaming multiple items at once

To rename a group of files, first select them all; then right-click anywhere in your selection and choose Rename from the contextual menu. A dialog appears with options for adding or replacing text in the existing filename, or creating a custom format with indexes, counters, and dates before or after whatever new filename you choose.

Compressing files

TIP

If you're going to send files as an email enclosure, creating a compressed archive of the files first and sending the archive instead of the originals usually saves you time sending the files and saves the recipient time downloading them. To create this compressed archive, simply select the file(s) or folder(s) and then choose File ⇨ Compress. This command creates a compressed file in the widely used zip format containing the files or folders you selected. If those items are compressible, the zip file is smaller than the original items, sometimes substantially smaller; if the items aren't compressible, the zip file may actually be bigger than the items — but even so, it's easier to handle. Double-click a zip file to decompress it.

Getting rid of files and folders

To get rid of a file or folder, simply drag it onto the Trash icon in your Dock.

REMEMBER

Trashing an alias gets rid of only the alias, not the parent file. But trashing a document, a folder, or an app icon puts it in the Trash, where it *will* be deleted permanently the next time you empty the Trash. The Finder menu offers a couple of commands that help you manage the Trash:

>> **Finder ⇨ Empty Trash:** This command deletes all items in the Trash from your hard drive, period.

WARNING

Use the Empty Trash command with a modicum of caution. After a file is dragged into the Trash and the Trash is emptied, the file is gone, gone, gone unless you have Time Machine or other backup. (Okay, maybe ProSoft Engineering's Data Rescue or some other third-party utility can bring it back, but don't bet the farm on it.)

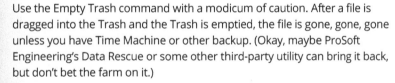

TIP

If you put something in the Trash by accident, you can almost always return it to whence it came: Just click the Trash icon in the Dock to open its window, Control-click or right-click the item you want to return, and choose Put Back from the contextual menu.

>> **Edit ⇨ Undo:** You can also invoke the magical Undo command by choosing Edit ⇨ Undo or pressing ⌘+Z. The accidentally trashed file returns to its original location. Usually. Unfortunately, Undo doesn't work every time — and it remembers only the very last action that you performed when it

does work — so don't rely on it too much. (The Control-click or right-click trick, however, works every time.)

TIP

One last thing: If you have two or more items you want to move to a new folder, select the items and choose File ⇨ New Folder with Selection, press ⌘+Control+N, or Control-click or right-click one of the selected items and choose New Folder with Selection from the contextual menu. All three techniques will create a new folder, move the selected items into it, and select the name of the new folder (which will be New Folder with Items) so you can type its new name and press Return.

Using iCloud, iCloud+, and iCloud Drive

iCloud has been around in various forms for years providing Internet-based storage for Macs, iPhones, iPads, and other Apple devices. iCloud Drive is a component of iCloud that lets you store files of any type in iCloud and access them from any device via your iCloud account. iCloud Drive is built into macOS, so it works like any other folder on your Mac. In other words, you can drag documents of any type into it, organize them with folders and tags (see Chapter 4) if you care to, and find them with Spotlight (see Chapter 9).

The best part is that the files are available not only on your Mac, but also on your iPhone, iPad, or Windows PC as well. That's the good news. The bad news is that if you need more than the 5GB of free storage space that you get in a standard iCloud account, you need to move up to the paid tier, which is called iCloud+. As of this writing, iCloud+ storage costs 99 cents per month for 50GB, $2.99 per month for 200GB, and $9.99 per month for 2TB.

iCloud Drive is normally enabled by default. To see whether it is, pop open a Finder window; expand the iCloud category, if it's collapsed; and look for the iCloud Drive item. If you don't see it, you may need to enable iCloud Drive: Click the System Settings icon on the Dock, click the Apple ID icon in the sidebar, click the iCloud button to display the iCloud screen, and then set the iCloud Drive switch to On.

If you've set the iCloud Drive switch to On but still don't see iCloud Drive in your sidebar, Finder may be set to suppress iCloud Drive. With a Finder window active, choose Finder ⇨ Finder Settings to open the Finder Settings window, click the Sidebar tab at the top, and then select the iCloud Drive check box in the iCloud section of the Show These Items in the Sidebar box.

One last thing: If your start-up disk is getting close to full, you can choose to store the contents of your desktop and Documents folders on your iCloud Drive instead of your start-up disk. The up side is that files in those folders are available to all your Macs and iDevices and via the iCloud website. The down side is that you may need to have Internet access to access those files.

If storing your Desktop and Documents folders in the cloud appeals to you, follow these steps:

1. Click the System Settings icon on the Dock to open System Settings.

2. Click the Apple ID icon in the sidebar to display the Apple ID screen.

3. Click the iCloud button to display the iCloud screen.

4. Click the Options button on the iCloud Drive row to open the Options dialog for iCloud.

5. Make sure that the Documents tab is selected at the top of the Options dialog.

6. Select the Desktop & Documents Folders check box.

Chapter **9**

Eight Terrific Time-Saving Tools

V entura is packed with time-saving apps and shortcuts. This chapter makes sure you know what you need to exploit eight key tools to the full. I start with Siri, the voice-driven virtual assistant; touch on the Clipboard and the Universal Clipboard; and then move on to peeking at files with Quick Look, searching for files and folders with the Find feature, and searching for pretty much anything with Spotlight.

After queries, quizzing, and search, I move on to management. I dig into managing apps, windows, desktops, and spaces with the Mission Control feature, and then show you how to use Stage Manager, Ventura's new tool for marshalling your recent apps and flipping among them. Last, I review two essential tools you have already met: Control Center and Launchpad.

Are You Siri-ous?

If you aren't familiar with Siri, Apple's intelligent digital assistant, you will be after reading this section.

Siri is designed to help you get things done by using your voice, including capabilities designed specifically for your Mac, which means you can search for information, find files, send messages, and do much, much more with only your voice. As you'd imagine, your Mac needs an Internet connection for Siri to search online.

Finally, Siri is optimized to work well with your Mac's built-in microphones, so you don't have to buy or connect a mic. This optimization is a welcome move by Apple, but you'll find that Siri, along with other voice-driven features such as Dictation and Voice Control, work even better with a headset microphone. (More on this in Chapter 20.) A headset microphone is especially helpful if you're using Siri in a noisy environment.

If you haven't tried Siri, you should. And if you're already a Siri fan, the latest rendition works just as you'd expect.

What Siri can do for you

Before I get to the "how," I'll look at exactly what Siri can do for you. Here's a short list of some cool things you can ask Siri to do:

>> "Open the Microsoft Word document I worked on yesterday."

>> "Remind me to take the pizza out of the oven in 14 minutes."

>> "Add a meeting to my calendar at 11 a.m. tomorrow with Dr. Spock."

>> "Call Anna Connor with FaceTime."

>> "Play songs by The Beatles." (This one works only if you have songs by The Beatles in your iTunes Library or subscribe to Apple Music.)

>> "Call me 'Your Highness.'" (Replace "Your Highness" with, "Sir," "Madam," or anything else you like; Siri will refer to you by that name forevermore.)

>> "Who am I?" (If you forget who you are, Siri will remind you that you are Your Highness.)

>> "Call my wife on her cellphone."

- » "What song is this?" (If you've ever used Shazam to identify songs, Siri uses its technology, so like the Shazam app, it can identify millions of songs after a brief listen.)

- » "Send a message to Martina to reschedule dinner tomorrow."

- » "Find an ATM near here."

- » "Send an email to Jack Black that says, 'You rock.'"

- » "Show me pictures I took in Florence Italy" or "Show me all the pictures I took on Thanksgiving."

- » "What is the Dow at?"

- » "Send a tweet: 'Going on vacation. Smiley-face.'" (Siri will replace "Smiley-face" with a smiley-face emoji in the tweet.)

- » "I need directions to House of Blues."

- » "Who was the 19th president of the United States?"

- » "How many calories are in a blueberry muffin?"

- » "Wake me up at 8:30 in the morning."

- » "Who is pitching for the Yankees tonight?"

- » "Who won the Academy Award for Best Actor in 2003?"

- » "What is trending on Twitter?"

Siri is relatively intelligent and understands many things in context. So if you ask, "Will I need an umbrella this weekend?" Siri will get that you're looking for a weather forecast. Siri is also smart about using your personal information, so you can say, "Remind me to call Mom at 8 p.m." When the time comes, Siri will offer a list of your mom's phone numbers. And if Siri can't determine who "Mom" is, it will ask you — and then, in the future, Siri will remember your mother.

You can also ask things such as "What's the traffic like around here?" or "Where can I get cheap gas around here?" Siri knows precisely where "here" is based on your Mac's current location (assuming you have enabled Location Services).

Now that you've had a glimpse of the kinds of things Siri will do for you, dive in and take a look at how to *use* Siri.

Working with Siri

You can summon Siri in six easy ways. The first four ways are to click its menu-bar icon or its icon in Launchpad (shown in the margin), double-click its icon in the Applications folder, or use its keyboard shortcut (⌘+spacebar by default or whatever you selected in the Siri System Preferences pane). The fifth way is available only if you have a MacBook that includes the Touch Bar control strip above the keyboard; if so, tap the Siri icon in the Touch Bar.

If you pressed and held down ⌘+spacebar, and Spotlight appeared instead of Siri, you didn't press and hold down long enough. Keep both keys pressed for two or three seconds, and Siri will be at your beck and call. Pressing and releasing them any faster summons Spotlight, not Siri.

The sixth way is new: Say, "Hey Siri." Alas, this way is disabled by default. If you want to summon Siri by saying, "Hey Siri," enable the Listen for "Hey Siri" check box in the Siri System Preferences pane.

Whichever way you use to summon Siri, a bubble will appear near the top-right corner of your screen, waiting for your input, as shown in Figure 9-1.

FIGURE 9-1:
Speak to Siri now, or forever hold your peace.

Making Siri your own

Using Siri couldn't be easier: You summon it, ask or tell it to do something, and then wait for that something to be done. But you can invoke several tweaks that can help make Siri sound and behave the way you prefer.

You manage Siri in the Siri & Spotlight pane in the System Settings app (by choosing ➪ System Preferences ➪ Siri & Spotlight). Here's what you can customize and how to do it:

>> **Ask Siri:** Set this switch to On to enable Siri (if it's not enabled already).

>> **Keyboard Shortcut menu:** If you don't care for the default ⌘+spacebar keyboard shortcut, this menu lets you change it to anything you like. Several built-in keyboard shortcuts are available, but you can also click Customize and then press exactly the keys you want.

TIP

>> **Language menu:** Use this menu to choose the language Siri will speak and understand. The list is a long one, including nine varieties of English; four varieties each of Chinese, French, and Spanish; and dozens of others.

Siri is known to have difficulty understanding people with distinct accents. If Siri has trouble understanding you, look on the Languages menu for a different version of the language. Making a change couldn't hurt, and it might just help.

>> **Siri Voice row:** The readout shows the selected voice variety (such as American) and Siri voice (such as Voice 2). Click the Select button to display the Siri Voice dialog. In the Voice Variety list, click the voice variety, such as American or Australian if you set Siri to use the English language. Then choose one of the voices offered for that voice variety. The number of voices you see here depends on which language and voice variety you choose.

>> **Delete Siri & Dictation History button:** If you say something you shouldn't have said and want to eradicate any record of it, click this button.

>> **Siri Suggestions & Privacy button:** Click this button to display the Siri Suggestions & Privacy dialog. In the left pane, click the app you want to configure; then, on the right, choose options by setting the switches to on or off, as needed. Each app has the Learn from This App switch; some apps have the Show Siri Suggestions in App switch as well. Click Done when you're done.

>> **Siri Responses button:** Click this button to display the Siri Responses dialog. Here, you can set to the Voice Feedback switch to on or off to control whether Siri gives you voice feedback; set the Always Show Siri Captions switch to on or off to control whether what Siri says appears on screen; and set the Always Show Speech switch to on or off to specify whether what you've said (rather, what Siri thinks you've said) appears onscreen. Again, click Done when you're done.

Comprehending the macOS Clipboard

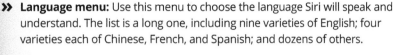

The *Clipboard* is a holding area for the last thing you selected and then cut or copied. That copied item can be text, a picture, a portion of a picture, an object in a drawing app, a column of numbers in a spreadsheet, any file or folder (except a drive), or just about anything else that can be selected.

Put another way, the Clipboard is your Mac's temporary storage area.

Introducing the Clipboard

Most of the time, the Clipboard works quietly in the background, but if you want to know what it currently contains, the Clipboard will reveal itself if you choose Edit ⇨ Show Clipboard when a Finder window (or the desktop) is active.

This command summons the Clipboard window, shown in Figure 9-2, which displays the type of item (such as text, an image, or sound) on the Clipboard, as well as either the item itself or a message letting you know that the item on the Clipboard can't be displayed.

FIGURE 9-2:
The Show Clipboard command displays whatever is on the Clipboard if it can.

When you cut or copy an item, that item remains on the Clipboard only until you cut or copy something else; you log out of your Mac, restart it, or shut it down; or your Mac crashes. When you cut or copy something else, the new item replaces the Clipboard's contents.

If you want to preserve something you've cut or copied, put it in longer-term storage rather than leave it on the Clipboard. You could paste the cut or copied item into a note in your Notes app, for example (or into any other document, as long as that document is saved somewhere).

TIP

Myriad third-party clipboard enhancers remember the last 100 things (or more) that you copy or cut to the Clipboard. These utilities also preserve their contents when you log out of your Mac or shut it down (or if it crashes). My favorites are CopyClip from FIPLAB (free) and its more powerful successor, CopyClip 2 ($7.99), both available from the Mac App Store (see Chapter 20).

TECHNICAL STUFF

The Cut, Copy, and Paste commands on the Edit menu are enabled only when they can be used. If the selected item can be cut or copied, the Cut and Copy commands on the Edit menu are enabled (black). If the selected item can't be cut or copied, the commands are unavailable and are dimmed (gray). If the Clipboard is empty, or the current document can't accept what's on the Clipboard, the Paste command is dimmed. And when nothing is selected, the Cut, Copy, and Paste commands are all dimmed.

One more thing: Files and folders can't be cut; they can only be copied (and pasted). So when a file or folder is selected, the Cut command is always gray.

Copying files and folders

One way to copy files and folders from one place to another is to use the Clipboard. Select a file or folder, or select multiple items; then choose Edit ⇨ Copy (or use its shortcut, ⌘+C) to copy what you've selected to the Clipboard. To paste the copied item or items in another location, navigate to that other location and then choose Edit ⇨ Paste (or use its shortcut, ⌘+V). The result is that you have two copies of the files or folders in two places.

Other methods of copying files and folders from one place to another include these:

>> **Drag the file or folder from one folder onto the icon of another folder while holding down the Option key.** Release the mouse button and Option key when the second folder is highlighted. This technique works regardless of whether the second folder's window is open.

When you copy something by dragging and dropping it with the Option key held down, the pointer changes to include a little plus sign (+) next to the arrow, as shown in the margin. Neat!

Note that when you drag an item to a different disk, macOS copies the item rather than moves it, whether or not you hold down the Option key. But you can move an icon from one disk to another by pressing ⌘ when you drag.

>> **Drag a file or folder into the open window for another folder while holding down the Option key.** Drag the file or folder that you want to copy into the open window for a second folder (or other hard drive or removable media, such as a USB flash drive).

>> **Choose File ⇨ Duplicate (⌘+D), or right-click or Control-click the item you want to duplicate and then choose Duplicate from the contextual menu that appears.** This command makes a copy of the selected item, adds the word *copy* to its name, and then places the copy in the same window as the original item. You can use the Duplicate command on any item except a disk.

You can't duplicate an entire disk onto itself. But you can copy an entire disk (call it Disk 1) to any other actual, physical, separate disk (call it Disk 2) as long as Disk 2 has enough space available. Just hold down Option and drag Disk 1 onto Disk 2's icon. The contents of Disk 1 are copied to Disk 2 and appear on Disk 2 in a folder named Disk 1.

If Disk 1 is a *start-up disk* (macOS has been installed on the disk, and it can start your Mac), Disk 2 will contain the same files but won't be a bootable start-up disk (that is, can't start a Mac). Also, some files may not be copied properly due to macOS permissions issues. See Chapter 16 for the story on permissions.

You can cut an item's name, but you can't cut the item itself; you can only copy an item.

There are two ways to achieve the same effect as cutting an item:

>> Select the item, copy it to the Clipboard, paste it in its new location, and then move the original item to the Trash.

>> Use the secret shortcut to move the item via Copy and Paste. The secret is that you press the Option key before clicking the Edit menu. When you do, the Paste command transmogrifies into Move Item Here, providing the functional equivalent of cutting and pasting the item. You can even use a keyboard shortcut — ⌘+Option+V — to move items from one location to another. Cool, eh?

When you copy a file, it's wise to change the name of the copied file after you paste it. See, having more than one file on your hard drive with the same name isn't such a good idea, even if the files are in different folders. Trust me — having 12 files all named *Expense Report* or 15 files named *Consulting Invoice* is confusing, no matter how well organized your folder structure is.

Add distinguishing words or dates to the names of files and folders you copy, such as *Expense Report Q3 2022* or *Landscape Bunnies Invoice 4-1-2023*.

You can have lots of files with the same name *on the same disk* (although it's probably not a good idea). But your Mac won't let you have more than one file with the same name and extension (.txt, .jpg, .doc, and so on) *in the same folder.*

Pasting from the Clipboard

To place the item that's on the Clipboard someplace new, click where you want the item to go, and choose Edit ⇨ Paste or use the keyboard shortcut ⌘+V to paste what you've copied or cut.

Pasting doesn't purge the contents of the Clipboard. In fact, an item stays on the Clipboard until you cut or copy another item; you log out, restart, or shut down your Mac; or your Mac takes matters into its own hands and crashes. This means that you can paste the same item over and over and over again, which can come in handy at times.

And don't forget that most apps have Edit menus and use the Clipboard, which means that you can usually cut or copy something from a document in one app and paste it into a document in another app.

Expanding your horizons with the Universal Clipboard

The Universal Clipboard lets you copy or cut an item on one device (say, your Mac), and then paste it on another device (say, your iPhone or iPad). Because it performs this magic by using iCloud, the requirements are as follows:

>> You must have an Internet connection (wired or wireless).

>> Bluetooth must be enabled.

>> Both devices must have Handoff enabled. (On your Mac, choose System Settings ➪ General ➪ AirPlay & Handoff and then set the Allow Handoff Between This Mac and Your iCloud Devices switch to on. On your iPhone or iPad, choose Settings ➪ General ➪ AirPlay & Handoff and then set the Handoff switch to on.)

>> Both devices must be logged into the same iCloud account.

>> The devices must be within a few feet of each other.

When these conditions are met, Universal Clipboard just works. If you cut or copy something on one device, you can paste it on another device for approximately 2 minutes after you cut or copy it; after a couple of minutes, however, all bets are off.

If Universal Clipboard doesn't work for you, check the Apple website (`www.apple.com/macos/continuity`) to make sure that both devices meet the system requirements. If both are supported, and you still can't make Universal Clipboard work, try turning off Handoff on both devices, wait a minute or two, and then turn it back on. You might also try logging out of iCloud on both devices, restarting them, and then logging back into iCloud on both. Finally, some older Macs have issues with the set of features Apple calls Continuity, which include the Handoff and Universal Clipboard features, even though these Macs meet the specifications.

With a Quick Look

The Quick Look command displays the contents of the selected file in a floating window, letting you see what's in a file without double-clicking (to open) it and without launching an app. Quick Look is great when you want to peek at the contents of a file without having to open it.

To take a Quick Look yourself, select an icon and then do any of the following:

» Choose File ⇨ Quick Look.

» Right-click or Control-click the file's icon, and choose Quick Look from its contextual menu.

» Choose Quick Look from the Action icon/menu on the toolbar.

» Use one of its two keyboard shortcuts: Press ⌘+Y or (the easiest shortcut ever) press the spacebar while an icon is selected.

Quick Look is especially useful for a folder full of images, such as the one shown in Figure 9-3.

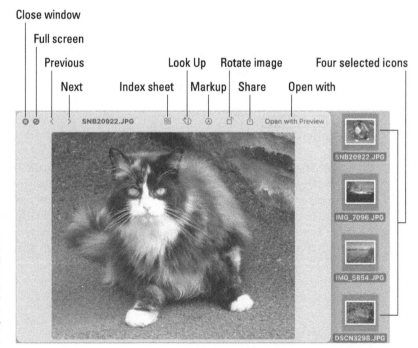

FIGURE 9-3:
The Quick Look window (right) displaying an image from one of the four selected icons in a folder full of pictures (left).

While the Quick Look window is open, you can select different icons in the Finder window — use the arrow keys to select the next or previous icon — and see their contents in the Quick Look window!

The bad news is that although Quick Look works with many types of files — Microsoft Office, Apple iWork, plain-text, PDF, TIFF, GIF, JPEG, PNG, and most types of audio and video files — it doesn't work with *all* files. You'll know it doesn't work if Quick Look shows you a big document, folder, or app icon instead of the contents of that file.

If you select multiple items before you invoke Quick Look, as in Figure 9-3, the Previous (<) and the Next (>) icon appear at the top of the Quick Look window near the left side, enabling you to navigate to the previous item or the next item; you can also press the left-arrow key for the previous item or the right-arrow key for the next item. To the right of the current item's name is the Index Sheet icon, which shows four small squares. You can click Index Sheet to view all selected items at the same time as an *index sheet*.

You can invoke Markup from the Quick Look window. Just click the Markup icon, and the Markup tools appear. (Markup is described in loving detail in Chapter 5.)

Share and share alike with the Share menu

If you use an iPhone or iPad, you're surely familiar with the Share icon, the rectangle with an arrow escaping from it, as shown in the margin and on the toolbar in Figure 9-3. Clicking the Share icon opens the Share menu, which gives you seven or more options (depending on the type of file you selected):

>> **Mail:** Launches the Mail app and attaches the selected file to a blank message, ready for you to address and send.

>> **Messages:** Launches the Messages app and puts the selected file in an outgoing message, ready for you to address and send. You become well acquainted with the Messages app in Chapter 15.

>> **AirDrop:** Sends the selected file to other Mac users or Apple-device users. As long as you're on the same Wi-Fi network, your file transfer takes but a single click (or a single tap on the iPhone or iPad).

>> **Notes:** Sends the selected file to the Notes app, where you can add it to an existing note or create a note for it. (You discover the Notes app in Chapter 10.)

>> **Reminders:** Creates a new reminder in the Reminders app. (To discover more about the Reminders app, see Chapter 10.)

>> **Add to Photos:** Adds the selected item to the All Photos album in the Photos app.

>> **More:** Lets you add other services (such as Vimeo or LinkedIn) and apps (such as Photos or Aperture) to your Share menu via macOS's extensible architecture. To manage these extensions, choose More from the Share menu. Alternatively, you can launch the System Settings app, click the Privacy & Security button, click the Extensions icon, and then click Sharing in the Extensions pane. In the Select Extensions for Sharing with Others dialog that opens, select the check box for each extension you want to enable and then click Done.

If the file or folder you select is on your iCloud Drive, you'll see an additional option that lets you share the file or folder with others. You specify who can see it, who can modify it, and who can share it with others before sending them an invitation via Mail, Messages, Link, or AirDrop.

Slide into Slideshow (full-screen) mode

Quick Look really shines in its Slideshow (full-screen) mode, which you can start with any of these techniques:

>> Hold down Option and choose File ➪ Slideshow.

>> Press ⌘+Option+Y.

 If your file is already open in the Quick Look window, click the full-screen icon, as labeled in Figure 9-3 and shown here in the margin.

When you're in Slideshow mode, a completely different set of controls appears onscreen automatically, as shown in Figure 9-4.

FIGURE 9-4:
The Slideshow controls appear automatically in full-screen Slideshow mode.

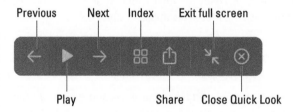

The Slideshow controls disappear after a few seconds of inactivity; if you don't see them when you need them, just wiggle the pointer anywhere onscreen to make them pop up.

TIP

To exit Slideshow (full-screen) mode, press Esc or click the Exit Full Screen icon to return to the Quick Look window, or click the Close Quick Look icon to both exit Slideshow mode and quit Quick Look.

When you're finished with the Quick Look window, click the X icon in the top-left corner (refer to Figure 9-3). If you're in full-screen mode, click the X icon on the control bar, as shown in Figure 9-4, or press ⌘+Y, which works in either mode.

Spotlight on Finding Files and Folders Faster

Even if you follow every single bit of advice provided in this chapter, a time will come when you won't be able to find a file or folder even though you know for certain that it's somewhere on your hard drive. Fortunately, macOS includes a fabulous search technology called Spotlight, which can help you find almost anything on any mounted disk in seconds. Spotlight can search for

>> Files

>> Folders

>> Text inside documents

>> Files and folders by their metadata (creation date, modification date, kind, size, and so on)

Spotlight finds what you're looking for and then organizes its results logically, all in the blink of an eye (on most Macs).

Spotlight is both a technology and a feature. The technology is pervasive throughout macOS and is the underlying power behind the Search boxes in many Apple apps and utilities, such as Mail, Contacts, System Preferences, and Finder. You can also use it by clicking the Spotlight menu — the little magnifying glass on your menu bar. Finally, you can reuse Spotlight searches in the future by turning them into smart folders (see Chapter 8).

Finding files and folders has never been faster or easier than it is in Ventura. The following sections show you the two separate but related ways that Spotlight helps you find files, folders, and even text inside document files and on the web: the Search box in the toolbar of Finder windows and the main Spotlight menu. Searching in Finder windows searches only your Mac's file system. Searching with the Spotlight menu searches both your Mac and the web.

Using the Find command

Here's how to use the Find feature to find things on your Mac:

1. **Click open space on the desktop to make Finder active.**

If you've smothered the desktop with windows, click the Finder icon in the Dock.

If you've already got a Finder window open that you want to use, click that window.

2. **Choose File ➪ Find or press ⌘+F to begin a new search, or click the Search box of your open window.**

If you want to limit the search to a specific folder (and its subfolders), open that folder first and then click its Search box or press ⌘+F.

You can search for files by clicking This Mac (all files) or the active window's name, if there is one. If no windows are open, This Mac (all files) is used by default, as shown in Figure 9-5.

3. **In the Search box, type a single character.**

I typed the letter *s,* and the window started displaying the results, as shown in Figure 9-5.

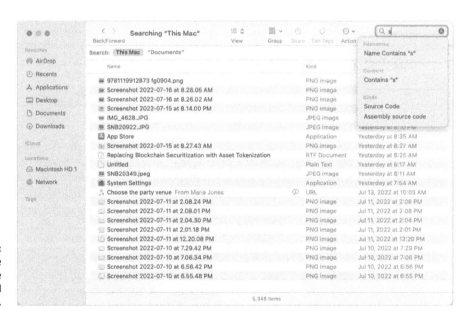

FIGURE 9-5:
Type one character in the Search box, and the magic begins.

At the same time, a menu drops down below your pointer to offer search suggestions, in categories such as Filenames, Content, and Kinds, as shown in Figure 9-5. Choose an item from the menu to narrow the scope of your search, or type additional characters: The more you type, the fewer matches and suggestions you'll see.

Spotlight's default behavior is to search files' contents if it can (and it can search the text inside files created by many popular apps).

TIP

Third-party Spotlight plug-ins are available that let you search the contents of file types not supported by Ventura, including old WordPerfect and QuarkXPress files and many others. Search the Internet for *Spotlight plug-ins,* and you'll find plug-ins for dozens of popular apps.

If you know all or part of the file's name, you can limit your search to filenames (that is, exclude text in files and search only for files by name). Just choose Name Matches (it's *s* in Figure 9-5) from the drop-down menu.

4. **When you find the file or folder you want, open any item in the window by double-clicking it.**

REMEMBER

Keep these points in mind when you perform a search:

>> You have a choice of where to search. This Mac is selected in Figures 9-5 and 9-6.

>> You can choose additional search criteria — such as the kind (Text with the subcategory Rich Text in Figure 9-6) and the date the file or folder was created (Within Last 7 Days in Figure 9-6) — as well as other attributes, including Modification Date, Creation Date, Keywords, Label, File Contents, and File Size.

>> To add another criterion, simply click the + button on the right side of the window.

>> To save a search for reuse in the future, click the Save button in the top-right corner of the window.

FIGURE 9-6:
Search your entire Mac or a specific folder (and its subfolders) and then narrow your search by using one or more criteria.

TIP

Try choosing different options from the window's Group menu — Name, Kind, Date Last Opened, and so on — to see the search results presented in different ways.

Using the Spotlight menu and its keyboard shortcut

When you want to search both your Mac and the web, use the Spotlight menu. Click the magnifying-glass icon at the far-right end of your menu bar or press the keyboard shortcut ⌘+spacebar to open the Spotlight Search box. Then type a character, word, or series of words in the Search box to begin your search.

Spotlight floats elegantly in the middle of your screen, as shown in Figure 9-7, displaying a search for Ventura. As you can see, Spotlight brings in results from external sources, including the official website of Ventura, California, as well as results from your Mac.

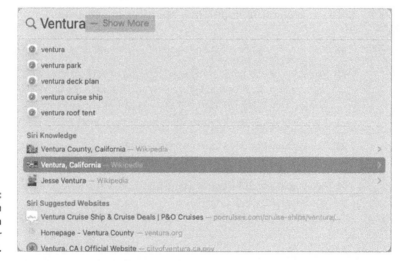

FIGURE 9-7:
Spotlight in Ventura searching for *Ventura.*

TIP

The Spotlight Search keyboard shortcut, ⌘+spacebar, could hardly be easier to remember. But if you prefer a different shortcut, you can change it in the Siri & Spotlight pane of System Settings.

Spotlight is more than just a menu and a Search box; it also uses a technology that's pervasive throughout macOS and apps, including (but certainly not limited to) Mail and Contacts. The reason why it's so spectacularly speedy is that it indexes your files when your Mac is idle. The upshot is that Spotlight knows file locations and contents soon after a file is created or modified.

Blast Off with Mission Control

If you use your Mac extensively (and you will), chances are that you'll use lots of apps at the same time and that some of those apps will have multiple windows open. Some apps may be full-screen. Oh, and you may have multiple desktops as well.

To navigate among your open windows, apps, and desktops, you can use Mission Control, discussed here. (You can also use Stage Manager, discussed in the upcoming section, "All the World's a Stage . . . and You're the Manager.")

Mission Control shows you big thumbnails of your open windows, apps, full-screen apps, and desktops so you can organize them or navigate swiftly to the one you want. Mission Control can also display all the open windows for the active app, which is great for navigating inside that app; this feature is called App Exposé. Less excitingly but still usefully, Mission Control can display the desktop, enabling you to get at the items you've parked on it; this feature has the does-what-it-says-on-the-tin name Show Desktop.

Before you start using Mission Control, you might want to configure it. Open the System Settings app, click the Desktop & Dock item in the sidebar, and then scroll down to the Mission Control section at the bottom of the Desktop & Dock pane.

Setting Mission Control parameters

The Mission Control section of the Desktop & Dock pane contains four switches: Automatically Rearrange Spaces Based on Most Recent Use; When Switching to an Application, Switch to a Space with Open Windows for the Application; Group Windows by Application; and Displays Have Separate Spaces. These long-winded switches will all start to make sense shortly; for now, just know that they do what their lengthy names imply. You should experiment with the settings, turning them on and off, to see which way you prefer them.

Below these four switches are two buttons: Shortcuts (discussed here) and Hot Corners (discussed in the next section, "Hot corners are hot stuff!").

Click the Shortcuts button to open the Keyboard and Mouse Shortcuts dialog for Mission Control. Open the Mission Control pop-up menu and set the keyboard shortcut for invoking Mission Control; open the Application Windows pop-up menu and set the keyboard shortcut for displaying just the active app's windows; and open the Desktop pop-up menu and set the keyboard shortcut for displaying the desktop, getting all open windows out of the way.

Hold down the ⌘, Option, Control, or Shift key (or any combination thereof) when you choose an item from any of the shortcut menus to add modifier keys to the shortcuts you create. So if you were to hold down ⌘+Shift when you choose F11 from a pop-up menu, the keyboard shortcut for that feature would be ⌘+Shift+F11.

Finally, most Apple keyboards made since April 2007 include a dedicated Mission Control shortcut key (on the F3 or F4 key). If you see a tiny picture that looks like the Mission Control icon (shown in the margin) on your F3 or F4 key, you can use that key in addition to the other shortcuts discussed in this section.

A picture is worth a thousand words, so check out Figure 9-8 as you read about each feature:

>> To see all open windows that aren't minimized or hidden in all open apps (as shown in Figure 9-8), press Control+↑ (up arrow).

>> To see all open windows belonging to the active app in a similar display, press Control+↓ (down arrow). This view is App Exposé view.

>> If you hover your pointer over a thumbnail in Mission Control, a blue border appears around it.

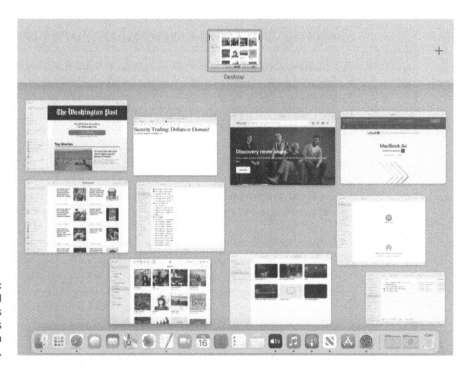

FIGURE 9-8:
Mission Control (Control+↑) gives you quick access to all your open windows.

If you press the spacebar while a thumbnail is highlighted, you'll see an overlay with a larger preview of the window's contents, which is especially helpful when a window is partially obscured by another window.

>> To hide all open windows so you can see icons on the desktop, press F11 or Fn+F11.

Note that when you're using Mission Control, windows appear as reduced-size thumbnails. Hover the pointer over a thumbnail in Mission Control to display the name of the app or window. Hover the pointer over a thumbnail in App Exposé to display the window's name below its thumbnail. Click a thumbnail to exit Mission Control or App Exposé and make that app or window active.

One last thing: If you use a trackpad, check out the More Gestures tab of the Trackpad pane in System Settings, where you can enable gestures to invoke Mission Control, App Exposé, Launchpad, and Show Desktop.

Hot corners are hot stuff!

In the bottom-right corner of the Mission Control section of the Desktop & Dock pane in System Settings is the Hot Corners button, which lets you designate any or all of the corners of your screen as hotspots to trigger Mission Control, App Exposé, Show Desktop, Notification Center, Launchpad, Quick Note, Screen Saver, Display Sleep, or Lock Screen. Click the menu for a corner, and select the feature you want to associate with that corner. Then, whenever you move your pointer to that corner and leave it there for a second or two, the feature executes.

WARNING

Hot corners can be great, but if you tend to park the mouse pointer in a particular corner of the screen as you work with the keyboard, either don't set a hot corner for that corner or add one or more modifier keys to the hot corner, as explained in the next tip.

Mission Control is enabled by default, but you can disable any or all of its features by turning off its trigger: Just choose the minus sign from a pop-up menu instead of a keyboard shortcut.

TIP

Hold down the ⌘, Option, Control, or Shift key (or any combination thereof) when you choose an item from any of the Active Screen Corner menus to add modifier keys to the hot corners you create. So if you were to hold down ⌘+Shift when you select Mission Control as the shortcut assigned to the top-left corner, you'd have to press ⌘ and Shift and move the pointer to the top-left corner to trigger it. Or if you were to hold down Shift when you choose Application Windows from the pop-up menu, you'd have to hold down Shift when you move the pointer to the top-left corner to invoke the command. If you don't press a modifier key when you select an item from a hot-corner menu, merely moving the pointer to that corner invokes the command.

Organizing desktops and spaces with Mission Control

Mission Control is great for organizing your windows, but it's not content to stop there: It also lets you manage spaces and desktops and switch among them with a keystroke or a trackpad gesture.

This feature is fantastic, but the terminology is awkward. A *desktop* is an area on which you can arrange windows, as you're used to doing on the main desktop. A *space* is either an app running full-screen or multiple app windows arranged to take up a full screen. So, depending on how you look at it, a desktop is a special kind of space — or a space is a special kind of desktop.

Before you slap your forehead in frustration, take a look at Figure 9-9. Here, you see three desktops called Desktop 1, Desktop 2, and Desktop 3. So far, so clear. But there are also two spaces: one called Safari & Finder, in which those two apps split the screen 50–50, and one called TextEdit, in which your favorite text editor gets to hog the whole screen.

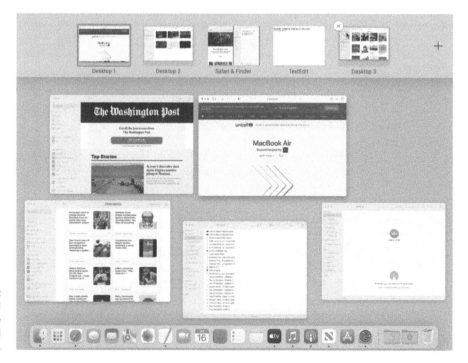

FIGURE 9-9: Mission Control showing off three desktops and two spaces.

If you find yourself spending too much time moving and resizing windows onscreen, consider setting up desktops and spaces for specific tasks. You might have one desktop dedicated to a specific project, a full-screen space for web surfing, a second desktop for email and scheduling, and a third desktop for media. In each desktop and space, you can keep the windows arranged just the way that works best for you.

To navigate your desktops, invoke Mission Control by pressing the keyboard shortcut (by default, Control+↑ or the dedicated F3 or F4 key). If you have a trackpad, you can also swipe upward with three fingers (unless you've disabled this gesture).

At first, the bar at the top of the screen shows each desktop and space as just a name with no thumbnail: Desktop 1, Desktop 2, Safari & Finder, and so on, continuing the preceding example.

Move the pointer up over the bar to display the thumbnails of the desktops and spaces, as in Figure 9-9. Then you can take the following actions:

>> **Add a new desktop.** Click the Add (+) button at the right end of the bar.

   To add a new desktop containing a particular window, drag that window to the Add (+) button.

>> **Delete a desktop.** Move the pointer over the desktop's thumbnail and then click the X-in-a-circle button that appears the upper-left corner of the thumbnail.

   When you delete a desktop, macOS moves all its windows to the previous desktop.

>> **Rearrange your desktops and spaces.** Grab a desktop or space, and drag it left or right along the bar.

>> **Reduce a space to windows.** Move the pointer over the space's thumbnail and then click the Exit Full Screen button (two diagonal arrows butting heads) that appears. The space vanishes, and macOS migrates the windows to the previous desktop.

>> **Move a window to a different desktop.** Drag the window's thumbnail to the desktop's thumbnail.

>> **Display a desktop or space.** Click the desktop or space. Mission Control closes.

>> **Return to the desktop or space whence you came.** Press Esc, the Mission Control key, or the Mission Control keyboard shortcut.

To move quickly among your desktops and spaces with the trackpad, swipe left or right with three fingers. If this gesture doesn't work, open System Settings, click Trackpad in the left pane, click the More Gestures tab, and then configure the Swipe Between Full Screen Apps setting.

macOS takes full advantage of multiple displays no matter how many displays are connected to your Mac. So you can work in Finder's desktop on one display and use a full-screen app on another, for example. Each display has its own exclusive set of Mission Control desktops and spaces associated with it.

If you use multiple monitors (as I do), you can drag and drop a desktop or space from one display to another. Try it — it's way cool!

All the World's a Stage . . . and You're the Manager

Ventura adds a completely new method of multitasking to macOS: Stage Manager.

If you're feeling that the Dock, the app switcher, and Mission Control provide quite enough multitasking firepower for you, yes, you have a point. But even if you're happy multitasking with those tools, it's worth your spending a little while playing with Stage Manager, because you may find it helpful. And if you don't, you're under no obligation to use Stage Manager.

If you've used Stage Manager on an iPad, you'll find that it works pretty much the same way on the Mac.

So: Stage Manager. What is it, and what does it do? Why? How? (And when?)

Enabling Stage Manager

To get started, open a handful of apps — at least five of your choice — to give Stage Manager enough raw material to work with. Figure 9-10 shows five apps — Music, Contacts, Calendar, Safari, and Photos — jostling for space on a small screen. The app windows overlap, and though you can bring any window to the front by clicking it (or using the Dock, the app switcher, or Mission Control), the effect is cluttered, and the use of desktop real estate is poor.

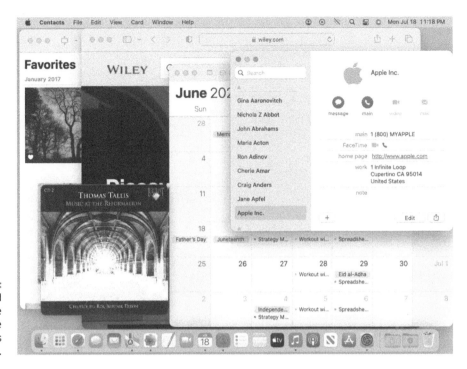

FIGURE 9-10:
A cluttered
desktop — the
problem Stage
Manager was
built to solve.

To bring order to your desktop when it's like this, enable Stage Manager in Control Center. Click the Control Center icon (shown in the margin) on the menu bar to open Control Center; then click the Stage Manager button below the Do Not Disturb icon, so that the button shows a white background (see the left screen in Figure 9-11) rather than a background based on the wallpaper behind it. macOS displays the Stage Manager dialog, which briefly explains the feature. Click the Turn On Stage Manager button to dismiss the dialog and enable Stage Manager.

TIP

To give yourself quick access to Stage Manager, open Control Center, and drag the Stage Manager icon to the menu bar so that you can display it directly from the menu bar (see the right screen in Figure 9-11) without having to open Control Center.

Using Stage Manager

Now Stage Manager is on, and you'll see that it has rearranged your recent windows (see Figure 9-12). The active window now sits centrally on the screen, whereas the other apps appear as a column of thumbnails on the left side of the screen. This column is the Recent Apps list. The number of apps in the Recent Apps list varies depending on the screen resolution. For a low-resolution screen, as in the example, Stage Manager typically provides four app thumbnails, whereas a higher-resolution screen gets six app thumbnails.

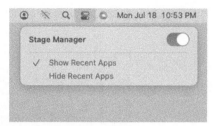

FIGURE 9-11:
Enable Stage
Manager
in
Control Center,
so that the button
has a white
background.
(left). Add Stage
Manager to the
menu bar (right)
so you can enable
and disable
it quickly.

FIGURE 9-12:
Stage Manager
quickly imposes
order, placing the
active window
centrally and
lining up the
other windows in
the Recent Apps
list on the left of
the screen.

Click one of these thumbnails. In the example, I clicked the Safari thumbnail. Figure 9-13 shows what happens: Stage Manager displays that window centered on the screen, replacing the previous window, which it displays as a thumbnail where the new app's thumbnail was in the Recent Apps list. Stage Manager resizes the central app window as needed to provide space for the Recent Apps list. Stage

Manager also leaves some space free on the right side of the screen, perhaps to create the illusion of balance.

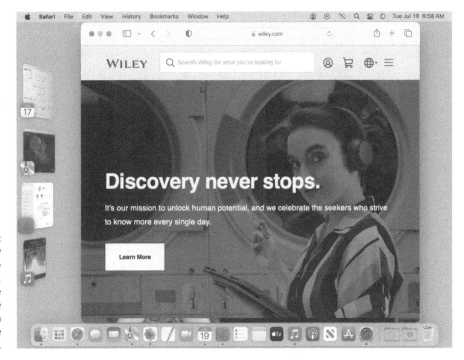

FIGURE 9-13:
Clicking a window brings it to the central position, moving the previous active window to a thumbnail on the Recent Apps list.

TIP

You can resize the central window as needed by dragging its borders. You can expand the window to take up the space on the right side of the screen, for example. Or you can expand it to the left, taking up the space the Recent Apps list occupies; when you do, Stage Manager hides the Recent Apps list to get it out of your way.

Now try dragging an app thumbnail on top of the central window. In the example, I dragged the Calendar thumbnail. Figure 9-14 shows the result: The two apps appear together in the central position. You can rearrange them as necessary. You might position the apps so that you can see the contents of both their windows, for example.

Now the apps are a group, and Stage Manager treats them as a unit. That means there's a free place in the Recent Apps list. In Figure 9-14, you can see that Stage Manager has added the Photos thumbnail to take up the free place (the top place in the Recent Apps list).

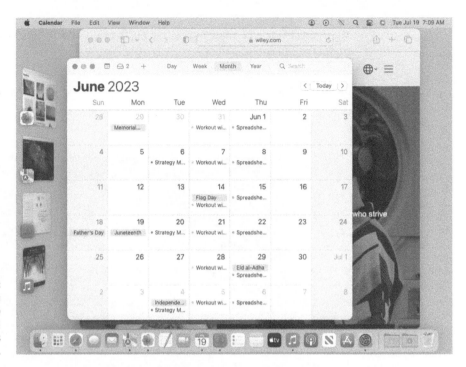

FIGURE 9-14:
Dragging a
thumbnail onto
the central
window groups
the apps.

Now if you click another app thumbnail to make it active, the grouped apps that were active move to the Recent Apps list, where the group appears as a thumbnail. Figure 9-15 shows what happened when I clicked the Maps thumbnail to make Maps active: The Calendar-n-Safari group appeared as a thumbnail.

Now you know how to use Stage Manager to flip among your recent apps. Here are four more things that are helpful to know to make the most of Stage Manager:

» If your desktop contains files, folders, drives, and so on, Stage Manager hides them to help keep the view uncluttered. If you need to work with them, click open space on the desktop, and Stage Manager hides the active app. Click open space on the desktop again when you're ready to summon the active app back.

» If you don't want to dedicate space to the Recent Apps list, hide the list. Click the Control Center icon on the menu bar to open Control Center; click the Stage Manager button to display the subpanel; and then click Hide Recent Apps, placing a check mark next to it.

» If you open three or more windows of the same app, Stage Manager automatically shuffles them into a group.

» To switch to another app that's not in the Recent Apps list, you can use Launchpad, the Dock, or the app switcher, as usual. Stage Manager works well with Mission Control, with desktops and spaces, and with the Dock. You can even position the Dock on the left side of the screen, where it will coexist peacefully with the Recent Apps list (whether you've chosen to show this list or to hide it).

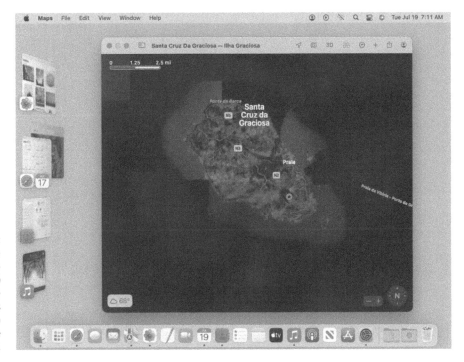

FIGURE 9-15: When you make another app (Maps here) active, the grouped apps appear as a thumbnail in the Recent Apps list.

And when — if — you want to stop using Stage Manager, open Control Center, click the Stage Manager button to display the subpanel, and then set the Stage Manager switch to off (white).

Taking Control of Essential Settings

Control Center lets you manage Wi-Fi, Bluetooth, AirDrop, and other settings quickly, easily, and without opening the System Settings app.

 To access Control Center, click its icon on the menu bar, as shown on the left in Figure 9-16 (and in the margin). To see the options for each control, move the pointer over the control, and then click the chevron (>) that appears. The options for Wi-Fi are shown on the right side of Figure 9-16.

FIGURE 9-16:
The default
Control Center
(left) and its Wi-Fi
controls (right).

To add controls to Control Center, open the System Settings app, and click Control Center in the sidebar. Then go to the Control Center Modules list and use the pop-up menus to specify which items appear in the menu bar.

Launchpad: The Place for Apps

Launchpad presents all the apps in your Applications folder in a view that looks somewhat like the home screen of an iPhone or iPad.

 Click the Launchpad dock icon (shown in the margin). It fills your screen with big, beautiful app icons, as shown in Figure 9-17.

If your Launchpad has more than one page of apps, you'll see dots near the bottom of the screen. To switch pages, click a gray dot; press ⌘+right arrow (→) or ⌘+left-arrow (←) to move to the next or previous page, respectively; or click anywhere (except on an icon) and flick left or right. Trackpad users can also use a three-finger swipe left or right to move from page to page.

To launch an app, click its icon. Launchpad disappears, and the app replaces it on your screen.

FIGURE 9-17:
Launchpad, in all
its glory.

You can configure Launchpad by rearranging the app icons, organizing them in folders, and deleting them. These are the moves you need to know:

>> **To find an app:** Type the first few characters of its name in the Search box at the top of the screen.

>> **To rearrange app icons on a page:** Click and drag the app to its new location.

>> **To move apps to the next or previous page:** Click and drag the app to the left or right edge of the screen. When the next page of apps appears, drag the app to its new location on that page.

>> **To add an app to your Dock:** Click and drag the app onto the left side of the Dock.

>> **To create a folder for apps:** Drag one app's icon on top of another app's icon to create a folder. macOS gives the folder a default name, but you change it by selecting it, typing the name you want, and then pressing Return.

>> **To add an app to a folder:** Drag the app onto that folder to add it.

>> **To move an app out of a folder:** Click the folder to open it and drag the app out of the folder to a new location.

>> **To change a folder's name:** Click to open the folder, click the current name, and then type a new name.

>> **To uninstall apps:** Click an app's icon, but don't release the mouse button until all the icons begin to wiggle. Apps that can be uninstalled display a Delete icon (X); click to uninstall the app.

>> **To stop the wiggling:** Press Esc or click the background.

TIP

Many Apple apps don't have a Delete icon because they're integral pieces of macOS and can't be removed.

Chapter **10**

Organizing Your Life

Apple supplies macOS Ventura with a folder full of apps that you can use to do everything from surf the Internet to play movies to perform numeric calculations. In this chapter, I look at three of these apps that help you organize and simplify your everyday affairs: Calendar, Reminders, and Notes. Like most apps, these three live in the Applications folder, and you can run them from there, from the Dock (on which they appear by default), or from Launchpad. I also dig into applying the Focus feature to minimize distractions and maximize productivity, as well as tracking your own activity or a family member's activity with the Screen Time feature.

Keeping Track with Calendar

Calendar is a powerful app that provides one or more appointment calendars with alerts. You can have multiple color-coded calendars; several types of visual, audible, and emailed alerts; repeating events; and more. You can publish your calendars on the web for others to view (which requires an iCloud account or other

WebDAV server), and you can subscribe to calendars published by other Calendar users. In the following sections, you meet Calendar's most useful features.

Navigating Calendar views

Calendar lets you display the main Calendar window just the way you like it. You can find the following useful items (most of which have shortcuts) on the View menu, which provides close control of what you see and how you navigate:

>> **To move back or forward:** Click the arrow buttons on either side of the Today button (top right), or use the keyboard shortcuts ⌘+left arrow and ⌘+right arrow, respectively. Then you see the previous or next week in Week view, yesterday or tomorrow in Day view, and so on.

>> **To go to today's date:** Click the Today button or use its keyboard shortcut, ⌘+T.

>> **To add a new calendar:** Choose File ➪ New Calendar or use its keyboard shortcut, ⌘+Option+N.

>> **To view your calendar by day, week, month, or year:** Click the Day, Week, Month, or Year button at the top of the calendar. Figure 10-1 shows Week view (keyboard shortcut: ⌘+2). Other views on the View menu include By Day, By Month, and By Year; you can use the keyboard shortcuts ⌘+1, ⌘+3, and ⌘+4, respectively.

Understanding the Calendar list

In Figure 10-1, you can see the Calendar list in the sidebar on the left. Here, the Calendar list includes two categories: iCloud and Other. The iCloud category contains the calendars in your iCloud account — in the example, calendars such as Home, Family (Core), Family (Everyone), Work, and Softball Team. The Other category contains the Birthdays calendar, which Calendar creates and maintains automatically from the birthday dates in your contact data; the US Holidays calendar, which is a public shared calendar; and Siri Suggestions, which presents potential dates that Siri has gleaned from incoming messages in the Mail app, the Messages app, and similar sources.

If you've set up another Internet account that includes calendaring, that account appears as another category in the Calendar list, with its calendars listed below the category name. You can add another account in the Internet Accounts pane of System Settings (choose System Settings ➪ Internet Accounts) or in the Accounts pane of Calendar Settings (choose Calendar ➪ Settings ➪ Accounts).

Calendar list   Events Selected event   Today button

Event info for selected event

FIGURE 10-1:
The Calendar
main window
displaying
Week view.

In the Calendar list, select a check box to display the calendar's events in the main pane; deselect a check box to hide the calendar's events. Displaying only the calendars you need to see can help you focus on work, leisure, or whatever.

Creating calendars

To create a calendar in Calendar, follow these steps:

1. Choose File ⇨ New Calendar.

If you have more than one account enabled, choose File ⇨ New Calendar ⇨ iCloud (or whichever account you want to use for this calendar).

TIP

Some third-part account providers don't let Calendar create new calendars. If you find the New Calendar command isn't available for the third-party account in which you want to create a calendar, go to the account provider's site and create the calendar there.

Calendar creates a new calendar named Untitled and adds it to the appropriate account in the sidebar.

2. Type a descriptive name for the calendar over the default name, Untitled.

3. **To change the default color that Calendar assigned, Control-click or right-click the new calendar in the Calendar list and then choose a color from the contextual menu.**

   The contextual menu offers seven canned colors — red, blue, green, and so on — but you can click Custom Color to crank up the Colors window, whose five tabs let you create any color you can visualize.

Sharing and publishing calendars

If you have an iCloud account (or access to another server that supports the WebDAV protocol), you can share your calendars with specific people or publish them to the web so that anyone can view them. To share a calendar, follow these steps:

1. **Control-click or right-click the calendar in the Calendar list and then choose Share Calendar from the contextual menu to display the Share dialog.**

2. **Click the Share With line, and start typing the email address of the first person you want to share with.**

   Calendar displays matching results from your contacts. Click the right one, and it appears as a button in the Share dialog.

3. **Move the pointer over the button, click it to open a pop-up menu, and then choose View Only or View & Edit.**

   View & Edit is the default setting, but you may want to put some people in the look-but-don't-touch category.

4. **Repeat Steps 2 and 3 until you've added everyone you want to share the calendar with.**

5. **Click Done to close the Share dialog.**

   Calendar sends an invitation to each person you specified. If they accept, they can view your calendar and can edit it if you specified View & Edit for them.

If you want the whole world and its dog to be able to view your calendar, Control-click it or right-click it in the Calendar list, choose Share Calendar from the contextual menu, select the Public Calendar check box in the Share dialog, and click Done. Then you can tell everyone (and the dog) about the calendar by Control-clicking or right-clicking it; from the contextual menu, choose Send Publish Email to send out an email, or choose Copy URL to Clipboard if you want to share the web address via another means, such as social media.

Deleting a calendar

To delete a calendar, select it in the list and press ⌘+Delete. An alert will appear to ask if you're sure.

This alert has a useful button, Merge, which provides an opportunity to merge the calendar with another rather than just blowing it (and all the events it contains) away. You can only merge calendars that live in the same account, not calendars from different accounts. For example, you can merge two iCloud calendars, but you can't merge an iCloud calendar with a Google calendar.

Click Merge to select another calendar to merge this one with, click Delete to delete it, or click Cancel to do neither thing. Note that you can't merge calendars in the Other category; you can only suppress their display by deselecting their check boxes.

WARNING

When you delete a calendar, all the events and reminder items in that calendar are also deleted. Although you *can* undo a deleted calendar (choose Edit ⇨ Undo or press ⌘+Z), you must do so before you quit Calendar. If you quit Calendar without undoing a calendar deletion, everything on that calendar (or calendars) will be gone forever (unless you have Time Machine or another backup, covered in Chapter 21).

WARNING

If you sync your calendars with iCloud or another cloud-based service, deleting the calendar will delete it from all your devices.

Creating and managing events

The heart of Calendar is the event. To create a new one, follow these steps:

1. **Choose File ⇨ New Event, press ⌘+N, double-click a date or time on the calendar in any view, or drag up or down anywhere on a date in Week view or Day view.**

    TIP

    If you double-click or click and drag on the day of the event, you can skip Step 2, and you don't need to specify the date in Step 3.

2. **If the event doesn't appear in the proper place, just click it and drag it wherever it belongs.**

3. **To edit an event quickly, double-click it to open a bubble containing its details.**

    All the items can be edited. Click the date or time to change it, for example. The other items — Repeat, Travel Time, and Alerts — are pop-up menus.

TIP

The colored square in the top-right corner of the event's Info window is a pop-up menu that lets you assign this event to a different calendar.

The Travel Time item lets you add travel time to and from an event (and blocks out that time on your calendar) while preserving the event's start and end times.

4. **When you've fixed all the details, press Return or click anywhere outside the event bubble.**

Editing an event's details in a bubble is easy enough, but Calendar offers you two alternatives: the Info window and the Inspector window. Confusingly, the Inspector window has the title Info, so it looks the same as the Info window. What's the difference? Glad you asked! Here's what you need to know:

>> **Info window:** Control-click or right-click the event and then choose Get Info from the contextual menu; alternatively, click the event and then press ⌘+I or choose Edit ⇨ Get Info. Each event has its own Info window, and you can open as many Info windows as you need, which makes the Info window good for comparing the details of different events; just pop open an Info window for each event, and you're in business.

>> **Inspector window:** Click the event and then choose Edit ⇨ Show Inspector or press ⌘+Option+I. There's only one Inspector window, and it displays the details of the selected event. Click another event to display its details. The Inspector window is great for working with a series of individual events, because you can park the window in a handy part of the screen and simply click each event in turn.

Inviting others to attend an event

To invite other people to your event, open the Contacts app (choose Window ⇨ Contacts) and drag the contacts onto the event in Calendar. Alternatively, you can type the first few letters of the name in the Invitees field for an event, and names that match magically appear. Figure 10-2 shows the result of typing the letter *j*: a list of three contacts with names that start with that letter. Sweet! (If you're unfamiliar with Contacts, flip to Chapter 14 for details.)

After you add one or more invitees, click the Send button to invite them to the event. If the invitees have a compatible calendar app (Calendar, Microsoft Outlook, and most calendar apps on most platforms), they can open the enclosure (included with your invitation email), which adds the event to Calendar with Accept, Decline, and Maybe buttons. All they have to do is click the appropriate button, and you receive an email informing you of their decision along with an enclosure that adds their response to the event in Calendar.

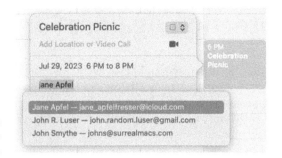

Invitations don't always work with some third-party mail apps, but the majority of people use Apple Mail, Google Calendar, or Microsoft Outlook, which can handle Calendar invitations.

If the invitee doesn't have a compatible calendar app (or doesn't open the invitation), they have to respond the old-fashioned way: by replying to your email, texting, or calling you on the telephone.

Setting an alert

What's the point of putting an event on your calendar if you forget it? If you set an alert, Calendar won't let you forget. To set an alert, click None (just to the right of the word *alert)* in the Info window or Inspector window for an event. Now choose a time for the alert from the menu or choose Custom, which lets you set Calendar to display a message with a sound, send you a reminder email, or open a file. Opening a file can be particularly effective; you're much less likely to put off updating your Microsoft Excel timesheet if Calendar opens it right in your face.

Depending on the calendar account, you can usually create multiple alerts for an event. When you add the first alert to an event, a +-in-a-circle will appear to its right when you hover the cursor over the alert pop-up menu; click the + to create a second (or third or further) alert. If the + no longer appears, you've likely hit the limit for the calendar account.

To remove an alert, click the pop-up menu to the right of the word *alert* and choose None from the pop-up menu.

TIP

You can choose separate default alerts for Events, All Day Events, and Birthdays in Calendar Preferences. Choose Calendar ⇨ Settings or press ⌘+, (type the comma) and then click the Alerts tab at the top of the window.

Calendar on your Mac alone is pretty wonderful, but syncing your events and alerts with all your devices — your iPhone, iPad, and Apple Watch as well as your Mac — is the killer feature. Create an event on one device, and it appears on all the other devices within seconds, thanks to the magic of iCloud.

Reminders: Protection Against Forgetting

Reminders help you stay organized. Unlike an event, a reminder item isn't necessarily associated with a particular day or time (although it can be). Furthermore, reminders can be associated with a location, which is handy on a MacBook but even handier on an iPhone, iPad, or Apple Watch. Finally, reminders can have a priority level of low, medium, high, or none.

If you have multiple Apple devices and sync with iCloud, Microsoft Exchange, or Office 365, your reminders will appear simultaneously on all your Apple devices — other Macs, iPhones, iPads, and Apple Watches — which means that you should never miss a reminder.

To get started with Reminders, launch the app by clicking the Reminders or Launchpad icon on the Dock and then clicking Reminders on the Launchpad screen. If you're a fan of the Applications folder, you can double-click the Reminders icon there instead.

The first time you launch Reminders, the app asks to use your current location. Click Yes so that you can use arriving at or leaving a location as the trigger for receiving a reminder.

Getting started with Reminders

The Reminders app enables you to divide your reminders into different lists. You might want a Home list, a Work list, a Shopping list, a Dreams list, and so on so that you can keep home tasks separate from work tasks and avoid shopping for dreams. Reminders starts you off with a default list called simply Reminders, but you can rename it or delete it if you want.

To create a new list, follow these steps:

1. **Click the Add List (+) button in the bottom-left corner of the window — or choose File ⇨ New List, or press ⌘+Shift+N — to open the New List dialog (see Figure 10-3).**

2. **Click the New List tab at the top.**

   When you've created list templates containing your preferred settings for lists, you can click the Templates tab and choose a template there.

3. **Type a descriptive name in the Name box.**

4. **Click the color you want the list to have.**

5. In the Icon area, click either the Emoji icon (the smiley) or the Glyph icon (which shows a house in Figure 10-3) and then click the emoji or glyph you want on the pop-up panel.

6. Select the Make into Smart List check box if you want to be able to organize the list by using tags and filters.

7. Click OK.

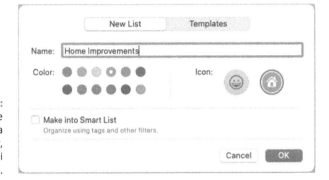

FIGURE 10-3:
When you create
a list, assign it a
name, a color,
and an emoji
or glyph.

Reminders creates a separate section for completed items after you click the circle before a reminder's name to indicate that a task is done, such as *Unblock the garage drain* in Figure 10-4.

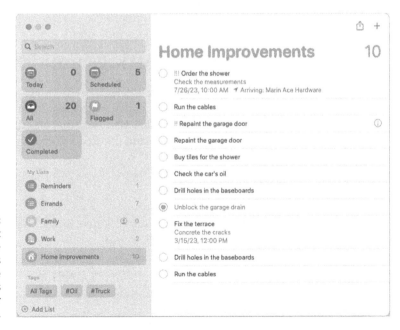

FIGURE 10-4:
When a list
(here, Home
Improvements) is
selected in the
sidebar, its
reminders appear
in the main pane.

After you select the circle for an item, Reminders moves the item to the completed list. To see completed items, click the Show button in the upper-right corner of a list or choose View⇨ Show Completed or press ⌘+Shift+H. When shown, completed items appear at the end of the list below uncompleted items. To hide the completed items again, click the Hide button (which replaces the Show button) or choose View⇨ Hide Completed or press ⌘+Shift+H again.

Here are further helpful techniques for working with lists:

>> **Rename a list:** Control-click or right-click the list, choose Rename from the contextual menu, type the new name, and press Return when you're done. Or select the list, press Return, type the new name, and then press Return again when you're done.

>> **Display a list in a separate window:** Double-click the list name; or Control-click or right-click the list, and choose Open List in New Window from the contextual menu.

>> **Show or hide the sidebar:** Choose View ⇨ Show/Hide Sidebar or press ⌘+Option+S.

Finally, the boxes near the top of the sidebar — Today, Scheduled, All, Flagged, and Assigned (which appears only if one or more tasks is assigned to you by someone else or by you to someone else) — are preconfigured smart lists. To hide a smart list, Control-click or right-click the list and then choose Hide from the contextual menu. Alternatively, choose View⇨ Show Smart List⇨ and then select the smart list to remove its check mark.

To do or not to do: Setting reminders

You're good on lists now, so it's time to create some reminders to go in them. Click the list to which you want to add the new reminder and then choose File⇨ New Reminder; press ⌘+N; click the + in the top-right corner of the Reminders window; or click the first blank line in a list and begin typing.

Type the text for the reminder — its name, if you will. Then you can do more, including

>> Reminding you at a specific time on a specific date (as shown in Figure 10-4)

>> Repeatedly reminding you at a specified interval

>> Reminding you at a specific location (as shown in Figure 10-5)

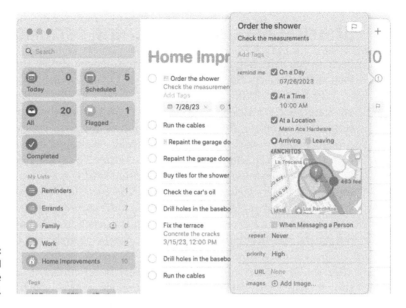

FIGURE 10-5:
Location-based
reminders are
super-handy.

If you have an iPhone, location-based reminders are the best for making sure that you don't miss completing tasks. As you can see in Figure 10-5, the alert triggers not just at a particular day and time, but also on arrival at Marin Ace Hardware, which should make ordering the shower impossible to forget.

As well as text notes, which you can type in on the line after the reminder's name, a reminder can also have a priority, a URL, and images. To access these features, move the pointer over the reminder and click the i-in-a-circle that appears on the right; you can also click in the reminder and choose View ⇨ Show Reminder Info. Either way, the info bubble opens. Then you can open the priority pop-up menu at the bottom and assign the priority, click in the URL field and add a URL, or click Add Image and add an image either from the Photos app or by scanning or shooting with your iPhone's or iPad's camera.

To change the order of reminders in a list, choose View ⇨ Sort By and then choose Due Date, Priority, Creation Date, or Title. Or choose Manual and control the item order yourself by clicking a blank spot on any reminder and then dragging it to its new position.

Reminders can have subtasks, which you create by choosing Edit ⇨ Indent Reminder or pressing ⌘+]; to promote a subtask, choose Edit ⇨ Outdent Reminder or press ⌘+[. If the subtask is below the wrong reminder, click a blank spot on the subtask and drag it where you want it. You can show all subtasks by choosing View ⇨ Show All Subtasks or pressing ⌘+E and hide all subtasks by choosing View ⇨ Hide All Subtasks or pressing ⌘+Shift+E.

Sharing lists and assigning reminders

Because you can assign a reminder only to someone you've shared a list with, I'll look at sharing lists first.

To share a list, Control-click or right-click the list and choose Share List from the contextual menu, or click the list to select it and then choose File ⇨ Share List. A bubble appears with options such as Mail, Messages, Notes, and Invite Link. Near the top is a sharing readout that says either *People you invite can add others* or *Only people you invite have access*; if the current setting suits you, leave it, but if you want to change it, click the > button to reveal the Allow Others to Invite check box and then select it or clear it as needed. Click the appropriate sharing method, such as Mail, and send the message. The recipient gets a link that adds the list to their reminders, synchronizing changes in (almost) real time.

After you've shared a list, you can assign its reminders to anyone with whom you've shared the list. To assign a reminder, Control-click or right-click the reminder and then choose Assign ⇨ *person's name* from the contextual menu, or click the reminder to select it and then choose Edit ⇨ Assign ⇨ *person's name.*

One more thing: You can view your Reminders in any web browser on any device by logging in to www.icloud.com and clicking Reminders. You'll see the same lists and reminders that you see on your Macs and Apple devices. You can't share lists or assign reminders (at this time), but you can manage existing reminders or create new ones, which can be handy when you're stuck somewhere without your Apple devices.

Everything You Need to Know about Notification Center

The item in Figure 10-6 should look familiar to those of you who use an iPhone or iPad: It's Ventura's rendition of Notification Center.

Notification Center manages and displays alerts from any app that supports Apple's notifications protocol. You can show or hide Notification Center by clicking the clock icon in your menu bar or by swiping left from the right edge of your trackpad with two fingers.

FIGURE 10-6:
Calendar and
Reminders alert
banners (top),
Calendar's Up
Next widget
(second row, left),
Weather widget
(second row,
right), the World
Clock widget, and
the News widget
(bottom).

Tweaking Notification settings

You manage which apps display notifications by using the Notifications pane of System Settings. Choose System Settings ⇨ Notifications to display the main Notifications pane and then navigate to its subpanes as necessary.

Start by configuring the following four settings in the Notification Center section at the top of the main Notifications pane:

>> **Show Previews:** Open this pop-up menu, and choose Always, When Unlocked, or Never, as needed. Always is indiscreet and Never is laconic, so When Unlocked usually is the best choice.

>> **Allow Notifications When the Display Is Sleeping:** Set this switch to on (blue) or off (white), as needed.

>> **Allow Notifications When the Screen Is Locked:** Set this switch to on (blue) or off (white), as you prefer.

>> **Allow Notifications When Mirroring or Sharing the Display:** Set this switch to on (blue) or off (white). Off usually is the better choice unless you're demonstrating how to deal with notifications.

Next, move on to the App Notifications section of the main Notifications pane, which contains a button for each app or feature for which you can configure notifications. Click the button to display the pane for the app or feature, such as the Calendar pane of the Calendar app. Then you can choose settings as follows:

>> **Allow Notifications:** Set this switch to on (blue) to allow the app to raise notifications. Set the switch to off (white) to suppress notifications.

>> **Alert Style:** In the box, click None, Banners, or Alerts. Alerts remain onscreen until you dismiss them, so they're good for notifications you can't afford to miss; banners appear in the top-right corner for a few seconds before slipping away.

TIP

To make a banner reappear after it disappears, just click the clock on your menu bar or swipe left from the right edge of the trackpad with two fingers.

>> **Allow Time Sensitive Alerts:** Set this switch to on (blue) to allow time-sensitive alerts to clamor for your attention.

>> **Show in Notification Center:** Set this switch to on (blue) to include this app's notifications in Notification Center.

>> **Badge App Icon:** Set this switch to on (blue) to have the app's Dock icon display a red badge showing the number of notifications.

>> **Play Sound for Notification:** Set this switch to on (blue) to allow the app to accompany a notification with a sound.

>> **Show Previews:** Open this pop-up menu and choose Default, Always, When Unlocked, or Never. Choose the Default item to have this app use your choice in the Show Previews pop-up menu in the main Notification pane.

>> **Notification Grouping:** Open this pop-up menu and choose Automatic, By App, or Off to control how macOS groups notifications for this app.

Managing Widgets 101

To manage the Widgets displayed in Notification Center, click the clock to display Notification Center and then click the Edit Widgets button at its bottom. You may need to scroll down to reach the Edit Widgets button.

A list of widgets available in Notification Center appears on the left side of the screen, with details displayed in the middle. Many widgets offer three sizes — small, medium, and large, which you select by clicking the three little buttons (S, M, L) below the widget in the middle column. As you'd imagine, small widgets display less information than medium widgets, which in turn display less than large widgets, and not all widgets come in all sizes. Experiment with different sizes of widgets to find which work best for you.

To add a widget to Notification Center, start by clicking a size button (if available) and then click the widget. A green circle containing a white + sign appears when you move the pointer over the widget. You can click this + sign if you want, but clicking the widget is much easier.

To move a widget to a different spot, click and drag it (on the right side of the screen) to its new location.

Finally, many widgets offer additional options. To access such options, click the widget on the right side of the screen. If options are available, the widget spins around to display them on its reverse. When you've finished working with a widget's options, click Done.

When you're happy with your widget lineup and arrangement, click the Done button at the bottom of the right pane.

Using Notification Center

Now, here's a quick rundown of ways you can use Notification Center:

TIP

» **To respond to a notification:** Click the banner or alert before it disappears. Or open Notification Center and then click the notification to launch its app.

   Hover the pointer over a banner to display additional options such as the ability to reply to an email or message without launching Mail or Messages.

» **To repeat a notification in nine minutes:** Click its Snooze button.

» **To clear all notifications for an app:** Hover the pointer over a notification. If the app has more than one notification, the little X in its top-left corner (which would clear only this notification) changes to a Clear All button. Click Clear All to clear all notifications from that app.

Getting focused

Versions of macOS before Monterey offered the Do Not Disturb feature, which silenced all alerts and notifications. But Do Not Disturb was on or off, period. Monterey replaced Do Not Disturb with Focus, which did everything DND used to do but also enabled you to customize who and what could notify you and when. Ventura builds on Focus by adding new features, including focus filters, which enable you to customize how key apps (such as Mail and Messages) behave while the focus is on.

You can have one or more focuses, which you manage in the Focus pane in System Settings. In the Focus tab, you'll find several prefab focuses, such as Do Not Disturb, Driving, and Sleep. You can activate other canned focuses (such as Reading, Gaming, and Mindfulness) that typically lurk shyly at first, and you can create your own custom focuses from scratch. And you can configure each focus to specify exactly which apps you're prepared to acknowledge and which Hollywood agents you might be interested in taking calls from while you're meditating.

If the Focus pane doesn't show the focus you want, click Add Focus to open the What Do You Want to Focus On? dialog. If the focus you want appears here, click it; macOS closes the dialog, adds the focus to the list in the Focus pane, and displays the focus's configuration screen, where you can proceed as explained next. If the dialog doesn't show the focus you want, click Custom. In the Custom dialog that opens, type the name for the focus; click a color circle; click the emoji or glyph you want to use (yes, this part is like creating a list in Reminders); and click OK. The Custom dialog closes, the new focus takes its place in the Focus pane, and the focus's configuration screen appears.

If you just want to configure one of the focuses that was already in the Focus pane, click it there, and its configuration screen appears.

You're ready to configure the focus.

Use the Allow Notifications section to specify which people and apps (if any) can notify you while the focus is enabled.

To add a person or group, click the Allowed People button, and work in the Allowed People dialog. From the pop-up menu at the top, choose the Allow Some People item or the Silence Some People item. Then click Add (+), and add people to the list. If you chose Allow Some People, you can open the Allow Calls From pop-up menu and choose Everybody, Allowed People Only, Favorites, Contacts Only, Colleagues, or Friends, as appropriate. You can also set the Allow Repeated Calls switch to on (blue) to let people crash into the focus by calling twice within 3 minutes (which might signal an emergency). If you chose Silence Some People, set the Allow Calls from Silenced People to on (blue) or off (white), as appropriate. Click Done when you finish working in the Allowed People dialog.

To add an app, click the Allowed Apps button, and work in the Allowed Apps dialog. From the pop-up menu at the top, choose Allow Some Apps or Silence Some Apps. Then click Add (+), and add apps to the list. Set the Time Sensitive Notifications switch to on (blue) or off (white), as needed. Click Done when you finish working in the Allowed Apps dialog.

Back on the configuration screen for the focus, click the Add Schedule button in the Turn On Automatically section if you want to run this focus on a schedule rather than enable and disable it manually.

In the Focus Filters section, click Add Filter if you want to add a focus filter. In the App Filters dialog, click the app you want to affect, such as Safari. In the following dialog, which varies depending on the app, choose suitable options for the focus. In Safari, for example, you can allocate a specific tab group to the focus and decide whether to allow opening links that lead outside that tab group. Click Add to add the focus filter to the configuration screen for the focus.

 To enable or disable a focus, click the Control Center icon on the menu bar (and shown in the margin), click Focus, and then click the focus you want to use.

Use Notes for Making Notes

Notes is an electronic notepad for your Mac. A note is a convenient place to jot quick notes, recipes, phone numbers, or whatever. Figure 10-7 shows some notes.

To create a new note, choose File ➪ New Note; press ⌘+N; or click the button with the little square and pencil on the toolbar.

Notes is supremely flexible. Here are key moves to get you started:

TIP

» **Double-click a note to open it in its own window** so you can drag it around onscreen by its title bar.

After opening a note in its own window, if you want the note to float in front of other windows so it's always visible, choose Window ➪ Keep on Top.

» **Change the text** to any font, color, size, and style by selecting it and using the myriad tools on the Format menu and the Format pop-up menu (the Aa icon) on the toolbar.

» **Search for a word or phrase** in any note by typing your query in the Search box.

» **Create bulleted, numbered, or dashed lists** by selecting the text and choosing Format ➪ Bulleted List (⌘+Shift+7), Format ➪ Dashed List (⌘+Shift+8), or Format ➪ Numbered List (⌘+Shift+9).

In Figure 10-7, Ingredients is a bulleted list, and Method is a numbered list.

>> **Create folders** (such as Family and Recipes in Figure 10-7) to organize your notes by choosing File ⇨ New Folder, pressing ⌘+Shift+N, or clicking the New Folder button at the bottom of the Folder list.

REMEMBER

Folders in the Notes app are exclusive to Notes. In other words, the folders described in the following bullets aren't folders in Finder. You won't find them on your hard drive; they live only in the Notes app (and in iCloud or other Internet accounts if you've enabled them). Also keep in mind the fact that folders are optional. If you don't have a ton of notes, keeping them all in a single folder and using the Search box to locate those you need may work for you.

>> **Show or hide the Folders list** by choosing View ⇨ Show/Hide Folders or pressing ⌘+Option+S.

>> **Show only notes in a specific folder** by clicking the folder name in the Folders list, or click All iCloud to see all your notes.

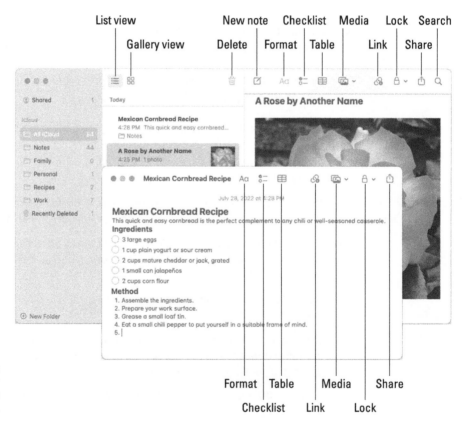

FIGURE 10-7:
Notes is for making notes on your Mac.

- >> **Automatically sync notes with your Apple devices by using iCloud or other Internet Accounts** by choosing Notes ➪ Accounts, which opens the Internet Accounts pane in System Settings. Then click the appropriate Internet account — such as Office 365 or Gmail — and set its switch to on (blue) to sync Notes.

- >> **Send the contents of the active note via the Mail or Messages app** by choosing File ➪ Share or clicking the Share icon.

- >> **Print a note** by choosing File ➪ Print or pressing ⌘+P.

TIP

Whatever you type in a note is saved automatically as you type it, so you don't have to give the Save command in Notes. To duplicate the active note, choose File ➪ Duplicate Note or press ⌘+D.

Moving right along, here are more useful features in Notes:

- >> You can drag and drop photos, PDFs, videos, and other files into any note.

- >> The Attachments browser displays every external file you've dragged into every note in a single place, making it easier to find things. Choose View ➪ Show/Hide Attachments Browser or use its keyboard shortcut ⌘+3 to see the Attachments Browser in action.

- >> Use the Share menu in apps such as Safari and Maps to add content to Notes.

- >> You can add checklists (in addition to bulleted, numbered, and dashed lists) by clicking the Checklist icon on the toolbar (shown in the margin), by choosing Format ➪ Checklist, or by using the shortcut ⌘+Shift+L.

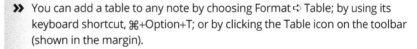

- >> You can add a table to any note by choosing Format ➪ Table; by using its keyboard shortcut, ⌘+Option+T; or by clicking the Table icon on the toolbar (shown in the margin).

- >> You can format text as a title, heading, or body by choosing Format ➪ Title, Format ➪ Heading, or Format ➪ Body or by using the keyboard shortcut ⌘+Shift+T, ⌘+Shift+H, or ⌘+Shift+B, respectively.

  To specify the style with which each new note starts, choose Notes ➪ Settings and choose the style in the New Notes Start With pop-up menu.

- >> Notes appear in the list in chronological order with the most recently edited note on top. You can pin a note to the top of the list, where it remains until you unpin it. To pin or unpin a note, click it once to select it and then choose File ➪ Pin Note (or Unpin Note). Or Control-click or right-click the note in the list and choose Pin Note (or Unpin Note) from the contextual menu. The note appears in the Pinned section at the top of the list.

You can also share your notes with others and allow them to edit them. Here's how the process works: Select the note, and click the Share icon on the toolbar to open the Share panel. At the top, choose Collaborate from the pop-up menu. (The other choice is Send Copy.) Then choose how you'd like to send your invitation: Mail, Messages, Invite with Link, or AirDrop.

If the people you invite are also running Ventura or another recent version of macOS, they'll see the note in their copy of Notes; if they're running any other operating system, the note will open in the iCloud website for editing. When they're done, you'll see their edits in Notes on your Mac (and on your iPad and iPhone) within a few minutes.

Other Notes goodies include a spelling and grammar checker, spoken notes, text substitutions (such as smart quotes and smart dashes), and transformations (such as Make Upper Case and Make Lower Case). You can find all these options on the Edit menu.

When you need to find out what changes have been made in a note, select it and then choose View ⇨ Show Note Activity or press ⌘+Control+K. Similarly, when you want to learn about changes at the folder level, select the folder and choose View ⇨ Show Folder Activity.

When you're feeling logical, folders can be a great way to organize your notes. But when you need more flexibility, use tags instead to not only organize your notes, but also filter them. To create a tag, simply put # before the tag word, such as #*Ventura* or #*efficiency*. After you create a tag, it appears in the sidebar's Tag Browser as a button that you can click to display all notes that bear that tag. Or click All Tags to see notes that have any tag.

TIP

If you've created one or more tags but don't see buttons in your sidebar, hover your cursor over the word Tags and click the > that appears to its right.

One more thing: Don't forget that you can use your iPhone or iPad as a camera or scanner by using Continuity Camera. (Chapter 20 has the details.)

Taking a Quick Note with Quick Note

When you need to jot down a note instantly, use Quick Note. To do so, move the pointer to the bottom-right corner of your screen, and click the blank note that appears. The Notes app launches (if it's not already open), and a new note appears in the middle of the screen.

If you click the link icon, you can add an app link to the note. Then, because Notes knows which website you're on, what story you're reading in the News app, who you're communicating with in the Messages app, and much more, the next time you visit that website or store or correspond with a person, Notes will automatically display that Quick Note in the bottom-right corner.

The links are contextual, so the Quick Note will appear when Notes thinks you need it. There's also a smart list in the Notes app with all Quick Notes you've created.

Tracking Productivity with Screen Time

We can all use a break from our digital devices, and Apple's solution is Screen Time. Although Screen Time includes the parental controls that used to appear in the Parental Controls System Preferences pane in older versions of macOS, Screen Time also encourages you to police your own behavior.

If you have an iPhone or iPad, you're probably familiar with Screen Time, which provides insight into how you spend your time on your iPhone or iPad, including which apps you used and websites you visited, and for how long. On the Mac, Screen Time manifests itself as a pane in System Settings, so choose System Settings ⇨ Screen Time to get started.

At the top of the Screen Time pane, open the Family Member pop-up menu, and choose yourself or the family member for whom you want to configure Screen Time. Then set the Screen Time switch to on (blue) to enable Screen Time.

Near the bottom of the Screen Time pane, set the Share Across Devices switch to on (blue) if you want Screen Time to report data for every iPhone, iPad, and Mac that signs in to this iCloud account. This setting usually is what you want; there's no sense monitoring your teenager's Mac use closely while letting them run riot on their iPad.

Also at the bottom of the Screen Time pane, set the Use Screen Time Passcode switch to on (blue), and follow the prompts to set a four-digit password that will prevent anyone from switching off or reconfiguring Screen Time without your okay.

Now use the eight buttons in the main part of the Screen Time pane to view usage and set suitable restrictions:

>> **App Usage:** Displays details about the apps the user used and how long they used them.

>> **Notifications:** Displays the number of notifications the user received on this day and the times received.

>> **Pickups:** Shows you how many times the user picked up their devices.

>> **Downtime:** Sets a schedule for times when only apps specifically allowed during downtime are available. A reminder appears 5 minutes before downtime starts.

>> **App Limits:** Sets time limits for apps and app categories such as Social, Games, and Productivity & Finance.

>> **Communication Limits:** Specifies who is allowed to contact the user via phone, FaceTime, or iMessage during Screen Time and downtime.

>> **Always Allowed:** Specifies the contacts and apps available to the user during downtime.

>> **Content & Privacy:** Replaces the Parental Controls options in earlier versions of macOS. Enable or disable content by type, Apple online store, or specific app, as well as allow or disallow passcode changes, account changes, and other options for which you may want to restrict changes.

Chapter **11**

Maps Are Where It's At

I f you know how to use the Maps app on your iPhone or iPad, you already know most of what you need to know to use Maps on your Mac. But if you don't have an iPhone or iPad, don't worry — this chapter will get you up to speed in next to no time.

Finding Your Current Location with Maps

If you're wondering where you're at, Maps can set you straight. Launch Maps from the Dock, from Launchpad, or from the Applications folder and then click the Current Location icon, which is a little arrowhead (shown in the margin) on the toolbar at the top of the window. Your location is indicated by a blue dot.

REMEMBER

If you click or drag the map, your Mac continues to update your location but won't re-center the blue marker — meaning that the blue dot can scroll (or zoom) off the screen. If that happens, click the Current Location icon again to center the map on your current location again.

This feature and many other Maps features rely on an active Internet connection and having Location Services enabled. To check about Location Services, click System Settings on the Dock, click Privacy & Security in the sidebar, click Location Services to display the Location Services screen, and then set the Location Services switch to On. Set the switch on the Maps row to On as well.

TIP

Use the − and + icons in the bottom-right corner (or the scroll control on your mouse or trackpad) to zoom in and out on the map.

Finding a Person, Place, or Thing

To find a person, place, or thing with Maps, choose Edit ⇨ Find, press ⌘+F, or click the Search field in the sidebar (where it says Search Maps) and then type what you're looking for. You can search for addresses, zip codes, intersections, towns, landmarks, and businesses by category and by name, or combinations, such as *New York, NY 10022*, *pizza 60645*, or *Texas State Capitol*.

TIP

If the letters you type match names stored in your Contacts list (see Chapter 14), the matching contacts appear in a list below the Search field. Click a name to see a map of that contact's location. The Maps app is smart about it, too, displaying only the names of contacts that have a street address.

If you don't find a match in the list, press Return, and with any luck, a map will appear within a few seconds. If you search for a single location, it's marked with a single bubble. If you search for a category (*coffee 02108*, for example), you may see multiple bubbles, one for each matching location (a terrifying number of coffee shops in Boston), as shown in Figure 11-1.

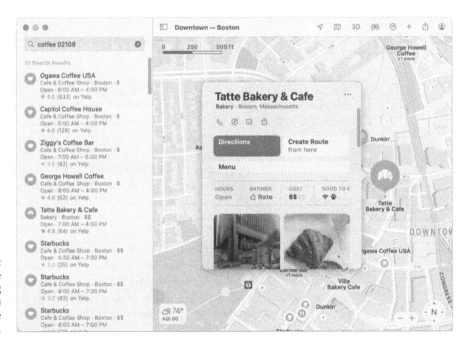

FIGURE 11-1: Bubbles indicate matching locations; click a bubble to see its details.

TIP

You can search for all sorts of things, including intersections, neighborhoods, landmarks, restaurants, and businesses. Furthermore, you can combine several items, such as pizza and a zip code. The Maps app is adept at interpreting search terms and finding the right place.

To find out more, click a name in the list below the Search field or click a pin. An overlay with details appears (refer to Figure 11-1).

This handy little info window sometimes contains reviews, photos, or both (only photos are visible in Figure 11-1), so scroll down through the overlay to read reviews or view pictures.

Views, Zooms, and Pans

The preceding section talks about how to find just about anything with Maps, and the following section shows ways to use what you find. But before doing that, I'll take a little detour and explore how you can work with Maps.

Click the Map Mode icon on the toolbar to choose Explore view, Driving view, Transit view, or Satellite view (see Figure 11-2), all of which can be viewed also in 3D. Satellite view uses satellite imagery, as you see in Figure 11-3; this figure also uses 3D view, which lets you look at the map from an angle rather than from directly overhead.

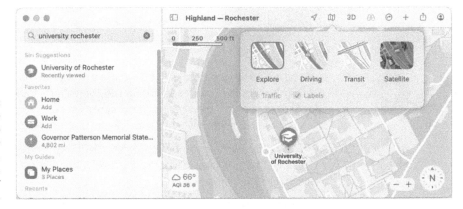

FIGURE 11-2:
Click the Map
Mode icon to
choose Explore
view (shown),
Driving view,
Transit view, or
Satellite view.

WARNING

3D maps aren't available in every area. It appears that the more populated an area is, the more likely it is to be available in 3D.

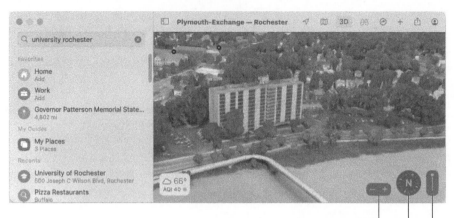

Zoom In and Zoom Out buttons

Rotate map compass

3D camera angle slider

FIGURE 11-3:
A 3D satellite
view.

Speaking of which, to display a 3D map, click the 3D icon on the toolbar (shown in the margin), choose View ⇨ Show 3D Map, or press ⌘+D. You may have to zoom in for the map to appear in 3D.

Moving right along, these tools are available in all views, in 2D or 3D:

>> **To zoom in:** Choose View ⇨ Zoom In or press ⌘++ (plus sign). If you have a trackpad, you can also expand (spread two fingers) to zoom in, just like on an iPhone or iPad.

>> **To zoom out:** Choose View ⇨ Zoom Out or press ⌘+− (minus sign). If you have a trackpad, you can also pinch to zoom out, just like on an iPhone or iPad.

If you have a scroll-wheel mouse, you can use the wheel to zoom in and out. You can also click the Zoom In (+) button and Zoom Out (–) button in the bottom-right corner of the window. If you want to get back to the default zoom percentage, choose View ⇨ Default Zoom or press ⌘+0.

If you click and then fling your mouse in any direction (or flick with two fingers on a trackpad), you'll "fly over" the ground below. This feature usually isn't useful, but it's fun and looks cool.

To get to Maps' Globe view, zoom out as far as you can. Then you can manipulate the globe with your mouse or trackpad and zoom in wherever you like to see additional details.

>> **To scroll:** Hold down the mouse or trackpad button and then drag left, right, up, or down. If you have a trackpad, drag with two fingers.

>> **To rotate the map:** Click the compass in the bottom-right corner, and drag. You can also place two fingers (or your thumb and a finger) on the trackpad and rotate them.

Finally, to adjust the camera angle in 3D views, press the Option key before you click and drag on the map (Option+drag with two fingers on a trackpad), or click and drag the little slider in the bottom-right corner (shown in Figure 11-3).

Maps and Contacts

Maps and Contacts (see Chapter 14) go together like peanut butter and jelly. If you want to see a map of a contact's street address, for example, type a few letters of the contact's name in the Search field, and click the name in the list that automatically appears.

If you're in the Contacts app, the process is even easier: Hover your pointer over a street address, and click the little blue pin that appears to its right, as shown in Figure 11-4. Maps opens, showing a pin at the address.

FIGURE 11-4:
Click the little blue pin to see this address in Maps.

After you find a location by typing an address in Maps, you can add that location to your contacts.

First, click the location's bubble on the map; then click the ellipsis in the top-right corner of the Info sheet and choose Create New Contact from the menu that appears.

You can also get driving directions to and from most locations, including a contact's address, to most other locations, including another contact's address. You see how in "Smart Map Tricks" later in the chapter.

Time-Saving Map Tools: Favorites, Guides, and Recents

The Maps app offers three tools in its sidebar that can save you from having to type the same locations over and over.

Favorites

Favorites in the Maps app, like favorites in Safari, lets you return to a location without typing a single character. To make a location a favorite, click its bubble on the map and then click the ellipsis in the top-right corner of the Info sheet and choose Add to Favorites or scroll to the bottom of the Info sheet and click the Add to Favorites button.

You can also add a favorite by clicking the little + that appears to the right of Favorites in the sidebar when you hover over it. The little chevron that also appears when you hover your cursor over Favorites is a disclosure triangle. Click it, and you'll see either all or none of your favorites.

After you add a favorite, you can recall it at any time.

TIP

The first items you should add as favorites are your home address and work address. You use these addresses all the time with Maps, so you might as well add them now to avoid typing them over and over.

Here's how to manage your favorites:

>> **To move a favorite up or down in the Favorites list:** Click and drag the favorite upward to move it higher in the list or downward to move it lower in the list.

>> **To delete a favorite from the Favorites list:** Control-click or right-click the favorite and then choose Remove from Favorites from the contextual menu.

Guides

Guides are collections of places that you can create and share with others. A few big cities, such as San Francisco, New York, London, and Los Angeles, have guides created by "brands you trust" (at least, according to Apple). The cool thing about guides is that they update automatically, so if you share them with others, their guides will update when you add or delete locations.

To create a guide, hover your cursor over the words My Guides in the sidebar and then click the little + that appears to its right. A new guide named New Guide appears. Change its name to something meaningful and then Control-click or right-click your new guide to do the following:

>> **Edit the guide.** Click Edit Guide to change the name of this guide, add or change its photo, or delete it.

>> **Add a new place.** Click Add New Place to open an overlay where you can search for a place or choose one from your Recents list by clicking its + button.

>> **Duplicate the guide.** Click Duplicate Guide to create a copy of this guide. Then you can edit it without affecting the original guide.

>> **Open the guide in a new tab or window.** Click Open in New Tab or Open in New Window, as needed.

>> **Share the guide.** Click Share to display the Share dialog, which enables you to share the guide via apps and services such as AirDrop, Mail, Messages, Notes, and Reminders. You can click Edit Actions in the Share dialog to add another means of sharing.

>> **Send the guide to a device.** Click Send to Device to display a list of all Apple devices nearby; select one to send this guide to it.

>> **Delete the guide.** Click Delete Guide and then click Delete in the confirmation dialog.

And there you have all you need to know to create and share guides in Maps.

Recents

The Maps app automatically remembers every location you've searched for in its Recents list, including the locations you'd rather forget. Click Recents to see your recent searches; click the item's name to see it on the map.

To remove a single location from your Recents list, Control-click or right-click it and choose Delete from the contextual menu.

To clear the Recents list, go to the very bottom of the list and then click Clear Recents. There's no confirmation dialog for this action.

Smart Map Tricks

The Maps app has more tricks up its sleeve. This section lists a few nifty features you may find useful.

Get route maps and driving directions

You can get route maps and driving directions to any location from any other location in a couple of ways:

>> **If a bubble is already on the screen:** Click it and then click the Directions button on its Info sheet. Click in the My Location field to choose where the directions begin.

>> **When you're looking at a map screen:** Click the Directions button on the toolbar (shown in the margin). The Directions overlay appears, with Start and End fields at the top. When you click either field, a drop-down list appears with your current location and a few recent locations. If you don't see what you need, type a few letters and choose the location from the list that appears. To swap the starting and ending locations, click the little swirly arrow to the right of the Start and End fields.

If you need to change the start or end location, click it, click the little x-in-a-circle to the right of its name to erase it, and try again.

Many journeys need only a start and a destination, but for others, you'll want to add stops along the way. Click Add Stop, type the location, and then select the appropriate match. Drag the stops into the appropriate order by using the handles at the right end of their buttons; Maps updates the route with the best fit, as shown in Figure 11-5.

When the start and end fields have been filled, press Tab or Return, and step-by-step directions appear in an overlay, as shown in Figure 11-6.

Maps will often suggest several routes, as in Figure 11-6. The suggestions appear on the map with the selected route in darker blue (the 1 hr 58–minute route is selected in Figure 11-6). The alternative routes are shown on the map in lighter blue, as are the balloons that tell you how long the alternative routes will take.

Click a balloon or alternative route in the list to select it. The selected route always appears in dark blue; alternative routes always appear in a lighter shade of blue. Click a blue line or a balloon to select the route you want.

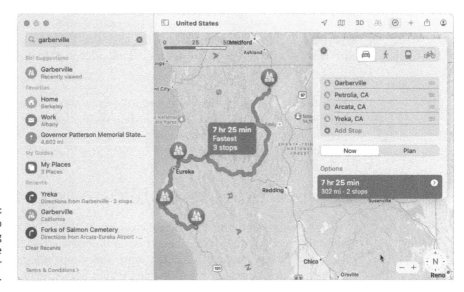

FIGURE 11-5:
Click Add Stop to add a stop along the way. Drag the stops into your preferred order.

FIGURE 11-6:
Routes from Weaverville to Weed, California.

Click the chevron to the right of a route in the overlay to see step-by-step directions for it.

After you've selected your route, you can print the directions (File ⇨ Print or ⌘+P), share them (File ⇨ Share), or send them to any nearby Apple device (File ⇨ Send to Device).

When you're finished with the step-by-step directions, click the Directions button to close the Directions overlay.

Get walking directions

For step-by-step directions for walking, click the Walk icon above the Start and End fields. Walking directions generally look a lot like driving directions except for your travel time.

WARNING

Check through walking directions carefully before attempting to follow them. Apple keeps improving the directions, but verify that they don't involve any impossible moves. Pedestrian-free tunnels and bridges have been sore points in the past.

Get directions for public transportation

Maps offers directions for using public transportation in more cities than ever. That's the good news. The bad news is that unless you live in a relatively large city, it may be a while (and possibly a long while, depending on the size of your city) before such directions are available for your hometown.

To get public-transit directions, specify your start and end points as usual and then click the Public Transit icon (the train icon) at the top of the overlay. Maps suggests as many viable routes via public transit as it can identify.

TIP

If you zoom in far enough, you can see the entrances to transportation facilities, such as train stations. Also, to see the effect of leaving at a time other than right now, click the Plan tab, and specify a departure or an arrival time.

Get traffic info in real time

You can find out the traffic conditions for whatever map you're viewing by choosing View ⇨ Show Traffic. When you do, major roadways are color-coded to inform you of the current traffic speed.

TIP

Reverse this process to hide traffic.

Here's the key to those colors: Orange means 25 to 50 miles per hour; red means under 25; and no color means that no data is available at this time.

Traffic info isn't available in every location, but the only way to find out is to give it a try. If color codes don't appear, assume that traffic information doesn't work for that particular location.

Enjoying flyovers and look arounds

Certain cities and landmarks include cool additional features such as 3D flyover tours and *look arounds,* which you can use to explore select cities in an interactive 3D experience, panning 360° and moving smoothly through streets.

Flyovers

To try a flyover, first search for a city or landmark by name and select it. If a 3D flyover tour is available for it, you'll see the Flyover Tour button on its Info sheet, as shown in Figure 11-7. Click the button to watch the flyover tour; click the little x-in-a-circle at the bottom of the window to end the tour.

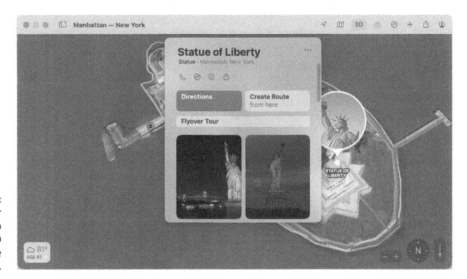

FIGURE 11-7:
Click the Flyover Tour button to watch the 3D flyover tour of the Statue of Liberty.

Look arounds

Look arounds are rare but interesting when you find them. You can start a look around by clicking the Look Around icon on the toolbar. The map screen changes to look around view, where you can click to move (or look) in any direction, as shown in Figure 11-8. If the Look Around icon is light gray, and nothing happens when you click it, a look around doesn't exist for that location.

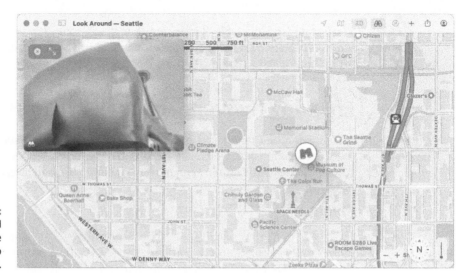

FIGURE 11-8:
A look around
view of the
Museum of Pop
Culture in Seattle.

Do more on the Info sheet

As I explain earlier in this chapter, after clicking a location's bubble, you can get directions to or from that location, add the location to your favorites or contacts, or create a new contact from it. But you can do three more things with a location from its Info sheet:

>> Click the phone number to call it.

>> Click the email address to launch the Mail app and send an email to it.

>> Click the URL to launch Safari and view its website.

Now you know how to get anywhere you want to go with Maps.

Chapter **12**

Apps Born in iOS

This chapter covers five apps that have been around on the iPhone and iPad for many years but made their debut on the Mac more recently. They should be familiar to anyone who uses an iPhone or iPad:

» Stocks lets you monitor information about specific stocks and the market in general.

» News gathers stories from myriad publications in one convenient place.

» Voice Memos lets you record (what else?) memos with your voice.

» Shortcuts lets you automate repetitive tasks.

» Home lets you control your HomeKit-enabled smart devices such as lights, thermostats, and locks.

None of the five is earth-shattering as a Mac app, but all can be useful if you need what they provide. More Mac apps that started as iPhone and iPad apps are coming up in Chapters 17 and 18. For now, just dive right in with Stocks.

Taking Stock of the Market with Stocks

If you're familiar with the Stocks app from your iPhone and iPad, you're in for a treat, because the Ventura version of the Stocks app makes it easy to view stock quotes, interactive charts, and top business news (from Apple News, which is covered in an upcoming section).

When you launch Stocks for the first time, it's populated with a default set of quotes and indexes that Apple thinks you might appreciate, as shown in Figure 12-1. Note that if you have an Apple ID and have already selected securities in the Stocks app, your selections will appear instead.

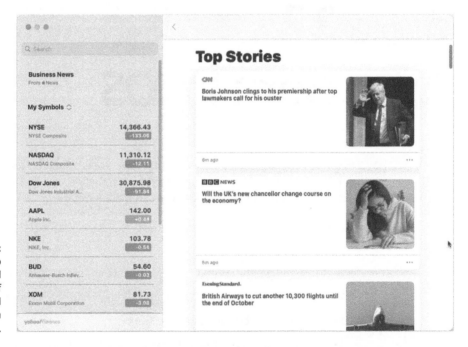

FIGURE 12-1: The Stocks app comes stocked with a handful of securities and indexes chosen by Apple.

The default stocks, funds, and indexes are listed in the sidebar on the left; news items appear in the pane on the right. Figure 12-1 shows only a handful of stocks and news items; scroll down either pane to see more.

When you open the Stocks app, it displays the latest price for the listed stocks, with two provisos:

>> The quotes are provided in near real time.

>> The quotes are updated only if your Mac can connect to the Internet.

Your stocks also appear by default in Notification Center. If you don't see stocks in yours, click the Edit Widgets button at the bottom of Notification Center to add the Stocks app. (See Chapter 10 if you don't know how to add widgets.)

Adding and removing stocks, funds, and indexes

Your chance of owning the exact group of stocks, funds, and indexes displayed by default is slim, so this section shows you how to add your own stocks, funds, or indexes and delete any or all default ones.

Here's how to add a stock, a fund, or an index:

1. **In the Search field in the top-left corner of the Stocks window, type the name of a stock, fund, or index you want to add.**

    As you type, the list updates with companies, indexes, and funds that match what you've typed so far, with items already in your watchlist appearing in a separate section.

2. **Do one of the following:**

    *   *Click the Add to Watchlist icon, the little + sign in a circle to the left of the item's name.*

    *   *Control-click or right-click the stock, fund, or index you want to add, and choose Add to Watchlist from the contextual menu.*

3. **When you finish adding stocks, funds, and indexes, click the Delete (X) button to the right of the Search field to clear the search results and return to your watchlist.**

To remove a stock, fund, or index, select it, press Delete, and then click Remove in the confirmation dialog that opens. Alternatively, Control-click or right-click the item and choose Remove from Watchlist from the contextual menu. Or even click the item and then click the Remove from Watchlist icon, the check-mark icon in the top-right corner of the Stocks window.

That's all there is to adding and removing stocks.

TIP

To change the order of the items on your watchlist, click an item, hold down the mouse button, and drag the item up or down to its new place in the list.

Details, details, details

To see the details for an item, click it; the right side of the window offers additional information on the item. The interactive chart described in the next section appears at the top of the pane. Scroll down for additional news; click See More Data from Yahoo! Finance for even more additional news.

Charting a course

When you select a stock, fund, or index, you'll see a graph with the following numbers and letters above it: 1D, 1W, 1M, 3M, 6M, YTD, 1Y, 2Y, 5Y, 10Y, and ALL. These symbols stand for 1 day, 1 week, 1 month, 3 months, 6 months, year to date, 1 year, and 2, 5, 10, and all recorded years, respectively. These numbers and letters are labels; click one, and the chart updates to reflect that period of time.

You can do two other very cool things with charts:

>> Hover your cursor over the chart to see the value for that day.

>> Click and drag to see the difference in values between two days.

By default, the Stocks app displays the change in a stock's price in dollars. You can see the change expressed as a percentage instead or as the stock's market capitalization. Just open the View menu and choose Price Change, Percentage Change, or Market Cap, as needed.

While the View menu is open, check out its other Stocks-related commands:

>> Refresh (⌘+R)

>> Hide Sidebar (⌘+Control+S)

>> Back (⌘+[)

>> Next Story (⌘+→)

>> Previous Story (⌘+←)

>> Actual Size (⌘+Shift+0)

>> Zoom In (⌘+plus sign)

>> Zoom Out (⌘+minus sign)

>> Enter Full Screen (⌘+Control+F)

Finally, Stocks lets you open multiple windows or tabs to keep more information available on the screen.

And that's about all you need to know to enjoy and be educated by the Stocks app.

Read All about It in News

The Apple News app gathers articles, images, and videos you might be interested in and displays them in a visually appealing fashion. Participating publishers include ESPN, *The New York Times,* Hearst (publisher of various newspapers), Time Inc., CNN, Condé Nast, and Bloomberg.

What are your interests?

You can customize what appears in your News app by choosing File ➪ Discover Channels, as shown in Figure 12-2.

FIGURE 12-2: The Follow Your Favorites screen with HuffPost, Yahoo! News, and Bloomberg selected to follow.

When the Follow Your Favorites screen appears, click the little red plus sign for each source you want to follow in the News app. When you click, a red check mark in a circle appears to indicate that you're following this source (such as HuffPost, Yahoo! News, and Bloomberg in Figure 12-2).

Click the item again, and the check mark turns back into a small red plus sign to indicate that you're not following this source.

When you've clicked all the sources you want to follow, click Done, and they'll appear in the Following section of your sidebar.

To remove an item from the sidebar's Following section, do one of the following:

>> Control-click or right-click the item, and choose Unfollow Channel from the contextual menu.

>> Select the item, and choose File ⇨ Unfollow Channel.

>> Select the item, and press ⌘+Shift+L.

How News works

News creates a customized real-time news feed based on the sources you're following, highlighting stories it expects you to be interested in. The more you read, the better its suggestions become, or at least that's what Apple says.

Click a story to read it; click < (Back) at the top of the pane to return to the main News screen. Or use the handy commands and shortcuts on the View menu, including the following:

>> Check for New Stories (⌘+R)

>> Next Story

>> Previous Story

>> Actual Size (⌘+Shift+0)

>> Zoom In (⌘+plus sign)

>> Zoom Out (⌘+minus sign)

Managing your news

In addition to the useful commands in the View menu, the News app's File menu offers myriad commands that help you manage your news.

To help News find stories you'll enjoy, for example, choose File⇨ Suggest More Stories Like This (⌘+L) if you love the story you're reading; choose File⇨ Suggest Fewer Stories Like This (⌘+D) if you don't love it.

The more you use these two commands, the more insightful News will be when suggesting stories of interest.

Choose File⇨ Save Story (⌘+S) to save the story for future reading (in the Saved Stories section near the bottom of the sidebar).

The History section in the sidebar can help you find that story you read the other day and now want to share.

Finally, check out the other commands on the File menu, which can help fine-tune what you see in News, including the following:

>> Follow Channel (⌘+Shift+L)

>> Block Channel (⌘+Shift+D)

>> Manage Notifications & Email

>> Manage Blocked Channels and Topics

>> Manage Subscriptions

In 2019, Apple began offering a subscription news service called News+, which offers access to hundreds of newspapers and magazines for $9.99 a month. Click News+ in the sidebar for more information or to begin a free one-month trial.

You can also get access to News+ by taking out a subscription to the Apple One service, which bundles up to six services in a single subscription payment. Depending on which other Apple services you want, getting them via Apple One might cost less than getting them individually.

And that's about all you need to know to customize and enjoy news in the News app.

Recording Memos with Voice Memos

The third addition from iOS is called Voice Memos, a simple one-trick pony of an app that lets you record, play back, and share short audio recordings. Any time you need to capture audio quickly without fuss or muss, fire up Voice Memos, and you're in business.

Recording a voice memo

Launch Voice Memos, and you'll see a simple window with a sidebar that sports your previous recordings (if you have them) and a big red button.

TIP

Recordings use your Mac's built-in microphone by default. If you prefer to use a different microphone, select it in the Sound pane of the System Settings app before you begin recording.

To record a voice memo, click the big red button. To pause the recording, click the red Pause button, which becomes the Resume button, as shown at bottom left in Figure 12-3. Click Resume to continue recording, or click Done to finish and save the recording.

FIGURE 12-3:
You can pause at any time and then click Resume or Done.

Listening to a voice memo

After you capture your thoughts or musings, you'll probably want to play them back. To do so, just click the voice memo you want to hear and then click the triangular Play icon to listen.

TIP

You can drag the playhead (the vertical blue line in the middle of the waveform) to move forward or back in the memo.

Naming a voice memo

When a memo is added to your list of recordings, it shows up with the date and length of the recording and the uninspiring title New Recording. If you've allowed Voice Memos to access Location Services, Voice Memos gives each memo a name based on the location it detects for you, but these names quickly get repetitive too.

To keep your voice memos straight, rename them like this:

1. **Click any Voice Memo in the sidebar.**

2. **Double-click the name Apple assigned (New Recording, New Recording 1, and so on).**

3. **Type your own name for the voice memo, and press Return.**

That's it. Your recording is duly identified.

Trimming a voice memo

Maybe the professor you were recording rambled on and on. Fortunately, it's easy to trim the audio. To do so, first click a recording and then choose Edit⇨ Trim Recording to display the controls.

Now drag the start marker (<), end marker (>), or both to specify the portion of the audio you want to keep. Click the Play icon to listen to what's left and make sure that it's the part you need. If so, click the Trim button and then click the Save button.

If you make a mistake, choose Edit⇨ Undo immediately to restore the audio you trimmed.

TIP

You may want to share a Voice Memo with others. No problem. Just click a Voice Memo to select it and then click the share icon (shown in the margin) on the toolbar. You have the option to email the memo or send it in a message. Or you can share it instantly with Mac, iPhone, or iPad users via AirDrop (covered in Chapter 4), or add it to the Notes or Reminders app.

When you have no further use for a recording, you can remove it from the Voice Memos app by selecting it in the sidebar and pressing Delete (or Backspace on a non-Apple keyboard). Alternatively, Control-click or right-click the recording in the sidebar and then choose Delete from the contextual menu.

TIP

To see all your voice memos on all your Apple devices, do one of the following:

>> **On your Mac:** Open System Settings, click Apple ID in the sidebar, click iCloud, click the Options button on the iCloud Drive row, click the Documents tab, and enable Voice Memos in the list of apps.

>> **On your iPhone or iPad:** Tap Settings ⇨ Apple ID (the button bearing your name) ⇨ iCloud and then set the Voice Memos switch to On.

Automating Repetitive Tasks with Shortcuts

The Shortcuts app which helps you automate repetitive tasks and trigger those automations from the menu bar, from Quick Actions, or with Siri. Shortcuts is a powerful feature that deserves an entire chapter — but not in this book and not today.

The best way to get started with shortcuts is to click the Gallery item in the sidebar. Doing so displays the Gallery (see Figure 12-4), which contains hundreds of premade shortcuts that you can use as they are or customize to suit your needs.

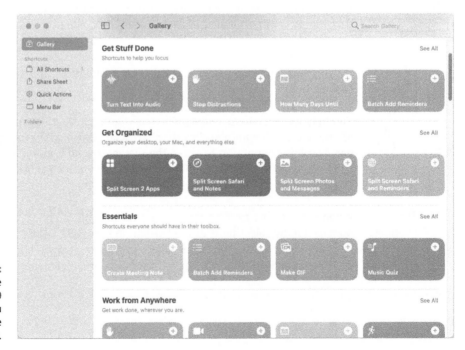

FIGURE 12-4: Explore more than 300 made-for-you shortcuts in the Shortcuts Gallery.

Click any shortcut to see a description of what it does. If you click the Turn Text Into Audio shortcut (the first shortcut in the Get Stuff Done category in the Gallery), you see the Turn Text Into Audio screen (see Figure 12-5). If you like it, click the Add Shortcut button. Depending on how the shortcut is configured, you may just see the message *Shortcut Added,* or the Setup dialog may open so that you can configure the shortcut for your Mac.

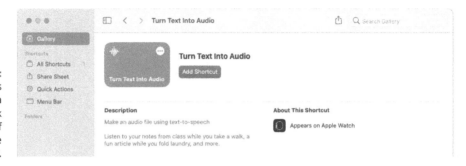

FIGURE 12-5:
On the details screen for a shortcut, click Add Shortcut if you want to use the shortcut.

After you've added a shortcut, drag it from your All Shortcuts folder to the Quick Actions folder if you want to be able to trigger the shortcut from the contextual menu or to the Menu Bar folder if you want to run the shortcut from the menu bar. You can also ask Siri to perform the shortcut by name.

When you've whetted your appetite with built-in shortcuts, you can graduate to creating custom shortcuts of your own. To get started, choose File ➪ New Shortcut or press ⌘+N.

Controlling Lights, Locks, and More with Home

The Home app lets you use your Mac to remotely control smart *HomeKit* accessories, such as smart door locks, lightbulbs, thermostats, garage-door openers, and other devices.

As of this writing, the Home app on macOS is something of a 98-pound weakling, as it can't yet add HomeKit accessories. Instead, you need to use the Home app on your iPhone or iPad to add the accessories before you can manage them with the Home app on your Mac. Apart from this severe limitation, the Home app on the Mac works in a similar way to the Home app on the iPad and iPhone.

3
Getting Along with Others

IN THIS PART . . .

Get the Internet working on your Mac (and find out what to do with it after that).

See how to surf the Internet with Safari.

Explore video chatting with FaceTime and SharePlay.

Make apps such as Mail, Contacts, and Messages work for you.

Share files and more.

» **Pre-surfing with the Network pane in System Settings**

» **Surfing the web with Safari**

» **Searching the web**

Chapter **13**

(Inter)Networking

These days, networking online is easier than finding a log to fall off: You simply use the Internet to connect your Mac to a wealth of information residing on computers around the world. Luckily for you, macOS Ventura has the best and most comprehensive Internet tools ever shipped with a Mac operating system.

macOS offers built-in Internet connectivity right out of the box. macOS Ventura comes with the following:

» Apple's Safari web browser, which you use to navigate the web, download remote files, and more

» The FaceTime app for video chats with other users of Macs, iPhones, iPads, and even Windows

» The Messages app, used for instant messaging (text), audio and video chatting, screen sharing, and file transfers

» The Mail app (for email)

This chapter and the two that follow cover the top things most people use the Internet for: surfing the web and video and audio chatting. You discover Safari in this chapter, Contacts and FaceTime in Chapter 14, and Mail and Messages in Chapter 15.

But before we can talk about any of those things, we need to make sure your Mac is connected to the Internet. The good news is that after you finish making the connection, you can play with your Internet-enabled apps to your heart's content.

And here's more good news: If you're already able to surf the web, send and receive email, or send and receive text messages, you're connected and could skip many (if not most) of the steps in the "Getting Connected to the Internet" section.

Getting Connected to the Internet

Before you can use (or surf) the Internet, you need to connect to the Internet. If you're a typical home user, you need three things to surf the Internet:

>> **A connection to the Internet,** such as a cable modem, digital subscriber line (DSL) modem, fiber, or a satellite Internet service. This connection will normally manifest itself as a physical device that establishes the Internet connection, maintains it, and shares it with your devices via a local area network. In technical terms, this physical device is usually a router and switch combined, and will often be a wireless access point as well. This section uses the term *Internet router* to refer to this type of device, but you're free to call it your *Internet box* if you prefer.

The local area network via which your Internet router shares its Internet connection with your Mac and your household's other devices can be a wired network, a wireless network, or (double brownie points) both. Almost all wired networks use the Ethernet family of standards. Almost all wireless networks use the Wi-Fi family of standards.

REMEMBER

All Mac models have Wi-Fi, from the sveltest MacBook Air up to the honking Mac Pro. Recent iMac models have optional Ethernet built into their external power brick. Monitor-free desktop Macs — the Mac mini, the musclebound Mac Studio, and the honking Mac Pro — have built-in Ethernet ports. The Mac Pro is not content with one Ethernet port, so it has two.

>> **An account with an ISP,** such as AT&T or Comcast.

TIP

If you like taking a minimalist approach, you can get online with free Wi-Fi, which is available almost everywhere — in stores, restaurants, parks, libraries, and other places. Instead of an ISP account, you can go a long way with a free email account from Apple's iCloud, Microsoft's Outlook.com, Google's Gmail, or Yahoo! Mail.

>> **A Mac,** preferably one running macOS Ventura.

After you set up each of these components, you can launch and use Safari, Mail, Messages, and any other Internet apps.

Choosing an Internet service provider (ISP)

You may have to select a company to provide you access to the Internet: an ISP. The prices and services that ISPs offer vary, often from minute to minute. Keep the following in mind when choosing an ISP:

>> **If your connection comes from a cable or telephone company, your ISP is probably that company.** In effect, the choice of ISP is pretty much made for you when you decide on cable or DSL service.

>> **Broadband access to the Internet starts at around $25 or $30 per month.** If your service provider asks for considerably more than that, find out why. Don't take "supply-chain issues" as a reason.

If you think you're paying too much for Internet service or you don't like your current provider, do your homework and determine what other options are available in your neighborhood.

Generally speaking, ISPs are (belatedly, some would say) getting better at setting up Internet connections so that they work reliably and don't require you to bug the ISPs' tech support departments constantly. But before your Internet connection flatlines, do make sure you know how to get in touch with your ISP's tech support department via phone or another means that doesn't involve your Internet connection.

TIP

I'm sure you know that the Number One solution to computer problems is *power cycling* — switching the darn thing off, cursing freely, and then switching it back on. Well, guess what: The Number One solution to Internet router problems is power cycling too. You don't even need to vary the curses, fun though that can be.

Connecting your Mac to a network via Wi-Fi

Once your network is up and running, you can connect your Mac to it via Wi-Fi either via Control Center or via the Wi-Fi pane in System Settings. Let's start with Control Center, because this is the method you'll probably want to use when you're out and about.

1. **Click the Control Center icon (shown in the margin) on the menu bar to open Control Center (shown on the left in Figure 13-1).**

2. **Click Wi-Fi to display the Wi-Fi panel (shown on the right in Figure 13-1).**

   Make sure the Wi-Fi switch at the top is set to On (blue).

3. **Click the network's name in the Other Networks list.**

   Control Center closes. A dialog opens to prompt you for the Wi-Fi network's password.

4. **Type the password in the Password box.**

   If you want to see the characters you're typing, select the Show Password check box. Seeing the characters can be a lifesaver when you're entering a murderously complex password.

5. **Click the Join button.**

FIGURE 13-1:
Click Wi-Fi in Control Center (left), and then click the network in the Wi-Fi pane.

If the Wi-Fi network you want to join doesn't appear in the Other Networks list, but you know the network exists, it's probably set to hide its name (in technical terms, its Service Set Identifier, or SSID). Click Other to open the Find and Join a Wi-Fi Network dialog (see Figure 13-2). Fill in the Network Name field and the Password field, and then click the Join button.

TECHNICAL STUFF

Most home Internet routers are set to use a technology called Dynamic Host Configuration Protocol (abbreviation: DHCP), which automatically provides connection information to computers on the network. This connection information includes the Internet Protocol address (IP address), a number that identifies the computer; the subnet mask, a number used to organize the network; and the IP address or name of the Internet router, which tells the computer where to find the on-ramp to the Internet.

FIGURE 13-2:
Use the Find and
Join a Wi-Fi
Network dialog to
join a Wi-Fi
network that
hides its name.

To connect your Mac to a Wi-Fi network via the Wi-Fi pane in the System Settings app, follow these steps:

1. **Open System Settings — for example, click the System Settings icon on the Dock or on the Launchpad screen.**

2. **Click Wi-Fi in the sidebar to display the Wi-Fi pane.**

   Make sure the Wi-Fi switch at the top is set to On (blue).

3. **In the Other Networks list, move the pointer over the Wi-Fi network you want to join, and then click the Connect button that appears on the right (see Figure 13-3).**

   A dialog opens to prompt you for the Wi-Fi network's password.

4. **Type the password in the Password box.**

   If you want to see the characters you're typing, select the Show Password check box.

5. **Click the Join button.**

   Once macOS has established the connection, the network's name appears near the top of the Wi-Fi pane, just under the Wi-Fi switch.

Managing your Wi-Fi networks

If your Mac connects to only a single Wi-Fi network, you may not need to perform any management — you can just let it connect with default settings. But if your Mac connects to multiple Wi-Fi networks, take a minute to make yourself familiar with the controls for managing Wi-Fi networks. This is especially important if your Mac connects to two or more Wi-Fi networks in the same location — for example, if you have multiple Wi-Fi networks in your home, in your workplace, or in your favorite espresso emporium.

FIGURE 13-3:
From the Wi-Fi
pane in System
Settings, you can
set up and
configure Wi-Fi
network
connections.

1. **Open System Settings — for example, choose ⌘ ➪ System Settings.**

2. **Click Wi-Fi in the sidebar to display the Wi-Fi pane (see Figure 13-4).**

   The current Wi-Fi network appears at the top, with a green circle and a *Connected* readout. Below that, the Networks section shows three lists:

   - **Personal Hotspot:** These are hotspot Wi-Fi networks provided by devices such as your iPhone or cellular iPad.

   - **Known Networks:** These are the available Wi-Fi networks your Mac has previously connected to and for which it knows the password (if the network is secured, indicated by the lock icon).

REMEMBER

   Your Mac will automatically connect to networks in the Known Networks list when they are available. If you don't want your Mac to connect to a particular known network, you need to tell macOS (we'll get to this in a moment).

   - **Other Networks:** These are Wi-Fi networks your Mac hasn't previously connected to or which it has connected to but which you've made it forget.

3. **Set the Ask to Join Networks switch to on (blue) if you want your Mac to prompt you to join an available Wi-Fi network when none of its known networks is available.**

   These prompts may be helpful, so try turning on Ask to Join Networks and see how it suits you.

FIGURE 13-4:
In the Wi-Fi pane,
choose whether
to automatically
join known
networks and
hotspots.

4. **Set the Auto-Join Hotspots switch to on (blue) if you want your Mac to automatically glom on to available Wi-Fi hotspots.**

   Some hotspots are run by malefactors keen to slurp up unwary users' credentials, bank information, and cookie recipes, so it's best to turn off Auto-Join Hotspots.

5. **Click the Advanced button at the bottom of the Wi-Fi pane to display the Advanced dialog (see Figure 13-5).**

6. **Configure Auto-Join and prune the Known Networks list as needed:**

   - **Toggle Auto-Join for the network.** Click the ellipsis (. . .) button, and then click Auto-Join to place or remove the check mark.

   - **Remove a network.** Click the ellipsis (. . .) button, and then click Remove from List.

TIP

The Advanced dialog gives you access to two nuggets of information you may sometimes need to know. First, the ellipsis (. . .) pop-up menu also contains the Copy Password command, which lets you copy a known network's password. Second, the Wi-Fi MAC Address readout at the very bottom of the dialog (which is not visible in Figure 13-5) gives the Media Access Control (MAC, usually all caps to reduce confusion) address of your Mac's network interface. You may need the MAC address to whitelist your Mac with your Internet router.

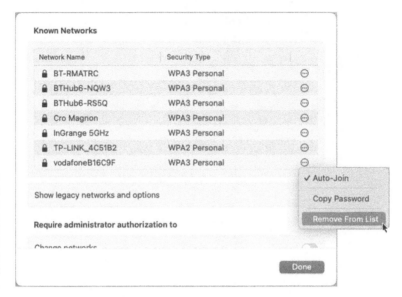

FIGURE 13-5:
In the Advanced
dialog, you can
control automatic
joining and
remove Wi-Fi
networks you no
longer want
to use.

7. **Set the Show Legacy Networks and Options switch to Off (white).**

   Legacies are generally a positive thing, but a *legacy network* usually means one that has poor network speeds and worse security. Avoid.

8. **In the Require Administrator Authorization To section, set the Change Networks switch and the Turn Wi-Fi On or Off switch to on (blue) or off (white), as needed.**

9. **Click Done to close the Advanced dialog.**

From the Wi-Fi pane in System Settings, you can click the Details button to display the Details dialog, which provides options for configuring the current Wi-Fi network. In this dialog, you can set these three switches:

» **Automatically Join This Network.** This switch gives you another way to control whether your Mac automatically joins this particular network when it's available.

» **Low Data Mode.** Set this switch to on (blue) to reduce your Mac's data usage as far as is practical. You'd use Low Data Mode when connecting your Mac to a metered network, such as the extortionate Internet connections some hotels provide. (If the Wi-Fi network is connected to an all-you-can-eat Internet connection, you probably won't want to use Low Data Mode.)

» **Limit IP Address Tracking.** Set this switch to on (blue) to have macOS hide your IP address from known address trackers in Safari and Mail. Limiting tracking is usually a good idea.

The Details dialog also contains readouts showing the IP address your Mac's wireless connection is using and the IP address of the router through which it is connected to the Internet. Lastly, there's a Forget This Network button that you can click to command your Mac to forget this network.

Use only wireless networks that you know and trust, especially in public places such as hotels and airports. If you must connect your Mac to a network that might be untrustworthy, use a virtual private network (VPN) to encrypt the data your Mac sends and receives.

Finally, if you have any reservations about using public Wi-Fi, use your mobile phone's hotspot feature (if it has one) instead of a public Wi-Fi network. Why? Because cellular networks encrypt all traffic, making them more secure than Wi-Fi networks.

Also look for *https* (not *http*) at the beginning of URLs to ensure your wireless connection to that website is encrypted (more secure).

Connecting your Mac to a network via Ethernet

If your Mac has an Ethernet port, you can connect the Mac to a network in seconds by plugging one end of an Ethernet cable into that port and the other end into your Internet router. Take a few more seconds to arrange the cable so that nobody will trip over it and your cats can't use it as a slackline while you're online with the Slack collaboration app (okay, that was a stretch).

Once you've made the physical connection, macOS normally configures it automatically within a few seconds. To see the details of the connection, open the System Settings app, click Network in the sidebar, and then click Ethernet in the Network pane. The Ethernet pane appears (see Figure 13-6), showing the connection's details, including the IP address and the router address.

From here, you can click the Advanced button to open the Advanced dialog, which enables you to perform heavy-duty configuration of the connection. With the Ethernet category selected at the top of the sidebar, make sure the Limit IP Address Tracking switch is set to on (blue). Beyond this, it's best not to change the settings in the Advanced dialog unless *a)* you know what you're doing, or *b)* you're following directions from a network administrator to solve a particular problem.

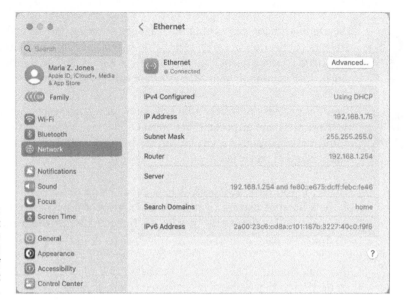

FIGURE 13-6:
Use the Ethernet
pane to learn the
IP address and
other details of
an Ethernet
connection.

Browsing the Web with Safari

With your Internet connection set up, you're ready to browse the web. The following sections use Safari because it's the web browser installed with macOS Ventura.

TIP

If you don't care for Safari, check out Firefox or Chrome, which are both free
browsers and have features you won't find in Safari. It never hurts to have a spare
in case Safari has issues with a particular website.

To begin, just open Safari in any of these ways:

>> Click the Safari icon on the Dock or Launchpad (look for the big blue compass
that looks like a stopwatch, as shown in the margin).

>> Double-click the Safari icon in your Applications folder.

>> Click a URL link in an email, an iMessage, or a document.

>> Double-click a URL link document (a .webloc file) in Finder.

The first time you launch Safari, you see a generic start page, as shown in
Figure 13-7. (If you've upgraded to Ventura from an earlier version of macOS,
Safari will open to the same page it opened to before you upgraded.)

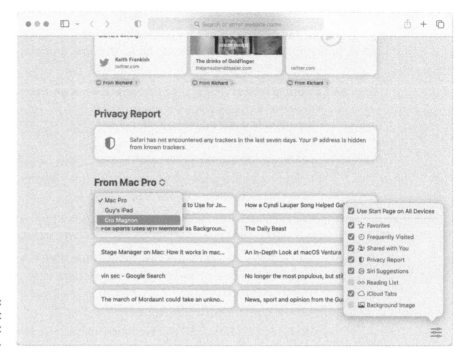

FIGURE 13-7:
Safari first
displays a generic
start page.

 You can customize your start page by clicking the little settings icon in the lower-right corner of the start page (shown in Figure 15-1 and in the margin). Enable or disable an item by selecting or clearing its check box, respectively.

TIP

The iCloud Shared Tabs section of the start page shows web pages you've recently accessed on your other computers and devices that log into the same iCloud account. To change the device providing the list, hover the pointer over the current device's name (Mac Pro, in the example) in the From list, click the little up-and-down arrow that appears, and then click the device you want.

TIP

You can choose what appears in new Safari windows and tabs by choosing Safari ➪ Settings and clicking the General tab at the top of the Settings window.

Owning your toolbar

The Safari toolbar, at the top of every Safari window, consists of a narrow row of icons and the Search or Enter Website Name field. The icons do pretty much what their names imply. From left to right, they are

>> **Show/Hide Sidebar:** Click to see your favorites or Reading list in the sidebar; click it again to hide the sidebar.

>> **New Tab Group:** Click this icon (shown in the margin) to create a new empty tab group. And if you don't already know what a tab group is, you will shortly. This icon appears when the sidebar is displayed.

>> **Tab Group Picker:** Click this icon (shown in the margin) to display a pop-up menu containing the list of tab groups, together with the New Empty Tab Group command and the New Tab Group with This Tab command. This icon appears when the sidebar is hidden.

>> **Back/Forward:** When you open a page and move to a second page (or third or fourth), Back takes you to previously visited pages. Remember that you need to go back before the Forward icon will work.

>> **Privacy Report:** Click to see an overlay with a brief privacy report; click the little *i*-in-a-circle on the overlay to see a more comprehensive report.

>> **Search or Enter Website Name (aka address box):** This field, to the right of the Show Sidebar button, is where you enter web addresses, or URLs (Uniform Resource Locators) that you want to visit. Just type one — or paste if you prefer — and press Return to surf to that site.

To the right of the Search or Enter Website Name field are three more icons. Keep reading.

>> **Share/More:** When you find a page of interest or a page you know you'll want to remember, click this icon (which is actually a drop-down menu) to tell Safari to remember it for you in its cool Reading list or as a bookmark — two topics covered later in this chapter. Or send a link to it via Mail or Messages, both covered in Chapter 15, or post it on Facebook or tweet it on Twitter.

>> **New Tab (+):** Click to open a new tab; press and hold down to see a drop-down menu of recently closed tabs, and then click the one you want to return to.

>> **Show/Hide Tab Overview:** Click the Show/Hide Tab Overview icon to see previews of all your open tabs (which you learn about shortly) or all tabs in the selected tab group. If you have other Macs or Apple devices, you'll also see the open tabs in Safari on other devices that have Safari enabled in iCloud. This feature is so handy you can also find it in the View menu, where you'll also spy its handy keyboard shortcut, ⌘+Shift+\.

TIP

You can add other useful icons to your toolbar by choosing View ➪ Customize Toolbar and then dragging icons such as Home Page, History, Bookmarks, Auto-Fill, and Print from the Customize Toolbar dialog to the toolbar.

Using the Safari sidebar

Click the Sidebar icon on the toolbar, choose View⇨ Show Sidebar, or press ⌘+Shift+L to display the sidebar, where you'll find links to your start page, tab groups, received links, and collected links (where you'll find Bookmarks and Reading List).

Click the first sidebar item, Start Page, to see your Start Page (as discussed previously).

Tab groups are the new pinned tabs

NEW

Earlier releases of macOS offered pinned tabs that persisted until you unpinned them. In Ventura, they've been replaced by tab groups, a more flexible approach for managing multiple tabs.

Here's how to set up and use tab groups:

To create a new tab group, click the New Tab Group icon on the right above the sidebar (shown in the margin) and choose New Empty Tab Group. Or, if you currently have more than one tab open, and you want to create a group containing those tabs, choose New Tab Group with *x* Tabs (where *x* is the number of open tabs).

Another way to create a new empty tab group is by choosing File⇨ New Empty Tab Group or pressing ⌘+Control+N.

You can add a web page to a tab group in these ways:

>> **If the sidebar is displayed:** Drag the web page's tab from the tab bar onto the appropriate tab group in the sidebar. If the sidebar is hidden, you can display it by choosing View ⇨ Show Sidebar or pressing ⌘+Shift+L.

>> **If the sidebar is hidden:** Click in the address box to make it active, and then drag the little icon that appears left of the address to the left side of the Safari window and pause. When the sidebar slides nonchalantly into view, drag the icon to the appropriate tab group and drop it there.

To see the Tab Overview page for a tab group with thumbnails of all the pages it contains (as shown in Figure 13-8), move the pointer over the tab group's name, click the ellipsis (. . .) button that appears, and then click Show Tab Overview on the pop-up menu.

To activate a tab group, click its name in the sidebar. The tab group's tabs replace your current tabs.

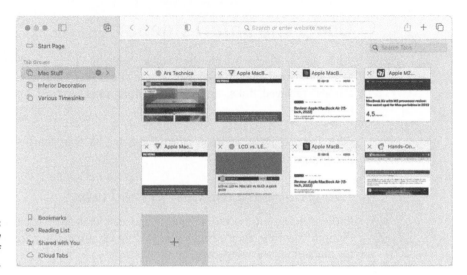

FIGURE 13-8:
The Tab Overview
for the Mac Stuff
tab group.

Note that if you open a new tab when a tab group is active (selected in the sidebar), the new tab becomes part of the active group. Conversely, if you close a tab when a tab group is selected in the sidebar, the tab is removed from the group.

Shared with You: Links from others

The Shared with You entry in the sidebar automatically gathers content that's been shared with you. Click Shared with You and an overview page appears with thumbnails of all the photos, videos, articles, and more that have been shared with you by friends and family in the Messages app.

Bookmarking your favorite pages

When you find a web page you want to remember and return to, you *bookmark* it. Here's how it works:

1. **Choose Bookmarks ⇨ Add Bookmark, press ⌘+D, or click the Share icon and choose Add Bookmark.**

2. **Choose where to store the bookmark from the pop-up menu.**

   By default, Safari puts new bookmarks in the Favorites folder. The Favorites folder can get full pretty quickly, so it's best to organize your bookmarks into a folder structure that suits your browsing needs.

3. **Rename the bookmark or use the name provided by Safari.**

4. **(Optional) Add a brief description in the Description field if you care to.**

5. **Click the Add button to save the bookmark.**

Finding your bookmarks in the sidebar

To return to a bookmarked page, click it in the Favorites bar, choose Bookmarks⇨ Show Bookmarks, press ⌘+Option+B, or click the Show Sidebar icon and then click Bookmarks to see all your bookmarks.

If you add a bookmark to the Favorites folder, it automatically appears in the Favorites bar. If you add the bookmark outside the Favorites folder in the sidebar, it will not appear in the Favorites bar but will be available at the bottom of the Bookmarks menu and in the Bookmarks sidebar.

Open bookmarked pages in the sidebar by clicking them once. View the contents of a folder by clicking the folder name in the list.

To delete a bookmark, Control+click or right-click it and choose Delete.

TIP

⌘+click a folder in the Bookmarks window or Favorites bar to simultaneously open all the bookmarks it contains.

Managing your favorites and the Favorites bar

Below the Search or Enter Website Name field is the Favorites bar, which is populated by default with icons for web pages that Apple thinks you might enjoy, including Apple, Yahoo!, Google Maps, YouTube, and Wikipedia.

TIP

If you don't see your Favorites bar, choose View⇨ Show Favorites Bar or press ⌘+Shift+B. If you want to access a ton of bookmarks from your Favorites bar, put folders of bookmarks rather than individual bookmarks on the Favorites bar. The Favorites bar displays the folders as drop-down menus, and you can quickly navigate down the menus to the bookmarks you want to display.

One last thing: Favorites and bookmarks are not exactly the same in macOS. Favorites is a folder of bookmarks that appear in the Favorites bar and Favorites page. Not all bookmarks are favorites, but all favorites are bookmarks. Which makes total sense when you think about it.

What's on your Reading list?

The Safari sidebar also contains your Reading list, which serves as a repository for pages or links you want to read sometime but don't want to read right now. A Reading list item is a lot like a bookmark but easier to create on the fly, which makes the Reading list perfect for sites or links you don't need to keep forever (that's what bookmarks are for).

To add the page you're viewing to your Reading list, hover your cursor over the left side of the Search or Enter Website Name field and then click the +-in-a-circle that appears. (You can also use the keyboard shortcut ⌘+Shift+D or click the Share icon and choose Add to Reading List from its menu.)

To add a link to your Reading list without visiting the page, just press the Shift key before you click that link. It's fast and easy, and it works even if the sidebar is closed. Or you can Control-click or right-click the link and choose Add Link to Reading List from the contextual menu.

Right-click any item in your Reading list for additional options.

To delete an item from the Reading list, Control-click or right-click the item and then choose Remove Item. To remove all items from the Reading list, Control-click or right-click any item and then choose Clear All Items.

TIP

If you have other Macs or Apple devices that sync with the same iCloud account, you can sync your Reading list among your devices by enabling Safari in the iCloud pane in the System Settings app.

Website-specific settings

To specify settings for the active website, choose Safari ➪ Settings for *website name*. The website-specific settings overlay appears with the following options:

>> **Use Reader when available.** Select this check box to use Reader view when it is available.

>> **Enable content blockers.** Select this check box to enable content blockers.

>> **Set page zoom.** Click this pop-up menu and set the zoom percentage at which you want to display this site.

>> **Auto-Play.** Click this pop-up menu and choose Allow All Auto-Play; Stop Media with Sound; or Never Auto-Play, as needed.

>> **Pop-up Windows.** Click this pop-up menu and choose Block and Notify; Block; or Allow, as needed.

>> **Camera, Microphone, Screen Sharing, and Location.** Open each pop-up menu and choose Ask, Deny, or Allow, as needed.

Reader view

 Finally, Reader view reformats the page for easier reading while hiding ads, navigation, and other distractions. It's available for a page if the icon in the margin appears at the left edge of the Search or Enter Website Name field.

Click the icon to enter Reader view; click it again to exit Reader view. Alternatively, press Shift+⌘+R to toggle Reader view on or off.

Controlling audio and video playback

In the bad old days of the web, a web page could start playing audio of its own accord, leaving you leaping for the volume control or trying to find which of your hundred open tabs was emitting Gothic yodeling drenced with guitar feedback.

Apple has improved matters considerably by making Safari block audio and video from playing by default. If you want to enable automatic playback of audio and video for all sites or specific sites, follow these steps:

1. **Choose Safari ⇨ Settings to open the Settings window.**

2. **Click Websites on the tab bar at the top of the window to display the Websites pane.**

3. **Click Auto-Play in the sidebar to display the Auto-Play controls.**

4. **For each website in the Currently Open Websites list, open the pop-up menu and choose Allow All Auto-Play, Stop Media with Sound, or Never Auto-Play, as needed.**

5. **Open the When Visiting Other Websites pop-up menu and choose Allow All Auto-Play, Stop Media with Sound, or Never Auto-Play, as needed.**

And when the noise starts (*The bells! The bells!*), go to the little blue speaker icon that appears on the right side of the address box whenever audio is playing on a web page. Click that icon, and Safari will fall silent even if the audio is coming from an inactive tab or a hidden window.

Chapter **14**

Dealing with People

I n this chapter, you see how to use the Contacts app built into macOS to store, manipulate, and use your contacts' information. You start by adding new contacts manually; then you move on to importing contacts from other contact-management apps and services, organizing your contacts in both conventional lists and self-updating smart lists, and setting your contact information to sync itself automatically through iCloud or another service.

Toward the end of the chapter, I explore how to make audio and video calls with Apple's FaceTime communications technology and how to use macOS's innovative SharePlay feature to enjoy media — TV shows, videos, songs, and more — with the other participants in your FaceTime calls.

Collecting Your Contacts

Contacts stores and manages information about your family members, friends, companies, and any other entities you want to keep in touch with. Contacts works seamlessly with the Mail, Messages, and Maps apps, enabling you to quickly look up phone numbers, email addresses, or physical locations when you're ready to communicate with someone or make tracks to their door.

In fact, Contacts works with a stack of apps, both on and beyond your Mac, including the following:

>> Use it with FaceTime (covered later in this chapter) to video-chat with friends and family.

>> Use it with Calendar (covered in Chapter 10) to display your contacts by choosing Window ⇨ Contacts. Then you can drag any person in your contacts list from the Contacts window to any date and time on the calendar, and Calendar automatically creates a special meeting event. The event even has a Send Invitation button; clicking it launches Mail and sends the person an invitation to this meeting.

>> The Contacts app can also work with any other app whose programmers choose to make the connection or with any device that's compatible with Contacts.

>> Contacts is available also in most apps that have a Share icon or menu so you can share with your contacts via whichever method is appropriate — usually their phone number, email, or icloud.com or mac.com address (for an iMessage).

>> If you use iCloud, you can choose to sync contacts with devices that include (but aren't limited to) other Macs, iPhones, and iPads. You can also sync contacts via Google, Microsoft Exchange, Microsoft Office 365, or any combination.

In the following sections, you find out the best ways to fill Contacts with your own contacts and how to keep those contacts organized. You'll start with adding contacts manually by creating new contact entries, because you'll likely need to do this now and then. But if you already have your contact data in another contacts app, skip to the "Importing contacts from other apps" section.

Adding contacts

Follow these steps to create a new contact record in Contacts:

1. **Launch the Contacts app by clicking its icon on the Dock or on the Launchpad screen or by double-clicking its icon in the Applications folder.**

   The Contacts window appears. The first time you open Contacts, you see two cards: Apple Inc. and the card with whatever personal identification information you supplied when you created your account.

2. **To create a new contact record, click the + button in the bottom-left corner of any Contact card, and choose New Contact from the pop-up menu.**

   An untitled address card appears, with the First text field selected.

3. **In the First text field, type the person's first name.**

4. **Press Tab.**

   Your cursor should be in the Last text field.

TIP

   You can always move from one field to the next by pressing Tab. In fact, this shortcut works in almost all Mac apps with fields. (Move to the previous field by pressing Shift+Tab.)

5. **Type the last name for the person you're adding to your Contacts.**

6. **Continue this process, filling in each field for which you have the contact's information (see Figure 14-1).**

   If you're creating a contact record for a company, select the Company check box just below the Company field at the top of the window to make Contacts list the contact record by the company name rather than first name and last name.

TIP

   If you don't see the field you need, click the + icon at the bottom of the card to open the pop-up menu (shown in Figure 14-1). The Add Field to Card section of this menu contains frequently used fields. The More Fields submenu contains less-used fields, including Phonetic First/Last Name, Lunar Birthday, and Department. Click the field you want to add to the contact record.

7. **When you've finished entering information, click the Done button to exit editing mode.**

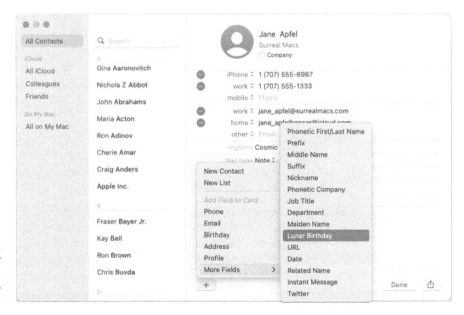

FIGURE 14-1: Creating a new contact record in the Contacts window.

TIP

The up and down arrows between the labels and their content fields in Figure 14-1 are pop-up menus that offer alternative labels for the field. You can click the arrows next to Mobile, for example, to choose iPhone, Apple Watch, Home, Work, and so on instead.

To add more info about any Contacts record, click the name in the list of contacts. Click the Edit button at the bottom of the Contacts window (where the Done button appears in Figure 14-1), make your changes, and click Done.

Repeat these steps for each new contact record you want to add to your Contacts list.

Importing contacts from other apps

If your contacts are on another Mac or an iPhone or iPad, or stored by Google or Microsoft, you won't need to import your contacts. Just add the appropriate account in the Internet Accounts pane of System Settings (if you haven't added it already) and then enable syncing for contacts.

If you have contacts in another app (such as FileMaker Pro or ACT), you can export the contact data to a file and then import it into Contacts.

Contacts can import data in five file formats:

>> **vCard:** vCard files are virtual address cards and use the .vcf file extension. A vCard can contain data for a single contact or multiple contacts. If the app that contains your contact data can export to vCard, this format is your best choice.

>> **Archive:** Early versions of OS X used archive files with the .abbu file extension. OS X has since become macOS, and Address Book has become Contacts, but the Archive format persists. If you have a file in this format, you can import it into Contacts.

>> **LDAP Data Interchange Format (LDIF):** LDAP is the acronym for Lightweight Directory Access Protocol, so LDIF is impressively long if you spell it out all the way. You might have an LDIF file (with the .ldif file extension, naturally) exported from a corporate address book.

>> **Comma-Separated Values (CSV):** This text-file format has commas separating the fields. CSV files usually have the .csv file extension. CSV files are a good way to export contact data from a Microsoft Excel worksheet for import into the Contacts app. You may also need to create a CSV file when you're exporting from an address book that doesn't support vCard format.

>> **Tab-Separated Values:** This text-file format has tabs separating the fields. The files use the .tsv or .txt file extension. You might use tab-separated values to export contact data from an app that supports neither vCard nor CSV format.

After you've exported the contact data, it's plain sailing. Go back to the Contacts app, choose File ➪ Import, select the exported data file in the Open File dialog, and then click the Open button. The imported contacts appear, and you can start working with them.

Creating a basic list

To organize your contacts in the Contacts app, you can create lists, which macOS used to call *groups*. A list can contain whatever logical (or illogical) selection you want, such as Friends, Colleagues, or Softball Team. After you've created the list and added the appropriate contacts to it, you can treat the list as a single unit. You can send an email to the Softball Team list, for example, without having to mess about with multiple addresses and maybe forget someone, causing them to stomp off in fury and join another team.

Here's how to create a list and add contacts to it:

1. **If the Contacts app isn't running, launch it by clicking its icon on the Dock or on the Launchpad screen.**

2. **Create the new list by choosing File ➪ New List, pressing ⌘+Shift+N, or clicking the + icon at the bottom of the window and choosing New List from the pop-up menu.**

   An untitled list appears in the List pane with *untitled list* selected.

3. **Type a descriptive name for this list and then press Return.**

   This example uses *Softball Team*.

4. **Click All Contacts in the list pane to show all your contacts in the second pane.**

5. **Click the contacts you want to include in the new list.**

   To select more than one contact, click the first contact and then ⌘-click each other contact.

   You can use the Search field at the top of the window to find a contact or contacts and then drag them to the list to add them.

TIP

6. **Drag the selected contact names to the new list, as shown in Figure 14-2.**

Contacts displays the number of contacts you're dragging, which happens to be six in this example.

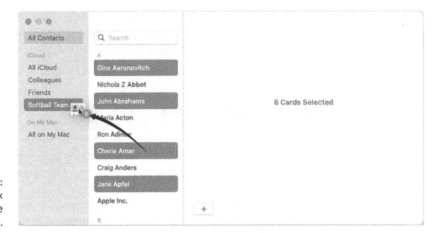

FIGURE 14-2:
Adding six
contacts to the
Softball Team list.

TIP

Another way to create a list is to select contacts by clicking, ⌘-clicking, or Shift-clicking contacts and then choosing File⇨ New List from Selection.

Setting up a smart list (based on contact criteria)

A second type of list — a smart list — might be even more useful to you because it gathers contacts in your Contacts based on criteria you specify. You might create a smart list that automatically selects contacts who have email addresses that use your company's domain name (such as surrealmacs.com).

REMEMBER

The big advantage of using a smart list instead of a regular list is that when your company hires or fires people, Contacts updates the list appropriately, with no action needed on your part.

To create a smart list, follow these steps:

1. **Choose File⇨ New Smart List or press ⌘+Option+N.**

The Smart List dialog opens (see Figure 14-3).

2. **Give the smart list a name.**

This example uses Company Staff.

3. **Choose the appropriate items from the menus: Company, Contains, Email, and so on.**

   Figure 14-3 shows the criteria for a smart list that picks any contact with the company name Surreal Macs Corp. or an email address that ends with *surrealmacs.com*.

4. **When you're happy with the criteria specified, click OK.**

   The smart list appears in the Smart Lists section of the Lists pane.

FIGURE 14-3:
Creating a
smart list.

Deleting a list or smart list

To delete a list or a smart list from your Contacts, click to select it and then press Delete or choose Edit ⇨ Delete List.

Sync + Contacts = Your contacts everywhere

To get the most out of your Mac and your other Apple devices that use the same Apple ID, you must sync your contacts — and preferably other information, such as your calendars and reminders — via iCloud or the other online service in which you store them, such as Google or Microsoft 365.

Here's how to enable cloud syncing for Contacts via iCloud:

1. **Choose System Settings ⇨ Apple ID to display the Apple ID screen in System Settings.**

2. **Click the iCloud button to display the iCloud screen.**

3. **Set the Contacts switch to on (blue).**

4. **While you're here, make sure that the switches are set to on (blue) for any other data you want to sync via iCloud, such as Calendars, Reminders, and Notes.**

5. **Choose System Settings ⇨ Quit System Settings to quit System Settings.**

TIP

To add another Internet account, such as a Google account that includes contacts, choose System Settings ⇨ Internet Accounts and then click Add Account in the Internet Accounts pane. Follow the prompts to add the account, authenticating yourself as required. Then, on the configuration screen for the account, set the switch to on (blue) for each service you want to sync, such as Mail, Contacts, Calendars, and Notes.

Making Audio and Video Calls with FaceTime

FaceTime enables you to make and receive audio calls or video calls between Macs, iPhones, and iPads. You can even use Apple's SharePlay technology (discussed later in this chapter) during a FaceTime call to enjoy a movie or a game with friends or family members remotely. FaceTime works beautifully for audio calls and video calls between Macs, iPhones, and iPads.

As of this writing, Apple hasn't released a version of FaceTime for Windows, let alone for other operating systems, such as Android or Linux. But you can add users of these and other operating systems to your FaceTime calls by sending them links that they open in a web browser. This approach to FaceTime is clumsy compared with the slick implementation on the Mac, the iPhone, and the iPad, but it does work.

Making a FaceTime call

Start by clicking the FaceTime icon on the Dock or on the Launchpad screen to launch FaceTime. The FaceTime window opens.

TIP

When you want to enjoy a FaceTime call with someone outside the Apple ecosystem, send them a FaceTime link. Click the Create Link button in the top-left corner of the FaceTime window to display the FaceTime Link pop-up panel. If the person appears as a suggestion circle near the top of the panel, marked with an icon for the type of sharing, click it. Otherwise, click the means of sharing you want to use — Copy Link (so you can paste it wherever you like), AirDrop, Mail, Messages, Notes, or Reminders — and then complete the sharing. When you click Mail, for example, macOS starts a new message in the Mail app, embeds the FaceTime link in it, and enters the text *Join my FaceTime*. Then you address the message, type a subject line compelling enough to make the recipient open the message, and send it.

To make a FaceTime call, click the New FaceTime button. The New FaceTime dialog opens, with a field for typing the contact's name above a few suggestions, as shown in Figure 14-4. Type the contact's name or accept a suggestion, and click the FaceTime button in the bottom-right corner to start a video call.

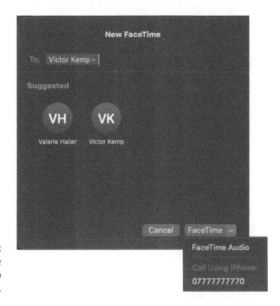

To make an audio FaceTime call instead of a video call, click the pop-up menu to the right of the FaceTime button and then choose FaceTime audio from the menu. If the Call Using iPhone item also appears on this pop-up menu, you can click it to place a FaceTime call via your iPhone's cellular connection rather than via your Mac's Wi-Fi connection.

If your contact appears in the list of recent calls in the sidebar, you can click the camera icon to initiate a video call that the recipient can answer on an iPad, an iPhone, or a Mac.

When the recipient accepts the FaceTime call, you see them, they see you, and you can socialize (see Figure 14-5).

TIP

FaceTime uses Contacts, so if you have friends or family members who have a Mac or any current or recent iPhone or iPad, type the contact name in the field, select them in the resulting list, and click the FaceTime button to begin your video chat.

FIGURE 14-5:
A FaceTime call.

Enjoying using SharePlay during a FaceTime call

After establishing a FaceTime call, you can use the SharePlay feature to watch a TV show or a movie along with the other call participants, enabling each of you to hear and see the other participants' reactions to what you're watching. You can also enjoy music via the Music app.

REMEMBER

To watch TV or a movie or to listen to a song via SharePlay, each participant must have access to the content independently, such as through a subscription to Apple TV or Apple Music. (A trial subscription is fine until it runs out.) You might wish that one participant could share their TV show or movie with everyone else, but no, that's not how SharePlay works. Anyone without access to the content will still be part of the FaceTime call but won't be able to see or hear the content. Instead, they'll receive prompts to get a subscription or to rent or buy the content.

To watch TV or a movie, simply open the TV app, and set the show or movie running. Because you're connected via FaceTime, macOS assumes that you want to use SharePlay and prompts you to confirm this desire. Click the Start SharePlay button, and you're in business. (If you click the Start Only for Me button instead, SharePlay will prompt you again next time.) The show or movie starts at the same time for each participant, and anyone can control playback by using the onscreen controls.

Sharing music via SharePlay works in a similar way. After connecting via FaceTime, open the Music app, and start playing a song to which each participant has access. The song starts at the same time for each participant, so you can all sing along. Each participant can control playback and can line up songs in the play queue.

TIP

If you want to stop SharePlay from bugging you to use it, open FaceTime, and choose FaceTime ⇨ Settings to display the Settings dialog for FaceTime. Click the SharePlay tab, and deselect the SharePlay check box.

Chapter **15**

Communicating with Mail and Messages

Y ou can see how to use Contacts and Maps to find people and places in Chapters 14 and 12, respectively. In this chapter, you dig into two more terrific apps — Mail and Messages — that work with Contacts to make managing your email and messages (chats) a breeze.

Sending and Receiving Email with Mail

TIP

This chapter covers a lot of material in relatively few pages, so if there's something you want to find out about Mail or Messages that it doesn't cover, try choosing Help⇨Mail Help or Help⇨Messages Help.

Mail is an app for sending, receiving, and organizing your email. Mail is fast and easy to use, too. Click the Mail icon on the Dock or Launchpad, or double-click the Mail icon in the Applications folder to launch Mail. The Mail icon looks like an envelope, as shown in the margin.

You can use other apps to read email. The App Store has dozens of other mail readers, and most versions of Microsoft Office include the Outlook app, which handles email and more. And most email services, including Google's Gmail and Apple's iCloud (to name a couple), offer a web-based interface you can use from a web browser in a pinch. You can continue to use any or all of these options for your email if you like, but when you're using your Mac, the easiest and best mail reader around (meaning the best one on your Mac by default) is almost certainly Mail. And you can't beat the price: It's free!

Setting up Mail

If you're launching Mail for the first time, you need to set up your email account(s) before you can proceed. A set of Choose a Mail Account Provider screens appears automatically. Just follow the instructions on each screen, fill in the fields as requested, and keep clicking the Continue button until you're finished.

If you've signed into your iCloud account on this Mac, your iCloud email should be set up already. If it's not, choose Mail ⇨ Accounts to display the Internet Accounts pane in the System Settings app, click the iCloud button, and then set the iCloud Mail switch to on (blue).

If you've enabled iCloud mail on this Mac for the first time, you'll also see a Mail Privacy Protection dialog the next time you launch Mail. Click the Protect Mail Activity button or the Don't Protect Mail Activity button, as appropriate, and then click Continue. (To change this setting at any time, choose Mail ⇨ Settings ⇨ Privacy and select or deselect the Protect Mail Activity check box. If you deselect Protect Mail Activity, you can select or deselect the Hide IP Address check box and the Block All Remote Content check box, as needed. When the Protect Mail Activity check box is selected, Mail manages the Hide IP Address check box and the Block All Remote Content check box for you.)

TIP

If you don't know what to type in one or more of these fields, contact your Internet service provider or mail provider for assistance.

After you set up one or more email accounts, you see a Welcome message, asking whether you'd like to see what's new in Mail. If you click Yes, Help Viewer launches and shows you the What's New in Mail page; the Mail main window, which looks like Figure 15-1, appears in the background. If you click No, the Mail main window appears immediately.

TECHNICAL
STUFF

The Mail main window is called a *viewer window* or *message viewer window.* You can have more than one of these windows on your screen, if you like; just choose File ⇨ New Viewer Window or press ⌘+Option+N. Using two or more viewer windows enables you to look at multiple mailboxes at the same time, which can be a great time-saver.

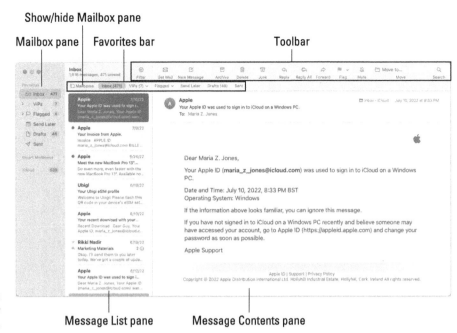

Show/hide Mailbox pane

Mailbox pane   Favorites bar   Toolbar

FIGURE 15-1:
The main window
in Mail.

Message List pane   Message Contents pane

A quick overview of the toolbar

Before you go any further, look at Figure 15-1, which shows the 12 handy icons and a Search field on the viewer window's toolbar by default:

>> **Filter:** Enables or disables filtering for this mailbox; click and hold down to change filtering criteria.

>> **Get Mail:** Checks for new email.

>> **New Message:** Creates a new, blank email message.

>> **Archive:** Archives the selected message or messages.

>> **Delete:** Deletes the selected message or messages.

To select more than one message in the list, click the first message; then ⌘-click each other message.

TIP

>> **Junk:** Marks the selected message or messages as junk mail.

Mail has built-in junk-mail filtering that can be enabled or disabled in Mail Settings. (Choose Mail ➪ Settings and click the Junk Mail icon on the tab bar.) If you receive a piece of *spam* (junk mail), select it and click the Junk icon to help train the Mail junk-mail filter. If a selected message has been marked as junk mail, the icon changes to read Not Junk.

>> **Reply:** Creates a reply to the sender only.

>> **Reply All:** Creates a reply to the sender and everyone who was sent the original message.

>> **Forward:** Creates a copy of this message you can send to someone other than the sender or other recipients.

>> **Flag/Unflag:** Toggles a flag on the selected message or messages. The flag has the color shown on the toolbar button. Open the pop-up menu to select a different color of flag. You can specify flags in searches and smart mailboxes (as you discover shortly).

>> **Mute:** Turns off notifications for new messages. Click this icon (or choose Message ⇨ Mute, or use the keyboard shortcut Control+Shift+M) to turn off notifications for new messages in the selected message thread.

>> **Move:** Moves the selected messages to the folder of your choice.

>> **Search field:** Finds a word or phrase in any item stored in Mail. When you begin typing, a pop-up menu appears so you can narrow the search to people or subjects matching your search phrase. Note that you can click the buttons on the Favorites bar to limit the search to a specific mailbox.

TIP

If you don't see the Favorites bar, choose View⇨ Show Favorites Bar or press ⌘+ Option+Shift+H.

TIP

Little numbers next to the mailbox buttons on the Favorites bar or Mailbox pane indicate the number of unread messages in that mailbox. A message is considered to be read after you display it for a second or two.

Searching in Mail should be familiar because it works the same way as searching in Finder. So, for example, if you want to save a search as a smart mailbox (Mail's version of a smart folder in Finder), click the + icon below the search field to add criteria.

Mail populates the Favorites bar with mailboxes it expects you to use often — namely, Inbox, VIPs, Flagged, Send Later, Drafts, and Sent. You can add your own favorite mailboxes by dragging them from the Mailbox pane to the Favorites bar or the Favorites section of the Mailbox pane.

Composing a new message

Here's how to create an email message:

1. **Choose File ⇨ New Message, click the New Message icon on the toolbar, or press ⌘+N.**

A new message window appears. This window is where you compose your email message, as shown in Figure 15-2.

Don't be concerned if your new message doesn't have a pop-up Signature menu like the one in Figure 15-2. That menu is displayed only after you've created at least one signature, as described later in this chapter.

2. **Click in the To field, and type someone's email address.**

   Use your own address if you don't know anyone else to send mail to.

   TIP

   If the recipient is in your Contacts, just type a few letters, and Mail's intelligent autocomplete function matches it up with names in your Contacts database. When the list appears, you can choose an item by clicking it or by using the arrow keys to select it and then pressing Return.

3. **Press the Tab key twice, and type a subject for this message in the Subject text field.**

4. **Click in the main message portion of the window, and type your message there.**

   TIP

   If you don't finish writing the message now, or if you finish it but want to read it again later before sending it (often wise!), you can save the message as a draft. Just click the red Close button (the red gumdrop) in the top-left corner of the message window, choose File ⇨ Close, or press ⌘+W. When the Save This Message as a Draft? dialog appears, click Save; Mail saves the message as a draft in the Drafts folder. You can resume work on the message by opening the Drafts mailbox and then double-clicking the message to open it in a window. When the message is finished, click the Send button to send it on its merry way.

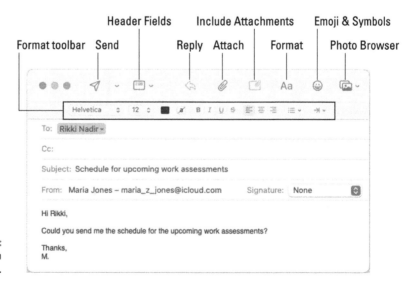

FIGURE 15-2:
Composing an
email message.

5. **When you're finished writing your message, click the Send button if you want to send the email immediately.**

If you realize that you shouldn't have sent the message, click the Undo Send button in the bottom-left corner of the Mail window immediately (see Figure 15-3). This button disappears after 10 seconds, so you need to act quickly. When you click the button, the message opens in its own window so that you can continue editing it and fix whatever problem you discovered.

TIP

If 10 seconds isn't long enough for you to undo sending, you can increase the delay to 20 seconds or 30 seconds. Choose Mail ➪ Settings ➪ Composing to display the Composing pane in Mail Settings, open the Undo Send Delay pop-up menu, and choose the setting you want. (You can also choose Off to disable Undo Send.)

If you want to send the message later, click the Send pop-up menu. Then you can choose a scheduled sending time, such as Send 8:00 AM or Send 9 PM Tonight, or click Send Later to open the Send Later dialog (see Figure 15-4). In the Send Later dialog, select the date, specify the time, and then click the Schedule button. Mail closes the message (confusingly, it plays the whooshing Send sound immediately), lines up the message for later sending, and sends it at the date and time you specified.

FIGURE 15-3:
Made a dreadful
mistake? Click the
Undo Send
button this
instant.

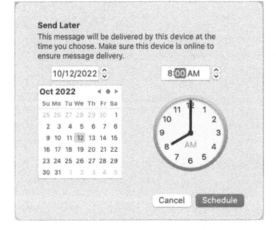

FIGURE 15-4:
Use the Send
Later dialog to
schedule a
message to go in
the mail later
rather than right
this moment.

Just for the record, here's what the icons on the toolbar in Figure 15-2 are all about:

>> **Send:** Sends the message right now. Click the pop-up menu to send the message later, as just explained.

>> **Header Fields:** Lets you select which header fields — Cc Address Field, Bcc Address Field, Reply-To Address Field, and Priority Field — you want to see in the message window. The Cc Address field appears by default, because many messages need Cc recipients. Fewer messages need Bcc (blind carbon copy, straight to the future from the days of typewriters, when people used carbon paper to make copies), but you can add the Bcc Address Field when you need it.

TIP

Use the Reply-To Address field when you want any reply from the sender to go to a different address (which you specify in this field) rather than to the address you're using to send the message.

TIP

Using the Priority Field to mark a message as High Priority (symbolized by two exclamation marks, !!), Normal Priority (one exclamation mark, !), or Low Priority (a dearth of exclamation marks) may seem to be helpful — but spammers have abused Priority so severely that few people pay attention to it anymore.

>> **Reply:** Lets you reply to the sender directly from the message window. This icon is inactive in Figure 15-2 because this message is brand-new, so there's no sender to reply to.

>> **Attach:** Displays a standard Open File dialog so you can choose a file or files to attach to this message. To attach multiple files, click the first; then ⌘+click each of the others.

If the recipients of this message use Windows, you probably want to click the oddly named Show Details button and select the Send Windows-Friendly Attachments check box, which appears in the details area at the bottom of the Open File dialog.

TIP

Select the Send Windows-Friend Attachments check box even if you don't think you have Windows-using recipients, because there's no downside for macOS or iOS users.

>> **Include Attachments:** Lets you include any files that were attached to the message you're replying to or forwarding. This icon is inactive in Figure 15-2 because this message is a new one, not a reply.

>> **Format:** Shows or hides the Format toolbar, which is displayed (between the toolbar and the To field) in Figure 15-2.

» **Emoji & Symbols:** Opens the Emoji & Symbols picker, in which you can double-click an emoji or a symbol to add it to your message at the insertion point.

» **Photo Browser:** Opens the Photo Browser panel, which displays the images in your photo library and lets you drag and drop them into a mail message.

Sending email from the Contacts app

If you're working in the Contacts app, you can quickly start an email message to a contact. With the contact record displayed, click the field label next to the email address you want to use and then choose Send Email from the pop-up menu that appears, as shown for the Work label in Figure 15-5. Or move the pointer over an email address and then click the tiny envelope icon that appears to the right of its name.

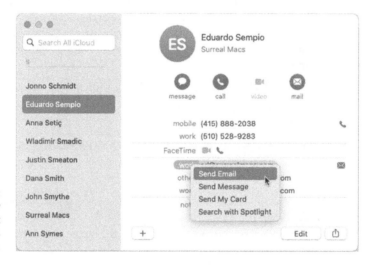

FIGURE 15-5:
Starting a new email to a contact is as easy as clicking twice.

The Mail app becomes active, and a blank email message addressed to the selected contact appears on your screen. Just type your email as you normally would.

As you can see in Figure 15-5, the pop-up menu next to email addresses lets you do the following:

» Send an email.

» Send a message (see the "Communicating with Messages" section later in this chapter).

>> Send your vCard (see the following Tip) to this email address.

>> Search for this email address in documents on your Mac by using Spotlight (see Chapter 9).

TIP

You can send a contact's information to other people in an industry-standard file format known as a *vCard* (virtual business card). Choosing Send My Card works the same as Send Email, but instead of starting with a blank email message, Mail creates a message with your vCard attached. When the recipient opens the vCard file, all your contact information will be added to their Contacts (or other contact manager in Windows).

Checking your mail

How do you check and open your mail? Easy. Just click the Get Mail icon at the top of the main Mail window (refer to Figure 15-1) or press ⌘+Shift+N.

>> **To read a new message:** Select it. Its contents appear in the Message Content pane.

>> **To delete a selected message:** Click the Delete icon on the toolbar or press Delete (or Backspace) on your keyboard.

You can delete a message in one other way if you have a trackpad. Swipe with two fingers from right to left a short way on the message in the Message List, and the Trash icon appears. Now you can either click the Trash icon or continue your swipe farther to the left until the Delete button takes up the full width of the Message List. Either way, the message disappears into Mail's Trash folder.

>> **To retrieve a message you accidentally deleted:** Click Trash on the left and drag the message to the Inbox or another mailbox. If the mailbox you want is out of sight, Control-click or right-click the message to display the contextual menu, click or highlight Move To, navigate to the right mailbox on the submenus, and then click it. Mail moves the message there.

TIP

>> **To configure Mail to send and check for your mail every *x* minutes:** Choose Mail ➪ Settings, and click the General icon at the top of the Settings window. Click the Check for New Mail pop-up menu, and make a choice: Automatically; Every Minute, Every 5 Minutes, Every 15 Minutes, Every 30 Minutes, or Every Hour; or Manually. The default is to check for new mail automatically, which means every few minutes. If you don't want Mail to do that, choose Manually. You can configure your focus settings to suppress new mail notifications, so you don't have to switch off checking for Mail to prevent the lure of new messages from interrupting a focus.

>> **To add a sender to Contacts:** When someone who isn't already in your Contacts sends you an email message, simply choose Message ⇨ Add Sender to Contacts.

Adding a sender to your Contacts has an additional benefit: It prevents future messages from that sender from being mistaken for junk mail. If a sender appears in your Contacts, their messages will never be mistakenly marked as junk mail. In other words, your Contacts is a whitelist for the spam filter. See the next section of this chapter to find out how to deal with spam.

When you receive an email containing details for an event, such as a flight or a dinner reservation, or even an invitation that says something like "Let's have brunch at 10:30 on Saturday," a smart suggestion appears between the message's header and body, so you can add the event to Calendar with just a click if you so desire.

>> **To receive a reminder to deal with a message:** Control-click or right-click the message in the Message List pane; click or highlight Remind Me on the contextual menu; and then click your choice on the Remind Me submenu, such as Remind Me in 1 Hour, Remind Me Tonight, or Remind Me Tomorrow. To set a specific date and time for the reminder, click Remind Me Later, choose the date and time in the Remind Me dialog (see Figure 15-6), and then click the Schedule button.

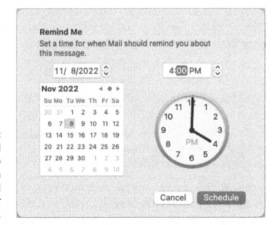

FIGURE 15-6: Use the Remind Me dialog to schedule a reminder to deal with a particular email message.

Dealing with spam

Speaking of junk mail . . . Although email is a wonderful thing, some people out there try to spoil it. They're *spammers* — lowlifes who share their lists among themselves. Before you know it, your email inbox is flooded with get-rich-quick schemes, advertisements for pornographic websites and chat rooms, pills and powders that claim to perform miracles, and plenty of the more traditional buy-this-now junk mail.

Fortunately, Mail comes with a powerful junk-mail filter that analyzes incoming message subjects, senders, and contents to determine which ones are likely to contain bulk or junk mail. Start by choosing Mail⇨ Settings and clicking the Junk Mail tab (see Figure 15-7). Make sure that the Enable Junk Mail Filtering check box is selected, and click the Mark As Junk Mail, But Leave It in My Inbox radio button.

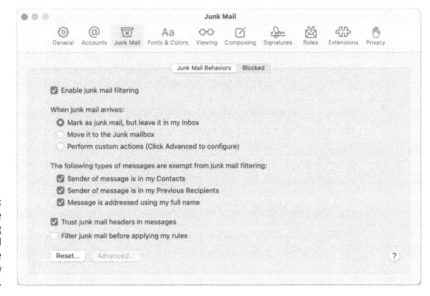

FIGURE 15-7:
Configure junk-mail filtering on the Junk Mail tab of the Settings window for Mail.

In the section titled The Following Types of Messages Are Exempt from Junk Mail Filtering, select or deselect the following three check boxes, as needed:

» **Sender of Message Is in My Contacts:** This setting is the one you found out about just a moment ago. If you've added the sender to your Contacts list, Mail won't treat their messages as junk mail. Normally, you'll want to keep this check box selected.

» **Sender of Message Is in My Previous Recipients:** Your previous recipients are the addresses to which you've sent email. So selecting this check box says that if the sender of an incoming message is someone to whom you've sent email, that incoming message isn't junk.

TIP

To see your list of previous recipients, choose Window⇨ Previous Recipients. Mail opens the Previous Recipients window, which shows the name, email address, and last-used date for each recipient. You can browse the list or search by terms you type to locate entries of interest. Click the Remove From List button to remove the selected entry, or click Add to Contacts to create a new contact record from the selected entry.

>> **Message Is Addressed Using My Full Name:** Spammers often use email addresses without associated full names (usually because they have don't have the full names). Selecting this check box says that if a message includes your full name, it's not spam. This test is less convincing than the previous two, so you may want to deselect this check box.

Select the Trust Junk Mail Headers in Messages check box if you want Mail to use the junk-mail marking that Internet service providers put in message headers to help Mail's assessment of what's junk and what's not.

Select the Filter Junk Mail Before Applying My Rules check box if you use rules to process your email. (If you don't create rules, this setting doesn't apply.)

When you close the Settings window, Mail is running in a sort of training mode, which is how it learns to differentiate between what it considers to be junk mail and what you consider to be junk mail; all it needs is your input. Mail identifies messages that it thinks are junk, but if you disagree with its decisions, here's what you do:

>> Click the Not Junk icon on the toolbar for any message that *isn't* junk mail.

>> Conversely, if a piece of junk mail slips past Mail's filters and ends up in the Inbox, select the message and click the Junk icon on the toolbar.

After a few days (or weeks, depending on your mail volume), Mail should be getting it right almost all the time. When you reach that point, choose Mail ⇨ Settings ⇨ Junk Mail again, but this time, select the Move It to the Junk Mailbox radio button. Now Mail starts automatically moving junk mail out of your Inbox and into the Junk mailbox, where you can scan the items quickly and trash them when you're ready.

If you prefer to use your email provider or third-party spam filters, you can turn off junk-mail processing in Mail by deselecting the Enable Junk Mail Filtering check box on the Junk Mail tab of the Settings dialog. Or use both.

Mailboxes smart and plain

After reading mail, you can either delete it or file it in a mailbox. The following sections take a closer look at the two types of mailboxes you have at your disposal: plain and smart.

Plain old mailboxes

Plain mailboxes are just like folders in Finder; you create them and name them, and they're empty until you put something in them. They even look like folders in the Mailboxes sidebar in Mail. You use mailboxes to organize any messages you want to save.

Here are three ways to create a plain mailbox:

>> Choose Mailbox ⇨ New Mailbox.

>> Click the + that appears to the right of each top-level Mailbox in the mailbox pane. If you don't see the +, it magically appears if you hover your cursor over mailbox name (such as iCloud or Gmail).

>> Control-click or right-click the Mailboxes sidebar, and choose New Mailbox from the contextual menu.

Whichever way you choose, the New Mailbox dialog opens. Open the Location pop-up menu, and choose the location: On My Mac to store your filed messages locally on your Mac's drive or iCloud (or another email provider) to store filed messages remotely on the mail server.

TIP

Choosing iCloud or your email provider means that messages you move to that mailbox will be stored remotely. If you access your email from more than one device, create all your mailboxes on the email server so that they'll be available to you no matter where you are or what device you're using to check your mail.

Type the name for the mailbox in the Name box; then click OK. Mail creates the mailbox, and it appears in the Mailboxes sidebar.

If you Control-click or right-click a mailbox and choose New Mailbox from the contextual menu, the Location menu in the resulting sheet will show the name of the mailbox you clicked, enabling you to create a submailbox of the mailbox you clicked. You can create a whole hierarchy of mailboxes, if you like.

You can also drag and drop a mailbox from the top level of the list into another mailbox to turn that mailbox into a submailbox.

To delete a mailbox (and its submailboxes, if it has any), do one of the following:

>> Click it to select it and then choose Mailbox ⇨ Delete Mailbox.

>> Control-click or right-click the mailbox and then choose Delete Mailbox from the contextual menu.

Smart mailboxes

A smart mailbox is Mail's version of Finder's smart folder. In a nutshell, a *smart mailbox* is a mailbox that displays the results of a search. The messages you see in a smart mailbox are *virtual;* they aren't stored in the smart mailbox itself. Instead, the smart mailbox displays a list of messages stored in other mailboxes that match whatever criteria you defined for that smart mailbox. Like smart folders in Finder, smart mailboxes are updated automatically when new messages that meet the criteria are received.

TIP

Smart mailboxes don't take up any additional disk space, so they're a great way to organize mail, automatically making it easier to find a message with no effort on your part (after you set them up).

To create a smart mailbox, do one of the following:

>> Choose Mailbox ⇨ New Smart Mailbox.

>> Click the +-in-a-circle on the right side of the Smart Mailboxes header in the Mailboxes pane.

Whichever method you choose, Mail displays the New Smart Mailbox dialog, which has a field for the smart mailbox's name, plus some pop-up menus, buttons, and check boxes, as shown in Figure 15-8. This smart mailbox gathers messages with the words *Ventura* in either the body or subject.

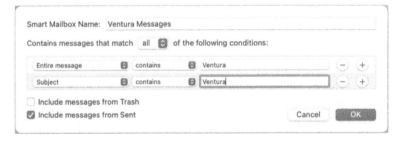

FIGURE 15-8:
Set criteria for a smart mailbox.

Name your smart mailbox, determine its criteria (by using the pop-up menus, plus and minus buttons, and check boxes), and then click OK. Then the smart mailbox appears in the Smart Mailboxes section of the Mailboxes pane with a little gear icon to denote that it's smart.

TIP

When you select a mailbox or multiple mailboxes (plain, smart, or both) in the Mailboxes pane, you'll see how many mailboxes are currently selected, along with how many messages they contain, displayed above the message list.

Changing settings for Mail

Mail's Settings window (choose Mail ➪ Settings or press ⌘+,) is the control center for Mail, where you can do the following:

>> **Create and delete email accounts.** Visit the Accounts pane.

>> **Determine which fonts and colors are used for your messages.** These settings are in the Fonts & Colors pane.

>> **Decide whether to download remote images.** This setting is in the Privacy pane.

>> **Decide whether to send formatted mail or plain text.** Go to the Composing pane.

>> **Decide whether to turn on the spell checker.** The default setting is to check spelling as you type, which many people find annoying. This setting, too, is in the Composing pane.

>> **Decide whether to have an automatic signature appended to your messages.** Use the Signature pane, as described below.

>> **Establish rules to process mail that you receive.** Visit the Rules pane (see "Mail rules rule" later in this chapter).

The first five items are up to you to decide. The last two are the most important features of the Settings window — namely, automatically adding your signature(s) to outgoing messages and inbound-mail processing rules.

Sign here, please

Would you rather not type your entire signature every time you send an email message? Yes? That's the right answer, because you don't have to with Mail. Instead, you can create as many canned signatures as you need and then insert them into outgoing messages without typing a single character.

Here's how it works:

1. Choose Mail ➪ Settings or press ⌘+, (comma) to open the Settings window.

2. Click the Signatures tab to display the Signatures pane (shown in Figure 15-9).

3. In the left column, click the name of the mail account for which you want to create this signature.

4. **To create a new, blank signature, click the little + sign at the bottom of the middle column.**

5. **Type a descriptive name for this signature to replace the default name, such as Signature #1.**

6. **In the right column, type the signature exactly as you want it to appear in outgoing messages.**

7. **(Optional) Drag a scanned image of your signature to the appropriate place in your document.**

   You can also Control-click or right-click the signature box and then insert a photo or a sketch from your iPhone or iPad by choosing the appropriate command from the contextual menu.

If you have more than one signature, you can select the one you want to use as the default: Select the account in the column on the left and then choose the signature from the Choose Signature pop-up menu at the bottom.

TIP

As soon as you add your first signature, another cool thing happens: The Signature pop-up menu appears in new messages and replies, so you can choose a different signature (or no signature) in seconds.

FIGURE 15-9:
You can include an image in a custom signature.

Mail rules rule

If you really want to tap the power of Mail, set rules to process your messages automatically. With rules, you can automatically tag messages with a color; file them in a specific mailbox; reply to, forward, or redirect the messages automatically (handy when you're going to be away for a while); reply to messages automatically; and *kill-file* messages (delete them without even bothering to look at them).

Rules are a huge topic that you'll likely want to explore in depth. This section gives you a quick look at how to create a rule by specifying a couple of simple conditions and the action for Mail to take when that condition is met. This example creates a rule called Mail from Boss Alert that plays an alert sound when Mail receives an incoming message from either of two specified email addresses. Figure 15-10 shows how the rule looks.

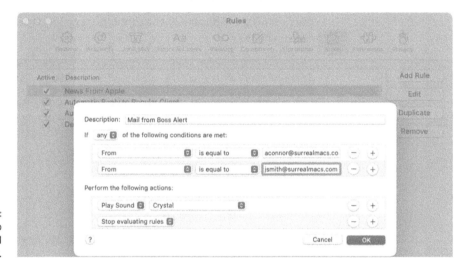

FIGURE 15-10:
Creating a rule to process email automatically.

Here are the steps:

1. **Choose Mail ⇨ Settings or press ⌘+, (comma) to open the Settings window.**

2. **Click the Rules tab to display the Rules pane.**

3. **Click the Add Rule button to open the Add Rule dialog.**

4. **In the Description field, type a description — in the example, Mail from Boss Alert.**

5. **Click the first pop-up menu (which is set to Any in Figure 15-10) to determine when to apply this rule.**

The options are Any and All. Choose Any to make the rule run when either (of two) or any (of more than two) of the conditions is true. Choose All to make the rule run only when each condition is met. (If your rule has only one condition, you can choose either Any or All, because your choice won't make any difference.)

6. **Click the first pop-up menu in the conditions section, and start defining the condition.**

   The example rule uses From, but you have a couple dozen other options: Date Sent, Date Received, Sender Is in My Contacts, Sender Is VIP, and so on. Mail gives you plenty of flexibility in creating rules.

7. **Click the second pop-up menu in the conditions section, and make a choice.**

   The example rule uses Is Equal To. The other choices are Contains, Does Not Contain, Begins With, and Ends With.

8. **In the field on the right side of the conditions section, type the text for the comparison.**

   The example rule uses the email address aconnor@surrealmacs.com, so the condition reads From Is Equal To aconnor@surrealmacs.com.

9. **Click the Add (+) button at the right end of the first condition to add a condition row, and use the same techniques to create the second condition.**

   The example rule uses this second condition: From Is Equal To jsmith@ surrealmacs.com.

   As you'd imagine, the Remove (–) button to the left of the Add (+) button removes the condition on that line.

10. **Click the first pop-up menu in the Perform the Following Actions section, and make a choice.**

    The example rule uses Play Sound. Your other choices include Move Message, Copy Message, Reply to Message, and Delete Message.

11. **Click the second pop-up menu in the actions section, and make a choice.**

    In the example, you select the sound to play: Crystal.

12. **Click the Add (+) button at the right end of the first line in the actions section to add an action row.**

13. **Click the first pop-up menu on the new action row, and choose Stop Evaluating Rules.**

    Choosing this item makes the remaining controls on the row disappear, so you have no further choices to make.

What good does this action do? Well, if you use complex rules, it prevents another action (which you perhaps hadn't anticipated) from taking place.

14. **Click OK.**

Mail asks whether you want to apply your rule(s) to the selected mailboxes.

15. **Choose Apply if you want Mail to run this rule on the selected mailboxes, or choose Don't Apply if you don't.**

From this point forward, every time you get a message from either of the two email addresses specified in the rule, the Crystal sound alerts you.

Take a (Quick) look and (Slide) show me some photos

Like Finder, Mail has a Quick Look feature that can morph into a slideshow. When you receive a message with multiple photos attached, click the paper-clip icon and then choose Quick Look from the resulting pop-up menu to display a Quick Look window showing the first of the enclosed pictures.

If you don't see a paper clip, hover your cursor over the line between the message header and the message body; the paper clip magically appears. Or click any image in the message body to highlight it and then press the spacebar to take a Quick Look.

Click the Full Screen icon (the two arrows pointing apart) in the top-left corner of the Quick Look window to switch to full-screen. Then you can click the Play button on the floating control bar to play a slideshow of the photos. When you finish viewing, click Exit Full Screen on the floating control bar to display the Quick Look window again.

To close the Quick Look window, click the little X in its top-left corner or press the spacebar.

Markup and Mail Drop

Last but not by any means least are two more excellent Mail features: Markup and Mail Drop.

Markup

Markup lets you annotate images or PDF documents. When you're composing a message that has an image or a PDF you've attached or dragged in, hover the pointer over the picture, and a little chevron (v) appears in its top-right corner. Click it to use the Markup tools on this image.

Details on using Markup appear in Chapter 5.

Mail Drop

Mail Drop is an elegant solution for large email attachments. If you enclose files or a folder full of files in a message, and Mail thinks the enclosure(s) may be too big to send via email, it displays the Would You Like to Send This Attachment Using Mail Drop? dialog (see Figure 15-11).

FIGURE 15-11:
Choose Use Mail Drop in the alert box when you try to send a file that's too big for email.

When this dialog appears, select the Don't Ask Again for This Account check box and then click the Use Mail Drop button. Mail uploads the file to a secure location on iCloud and sends the email recipient a link to download it. The file is available for 30 days, which should give the recipient ample time to download it.

What if you click the Try Sending in Email button instead? If the file is large rather than enormous, it might get through, but there's a good chance that a mail server along the way will bounce it back to you. Mail Drop prevents this awkwardness and lightens the load on the mail servers.

TIP

You can turn Mail Drop on or off manually. Choose Mail ⇨ Settings ⇨ Accounts to display the Accounts pane of the Settings window. Then click the account in the sidebar, click the Account Information tab, and select or deselect the Send Large Attachments with Mail Drop check box.

Unsubscribe and Block Sender

Another neat feature in Mail is the Unsubscribe button. When you receive an email from a mailing list, just click the Unsubscribe button (between the header and the body of the message), and you're done — at least, you're done if the list honors unsubscribe requests, as some lists apparently don't.

You'll also find a toolbar icon (a bell with a slash) to mute the selected conversation. Clicking this icon (or choosing Message ➪ Mute, or using the keyboard shortcut Control+Shift+M) turns off notifications for new messages in this thread.

Finally, you can block a sender by Control-clicking or right-clicking a sender's name and choosing Block Contact from the contextual menu. You'll see This Message Is from a Blocked Sender, along with a Preferences button. Click the button to specify how you want your blocked mail to be handled: marked as blocked but left in your inbox or moved directly to the Trash.

Finally, to unblock a sender you've blocked, choose Mail ➪ Settings, click Junk Mail, and then click the Blocked tab. In the Enter Email Addresses to Block in the List Below box, click the blocked sender and then click Remove (–) below the box.

Communicating with Messages

Instant messaging (IM) enables interactive communication among users all over the world. Messages gives you immediate access to all the other users of Apple's iMessage system. All you need are their screen names or email addresses, and you're set to go.

 To get started, launch Messages from the Dock, from Launchpad, or from your Applications folder.

What the heck is an iMessage?

iMessage is Apple's interdevice messaging protocol. iMessage enables you to send unlimited messages to anyone who uses an iPhone, an iPad, or a Mac.

Think of iMessage as being MMS messaging, similar to what you find on smartphones, but you can send and receive messages from your Mac via its network connection. Better still, an iMessage can include photos, audio recordings, videos, locations, and contacts in addition (of course) to text. If you have more than one Apple device or Mac, iMessage keeps all your conversations going across all of them. You can also get delivery receipts letting you know that your messages went through. You'll know a message has been read, too, if your friend has enabled read receipts.

If you have an iPhone 7 or newer, the Continuity feature allows all SMS and MMS text messages you send and receive on your iPhone via your wireless carrier's messaging system to appear in the Messages app on your Mac and iPad almost simultaneously — even if the person you're messaging doesn't have an iPhone. Better yet, you can reply from whichever device is closest to you, regardless of what kind of cellphone the person has.

For this to happen, all devices need to be using the same Apple ID for Messages, and Enable Messages in iCloud must be enabled. (On your Mac, choose Messages ⇨ Settings, click the iMessage tab, and then select the Enable Messages in iCloud check box.)

TIP

Another way to start a new iMessage is to click a phone number in Safari, Contacts, or Calendar.

Chitchatting with Messages

Your chats can be one to one, or they can be group bull sessions. Messages is integrated with Contacts, so you don't have to enter your buddies' information twice.

Here's all the essential info you need to get started:

>> **To start a text chat,** open Messages, click the New Message icon above the Search field (shown in the margin) and then begin typing a contact's name in the To field or click the little plus-in-a-circle to see a list of contacts with its own search field.

If you've already shared a message with someone, click their name in the list on the left to send a new message, or use the Search field to find your chat with that person.

After you've chosen a recipient, type your text in the iMessage field at the bottom of the window, and press Return or Enter to send it. Figure 15-12 shows a text chat.

In a chat, each participant's text appears in a different color and orientation. Your words appear in blue bubbles with white text on the right, whereas the other person's words appear in gray bubbles with black text on the left. This is true only when both the sender and recipient are using iOS or macOS devices.

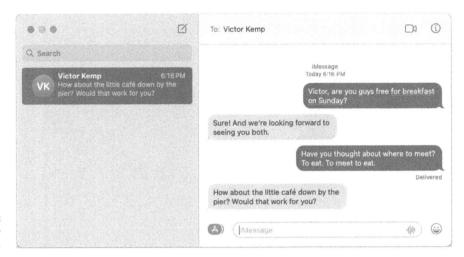

FIGURE 15-12:
A text chat in the
Messages app.

>> **To start a group text chat,** click the New Message icon, and add each person you want to include as described above.

When you finish adding names to the To field, type and send your message as just described; everyone in the To field will receive it. From then on, everyone will see every message from every participant.

TIP

Click the little *i*-in-a-circle at the top right to open the Info window for this conversation (see Figure 15-13). Now you can use your iPhone (if it's nearby) to call someone by tapping the Call icon below their name. Or select the Hide Alerts check box to mute notifications for this conversation only, which is great if one or more participants is a serial texter. Other options in the Info window let you share your location or your Mac's screen, send an email, start a FaceTime video call, and hide alerts for this conversation.

>> **To attach a picture to a person in your Contacts,** copy a picture of the person to the Clipboard in your favorite graphics app (Preview, for example). Now open Contacts, and display the card for the person for whom you want to add a picture. Click the empty picture box at the top of the card, and paste the picture from the Clipboard. Now you should see that picture on the Contacts card and also when you chat in Messages with the person. Neat!

TIP

If you've already attached a picture to a contact in Contacts, that picture will appear automatically when you chat.

>> **To transfer a file or files,** just drag the icon(s) to the iMessage field (where you type your messages) and then press Return. The file zips across the ether. This technique is a convenient way to share photos or documents without resorting to file sharing or email.

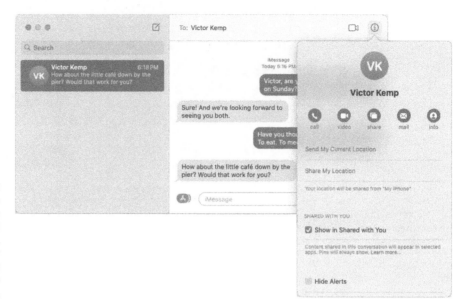

FIGURE 15-13:
In the Info
window, you can
start an audio call
or video call,
share your
screen, send
email, or simply
hide alerts.

When you drag an image file to the Messages window's message box, you see an oversize semitransparent preview, letting you know that you're sending the right image, not something totally embarrassing — another nice touch from Apple!

You could also choose Conversation ⇨ Send File and then select the file(s) in a standard Open File dialog, but the drag-and-drop method is faster and easier.

>> **To send a voice message,** click the sound wave to the right of the iMessage field, and begin talking. When you're finished, click the red Record icon and then click Send.

>> **To start a FaceTime video or audio call,** select the person you want to call in the list on the left and then choose Conversation ⇨ FaceTime Video or Conversation ⇨ FaceTime Audio.

>> **To share your Mac screen with a contact** (or ask a contact to share their Mac screen with you), choose Conversation ⇨ Invite to Share My Screen or Conversation ⇨ Ask to Share Screen.

TIP

This semi-hidden feature is awesome for providing technical support to other Mac users, such as members of your family. Solving a Mac problem is much easier when you can see the remote Mac's screen and control it from your Mac.

>> **To search for a person, a word, a phrase, or an image,** click the Search field (or press ⌘+F), and begin typing. Select the appropriate match in the list that appears.

>> **To pin a conversation to the top of the list,** Control-click or right-click the conversation, and choose Pin from the contextual menu. To unpin a pinned conversation, Control-click or right-click it, and choose Unpin from the contextual menu.

>> **To add message effects (balloons, confetti, lasers, fireworks, and more), create a memoji, use memoji stickers, or search for images on the Internet,** click the Apps icon (A) on the left side of the iMessage field and then choose Photos, Memoji Stickers, #images, or Message Effects from the pop-up menu.

>> **To send an email from Messages,** select a conversation in the list, and choose Conversation ⇨ Send Email (or press ⌘+Option+E). Mail launches (if it's not already open) and addresses a new message to the selected buddy, ready for you to begin typing.

Chapter **16**

Sharing Your Mac and Liking It

H ave you ever wanted to grab a file from your Mac while you were halfway around the world, around the corner, or in the next room? If so, rest assured that there's nothing scary or complicated about sharing files, folders, and disks — even printers — among computers as long as the computers are Macs. And even if some of the computers are running Windows, macOS makes the sharing as painless as possible.

Your Mac includes everything that you need to share files and printers, except the printers and the cables (and maybe a router). So here's the deal: You supply the hardware, and this chapter supplies the rest.

The first sections of this chapter provide an overview and tell you everything you need to know to set up new user accounts and share files successfully. When you've done all the required prep work and gotten all your virtual ducks in a line, the chapter shows you how to perform the actual sharing, starting with the "Connecting to a Shared Disk or Folder on a Remote Mac" section.

Before you start: If you're the only one who uses your Mac, you don't intend to share it or its files with anyone else, and you never intend to access your Mac from another computer in a different location, you can safely skip this chapter.

Introducing Networks and File Sharing

Ventura's file sharing enables you to use files, folders, and disks from other Macs on a network — including the Internet — as easily as though they were on your own local hard drive. If you have more than one computer, file sharing is a blessing.

Before diving in and sharing, you need to be clear on the following terms:

>> **Network:** For the purposes of this chapter, a *network* is two or more computers or devices connected by Ethernet cables or Wi-Fi (wireless networking).

>> **Ethernet:** This suite of network and cabling protocols lets you connect two or more computers or devices so that they can share files, disks, printers, or whatever.

>> **Ethernet port:** This port is where you plug an Ethernet cable into your Mac (as long as your Mac has one; most desktop Macs do).

WARNING

Be careful to match the cable to its specific jack. On your Mac and printer, the Ethernet ports look a lot like a phone jack, and the connectors on each end of an Ethernet cable look a lot like phone cable connectors — but they aren't the same. Ethernet cables are typically thicker, and the connectors (RJ-45 connectors) are a bit larger than the RJ-11 connectors that you use with old-fashioned telephones. (See examples of both types of ports in the margin.)

If your Mac didn't include an Ethernet port, but you'd like to have it, you can find Thunderbolt and USB adapters that enable you to add one.

>> **Local devices:** Such devices are connected directly to your computers, such as hard or optical drives. Your Mac's internal drive, for example, is a local device.

>> **Remote devices:** You access these devices over the network. The drive in a computer in the next room, for example, is a remote device.

>> **Protocols:** *Protocols* are the languages that networks speak. When you read or hear about networks, you're likely to hear the words *Bonjour, Ethernet, SMB,* and *TCP/IP,* all of which are protocols. Macs can speak several protocols, but every device (Mac or printer) on a network needs to speak the same protocol at the same time to communicate.

REMEMBER

Support for the TCP/IP protocol is built into every Mac, and macOS Ventura includes all the software you need to set up a TCP/IP network. The hardware you provide consists of Ethernet cables and a switch (if you have more than two computers) or Wi-Fi provided by a wireless router.

>> **Switch:** A *switch* is a device for connecting the devices on an Ethernet network. You might use a switch with eight Ethernet ports into which you plug the cables from your Mac mini, your desktop PC, your printers, and so on.

TECHNICAL STUFF

A switch is similar to a hub, which also enables you to connect devices via Ethernet cables, but a switch is smarter than a hub. A hub simply blasts out all data it receives to every device on the network; the device to which the data is addressed picks it off the wire, while every other device ignores it. By contrast, a switch makes a map of which device is where and directs data only to the device to which it's addressed. This smarter means of routing data reduces the amount of data crashing about the network and improves performance.

Portrait of home and home-office networking

A network can consist of as few as two devices, but these days, a typical home network or home-office network consists of the following:

>> A high-speed Internet connection, such as a fiber-optic connection, a digital subscriber line (DSL), or a cable connection.

>> An Internet router that shares the Internet connection on the network.

>> A wireless access point that enables computers and devices to connect to the network. Your MacBook, iPhone, and iPad might connect to the network via Wi-Fi; so might your Internet-enabled refrigerator.

>> An Ethernet switch that connects computers and devices via Ethernet cables. You might connect your desktop Macs and your printers via Ethernet rather than Wi-Fi.

REMEMBER

In many small networks, a single device plays multiple roles. If your Internet connection is a DSL, you might have a single device that combines a DSL router with a built-in Ethernet switch and a Wi-Fi wireless access point. The device acts as a one-stop shop for all your network needs.

Figure 16-1 shows a simplified example of such a network — simplified in that it shows only one phone, one tablet, one laptop, and one desktop rather that multiple devices for each member of the office or household.

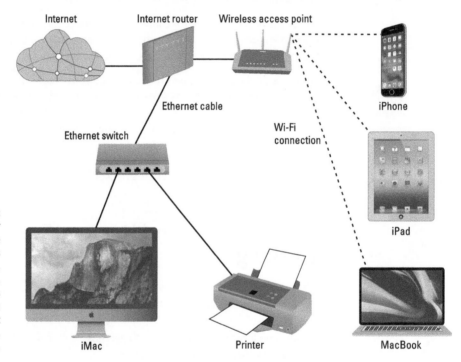

FIGURE 16-1:
A typical home or home-office network includes smartphones, tablets, laptops, and desktops sharing an Internet connection, files, and printers.

TIP

With the setup shown in Figure 16-1, you can set up each Mac on the network to access one another Mac's files, and each computer or device can print to the printer. And don't forget the most important thing: Each computer or device that connects to the network can access the Internet via the shared Internet connection.

TECHNICAL STUFF

A network can — and often does — have dozens or hundreds of users. Whether your network has two nodes (machines) or two thousand, the principles and techniques in this chapter apply.

FILE TRANSFER MADE EASY WITH AIRDROP

Perhaps all you want to do is transfer an occasional file — not necessarily a printer or a home Internet connection or a folder of music files or pictures. In that case, check out Apple's AirDrop, which is built into macOS, iOS, and iPadOS and which uses Bonjour, Apple's proprietary zero-configuration network protocol. Bonjour is a big part of the secret sauce in macOS that makes Mac networking so simple.

Here's how it works: If two devices speak Bonjour, you don't have to do any configuration other than possibly turning on the sharing capability (and getting the devices close to each other). Bonjour queries the other available networked devices to see what services they support and then configures the connections for you automatically. What could be easier?

AirDrop uses Bonjour to implement easy file transfer between Macs, iPhones, and iPads. On a Mac, AirDrop appears in the Favorites section of the sidebar in Finder windows. When you select the AirDrop favorite, as shown here, your Mac automatically locates all other AirDrop capable Macs and devices on your wireless network.

Drag from here...   ... to here

Control your Mac's AirDrop visibility

AirDrop uses both Bluetooth and Wi-Fi, and users must enable AirDrop from Control Center on iPhones and iPads or by selecting it in the sidebar of a Mac's Finder window.

(continued)

(continued)

To send a file (or multiple files and/or folders) to the other Mac, iPhone, or iPad, just drag it (or them) onto the icon for the appropriate Mac, iPhone, or iPad. AirDrop displays a dialog on the other Mac asking whether the user wants to accept delivery; if so, the items are transferred immediately to the Downloads folder on the Mac. If you're sending to an iPad or iPhone, its user sees a dialog asking whether to accept the file, and then is asked what app to open it in using the familiar Share sheet.

When you close the AirDrop window or tab, your Mac is no longer visible to other AirDrop users.

How to build your home or home-office network

To build a home network or home–office network, follow these general steps:

1. **Get an Internet connection that you'll share on the network.**

   If you've already got a high-speed Internet connection, you're good to go. If not, turn to section "Getting Connected to the Internet" in Chapter 13.

2. **Get a device for sharing the Internet connection on the network.**

   For DSL, cable, and fiber connections, many ISPs provide a single device or a pair of devices that establish and maintain the connection, share it with wired devices via Ethernet ports, and share it with wireless devices via Wi-Fi.

   If your ISP provides a less-complete solution, get either an Ethernet switch and a wireless access point or a device that combines both roles. Connect these devices (or this device) to the Internet router via Ethernet cables.

   TIP

   If you're buying an Ethernet switch, buy Gigabit Ethernet or faster. Regular Ethernet (10 Mbps) is already much too slow. Fast Ethernet (100 Mbps) is usable now but will soon be too slow, and Gigabit Ethernet (1000 Mbps) costs only a little more than Fast Ethernet.

3. **Connect each wired device to the Ethernet switch via an Ethernet cable.**

4. **Set up a Wi-Fi network on the wireless access point, and connect each wireless device to it.**

   TIP

   Many printers support both Ethernet and Wi-Fi connections. If your printer supports both, you'll probably want to use Ethernet for reliability — unless you need to position the printer somewhere that would be awkward to reach with a cable, in which case Wi-Fi is the better choice.

TIP

If your Mac doesn't have an Ethernet port built in, but you wish it did, pick up an inexpensive Ethernet-to-USB adapter for less than $20 at Amazon.com or your favorite tech store.

Setting Up File Sharing

Before you can actually share files, you must enable the appropriate type of file sharing. Follow these steps to do so:

1. **Choose System Settings ⇨ General ⇨ Sharing to display the Sharing pane of the System Settings app (see Figure 16-2).**

At the top of the pane, the Computer Name readout shows the name by which this Mac is known on the network.

2. **If you want to change the Mac's name, double-click the existing name and type the name you want.**

3. **Set the File Sharing switch to on (blue).**

FIGURE 16-2:
At the top of the Sharing pane, rename your Mac if you want and then set the File Sharing switch to on (blue).

4. **Click the Info (i) button to display the File Sharing dialog (see Figure 16-3).**

    Now other users on your network can access files and folders on your computer, as you see later in this chapter.

    By default, macOS shares only the Public folder that it creates automatically in your Home folder. Everyone on the network can see your Public folder but can't change its contents. Your Public folder contains a folder called Drop Box into which everyone on the network can put files but whose contents nobody but you can see. (I talk more about the Drop Box folder later in the chapter.)

TIP

    You can access your files or folders on this computer from another computer on the network by providing your username and password; you don't need to share your folders to give yourself remote access to them.

    Sharing only your Public folder is the safest setting. Don't share any other folders unless you're sure you need to.

REMEMBER

5. **If you want people who have accounts on your Mac to access shared files when they're using a Windows PC, click the Options button to display the Options dialog (see Figure 16-4), and then select the Share Files and Folders Using SMB check box.**

    For SMB to work, you must set macOS to store the user's password. To do so, select the check box to the left of the user's name in the On column of the list, type the user's account password in the Authenticate dialog that opens; then click OK.

6. **Click the Done button when you're done, and proceed to the following section to continue setting up your network.**

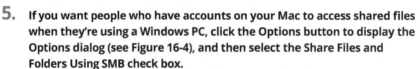

FIGURE 16-3:
In the File Sharing dialog, choose which folders to share and with whom to share them.

FIGURE 16-4:
In the Options dialog, specify which users can share files via SMB, and provide each user's password in the Authenticate dialog.

Access and Permissions: Who Can Do What

After you set up file sharing (as explained in the preceding section), tell your Mac who is allowed to see and access specific folders.

Users and groups and guests

Mac file sharing is based on the concept of users. You can share items — such as drives or folders — with no users, one user, or many users, depending on your needs.

Before you can understand how file sharing works, you need to know the terminology:

TIP

>> **Users:** People who share folders and drives (or your Mac) are *users*. A user's access to items on your local hard drive is entirely at your discretion. You can configure your Mac so that only you can access its folders and drives, or so that only one other person or group — or everyone — can share its folders and drives.

When you first set up your Mac, you created your first user. macOS automatically sets up this user as an administrator (see the next bulleted paragraph).

A user of your Mac can be either local (sitting at the Mac and thumping the keyboard) or remote, connecting across your local network or across the Internet. Or the user can log in locally sometimes and remotely at other times.

>> **Administrators:** Administrators have greater powers than standard users. Administrators' extra powers include creating and managing users, changing sensitive system settings, and accessing all folders on the Mac's drive.

TIP

If you try to take an action, and macOS prevents you, make sure that you're logged in as an administrator or can provide an administrator username and password when prompted.

TIP

You can upgrade a standard user account to an administrator account. Choose System Settings ➪ Users & Groups to display the Users & Groups pane, click the Info (i) button on the right of the user's row to display the Options dialog, and set the Allow This User to Administer This Computer switch to on (blue). Then click Done. You'll need to restart the Mac to make the change take effect.

>> **Groups:** As you may recall, macOS is based on the Unix operating system, and *groups* are the Unix-level designations for permissions consolidation. There are groups named Staff and Everyone, for example, as well as a bunch of others. A user can be a member of multiple groups. Your main account is in the Staff, Admin, and Everyone groups (and others too). Don't worry — you find out more about groups shortly.

>> **Guests:** macOS provides a special account called Guest for letting someone without a user account use your Mac temporarily. The Guest account has no password and provides limited functionality, the most important part of which is Internet access. A guest can't access files on your Mac. When the guest logs out, macOS automatically deletes all information and files in the Guest account's Home folder, leaving it pristine for the next guest.

TIP

To enable the Guest account, choose System Settings ➪ Users & Groups, click the Info (i) button at the right end of the Guest User row to display the Options dialog, and then set the switch titled Allow Guests to Log In to This Computer to on (blue). In the Options dialog, you can also set the Limit Adult Websites switch to on (blue) to reduce your guests' access to adult websites, and you can set the switch titled Allow Guest Users to Connect to Shared Folders to on (blue) to enable guests to reach files in shared folders.

Creating users

Before a user can share folders and drives, they must have an account on your Mac. You can create two kinds of user accounts for them:

>> **Standard user account:** macOS sets up each user account with its own Home folder and subfolders (Desktop, Documents, Downloads, Library, Movies, Music, Pictures, and Public). The Home folder bears the user's account name and is accessible only to that user.

>> **Sharing Only account:** macOS gives the sharing-only account access to the shared folders on the Mac — the Public folders that are shared automatically, plus any folders you've shared manually.

You can create a new *user* account only in the Users & Groups pane of System Settings. You can create a new *sharing only* account in either the Users & Groups pane of System Settings or in the Options dialog for a particular type of sharing (click the + button below the Users list).

When you add (create) a user, you need to tell your Mac who this person is. This is also the time to set a password and (maybe) administrative powers for this new user. Here's the drill:

1. **Choose System Settings ➪ Users & Groups to display the Users & Groups pane (see Figure 16-5).**

The Users & Groups pane displays the list of existing users. Each user's account shows its type: Admin, Sharing Only, or Standard.

2. **Click Add Account, and authenticate yourself if prompted, to open the Add Account dialog (see Figure 16-6).**

3. **Choose Standard from the New Account pop-up menu.**

4. **In the Full Name text box, type the full name of the new user.**

In the Account Name text box, macOS inserts a suggested account name derived from the full name — essentially, the same name, all lowercase, and minus spaces and punctuation. If you enter **Kay Tourney** in the Full Name text box, for example, macOS suggests *kaytourney* in the Account Name text box.

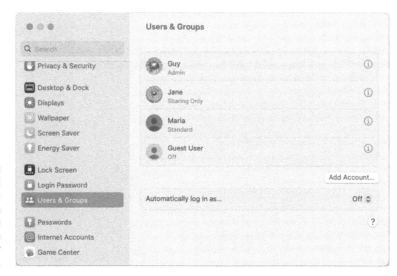

FIGURE 16-5:
Click the Add Account button in the Users & Groups pane to start adding a new user account.

5. Change the account name as needed.

macOS uses this name for the user's Home folder, so it's best to make the name readable. For a home or home-office network, you probably don't need a formal naming convention, so you may choose to use just the user's first name rather than the first name and last name smashed together.

TIP

Users can connect to your Mac by using the account name, rather than having to type their full names. The account name is also used in environments in which usernames can't have spaces and are limited to eight or fewer characters. Although macOS allows account names longer than eight characters (but no spaces), you might be better off keeping your account name to eight characters or fewer, just in case.

6. In the Password field, enter an initial password for this user.

Click the Password Assistant icon (the key icon) to the right of the Password field to display the Password Assistant (see Figure 16-6), which helps you generate passwords that will be hard for a cracking app to guess.

TIP

To make your password even harder to guess or crack, choose Random or FIPS-181–compliant from the Password Assistant's Type pop-up menu. It will also make it harder for you to remember, so make sure that you either memorize it or store it in a safe place.

7. If you're specifying a password manually rather than using the Password Assistant, type the password again in the Verify text field.

If you use the Password Assistant, it enters the password in the Verify text field for you.

8. (Optional) To help the user remember their password, type something in the Password Hint text box that will jog their memory.

FIGURE 16-6:
Name the new user, and your Mac suggests a shortened name and password.

TIP

If a user forgets the password and asks for a hint, the text that you type in the Password Hint field pops up. Creating a suitable password hint is difficult because you must strike a balance between preventing the user from getting locked out of their account because they can't remember the password and enabling unauthorized people to work out the password.

9. **Click the Create User button to create the account.**

The Add Account dialog closes, and the new user appears in the Users & Groups pane.

10. **(Optional) Click the account picture, and choose a different one.**

TIP

macOS assigns a picture from its default collection for each account, but you can select a different one by clicking the picture and working in the dialog that appears. You can select another built-in picture (from Suggestions), a memoji, an emoji, a monogram, or a photo from the Photos app. Alternatively, click Camera, and take a photo with an attached or built-in camera.

Changing a user

If circumstances dictate a change to a user's picture or administrator status, do the following:

>> **Change a user's picture.** Click the user's picture, and select a replacement. Click Save when you're done.

>> **Grant a user administrator status.** Click the Info (i) icon for the user you want to modify, set the Allow This User to Administer This Computer switch to on (blue), and then click Done.

Removing a user

What if you need to delete a user? You must be logged in with an Administrator account. In the Users & Groups pane, click the Info (i) icon for the user you want to delete and then click Delete Account in the dialog that opens. Click OK in the first confirmation dialog. A second confirmation dialog opens, offering three choices:

>> **Save the Home Folder in a Disk Image** saves a disk image of the user's Home folder in a folder named Deleted Users (which it creates inside the Users folder).

>> **Don't Change the Home Folder** removes the user from the Users & Groups pane of System Settings and from the login screen but leaves that user's Home folder in the Users folder. macOS appends *(Deleted)* to the folder's name.

>> **Delete the Home Folder** does what it says. You have the option of a secure erase (the contents get overwritten multiple times) if you select this option.

WARNING

Be certain that you really want to kiss that Home folder goodbye, because after you delete it, there's no way to get it back.

Select the appropriate option button and then click the Delete Account button.

REMEMBER

To remove the first user account ever created on this Mac, you must make at least one other user account an administrator account. Then you can log in with this administrator account and remove the first account.

macOS knows best: Folders shared by default

When you add a user account in the Users & Groups pane, macOS automatically creates a standard set of folders for that user account and makes some of them available for sharing.

Each time you add a standard or administrator user, macOS creates a Home folder hierarchy for that user in the Users folder. The user can create more folders (if necessary) and also add, remove, or move anything inside these folders. Unless you, as the owner of your Mac, give permission, the user can't see inside or use folders outside the Home folder (which has the user's name), with only three exceptions: the Shared folder in the Users folder, the top level of other user account folders, and the Public folder in every user's folder.

>> **Public:** Each user's Home folder contains a Public folder that is shared with every user who can log in to this Mac. The Public folder is also accessible to anyone who can reach your Mac by its IP address across your local network or across the Internet. Anyone who can reach your Public folder can view and copy its contents, but they can't add files or modify or delete existing files.

REMEMBER

To prevent outsiders from accessing your Public folder, activate the macOS firewall by choosing System Settings ⇨ Network ⇨ Firewall and then setting the Firewall switch to on (blue). You can also enable the firewall on your Internet router to protect the whole of your local network; consult your router's documentation to find out how.

Inside each user's Public folder is a Drop Box folder. As the name implies, this folder is where others can drop a file or folder for that user. Only the owner can open the Drop Box to see what's inside — or to move or copy the files that are in it. Imagine a street-corner mailbox: After you drop your letter in, it's gone, and you can't get it back out.

>> **Shared:** In addition to a Public folder for each user, macOS creates one Shared folder on every Mac for all users of this Mac. You can make the Shared folder available to the Guest user by clicking the Info (i) button on the Guest row of the Users & Groups pane, setting the switch titled Allow Guest Users to Connect to Shared Folders to on, and then clicking Done. You find the Shared folder within the Users folder (the same folder where you find folders for each user). The Shared folder is where to put stuff that everyone with an account on this Mac might want to use. (See Chapter 8 for an introduction to the macOS folder structure.)

Sharing a folder or disk by setting permissions

As you might expect, permissions control who can use a given folder or any disk (or partition) other than the start-up disk.

TECHNICAL STUFF

Why can't you share the start-up disk? Because macOS won't let you. Why not? Because the start-up disk contains the operating system and other stuff that nobody else should have access to.

You can set permissions for

>> The folder's owner

>> A subset of all the people who have accounts on the Mac (a group)

>> People who have the Mac's address, whether or not they have an account (guests)

Making sense of permissions

macOS distinguishes three kinds of users on the network:

>> **Owner:** The *owner* of a folder or disk can change the permissions to that folder or disk at any time. Your user account is the default owner of your Home folder and the folders it contains. Ownership can be given away (for more on that topic, see the "Useful settings for permissions" section later in this chapter). Even if you own the Mac, you can't change permissions for a folder on it that belongs to another user (unless you get Unix-y and do so as root, the superuser). The owner must be logged in to change permissions on their folders.

macOS is the owner of many folders outside the Users folder. If macOS owns it, you can see that "system" is its owner if you select the folder and choose File ➪ Get Info (or press ⌘+I).

Folders that aren't in the Users folder generally belong to system. Changing the permissions on any folder owned by system is almost always a bad idea.

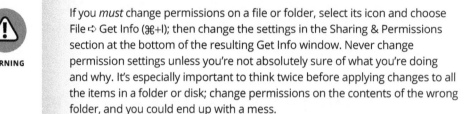

WARNING

If you *must* change permissions on a file or folder, select its icon and choose File ➪ Get Info (⌘+I); then change the settings in the Sharing & Permissions section at the bottom of the resulting Get Info window. Never change permission settings unless you're not absolutely sure of what you're doing and why. It's especially important to think twice before applying changes to all the items in a folder or disk; change permissions on the contents of the wrong folder, and you could end up with a mess.

>> **Group:** In Unix systems, all users belong to one or more *groups.* The group that includes everyone who has an account with administrator permissions on your Mac is called Admin. Everyone in the Admin group has access to Shared and Public folders over the network, as well as to any folder that the Admin group has been granted access to by the folder's owner.

For the purpose of assigning permissions, you can create your own groups the same way you create a user account: Choose System Settings ➪ Users & Groups to display the Users & Groups pane, click Add Account, choose Group from the New Account pop-up menu, type the name of the group in the Full Name text box, and then click the Create Group button.

The group appears in the Groups list in the Users & Groups pane. To assign users to the group, click the group's Info (i) button and then set the appropriate switches in the Options dialog (see Figure 16-7) to on (blue). Click Done when you finish.

>> **Everyone:** This category is an easy way to set permissions for everyone with an account on your Mac at the same time. Unlike the Admin group, which includes only users with administrative permissions, the Everyone group includes everyone with an account on this Mac.

REMEMBER

If you want people without an account on this Mac to have access to a file or folder, put that file or folder in your Public folder, where the people you want to see it can log in as guests.

Sharing a folder

Suppose that you have a folder you want to share, but it needs different permissions from those set up for the Public folder, for the Drop Box folder in the Public folder, or for your personal folders. You can set suitable permissions for the folder manually.

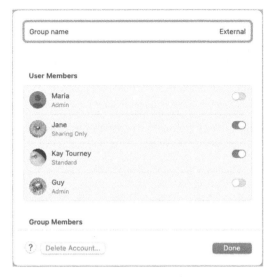

FIGURE 16-7:
In the Options
dialog for the
group, set the
switches to
on (blue) to
add users.

TIP

Share only those folders located in your Home folder (or a folder within it). Because of the way Unix works, the Unix permissions of the enclosing folder can prevent access to a folder for which you *do* have permissions. If you share only the folders in your Home folder, you'll never go wrong. If you don't take this advice, you could wind up having folders that other users can't access, even though you gave them the appropriate permissions.

You can set permissions for subfolders in your Public folder that are different from those for the Public folder itself. In fact, the Drop Box subfolder already has different permissions from the Public folder, its parent: Whereas the Public folder gives the Everyone group Read Only permission, the Drop Box subfolder gives the Everyone group Write Only (Drop Box) permission.

To share a folder with another user, follow these steps:

1. **Choose System Settings ➪ General ➪ Sharing to open the Sharing pane of the System Settings app.**

2. **Make sure that the File Sharing switch is set to on (blue).**

3. **Click the Info (i) icon on the File Sharing row to open the File Sharing dialog.**

   The lists of Shared folders and their users appear, as shown in Figure 16-8.

4. **Click the Add (+) button below the Shared Folders list, select the folder you want to share in the resulting dialog, and then click Add.**

   Alternatively, drag the folder from a Finder window to the Shared Folders list.

5. **If the user or group with which you want to share the folder doesn't appear in the Users list, click the Add (+) button below the Users box, click the user or group in the resulting dialog, and then click the Select button.**

    The user or group appears in the Users box.

6. **Click the double-headed arrow to the right of a user name or group name, and change its permissions.**

    Figure 16-8 illustrates changing the permission for the Everyone group from Read Only to Read & Write. You can choose among three types of access (in addition to no access) for each user or group, as shown in Table 16-1. If you're the folder's owner (or have administrator access), you can click the padlock icon and change the owner, the group, or both for the file or folder.

FIGURE 16-8: Changing the permissions of the Recipes folder for the group Everyone.

TABLE 16-1

Permissions

Permission	What It Allows
Read & Write	A user with Read & Write access can see, add, delete, move, and edit files just as though they were the owner of the files.
Read Only	A Read Only user can see and copy files that are stored in a shared folder but can't add new files or delete, move, or edit existing ones.
Write Only (Drop Box)	Users can add files to this folder but can't see what's in it. The user must have read access to the folder containing a write-only folder.
No Access	With no permissions, a user can neither see nor use your shared folders or drives.

Useful settings for permissions

The following sections show you some of the most common ways that you can combine permissions for a folder. You'll probably find one option that fits the way you work and the people you want to share with.

REMEMBER

Owner permissions must be at least as expansive as Group permissions, and Group permissions must be at least as expansive as Everyone permissions. So to set the Everyone permission to Read & Write, you must set the Group permission to Read & Write, and to set the Group permission to Read & Write, you must also set the Owner permission to Read & Write.

TIP

The following examples demonstrate setting permissions by working in the File Sharing dialog, which you access via the Sharing pane of the System Settings app. Another way to set permissions is to select a folder in Finder, choose File⇨ Get Info (⌘+I), and then change the settings in the Sharing & Permissions section at the bottom of the resulting Info window. The two methods are pretty much interchangeable, so you can use whichever is more convenient.

TIP

You can also set permissions in an Inspector window. Click the folder you want to affect and then press ⌘+Option+I to open the Inspector window; alternatively, Control-click or right-click the folder, press Option to change the Get Info command on the contextual menu to the Show Inspector command, and then choose Show Inspector. The Inspector window shows information for whichever folder is active, whereas the Info window shows information for only the folder for which you open it.

Here are six specific examples of setting permissions:

>> **Allow everyone access.** To give everyone access to the selected folder and let them create, modify, and delete files in it, open the pop-up menu to the right of the Everyone group and choose Read & Write.

>> **Allow everyone to read files but not change them.** To allow everyone to view files in the selected folder but not make any changes, give yourself Read & Write permission, give the Staff group Read Only permission, and give the Everyone group Read Only permission.

>> **Allow nobody but yourself access.** To allow nobody but yourself access to the selected folder, give yourself Read & Write permission, give the Staff group No Access permission, and give the Everyone group No Access permission.

>> **Allow all administrative users of this Mac access.** To give all administrative users access to the selected folder, give yourself Read & Write permission, give the Admin group Read & Write permission, and give the Everyone group No Access permission.

>> **Allow others to deposit files and folders without giving them access.** To allow others to deposit files and folders in the selected folder without letting them see its contents, set up the folder as a Drop Box. Give yourself Read & Write permission, but assign Write Only (Drop Box) permission to both the Staff group and the Everyone group.

>> **Apply the permissions to subfolders.** The Apply to Enclosed Items command (click the gear at the bottom of the Sharing and Permissions section of a Get Info window in Finder) does exactly what its name implies. This feature (which is available only in Get Info windows and doesn't appear in the Sharing pane of System Settings) is a fast way to assign the same permissions to many subfolders at the same time. After you set permissions for the enclosing folder the way you like them, issue this command to apply the same permissions to all folders inside it.

Be careful: There's no Undo command for applying a permission to subfolders.

Unsharing a folder

To unshare a folder that you own, change the permissions for every user and group to No Access. When you do, nobody but you has access to that folder.

Connecting to a Shared Disk or Folder on a Remote Mac

After you set up sharing and assign permissions, you can access folders remotely from another computer. (Just make sure that you have the correct administrative permissions to it.)

File sharing must be activated on the Mac that contains the shared files or folders; it doesn't have to be activated on the Mac that's accessing the files or folders. When file sharing is turned off, you can still use that Mac to access a remote shared folder on another machine as long as its owner has granted you enough permissions and has enabled file sharing. If file sharing is turned off on your Mac, others won't be able to access your folders, even if you've assigned permissions to them previously.

If you're going to share files, and you leave your Mac on and unattended for a long time, lock the screen or log out before you leave it to prevent other people from viewing your open apps and exploring your files.

REMEMBER

The following steps assume that you have an account on the remote Mac, which means you have your own Home folder on that Mac. If you need to know how to create a new user, see the "Creating users" section earlier in the chapter.

To connect to a shared folder on a Mac other than the one you're currently on, follow these steps:

1. **Open a Finder window.**

2. **If the Locations section of the sidebar is collapsed, click the Locations heading to expand its contents.**

3. **Click the Network item.**

   All available computers sharing files (or other services) appear in the main pane. You can see four computers in Figure 16-9: archer_d7, Mac Pro, mac-mini, and mac-pro.

4. **Click the Mac to which you want to connect — Mac Pro, in this example.**

   If the Mac is set to allow guest users to connect to shared folders, you'll see *Connected as: Guest* and a list of the shared folders, as shown in Figure 16-9.

   If the Mac is set to not allow guest users to connect to shared folders, you'll see *Not connected* and no list of shared folders. This is fine.

FIGURE 16-9:
The Mac is connected to Mac Pro as a guest and can see the Shared folder.

5. **Click the Connect As button.**

   The Connect dialog opens (see Figure 16-10). In the Connect As area, macOS automatically selects the Registered User radio button and enters in the Name field the account name under which you're logged into the Mac you're using.

6. **If your account on the remote Mac has another name, type it in the Name box.**

FIGURE 16-10:
In the Connect
dialog, enter your
password for the
remote Mac.

7. **Type your password in the Password box.**

8. **Select the Remember This Password in My Keychain check box if you want macOS to store your password so you won't have to type it in for future connections to this Mac.**

9. **Click the Connect button.**

   macOS establishes the connection, and the list of available drives and folders appears in the Finder window (see Figure 16-11). Now you can navigate the drives and folders as usual and work with their contents.

   When you connect to a shared folder or drive, macOS mounts it in your Mac's file system. When you finish using the shared folder or drive, you can eject it by clicking the Eject icon that appears to the right of its name (see Figure 16-12).

10. **When you finish using the remote Mac, disconnect by clicking the Disconnect button or by clicking the Eject icon to the right of the Mac's name in the Locations section of the Finder sidebar (see Figure 16-12).**

FIGURE 16-11:
The Mac is
connected to Mac
Pro as the user
guy and can see
the Mac's drives
and folders.

Click to disconnect from the remote Mac

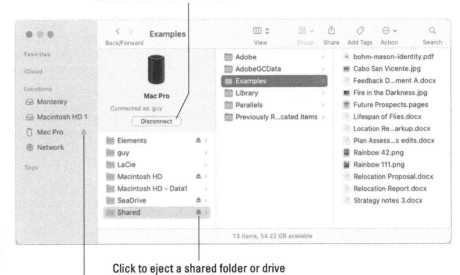

FIGURE 16-12:
You can quickly
eject a shared
drive or folder, or
disconnect from
the remote Mac.

Click to eject a shared folder or drive

Click to disconnect from the remote Mac

If you've finished working for the day, and you don't leave your Mac on 24/7 (as most folks do), choose ⇨ Shut Down or ⇨ Log Out. Shutting down or logging out automatically disconnects you from shared disks or folders. (Shut Down also turns off your Mac.)

TIP

Changing the Password for Your Account

You can change your account password at any time. Changing your password is a good idea if you suspect that someone else has learned your password. Follow these steps:

1. **Choose System Settings ⇨ Users & Groups to display the Users & Groups pane of the System Settings app.**

2. **In the Users list, click the Info (i) icon to the right of your name.**

   The Info dialog for your account appears.

3. **Click the Change Password button.**

   The Change Password dialog opens.

4. **In the Old Password field, type your current password to authenticate yourself.**

5. **In the New Password field, type your new password.**

   Click the Password Assistant icon (the key icon) to the right of the Password field to display the Password Assistant, which helps you generate hard-to-crack passwords. Look back to Figure 16-6 to see the Password Assistant.

6. **In the Verify field, retype your new password.**

7. **(Optional) In the Password Hint field, type a hint that will enable you to remember the password but won't let anyone else figure it out.**

8. **Click the Change Password button.**

9. **Click the Done button in the Info dialog.**

10. **Choose System Settings ⇨ Quit System Settings if you've finished working with System Settings.**

Resetting the Password for Another Account

To reset the password for a different account on your Mac, follow these steps:

1. **Choose System Settings ⇨ Users & Groups to display the Users & Groups pane of the System Settings app.**

2. **In the Users list, click the Info (i) icon to the right of the account whose password you want to reset.**

   The Info dialog for that user's account opens.

3. **Click the Reset Password button and then authenticate yourself if prompted.**

   The Reset Password dialog opens.

4. **In the New Password field, type the new password.**

   You can click the Password Assistant icon (the key icon) to use the Password Assistant to create a password and automatically enter it in both the New Password field and the Verify field.

5. **In the Verify field, retype the new password.**

6. **(Optional) In the Password Hint field, type a hint.**

7. **Click the Change Password button.**

   The Reset Password dialog closes.

8. Click Done to close the Info dialog.

9. Choose System Settings ⇨ Quit System Settings if you've finished working with System Settings.

More Types of Sharing

Apart from file sharing, macOS offers several types of sharing. You can configure all of them from the Sharing pane of the System Settings app (choose System Settings ⇨ General ⇨ Sharing).

Sharing a screen

Screen Sharing lets you control another Mac on your network from your Mac. You see the other Mac's screen on your Mac and control that Mac using your mouse and keyboard.

To set up Screen Sharing on the Mac you want to control remotely, follow these steps:

1. Choose System Settings ⇨ General ⇨ Sharing to display the Sharing pane of the System Settings app.

2. Set the Screen Sharing switch to on (blue).

3. Click the Info (i) button on the Screen Sharing row to open the Screen Sharing dialog.

4. Select the All Users radio button or the Only These Users radio button, as needed.

5. If you select the Only These Users radio button, click Add (+) below the list box to add the user or users whom you'll allow to use screen sharing.

   The Administrators group is included by default. You can remove it by clicking Administrators and then clicking Remove (–).

6. Click Done to close the Screen Sharing dialog.

To take control of your Mac from another Mac, follow these steps:

1. Open a Finder window.

2. If the Locations section of the sidebar is collapsed, click the Locations heading to expand its contents.

3. **Click the Network item.**

   All available computers sharing files or services appear in the main pane.

4. **Click the Mac to which you want to connect.**

5. **Click the Share Screen button.**

   A dialog opens, prompting you to sign in to the remote Mac.

6. **Type your user name and password for that Mac.**

7. **Click the Sign In button.**

   A window with the name of the remote Mac in its title bar appears. The window shows the remote Mac's screen.

8. **Do something.**

   Pull down a menu, or open a folder. You're controlling the remote Mac with your mouse and keyboard.

9. **When you're finished with your session, click the Disconnect button to end it.**

Sharing the Internet

If your Mac has an Internet connection, and another computer or device nearby doesn't, you can enable Internet Sharing, and the other computer or device can share your Internet connection.

REMEMBER

The Internet Sharing feature of macOS works reasonably well, but usually, you're better off sharing your home or home-office Internet connection via a hardware device such as an Ethernet switch or a wireless access point, as explained earlier in this chapter. A typical usage scenario for Internet Sharing would be when your desktop Mac has an Ethernet connection to the Internet but no connection is available for your other computers and devices.

To share Internet with other devices, follow these steps:

1. **Choose System Settings ⇨ General ⇨ Sharing to display the Sharing pane of the System Settings app.**

   At this point, the Internet Sharing switch may be dimmed because you haven't yet chosen settings for Internet Sharing.

2. **Click the Info (i) button on the Internet Sharing row to open the Internet Sharing dialog (see Figure 16-13).**

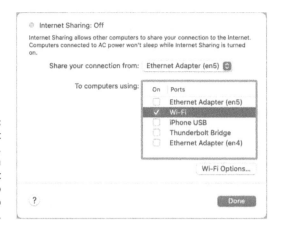

3. **Click the Share Your Connection From pop-up menu and then choose the connection you want to share.**

   Your choices typically are some or all of the following: Ethernet Adapter, Wi-Fi, and Thunderbolt Bridge. If you have an iPhone, the list may include iPhone USB as well.

4. **In the To Computers Using box, click the check box for the method you want to use for sharing with other computers and devices, such as Wi-Fi.**

5. **If you do choose Wi-Fi, click the Wi-Fi Options button to open the Wi-Fi Options dialog; then configure the wireless network your Mac will create to share the Internet connection.**

   Enter the name for the network in the Network Name box, and type a password in the Password box. Click OK to close the Wi-Fi Options dialog (see Figure 16-14).

6. **Click the Done button to close the Internet Sharing dialog.**

7. **Set the Internet Sharing switch in the Sharing pane to on (blue).**

FIGURE 16-14:
If you decide to
share the Internet
via Wi-Fi,
configure the
wireless network
in the Wi-Fi
Options dialog.

Three more ways to share

You may also want to explore the following three sharing methods that macOS offers:

>> **Printer (and Scanner) Sharing:** If you turn on Printer Sharing in the Sharing pane of System Settings, other people on your local network can use any printer or scanner that's connected to your computer. Printer Sharing is great for printers and scanners that connect to your Mac rather than to the network.

>> **Media Sharing:** Enable this option to allow devices on your network to browse and play downloaded music, movies, and TV shows from your Library.

>> **Bluetooth Sharing:** If you have a Bluetooth mobile phone or personal digital assistant, you can configure many of the behaviors for transferring files to and from your Mac. Figure 16-15 shows the Bluetooth Sharing dialog.

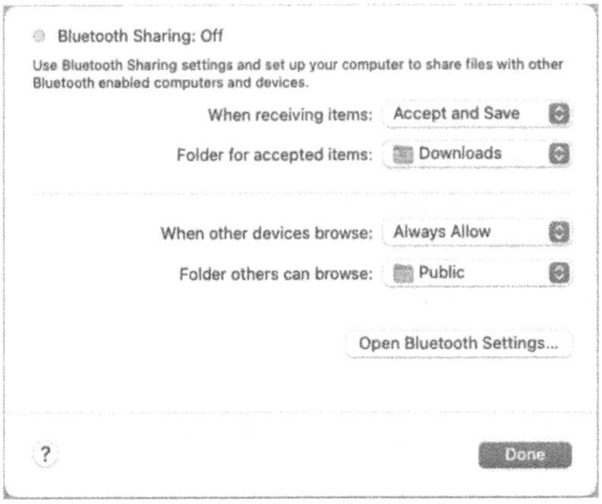

FIGURE 16-15:
In the Bluetooth Sharing dialog, choose settings for Bluetooth file transfers between other devices — such as iPhones and iPads — and your Mac.

4

Getting Creative

Enjoy music on your Mac with Music.

Read any good Books lately?

Work with photos.

Import and export media.

Get enough information about fonts and typefaces to impress your friends and family.

Set up a printer without tearing out your hair.

Make sense of the myriad print options.

Chapter **17**

The Musical Mac

Macs have long been known for their multimedia capabilities, and macOS Ventura proudly carries on that tradition, giving you the Music app for playing and managing music, the Podcasts app for enjoying podcasts, and the TV app for watching TV shows and other kinds of videos. This chapter digs into the Music app, and the next chapter gets you up and running with the Podcasts and TV apps.

Before you look at Music, however, you need to know a few things about the Apple Music and iTunes Match subscription services, because what you see in your Music app might be different if you subscribe to one or both.

Apple Music and iTunes Match Rock!

iTunes Match and Apple Music are a pair of subscription music services offered by Apple.

iTunes Match is the older of the two, designed to let you store all your music in iCloud so you can stream songs to any Mac, PC, iPhone, or iPad. iTunes Match performs its magic by first determining which songs in your iTunes library are already available in the iTunes iCloud library. Because Apple's vast iCloud repository contains tens of millions of songs, chances are that much of your music is already there. Then iTunes proceeds to upload a copy of every song it *can't* match (which is much faster than uploading your entire Music library). The result is that you can stream any song in your iTunes library on any of your Macs, PCs, iPhones, or iPads, regardless of whether the song file has been downloaded to the device. As a bonus, all the music iTunes matches plays back from iCloud at high quality — technically, 256 Kbps in Advanced Audio Coding (AAC) format, and without digital rights management (DRM) restrictions — even if your original copy was lower-quality. (You can even download higher-quality versions of those songs to replace your lower-bit-rate copies, if you want.)

As an iTunes Match subscriber, you can store up to 100,000 songs in iCloud, and songs you purchased from the iTunes Store don't count. Only tracks or albums you specify are stored locally on your devices, saving tons of precious storage space.

At just $24.99 a year, iTunes Match is a bargain for those with extensive collections of music *not* purchased from Apple.

But Apple Music may be a better option, albeit a more expensive one. For $9.99 a month (or $14.99 a month for you and up to five family members), an Apple Music subscription provides instant access to more than 90 million songs on all your devices. Whatever you want to hear is usually just a few clicks away.

You can even ask Siri to play whatever you want to hear on your Mac, as well as on your iPhone and your iPad. Try phrases such as these:

>> "Play popular songs by Elvis Presley."

>> "Play 'Running Up That Hill' by Kate Bush."

>> "Play *Greetings from Asbury Park, N.J.* by Bruce Springsteen."

>> "Play some hair metal."

>> "Play the number-1 song on December 31, 1999."

>> "Play 'Despacito' ten times. . . . No! Siri! Hey, Siri! Stop playing!"

If you find yourself with a song playing in your head (which some people call an earworm), just ask Siri to play it, and in seconds the song will be playing in real life. Usually.

TIP

Here are two quick tips. First, when asking for an album or song, include the artist's name to help Siri identify the item. So rather than saying "Play *Rubber Soul*," try saying "Play *Rubber Soul* by The Beatles." Second, before you travel by plane or commit yourself to a cruise ship, remember to tap the iCloud download button (or to Control-click or right-click and choose Download from the contextual menu) for all songs, albums, and playlists you want to listen to when Internet access isn't available.

WARNING

Make a complete backup of your Music library before enabling either iTunes Match or Apple Music, just in case. There were reports early in these services' existence that enabling one or both scrambled the data in some users' Music libraries.

Both subscription services require Internet access, but as long as you're connected, you can have your entire Music library (iTunes Match) or access to a library of more than 90 million songs (Apple Music) on your Mac, iPhone, or other device. You'll never have to worry about filling all of your device's storage space with your music.

Getting Started with the Music App

To open Music, click its icon on the dock or in Launchpad, or double-click its icon in the Applications folder. If you're opening Music for the first time, click the Start Listening button. An ad for the Apple Music subscription service appears. Click Try It Free or Already a Subscriber, or press the Esc key to dismiss the ad. Then the main Music window appears, as shown in Figure 17-1 with the key elements labeled.

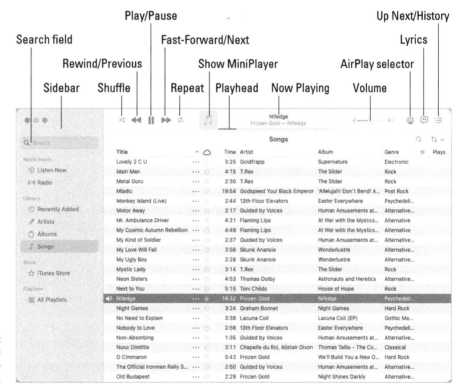

FIGURE 17-1:
What's what and where in the Music interface.

As usual, the sidebar on the left gives you access to different areas of the app and different categories of music. Whatever you select in the sidebar is displayed in the large pane on the right. In Figure 17-1, Songs is selected in the sidebar, so the list of songs appears in the large pane.

To play a song, double-click it, click it and then click the Play/Pause icon, or click it and choose Controls⇨Play.

TIP

The spacebar is the shortcut for Play/Pause. When Music is the active app, this shortcut is often the most convenient way to control playback. When an app other than Music is active, pressing the dedicated Play/Pause key on your Mac's keyboard is usually best.

After you've selected a song, you can use the Fast Forward/Next, Play/Pause, and Rewind/Previous controls to manage its playback.

Here are a few more things you should know about the Music app's interface:

>> When you don't want the full Music window taking up screen real estate, switch to the more manageable MiniPlayer (shown on the left side of Figure 17-2) by clicking the MiniPlayer icon (labeled in Figure 17-1), choosing Window⇨Switch to MiniPlayer, or pressing ⌘+Shift+M. When you give one of these commands, the main Music window hides; it comes back when you choose Window⇨Switch from MiniPlayer or simply press ⌘+Shift+M again.

TIP

>> If you look at the Window menu, you'll see that as well as the Switch to MiniPlayer command you just met, there's an unvarnished MiniPlayer command (Window⇨MiniPlayer), which has the keyboard shortcut ⌘+Option+M. What's it for? Well, the MiniPlayer command displays the MiniPlayer, or activates it if it's already open, but doesn't hide the main Music window. So if you want to navigate in both the MiniPlayer and the main window (don't ask why), use this command instead.

>> Music offers a ten-band graphic equalizer that can make your music (or video) sound significantly better. Just choose Window⇨Equalizer or press the shortcut ⌘+Option+E to invoke it onscreen. You can see the equalizer on the right side of Figure 17-2.

>> Don't miss Music's Visualizer, which offers a groovy light show that dances in time to the music. You turn it on by choosing Window⇨Visualizer or pressing ⌘+T. If you like the default Visualizer, also check out Classic Visualizer, which you'll find on the Visualizer Settings submenu.

When you've had enough of Visualizer, choose Window⇨Visualizer again or press ⌘+T again to make it disappear.

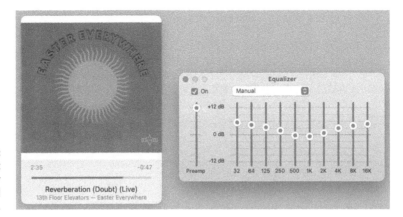

Working with Media

As you'd imagine, getting your music into the Music library is more than moderately vital. You can acquire media in several ways, depending on the type of media and where the files reside. You can add song files that you download from websites or receive as enclosures in email messages, for example, or you can add songs by ripping audio CDs. You can buy music at the iTunes Store (and, to be fair, from many other online vendors, including https://www.amazon.com). You can listen to all sorts of music on the Internet radio stations included with Music. Finally, Apple Music subscribers can listen to pretty much any song they can think of.

REMEMBER

To use the iTunes Store, Internet radio, or Apple Music, you must be connected to the Internet.

In the following sections, you discover the various ways to add music to your Music library; then you get a quick course in listening to Music's Internet radio stations.

Adding songs

You can add songs from pretty much any source, and how you add a song to Music depends on where that song comes from. Here are the main moves for adding songs:

>> **Add a song file (such as an MP3 or AAC file) from a disk drive.** Drag the document into the Music window, as shown in Figure 17-3, drag the song document (or documents or folders) to the Music icon on the Dock, or choose File ➪ Import (⌘+O) and choose the file or folder in the Open File dialog.

Drag from here...   ...to here

FIGURE 17-3:
Drag and drop
songs to the
Music content
pane or library to
add them to your
Music library.

>> **Add songs from a store-bought or homemade audio CD.** Insert the CD, and Music will launch itself and offer a dialog asking whether you want to import the CD into your Music library. Click the Yes button, and the songs on that CD are added to your Music library. If you don't see a dialog when you insert an audio CD, you can import the songs on that CD by selecting the CD in the sidebar's Devices section and then clicking the Import CD button.

TIP

If your Mac is connected to the Internet, Music magically looks up the song title, artist name, album name, song length, and genre for every song on the CD. Note that this feature works only for store-bought CDs containing somewhat-popular music; Music may not be able to find information about an obscure CD by an even-more-obscure band, even if the disc is store-bought. And in most cases, it can't look up information for homemade (home-burned) audio CDs. Finally, Music sometimes gets things wrong. To keep your library in good shape, look through the information that Music returns, and make any corrections needed.

>> **Buy your songs from the iTunes Store.** Click the iTunes Store in the sidebar to visit the iTunes Store. If you don't see the iTunes Store in the sidebar, choose Music ➪ Settings, click the General tab, and select the Show iTunes Store check box (in the Show section).

On the home page, you can either click a link or type the song title, album title, artist name, keyword, or phrase in the Search field. Press Enter or Return to start the search. When you find an item that interests you, double-click any song to listen to a short preview (or the entire song, if you're an Apple Music subscriber), or click the Buy button for the song or album to purchase the song or album, as shown in Figure 17-4.

>> **Buy your songs from other online vendors.** Amazon (https://www.amazon.com) has a huge downloadable music store on the web. Its MP3 Downloads section has more than a million songs, with more added every day. The prices at Amazon are often lower than the prices for the same music at the iTunes Store. If you're concerned about audio quality, read the details for each track or album carefully, and buy tracks that meet your criteria. Audiophiles insist on lossless compression, such as Apple Lossless Encoding, for their audio files, but most regular music fans find AAC audio files (Apple) and MP3 audio files (Amazon and most of the rest of the universe) encoded at the 256 kbps bit rate to be high-enough-quality for everyday listening.

WARNING

Run a quality check before buying any music tracks encoded at the 128 kbps bit rate, because they may have shortcomings that your ears can detect. Cymbal smashes, for example, may sound thin and incomplete (rather like the cymbals themselves after the drummer has been whaling on them).

Search field   Buy album   Buy song

FIGURE 17-4:
At the iTunes Store, buying music is as easy as clicking the Buy button for the song or the album.

To make a purchase from the iTunes Store, you have to create an Apple account, if you don't already have one. To do so, just choose Account⇨ Sign In and then click the Create New Apple ID button in the Sign In dialog. After your account is established, future purchases require just one or two clicks. *Note:* iTunes Store purchases made with this Apple account appear automatically on all other Apple devices that are signed into the same account.

Listening to Radio

Streaming audio is delivered over the Internet in real time. Think of streaming audio as being just like radio except that it uses the Internet rather than the air-waves as its delivery medium.

To listen to Radio, select Radio in the Music app's sidebar. The first thing you see, at the top of the screen, are Apple's own live radio stations: Music 1, Music Hits, and Music Country. These stations are on the air worldwide 24 hours a day, 7 days a week, offering world-class programming, interviews, and music. Scroll down to see more radio stations organized in categories such as Hosted by Artists, Discover New Shows, and Stations by Genre. To listen to a radio station, click it. Sadly, most radio stations are available only to Apple Music subscribers.

TIP

If you can't find a particular station in the Radio section of the Music app, search for the station's website, and find the URL for tapping into its stream. Copy this URL, go back to the Music app, and choose File⇨Open Stream URL or press ⌘+U. In the Open Stream dialog that appears, paste the URL into the URL box, and then click OK to start the station's stream playing.

Moving right along, the more music you have in your Music library, the more you're going to love Filter Field and Column Browser.

Finding songs quickly with the Filter Field

To enable Filter Field, choose View⇨Show Filter Field (or use its keyboard short-cut, ⌘+Option+F). The Filter Field appears in the top-right corner of the Music window. To hide the Filter Field, choose View⇨Hide Filter Field (or press ⌘+Option+F).

Type a word or phrase in Filter Field, and all items that match that word or phrase appear below it. You can type the name of a song, an album, an artist, a genre, or a composer; the results appear instantly as you type.

Enabling and using Column Browser

To enable Column Browser, choose View⇨Column Browser⇨Show Column Browser (or use its keyboard shortcut, ⌘+B). To hide it, choose View⇨Column Browser⇨Hide Column Browser (or press ⌘+B).

The Column Browser submenu allows you to choose which categories are displayed. Genres, artists, and albums are displayed by default. Disable or enable the Composers or Groupings columns by selecting them in the Column Browser submenu. A check mark next to a category means that it's enabled.

When it's enabled, Column Browser appears above the main content area. Narrow your search by clicking one or more items in each column. So, for example, if you selected Hard Rock in the first column (Genre by default) and Guns N' Roses in the second column (Artist by default), you'd see every Guns N' Roses album in every genre in the third (Albums) column.

Column Browser is an easy, visual way to narrow your search. It's especially useful if you have an extensive music library.

All about Playlists

Playlists are a big deal in Music; they let you manage otherwise-unmanageable amounts of media. Playlists let you create subsets of a large collection, so it's easier to enjoy exactly the kind of music you want in Music or on your Apple devices. If you're old enough to remember mixtapes, playlists are the high-tech equivalent.

You can create three types of playlists:

» **Regular playlists,** which contain the songs (or videos, podcasts, or radio stations) that you specify by adding them to the playlist.

» **Smart playlists,** which select songs from your library based on criteria you specify. Furthermore, you can set your smart playlists to update automatically when you add items to your library that meet the criteria.

» **Genius playlists,** which use artificial intelligence to choose songs from your library that the Genius thinks will go great together (and often do).

TIP

If you're an Apple Music subscriber, you can use songs from your personal Music library, as well as the more than 90 million songs available to Apple Music subscribers in any type of playlist.

Creating a regular playlist

To create a regular playlist, follow these steps:

1. **Choose File ⇨ New ⇨ Playlist, or press ⌘+N.**

   A new playlist named Playlist appears in the main pane.

2. **(Optional) The playlist's name, Playlist, is selected and ready to be edited, so you may want to type a new, somewhat meaningful name for it.**

   I typed *Morning Music* to create the playlist shown in Figure 17-5.

   If you decide not to name your playlist now, you can double-click it and type a new name any time.

   TIP

3. **(Optional) In the Add Description field, type a description of the playlist.**

4. **To add a song or songs to a playlist, click an item in your library and then drag the song or songs to the playlist's name in the sidebar.**

   The playlist (Morning Music in Figure 17-5) is highlighted, indicating that it's selected; the song or songs will be added to it when you release the mouse button.

   Note that adding a song to a playlist doesn't remove it from the library. And if you delete a song from a playlist, the song isn't deleted from your library. Furthermore, if you delete a playlist from the sidebar, the songs it contains aren't deleted from your library. Think of songs in playlists as being aliases of songs in your library.

FIGURE 17-5: Adding songs to a playlist is as easy as dragging them to the playlist.

5. **To listen to the songs in a playlist, click the playlist in the sidebar to select it; then click Play to hear all the songs in the list, or double-click a specific song to listen to it.**

If you don't want to drag songs to your playlist one by one, there's an easy way to do it in one fell swoop: Click the first song you want to include, ⌘-click each of the other songs, and then drag the whole bunch to the playlist. You can also create a new playlist from the songs you've selected; just choose File⇨New⇨Playlist from Selection or press ⌘+Shift+N.

Finally, you can add any song to a new or existing playlist by Control-clicking or right-clicking it and choosing Add to Playlist from the contextual menu.

Working with smart playlists

To create a *smart playlist* that gathers its contents based on criteria you specify and updates itself automatically, follow these steps:

1. **Choose File ⇨ New Smart Playlist or press ⌘+Option+N.**

   The Smart Playlist dialog appears, as shown in Figure 17-6.

2. **Use the pop-up menus to select the criteria — song or album name, genre, or other attributes — that will build your smart playlist.**

   To add more criteria, click the + button(s) on the far right.

3. **Click OK when you're done.**

   The playlist appears alongside your other playlists in the Music sidebar. You can tell that it's a smart playlist because its icon is a gear. To modify the criteria of a smart playlist after it's been created, click the playlist and then click Edit Rules (below the smart playlist's name and description in the main pane); alternatively, Control-click or right-click the smart playlist in the sidebar, and choose Edit Rules from the contextual menu.

Control-click or right-click any playlist to see additional options: Play, Shuffle, Play Next, Play Later, Love, Dislike, Open in New Window, Edit Rules (just mentioned), Burn Playlist to Disc, Copy to Play Order, Duplicate, and Delete from Library.

As you add to your music library and play the songs it contains, your smart play-lists update themselves automatically, so they're always current.

FIGURE 17-6:
Specify the
criteria for your
smart playlist.

Working with the Genius playlist

Regular playlists are great; smart playlists are even better; some playlists are pure Genius.

What is Genius?

Genius is more of a *what* than an *is:* a Music feature that lets you find new music (in your Music library or the iTunes Store) that's related to a song of your choice. Or, as Apple puts it: "Genius makes playlists and mixes from songs in your library that go great together. And the Genius selects music from the iTunes Store that you don't already have."

To use Genius, you must have an iTunes Store account, even though the information Genius sends to Apple about your Music library is stored anonymously, and no purchase is required. So sign in to your iTunes Store account if you have one, or create an account if you don't. After you agree to the terms of service, Genius gathers info about your Music library, sends the info to Apple, and then delivers your results. When all this is done, you can create Genius playlists and explore Genius suggestions.

How does Genius work?

Genius could hardly be easier to use. Select at least one song (or a bunch of songs) in your library or a playlist and then choose File⇨ New⇨ Genius Playlist. After a bit of cogitation, Music presents a Genius playlist based on the song you clicked, as shown in Figure 17-7.

 Or try a Genius shuffle, which is an instant Genius playlist without the playlist. Select a song and then choose Controls⇨ Genius Shuffle (or press Option+spacebar), and a selection of songs that go great together plays. To see the songs selected by Genius, just click the Up Next/History button on the toolbar (and shown in the margin).

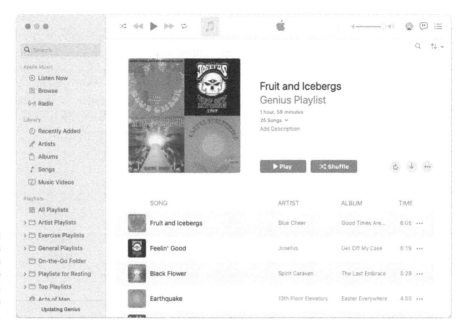

FIGURE 17-7:
Genius suggests
songs that go
nicely with the
song on which
the suggestions
are based.

Burning a playlist to CD

Another use for playlists is for burning audio CDs that you can listen to in almost any audio CD player. The only trick is making sure that the total playing time of the songs in the playlist is less than the capacity of the blank CD you're using, which is usually 74 to 80 minutes. Don't forget to account for the gap between tracks, which is 2 seconds by default. When you have all the songs you want on your CD in the playlist, choose File➪ Burn Playlist to Disc. The Burn Settings dialog appears.

Note that although the default type of disc Music burns is an audio CD, it can also burn two other types:

>> **MP3 CD** is a special format that can be played in many CD audio players and set-top DVD players. The cool thing about an MP3 CD is that rather than holding a mere 74 to 80 minutes of music, it can hold more than 100 songs! The uncool thing about MP3 CDs is that many older audio CD players won't play them.

>> **A data CD or DVD** is nothing more than a disc formatted to be read and mounted by any computer, Mac or Windows.

If you click the Burn button now, you'll get an audio CD. To burn an MP3 CD or Data CD or DVD, select the appropriate radio button in the Burn Settings dialog.

When you're satisfied, click the Burn button. In a few minutes, you'll have an audio CD that contains all the songs on the playlist — and plays the songs in the order in which they appeared in the playlist. Eject the freshly minted CD, label it lovingly before you forget, and take it for a test spin.

Chapter **18**

The Multimedia Mac

Media content is more than just music (the topic of Chapter 17), and your Mac is ready, willing, and able to handle almost any type of media (with almost any type of content) you can throw at it. Which is why, in addition to the aforementioned Music app, macOS includes apps for viewing and working with media (such as DVD movie discs and QuickTime movie files) as well as graphics in a variety of file formats (including PDF, TIFF, and JPEG).

In this chapter, you look at some bundled apps you can use to work with such media — namely QuickTime Player, TV, Books, Podcasts, Photo Booth, and Preview — followed by a brief section about importing your own media (photos and videos) into your Mac and the Image Capture app.

Playing Movies and Music in QuickTime Player

QuickTime is Apple's technology for digital media creation, delivery, and playback. It's used in myriad ways by apps such as Apple's iMovie, by websites such as YouTube (www.youtube.com), and in training videos delivered on CD or DVD.

QuickTime Player is the macOS app that lets you view QuickTime movies as well as streaming audio and video, QuickTime VR (Virtual Reality), and listen to many types of audio files as well. The quickest way to launch it is by clicking its icon in Launchpad or double-clicking its icon in the Applications folder. QuickTime Player is the default app for most QuickTime movie document files.

 I say most QuickTime movies because some will open QuickTime Player, and others will open the TV app or another video player. To change the app that opens for a particular movie, Control-click or right-click its icon in Finder and choose the app you prefer from the Open With submenu. However, this action opens the file with that app only this one time. To make the change permanent, press Option, and the Open With command becomes the Always Open With command.

TIP

To play a QuickTime movie, merely double-click its icon, and QuickTime Player launches itself.

Using QuickTime Player couldn't be easier. All its important controls are available right in the player window, as shown in Figure 18-1.

 The QuickTime Player's controls disappear when you're not using them. So, if you don't see the controls floating in front of your video, just hover the pointer over the QuickTime Player window and the controls will magically reappear.

TIP

FIGURE 18-1:
QuickTime Player
is simple to use.

Here are a few more QuickTime Player features you might find useful:

>> **The Movie Inspector window** (Window ⇨ Show/Hide Movie Inspector or ⌘+I) provides a lot of useful information about the current movie, such as its location on your hard drive and the file format, frames per second, file size, and duration.

>> **The Trim control** (Edit ⇨ Trim or ⌘+T) lets you delete frames from the beginning and end of a movie.

>> **The Share/More Menu** (click >> on the floating control bar) lets you send your movies to others via the Mail, Messages, Notes, or Photos apps or via AirDrop, or upload them to YouTube.

See Chapter 20 for details about the cool AirPlay Mirroring option, which lets you mirror what's on your Mac screen and view it on an HDTV wirelessly. The only thing you need is a smart TV with AirPlay or an Apple TV connected to your HDTV.

Watching TV

The TV app took over video storage and discovery duties from iTunes in 2019 (in macOS Catalina) — and it was about time. Now your video content lives in one place; it's easy to find more to rent or buy; and it's simple to add your own videos, too.

 The TV app's main window features five tabs: Watch Now, Apple TV+, Movies, TV Shows, and Library. All but Library suggest video content you can rent or buy from the iTunes Store.

Shopping for video is almost the same as shopping for music. Here are the steps:

1. **Select the appropriate tab.**

2. **Either click a link in the content pane or type in the Search field and press Return.**

   You can search for a movie title, a music video name, a TV show, an actor's or a director's name, or another keyword or phrase.

3. **When you find a video item that interests you, double-click it to see a preview or click the Buy button to purchase the episode or video.**

    Speaking of movies, don't forget to check out the picture-in-picture option, which works with most video content in the TV app, as well as videos on many websites. Just look for the little picture-in-picture icon (shown in the margin) at the bottom of the video player and click it to make your video float above all other pictures, as shown in Figure 18-2.

TIP

If you don't see a picture-in-picture icon on a video player, try Control-clicking or right-clicking the video. If it supports picture-in-picture, you'll see it in the pop-up menu.

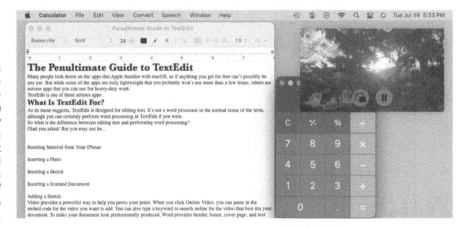

FIGURE 18-2:
The picture-in-picture video (upper right) continues to play and remains in front of TextEdit (left) and Calculator, even when one of those apps is active.

TIP

You can also add your own movies, TV shows, and home videos. To add a video file (such as MOV or MP4) from your hard drive, drag the file to the TV window or the TV dock icon, or choose File➪Import (⌘+O) and choose the file in the Open File dialog. In all cases, the file is added to your video library (click the Library tab to see it).

Using the Books App

Don't be surprised if you have to answer this question from an inquisitive child someday: "Is it true, Grandpa, that people once read books on paper?"

The Books app is Apple's answer to Amazon's Kindle. It's a combination ebook reader and bookstore. You can view your purchases (and free downloads) on any Apple device.

Everything that follows will make more sense if you have at least one ebook in your library. So the first thing to do is stock your virtual library with an ebook from the app's built-in Book Store. Don't worry. This won't cost you a penny unless you want it to — the store offers a healthy selection of free books!

So without further ado, here's how to acquire some ebooks (and audiobooks).

Buying an ebook or audiobook

First, launch the Books app in one of these ways:

>> Click Launchpad on the Dock, and then click Books.

>> Double-click Books in the Applications folder.

If this is your first time launching Books, you may be asked to sign in with your Apple ID and password. Do so (or don't) and then click the Get Started button.

Now, click Book Store (or Audiobook Store) in the sidebar.

TIP

If you've purchased Books from Apple in the past, they should appear automatically in your Books library.

You can look for books or audiobooks in many ways. After you select the Book Store tab, scroll down to see books organized into sections, which might include For You, Featured, Top Charts, New and Trending, More to Explore, and Bestsellers by Genre.

You can also search for a book or an author; just type a word or two in the Search field near the upper-left corner of the Books window and press Return.

When you see a book or ad that interests you, click it, and details will fill the screen, as shown in Figure 18-3.

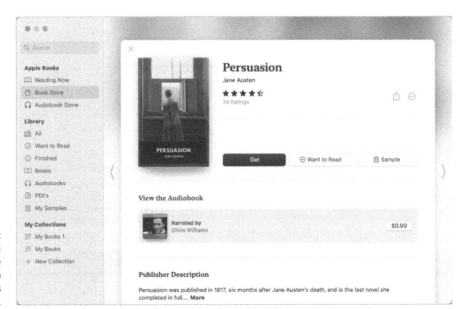

FIGURE 18-3:
Buy books from the Book Store and add them to your Books library.

Click the Buy button (which shows the price) to buy the book. Or for free books, click the Get button (shown in Figure 18-3) to add the book to your library for free.

TIP

Many books offer a free sample, or a chapter or chapters that you can download for free. Click the Sample button, and a sample will appear in your Books library within a few minutes.

One last thing: The big angle brackets to the left and right of the book description in Figure 18-3 are Previous and Next buttons. Click the one on the left to see the previous book in this section; click the one on the right to see the next book in this section.

When you finish shopping, click All in the sidebar's Library section to return to your Books library.

Shopping for ebooks without Apple

Books can also handle books you acquire elsewhere, and it supports a technical standard called *ePub*, which is a format that offers hundreds of thousands of free and public domain books on the web. You can import such files into Books, so you don't ever have to shop (or only shop) in the Book Store. The only possible gotcha is that the ePub titles must be *DRM-free*, which means free of any digital rights restrictions.

You can find ePub titles at numerous cyberspace destinations:

>> **Baen:** www.baen.com

>> **Feedbooks:** www.feedbooks.com

>> **Google Play:** Not all the books here are free, and Google has a downloadable app. https://play.google.com/store/books.

>> **Project Gutenberg:** www.gutenberg.us

>> **Smashwords:** www.smashwords.com

To import an ePub title, download the file to your Mac, fire up Books, and then do one of the following:

>> Choose File ⇨ Add to Library (or use its shortcut, ⌘+Shift+O), select the ePub file in the Open sheet, and click Add.

>> Drag the ePub file from Finder onto your Books library.

WARNING

You can't add books made for the Amazon Kindle to Books, not even ones that are DRM-free. You have to download the free Kindle app from the Mac App Store if you want to read Kindle books. Avoid book-conversion websites that claim to be able to convert Kindle-fomat ebooks to ePub-format ebooks. The conversion is unlikely to work, and the sites may try to install malware on your Mac.

TIP

You *can* add PDF files to Books; it works the same as adding an ePub title. After they're imported, they appear in the PDF section of your Books library.

Finally, for those who'd rather listen than read, you'll love that the Books app can read text aloud. To listen instead of reading, do the following:

1. Click at the spot where you want to begin from or select the text you want to hear.

2. Choose Edit ⇨ Speech ⇨ Start Speaking.

In a few seconds, a robotic voice will begin reading.

3. To stop, simply choose Edit ⇨ Speech ⇨ Stop Speaking.

It may not be quite like having Mom or Dad read you to sleep, but it can be a potential godsend for people with impaired vision.

Finding and Listening to Podcasts with the Podcasts App

Podcasts are like radio or television shows, except when you subscribe to them, you can listen to or watch them (using the Podcasts app on your Mac, iPad, or iPhone) at any time you like. Thousands of podcasts are available and many (or most) are free.

To find podcasts, launch the Podcasts app and follow these steps:

1. Click Browse or Charts in the sidebar.

2. Click a link in the content pane on the right or type a keyword or phrase in the Search field at the top of the sidebar.

3. When you find a podcast that appeals to you, do one of the following:

- *Click the Follow button to receive all future episodes of that podcast automatically.*

- *Click the Latest Episode button to listen to the latest episode immediately.*

- *Click the down arrow button to download the current episode of that podcast.*

4. **Click the ellipsis (. . .) for additional options.**

Figure 18-4 shows all these things for the Mac Geek Gab audio podcast from *The Mac Observer.*

For more information on most podcasts, just move the pointer over an episode of the podcast, and then click the ellipsis that appears, as shown in Figure 18-4.

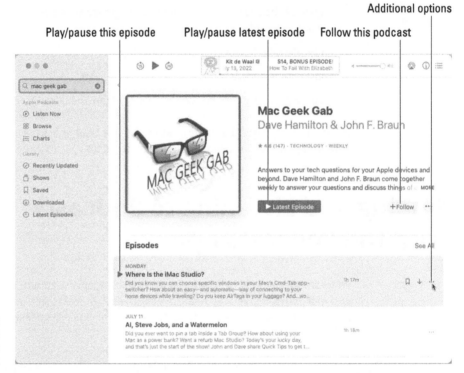

FIGURE 18-4:
The Mac Geek
Gab podcast from
The Mac Observer.

Following (formerly subscribing to) a podcast offers several options. You can configure how often the Podcasts app checks for new episodes (hourly, daily, weekly, or manually), what to do when new episodes become available (download the most recent one, download all episodes, or do nothing), and how many episodes to keep in your Podcasts library (all, all unplayed, or a specific number between 2 and 10). To specify these settings, click a podcast you've followed in your library, click the ellipsis (. . .), and choose the appropriate option from the shortcut menu.

When you start listening to a followed podcast on your Mac in the Podcast app and switch to an iPhone or iPad, the podcast will pick up where it left off on your Mac.

You're the Star with Photo Booth

The Photo Booth app provides all the fun of an old-time (or new-time) photo booth, like the ones you sometimes see in malls or stores. It lets you shoot one photo, shoot a burst of four photos in a row, or shoot a movie using your Mac's built-in camera. If yours is one of the rare Macs with no built-in camera (such as the Mac mini) or you own a USB webcam better than the built-in model, you'll be pleased to hear that most USB webcams work with Photo Booth right out of the box with no drivers or other software necessary. Just launch Photo Booth and look in the Camera menu, where all compatible cameras appear.

TIP

If you have an iPhone, you can use it as your Photo Booth webcam by using Ventura's Continuity Camera feature.

Photo Booth couldn't be easier to use. Start by clicking one of the three icons in the lower-left corner of the Photo Booth window — Burst (of four photos), Single Photo (selected in Figure 18-5), or Movie — and then click the big, red camera button to take a picture, as shown in Figure 18-5.

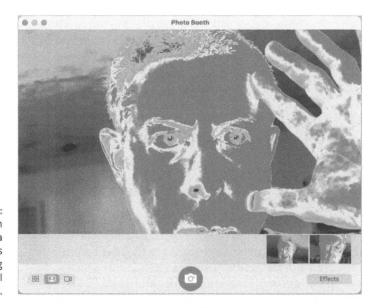

FIGURE 18-5:
Photo Booth about to take a picture of yours truly using the Thermal Camera effect.

Before you shoot, you may want to explore the five pages of special effects — Sepia Tone, Color Pencil, Pop Art, and dozens more — by clicking the Effects button (lower right) and then clicking the particular effect you want to try. If you like it, click the big, red camera button and shoot a picture, pictures, or video; if you don't, click the Effects button again and click another effect. Or if you prefer to shoot with no effects, click the Normal effect in the center of all the Effects pages.

TIP

Photo Booth includes a feature called Screen Flash, which uses your computer display as a camera flash by turning the screen all-white as it shoots the photo. If *your* screen isn't flashing when you shoot, look in the Camera menu and make sure that the Enable Screen Flash command has a check mark. Screen Flash is disabled when you're shooting movies.

After you shoot, your pictures or movies drop into the tray at the bottom of the window (there are two photos in Figure 18-5). You can then select one or more photos in the tray and then do any of the following:

>> **Delete them** by pressing the Delete or Backspace key.

>> **Share them** by clicking the Share button, which replaces the Effects button when one or more photos are selected in the tray.

>> **Export them as JPEG files** by choosing File ⇨ Export.

>> **Print them** by choosing File ⇨ Print or pressing ⌘+P.

>> **Drag them from the tray** to the desktop, a folder, an email, or an iMessage, where they appear as JPEG files; or drag them onto an image editor icon such as Photos (on the Dock or in the Applications folder). Note that they're not automatically saved in your Photos library or elsewhere, so if you don't drag them somewhere, they exist only in the tray of the Photo Booth app.

Viewing and Converting Images and PDFs in Preview

You use Preview to open, view, and print PDFs as well as most graphics files (TIFF, JPEG, PICT, and so on). *PDF files* are formatted documents that can include text and images. User manuals, books, and the like are often distributed as PDF files. You can't edit the existing text in a PDF file with Preview, but you can leaf through its pages, annotate and mark it up, and print it. You can often select text and graphics in a PDF file, copy them to the Clipboard (⌘+C), and paste (⌘+V) them into documents in other apps. Preview is also the app that pops open when you click the Preview button in the Print dialog, as I describe in Chapter 20.

Actually, that's not entirely true. You can edit one certain type of PDF file: a form that has blank fields. Preview allows you to fill in the blanks and then resave the document. And although it's technically not editing, you can annotate a PDF document by using the Annotate tools on the toolbar, and add, delete, or reorder pages in the sidebar.

One of the most useful things Preview can do is change the file format of a graphic file. For example, say you're signing up for a website and want to add a picture to your profile. The website requires pictures in the JPEG file format, but the picture file on your hard drive that you'd like to use is in the TIFF file format. Preview can handle the conversion for you:

1. **Double-click the TIFF file to open it with Preview.**

   If another app (such as Adobe Photoshop) opens instead of Preview, drag the TIFF document onto the Preview icon or launch Preview and choose File ⇨ Open (⌘+O) to open the TIFF file.

2. **Choose File ⇨ Export to open the Export dialog.**

3. **Choose the appropriate file format — such as JPEG or PNG — from the Format pop-up menu.**

4. **(Optional) If you want to make sure you don't confuse your original image with the one in the new format, change the name of your file in the Export As field.**

5. **(Optional) Add a tag or tags if you like.**

6. **Click Save.**

Preview lets you convert any file it can open to any of the following file formats: HEIC, JPEG, JPEG-2000, OpenEXR, PDF, PNG, and TIFF. Or choose File ⇨ Export as PDF to export the current file as a PDF.

HEIC is Apple's High Efficiency Image format, which creates smaller files with a higher image quality than JPEG. The upside is smaller files; the downside is that not all apps that will open a JPEG file will open an HEIC file.

You'll probably never need to convert a file to most of these formats, but it's nice to know that you can if you need to.

Almost every macOS app with a Print command allows you to save your document as a PDF file. Just click on the PDF button (found in all Print dialogs) and choose Save as PDF from the pop-up menu. Then, should you ever need to convert that PDF file to a different file format, you can do so by using the preceding steps.

Chapter **19**

Publish or Perish: Creating Documents and Printing

Your Mac is great for creating attractive documents and for printing them to create hard copies that you can share with others. In this chapter, I dig into four key aspects of the document-creation process. We start with the Font Book app, which enables you to get the fonts you need onto your Mac so that you can use them in your documents. We move on to creating text-based documents with Apple's TextEdit app or with more powerful alternatives. Then we examine how to connect printers to your Mac before examining how to print documents that look the way you want them to.

First up: Font Book and fonts.

Font Mania

You can jazz up your documents, or make them a little more serious, with different fonts. To a computer user, *font* means *typeface* — what the text characters look like. Although professional typographers will scream at this generalization, we'll go with this definition for this chapter.

Tens of thousands of fonts are available for the Mac. You don't want to use the same font for both a garage-sale flyer and a résumé, right? Luckily for you, macOS comes with hundreds of fonts. Some fonts are pretty staid, such as Times New Roman, but macOS gives you some artsy ones too, such as Brush Script.

If you *really* get into fonts, you can buy single fonts and font collections anywhere you can buy software. Plenty of shareware and public-domain fonts are also available from online services and user groups. Some people have thousands of fonts. Some people even *use* thousands of fonts.

To see how to manage the third-party fonts you collect, check out the upcoming section "Managing your fonts with Font Book."

Choosing font typefaces

macOS Ventura supports a wide variety of font formats, including OpenType, Mac TrueType, Windows TrueType, bitmap, and dfont. So pretty much any font you buy or download will probably work with macOS.

TECHNICAL STUFF

The big exception is PostScript fonts. macOS used to support most kinds of PostScript fonts, but Apple removed this support in macOS 10.15 (Catalina). So if your Mac runs macOS Ventura, you can't use PostScript fonts.

Managing your fonts with Font Book

The Font Book app lets you view your installed fonts, install new fonts, group your fonts in collections, and activate and deactivate installed fonts. Like any self-respecting app, Font Book lives in the Applications folder, so you can run it directly from there, or you can click the Launchpad icon on the Dock and then click the Font Book icon.

TIP

Before you install any fonts, know this: By default, Font Book installs new fonts only for the current user (which would be you). In this case, Font Book puts new fonts in your Home folder's Fonts folder, which is inside your invisible Library folder (/Users/Home/Library/Fonts). If you want to install fonts for all users of your Mac, choose Font Book ⇨ Settings, click the Installation tab of the Settings dialog, open the Default Install Location pop-up menu, and then click All Users. This setting makes Font Book put the fonts you install in the main Library folder (/Library/Fonts).

The easiest way to install a new font is to double-click it in Finder. Font Book opens and displays the font. Click the Install Font button to install the font.

Starting from Font Book, you can install a font by choosing File ⇨ Add Fonts. This command appears as Add Fonts to Current User if you've set the Default Install Location setting to Current User; if you've chosen All Users as the Default Install Location, the command appears as Add Fonts to All Users. Whichever way the command appears, you can also press ⌘+O to invoke it from the keyboard. A standard Open dialog appears. Select the font or fonts to install, and click the Open button.

Font Book can display the font list in three views:

>> **Grid:** Choose View ⇨ As Grid or press ⌘+1 to switch to this view. Each font appears as a thumbnail showing a character or two; you can drag the slider on the toolbar to increase or decrease the size of a thumbnail. Grid view is useful for getting a quick overview of the available fonts.

>> **Samples:** Choose View ⇨ As Samples or press ⌘+2 to use this view. Each font appears in a box that shows a healthy sample of the font. Samples view is great for seeing how each font looks, but you can see only a few fonts at a time.

>> **List:** Choose View ⇨ As List or press ⌘+3 for this view. All the fonts appear in a list, with each font family in an expandable section, like folders in List view in Finder. Click the > icon to expand a font family; click the resulting downward caret to collapse it again. Figure 19-1 shows Font Book in List view.

To view or find fonts, start by clicking the appropriate item in the sidebar. The sidebar contains three expandable lists: Fonts, which lets you choose among All Fonts (really all of them), All User Fonts (all the fonts installed for users), and My Fonts (just your fonts); Languages, which lets you choose any installed language; and Collections, which breaks the fonts into collections such as Fixed Width, Fun, Modern, Traditional, and Web.

So you might click All Fonts in the Fonts list to display all the fonts in the main part of the window (as in Figure 19-1), or click Fixed Width in the Collections list to display just fixed-width fonts.

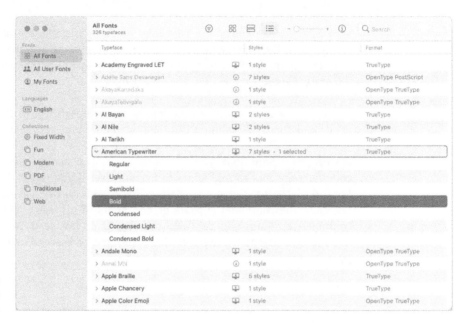

FIGURE 19-1:
Font Book in
List view.

To view a font or font family, double-click its name in the Font list. The font appears in the main part of the window, and you can switch between Specimen view (which shows a single style of the font) and Sample view (which shows all styles of the font deployed on the canonical *quick brown fox* sentence) by clicking the Specimen button or the Sample button on the toolbar. Figure 19-2 shows Sample view.

Drag the Text Size slider to change the size of the text, and click Back (<) when you want to return to the Font list.

To deactivate a font so that it no longer appears on any app's Font menu, Control-click or right-click it and then choose Deactivate from the contextual menu. To reactivate a previously deactivated font, Control-click or right-click it and then choose Activate from the contextual menu.

If a font's name is gray instead of black, that font is available but not yet downloaded to your Mac. To download and enable it, Control-click or right-click it and then choose Download from the contextual menu. After you download the font, Font Book activates it automatically, so you don't need to activate it manually.

Font Book looks out for your best interests, in that it won't allow you to deactivate or delete any fonts required by macOS itself — including (but not limited to) Lucida Grande, Helvetica, and Helvetica Neue.

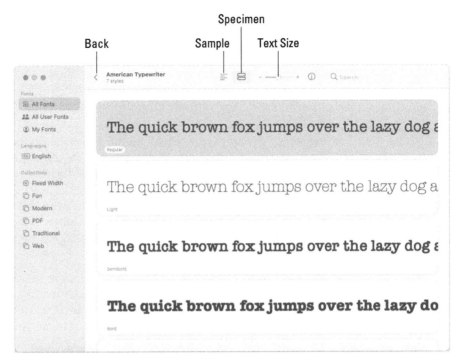

Specimen

Back   Sample   Text Size

FIGURE 19-2:
After displaying a
font, you can
switch between
Specimen view
and Sample view
(shown here).

WARNING

Refrain from installing more fonts than you'll use. Having tons of installed fonts can slow some apps and make the Font menu long and unmanageable. And the longer your Font menu gets, the longer it'll take the menu to appear after you click it. Bottom line: Install only the fonts you need. Your Mac will thank you.

Creating Documents

When you've sorted out your fonts, you're ready to create documents with them. This section quickly reviews your four main options for creating word-processing documents on your Mac, starting with TextEdit, which comes with macOS:

>> **TextEdit:** Like earlier versions of macOS, Ventura includes TextEdit, a powerful text editor that also offers modest word-processing capabilities. TextEdit lives in the Applications folder, so you can run it from there or from Launchpad. TextEdit is great for creating and editing text files, but it also supports basic formatting such as fonts and font sizes; boldface, italic, and underline; alignment; line spacing; and bulleted and numbered lists.

TextEdit can open files in Microsoft Word's .docx format, but you'll find that some formatting and most objects drop out. Compare Figure 19-3, which shows a Word document open in TextEdit, and Figure 19-4, which shows the same document open in the Pages app, retaining almost all the formatting and all the objects (including two images, the header, and the watermark).

>> **Pages:** Apple's Pages app, which you can download for free from the App Store, is a powerful word processor that runs on the Mac, the iPhone, and the iPad. You can also log in to your iCloud account and work with the web version of Pages. Pages syncs documents via your iCloud account, enabling you to work on them anywhere. As you can see in Figure 19-4, Pages has a clean interface and enables you to include a wide variety of objects — including tables, charts, shapes, and media files — in your documents along with text.

>> **Microsoft Word:** One of the main apps in the Microsoft 365 suite (formerly Microsoft Office), Word is a powerful word processor that's so widely used as to be the industry standard. Word runs on Windows PCs, Macs, iPhones, iPads, and Android devices; a web version is also available. Word provides soup-to-nuts word-processing capabilities, which means that you can use Word to create almost any kind of document.

Buying Word tends to involve complex decisions, but for most people, the best choice is one of the Microsoft 365 subscriptions, which include access to other key apps (such as Excel and PowerPoint) and provide bug fixes and new features via rolling updates. To see the available subscription plans, go to https://www.microsoft365.com. (This URL will redirect you to a site specific to your country or region.)

>> **Google Docs:** One of the leading apps in Google Workspace, Google Docs is an online-based word processing app. Google recommends its Chrome browser for accessing Google Workspace, but other browsers (such as Safari and Mozilla Firefox) usually work well. Google provides a Google Docs app for iOS and Android devices enables you to work on your documents easily without having to mess with a browser-based interface on a small screen. Google Docs has essential word-processing capabilities, including styles (for quick and consistent formatting) and revision tracking, but those features are much more limited than Microsoft Word's.

Google offers various plans for Google Workspace; see https://workspace.google.com.

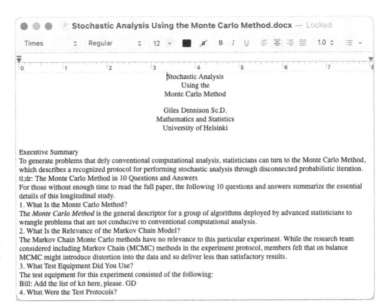

FIGURE 19-3:
A sample
Microsoft Word
document open
in TextEdit.

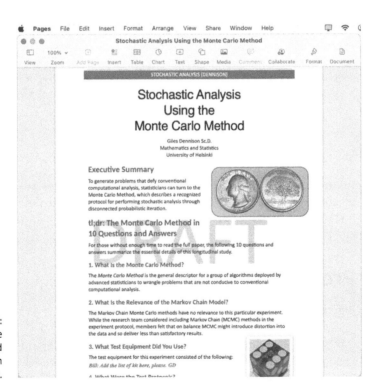

FIGURE 19-4:
The same
Microsoft Word
document open
in the Pages app.

WHAT'S THE DIFFERENCE BETWEEN A TEXT EDITOR AND A WORD PROCESSOR?

Glad you asked — but the answer is that the difference between the two isn't entirely hard and fast.

Generally speaking, a *text editor* is an app for writing and editing unadorned text — text without formatting or objects such as images or tables. Using a text editor should help you focus on the text without worrying about formatting and layout.

By contrast, a *word processor* is an app for writing, editing, formatting, laying out, proofing, reviewing, and revising documents that may include images and other objects as well as text. A word processor typically offers a WYSIWYG (What You See Is What You Get, pronounced *whizzy-wig*) mode that lets you see (almost) exactly how the document's pages will look when printed. Microsoft Word, for example, defaults to Page Layout view, which shows how the document's pages look, including any headers and footers.

In the olden days of the last millennium, most text editors and word processors maintained their distinctions pretty clearly. Nowadays, text editors increasingly provide features such as formatting, the capability to include images, and spelling checkers, so there's no longer a bright line between a text editor and a word processor.

Printing

Printing should be straightforward but often isn't. To make sure that you're set up to print without any headaches, this section walks you through the process of installing and configuring a printer, as though you've just unpacked a new printer and plugged it in.

Pre-printer prep

Before you start, keep these three essentials in mind:

>> **Read the documentation that came with your printer.** Hundreds of printer makes and models that work with the Mac are available, so if your printer's manual tells you to do something different from what this chapter recommends, follow the manual's instructions first. If that approach doesn't work, try the techniques in this chapter.

>> **The Print and Page Setup dialogs differ slightly (or even greatly) from app to app and from printer to printer.** Although this chapter's examples are representative of what you'll *probably* encounter, you may come across dialogs that look a bit different. The Print and Page Setup dialogs for Word, for example, include extra choices, such as Even or Odd Pages Only, Print Hidden Text, and Print Selection Only. If your Print dialog or Page Setup dialog contains commands that this chapter doesn't explain, they're specific to that app; look in its documentation for an explanation. Similarly, many graphics-related apps — such as Adobe Illustrator and Photoshop — have added their own Print dialog, which appears before the macOS Print dialog with check boxes, radio buttons, and other controls, to the point at which you might not even recognize them as being Print dialogs.

>> **Don't forget about Help.** Help is built into macOS and keeps getting better and better. Many third-party apps also support this excellent Apple technology, which can be the fastest way to figure out how to use a feature that has you stumped. Be sure to check out the Help menu before you panic.

Ready: Connecting and adding your printer

Before you can even think about printing something, you have to connect a printer to your Mac and inform it (and macOS) that the printer exists.

If you have a printer and are already able to print documents, you can skip to "Set: Setting up your document with Page Setup" later in this chapter. This section pertains only to setting up a new printer.

Connecting your printer

Read your printer's documentation for specific details on how to set up your particular printer model, such as how to load the ink or toner cartridges and remove any hidden seals they use.

Here are the general steps for connecting a printer to your Mac:

1. **Connect the printer to your Mac, with the cable snugly attached to both the printer and Mac.**

    Ignore this step if your printer supports wireless printing and you intend to print only wirelessly. Also ignore this step if your printer is a network-capable model and you've connected it to your network's switch or router with an Ethernet cable (again, snugly at each end).

For your printer to work, you have to connect it to a data source somehow. Connecting with a cable is usually more reliable than connecting wirelessly.

2. **Plug the printer's AC power cord into a power outlet in the wall, on a power strip, or on an uninterruptible power supply (UPS).**

Plugging an inkjet printer into a UPS works fine, but be careful with laser printers, because they typically draw a lot of power briefly while heating their fuser rollers in preparation for printing. This power draw can swamp the UPS and rob other devices of power. To avoid this potential problem, plug your laser printer into one of the surge-protected sockets on the UPS to protect the printer from power spikes; don't plug the laser printer into one of the battery-powered sockets.

3. **Turn on your printer.**

Look in the manual if you can't find the power switch. (The switch is on the printer, and the manual will tell you where.)

Setting up a printer for the first time

After you connect your computer and printer and provide a power source for your printer, you're ready to configure your Mac to communicate with the printer.

Many, if not all, of the steps involving the Printers & Scanners pane of System Settings require your printer to be turned on and warmed up — that is, already done with its diagnostics and start-up cycle. So before doing anything else, make sure that your printer is turned on, warmed up, and connected to your Mac.

The first time you connect your printer, you may see an alert asking whether you want to download and install software for your printer. You do, so click the Install button. At this point, you may see a License Agreement window. If so, click the Agree button to proceed. (You may click Disagree if you want, but you'll only halt the installation process.)

If you connect a new printer and *don't* see an alert, don't worry; just follow the upcoming instructions.

After you click the Install button and the Agree button, a Software Update window may appear, telling you that it's finding software. If it does, just leave it alone; it disappears after a minute or two. Don't click the Stop button unless you want to abort the installation.

Here are the steps for setting up a printer for the first time:

1. **Choose System Settings ⇨ Printers & Scanners to display the Printers & Scanners pane of System Settings.**

2. **Click the Add Printer, Scanner, or Fax button to open the Add Printer dialog (shown in Figure 19-5 with settings chosen).**

3. **At the top of the Add Printer dialog, make sure that the Default tab is displayed.**

   If it's not, click the Default button (the printer icon at the left end of the toolbar).

   The IP button (the globe icon in the middle of the toolbar) is for connecting to printers shared via =Internet Protocol (IP), including printers shared across the Internet.

   The Windows button (the printer icon at the right end of the toolbar) is for connecting to printers shared by Windows computers on the network.

4. **In the list box, select the printer you want to add.**

   The printer's default details appear in the Name box, the Location box, and the Use pop-up menu.

5. **(Optional) In the Name box, change the printer's name.**

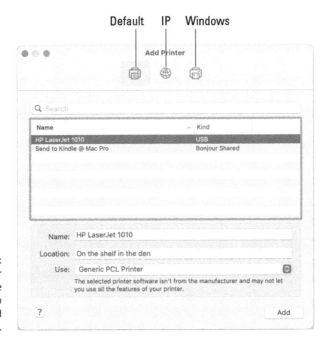

FIGURE 19-5:
Select your printer on the Default tab of the Add Printer dialog.

The printer normally appears listed by its model number, which usually isn't very informative. You may want to call the printer something more descriptive, such as *Little color printer*, especially if you'll be sharing it with other people on your network.

6. **(Optional) In the Location box, type a description of the printer's whereabouts.**

   Like the name, the location is important when you share the printer on the network. You may want to type **In the den** or **On top of the refrigerator** in this box.

7. **If the Use pop-up menu is set to Generic PCL Printer, try to find and choose a more-specific driver.**

   Click the pop-up menu and choose Select Software to open the Printer Software dialog (see Figure 19-6). Select the best driver match by browsing or by searching and then click OK.

   If there's no suitable match, click the Cancel button to close the Printer Software dialog. Download the latest driver from the printer manufacturer's website, and run its installer. Then open the Printer Software dialog again, select the new driver, and click OK.

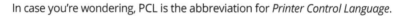

8. **Back in the Add Printer dialog, click the Add button.**

   If the Setting Up [printer name] dialog appears (see Figure 19-7), select or deselect the check boxes for any features that macOS suspects the printer may have, as needed. The HP LaserJet shown in the figure doesn't have a duplexer, for example, so you'd deselect the Duplexer check box.

TECHNICAL STUFF

FIGURE 19-6: Select a suitable driver in the Printer Software dialog.

FIGURE 19-7:
In the Setting Up
[printer name]
dialog, select or
deselect the
check boxes for
printer features.

9. **Click OK.**

The Add Printer dialog closes, and the printer appears in the Printers &
Scanners pane (see Figure 19-8).

10. **From the Default Printer pop-up menu, choose the printer you want to
use by default.**

Your choices are a specific printer (such as the printer you just installed) and
Last Printer Used.

11. **From the Default Paper Size pop-up menu, choose the default paper size
you want to use with this printer, such as US Letter.**

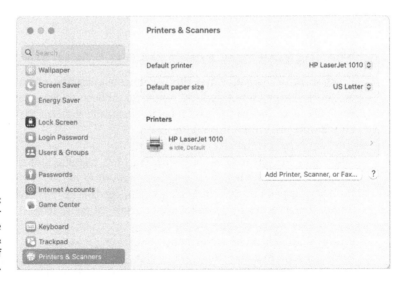

FIGURE 19-8:
The printer
appears in the
Printers &
Scanners pane of
System Settings.

GO FOR A DRIVER

Apple includes a library of printer drivers with macOS Ventura, which covers many popular printer brands and models. These drivers are installed by default. macOS also checks to see whether a newer driver is available — for every driver in its library — and if it finds one, it offers to download and install the new driver (as described earlier in this chapter).

If macOS can't find a driver for your printer, you need to install the appropriate printer drivers manually before your printer will appear in the Printers list in the Printers & Scanners pane of System Settings. So find and download the driver at the manufacturer's website, install it, and get ready to print.

One more thing: Most printer manufacturers introduce new drivers with enhanced functionality. If a CD came in the box with your printer (which happens less and less often these days), the driver on it is most likely out of date. So ignore the CD and let macOS take care of installing or updating the printer driver if possible. And if for some reason macOS can't manage it (which is rare), download the most recent version from the vendor's website rather than install the probably-outdated version on the CD that came with the printer.

12. **Close System Settings.**

You're ready to print your first document! Before you do, however, make sure that you have the document set up to look just the way you want it to look. See "Set: Setting up your document with Page Setup" later in this chapter for more info.

Sharing your Mac's printer on the network

If you want to share a printer that's connected directly to your Mac (with others on your wired or wireless local network), choose System Settings⇨ Printers & Scanners, click the printer to display its pane, and then set the Share This Printer on the Network switch to on (blue).

When you do, you may see a yellow warning triangle and the message *Printer sharing is turned off*. Click the Open Sharing Settings button to rock right on over to the Sharing pane of System Settings, and set the Printer Sharing switch to on (blue). If macOS prompts you to authenticate yourself, do so.

Printer sharing is on now. Normally, that setting means that everyone on the network can print to your printer. If you want to mitigate the onslaught of print jobs, click the Info (i) button to the right of the Printer Sharing switch and then work in the Printer Sharing dialog (shown in Figure 19-9 with the settings changed).

FIGURE 19-9:
In the Printer
Sharing dialog,
choose which
users can print to
your shared
printer.

By default, the only entry in the Users box is the Everyone group, which receives Can Print permission. To change this setting, click the Add (+) button, select the appropriate users or groups in the resulting dialog, and then click the Select button. The Users box in the Printer Sharing dialog shows the users and groups you chose with no permission entry (which means they can print), and the Everyone group with the No Access permission, which means that other people can't print. Click the Done button to close the Printer Sharing dialog.

Set: Setting up your document with Page Setup

After setting up your printer, you can print — but you need to make the right choices in the Page Setup dialog to get the printout to look the way you want. This dialog enables you to choose your target printer, paper size, page orientation, and scale. To open this dialog, you usually choose File ⇨ Page Setup. Some apps use a different command, such as File ⇨ Print Setup, so be prepared to look around if necessary. Figure 19-10 shows the Print Setup dialog for the TextEdit app.

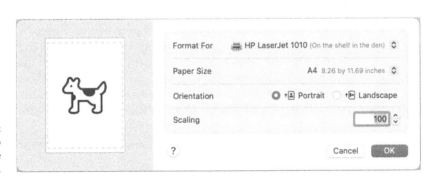

FIGURE 19-10:
The Page Setup
dialog in the
TextEdit app.

If you're using a network printer, the Print Setup or Page Setup dialog might look a bit different, but working out how to use it should be easy.

The options in the Page Setup dialog are as follows:

>> **Format For:** On this pop-up menu, you find the names of all recognized printers. If you have several printers configured, you can choose any of them from this menu.

   This menu usually defaults to Any Printer, which is the least-effective setting. Unless the printer you want to use appears here, you may not get full functionality when you print.

>> **Paper Size:** Use this pop-up menu to choose the type of paper that's currently in the paper tray of your printer or the size of the paper that you want to feed manually. The dimensions of the paper that you can choose appear after its name.

>> **Orientation:** Select the Portrait radio button to print the page in portrait orientation (like a letter, taller than it is wide). Select the Landscape radio button to print in landscape orientation (wider than it is tall).

>> **Scaling:** To print your page at a larger or smaller size, change this option to a larger or smaller percentage.

All these options remain in effect until you choose different settings. After you print an envelope, for example, don't forget to change the Paper Size setting back to Letter before trying to print on letter-size paper again.

Some apps offer additional Page Setup options. If your app offers them, they usually appear on the Settings pop-up menu in the Page Setup dialog. (Apps such as Photoshop and Word have extra options; TextEdit doesn't.)

Preview: Checking the page and setting PDF options in the Preview app

To see a preview of what your printed page will look like, click the PDF pop-up menu at the bottom of the Print dialog, and choose Open in Preview. This command makes the Preview app display the pages that you're about to print.

As you probably know, macOS can save any printable document as a PDF file. To do so, click the PDF pop-up menu at the bottom of the Print dialog and choose Save As PDF.

If you have any doubt about the way a document will look when you print it, check out Preview first. When you're happy with the document preview, just choose File ➪ Print, press ⌘+P, or click the Print button at the bottom of the Preview window. Or click the Cancel button to return to your app and make changes to the document.

Preview works with the Preview app. With the Preview feature, you can do cool things like these:

>> See all the pages in your document the way they'll be printed, one by one.

>> Zoom in or out to get a different perspective on what you're about to send to the printer. (Pretty cool!)

>> Rotate the picture 90 degrees to the left or right.

>> Insert (via drag and drop), delete, or reorder pages in Preview's sidebar.

>> Spot errors before you print something. A little up-front inspection can save paper, ink or toner, and frustration.

 Click the Show Markup Toolbar icon (shown in the margin) to display the Markup toolbar, which provides tools for marking up a document. See Chapter 5 for more information on Markup.

Check out the Preview app's View menu, where you'll find (among other things) four useful views: Content Only, Thumbnails, Table of Contents, and Contact Sheet, as well as the zoom commands (and more).

Also check out Preview's toolbar, from which you can add or delete icons by choosing View ➪ Customize Toolbar.

And speaking of tools, don't miss the selections in the Tools menu, which let you rotate pages, move forward or backward through multipage documents, and unleash the awesomeness of Magnifier.

TIP

The Magnifier tool is so cool that it has a rare single-key keyboard shortcut. That key is the ` (the backtick, which usually shares a key with the tilde); press it to show or hide Magnifier.

Print: Printing from the Print dialog

After you connect and configure your printer and set up how you want your document to print, you come to the final steps before that joyous moment when your printed page pops out of the printer. Navigating the Print dialog is the last thing standing between you and your output.

Although most Print dialogs that you see look like the figures shown here, others may differ slightly (or, occasionally, greatly). The features in the Print dialog depend on the app from which you're printing. Many apps choose to use the standard-issue Apple dialog, but not all do. If this section doesn't explain a certain feature that you see, chances are good that the feature is specific to the app or printer you're using, in which case the documentation for that app or printer should offer an explanation.

Printing a document

Follow these steps to print a document:

1. **Open the document that you want to print.**

2. **Choose File ⇨ Print (or press ⌘+P).**

   Some apps locate the Print command on a different menu or use a different shortcut, but you'll find the command easily enough.

   You see the basic Print dialog, shown in Figure 19-11.

3. **Click Print.**

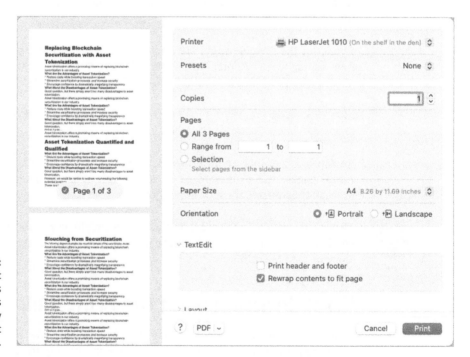

FIGURE 19-11:
A basic Print dialog. This one is from TextEdit, as you can tell by the TextEdit section.

4. **Wait a moment for your Mac to tell the printer what to do and for the pages to print.**

5. **Pick up the printed pages from the printer.**

Choosing among printers

Just as you can in the Page Setup dialog, you can choose which printer you want to use from the Printer pop-up menu at the top of the Print dialog.

REMEMBER

You can choose only among the printers you added via the Printers & Scanners pane of System Settings, as explained in "Setting up a printer for the first time" earlier in this chapter. This list includes printers connected to wireless base stations and routers, as well as Wi-Fi–enabled printers. After you've set up a Wi-Fi–enabled printer, Macs (and other devices) within range can print to it wirelessly.

Choosing custom settings

In addition to the drop-down Printer menu, your expanded Print dialog offers the following options:

» **Presets:** This pop-up menu lets you manage and save print settings, as described in "Saving custom settings" later in this chapter.

» **Copies:** In this text field, set how many copies you want to print. The Print dialog defaults to one (1) in most apps, so if you want a single copy, you don't need to change anything. To print more copies, replace the 1 with the appropriate number, either by typing it or by clicking the up- or down-arrow button.

» **Pages:** Here, you find three radio buttons: All, Range From, and Selection. The default behavior is to print your entire document, so the All option is preselected. To print only a specific page or range of pages, select the Range From radio button and type the desired page numbers in the From and To text fields. To print selected pages, select the Selection radio button; then, in the sidebar, select the circle at the bottom of each page you want to print (as shown in Figure 19-11).

» **Paper Size:** From this pop-up menu, choose the type of paper that's already in your printer's paper tray or the paper that you want to feed manually. The dimensions of the paper appear below its name.

TIP

The Paper Size setting is also in the Page Setup dialog. The difference is that the settings in the Print dialog apply only to *this document,* whereas the settings in Page Setup are the default for *all documents* and remain in effect until you change them.

>> **Orientation:** This setting also appears in the Page Setup dialog, and once again, the choice you make is the default for all pages you print. Choose the options here to tell your printer whether the page you want to print should be portrait- or landscape-oriented.

The settings you choose in the Print dialog apply only to this document.

Farther down the Print dialog, you can configure settings that are specific to the app you're using, as well as Layout, Paper Handling, Printer Options, and Printer Info settings. You won't need to change these settings frequently, but it's helpful to know which ones are available before you need them:

>> **App-specific settings (here, TextEdit):** The only TextEdit-specific options are two check boxes. Select or deselect the Print Header and Footer check box to control whether the printout includes the document's header and footer. Select or deselect the Rewrap Contents to Fit Page check box to control whether TextEdit rewraps lines to fit on the page or simply prints them as they stand.

The preview in the sidebar shows the effect of selecting and clearing these check boxes.

>> **Layout:** Expand the Layout section by clicking its heading. Then you can configure the following settings:

- *Pages per Sheet:* Open this pop-up menu and choose the number of document pages to print on each sheet of pager: 1 (the default, as you'd hope), 2, 4, 6, 9, or 16.

- *Layout Direction:* Choose one of the four icons to specify how multiple document pages are laid out on the printed page.

- *Border:* Your choices on this pop-up menu are None, Single Hairline, Single Thin Line, Double Hairline, and Double Thin Line.

- *Two-Sided:* If your printer supports two-sided (known as *duplex*) printing, the three radio buttons allow you to specify whether you're going to use two-sided printing, and if so, whether you'll be binding (or stapling) along the long or short edge of the paper or creating a booklet.

- *Reverse Page Orientation:* Set this switch to on (blue) to flip the pages upside down.

- *Flip Horizontally:* Set this switch to on (blue) to flip the pages horizontally.

>> **Paper Handling:** Expand the Paper Handling section if you want to collate the printed sheets, reverse the order in which the document's pages print, or print only the odd- or even-numbered pages. You can also specify whether the

document's paper size is to be used (in which case you might have lines that break across pages) or whether the output should be scaled to fit the chosen paper size.

>> **Printer Options:** Expand this section to reach the Paper Feed and Printer Features buttons. Click the Info (i) icon on the right of one of these buttons to display the Paper Feed or Printer Features dialog, in which you can choose further settings.

>> **Printer Info:** Expand this section to see information about the printer: its name, location, and model (actually the printer driver, not the printer model). The most useful information here is Supply Levels, which tells you how much ink or toner the printer has left. Sadly, the Supply Levels data isn't available for all printers.

Saving custom settings

After you customize your printer settings just the way you like them, you can save them for future use. Just click the Presets pop-up menu, choose Save Current Settings as Preset, and then provide a name for this preset. In the Available For area, select the radio button for the current printer to make the preset available only for that printer, or select the All Printers radio button to make the preset available to other printers as well.

From then on, the preset name appears as an option on the Presets pop-up menu. Choose your saved preset before you print any document, and all the individual settings associated with that preset are restored.

To manage your presets, choose Edit Preset List from the Print dialog's Presets pop-up menu. This nifty feature displays a list of your presets and their settings, and allows you to delete a present or rename it by double-clicking the current name and typing a new one.

5
Care and Feeding

Chapter **20**

Features for the Way You Work

This chapter delves into some macOS features that might very well improve the ways you interact with your Mac. These features are more esoteric than the mainstream apps and features you read about earlier in this book, so don't feel obliged to use them. But you should at least know about these features, because they can make you and your Mac a more productive team.

Get ready to roll up your sleeves and dig into these features. First up: Dark mode; the Mac App Store; and Continuity Camera, which lets you use your iPhone or iPad as a camera or scanner for your Mac.

Going Over to the Dark Side

macOS has long been celebrated for its bright and beautiful interface, which helps make computing a pleasure. But if you sometimes find the default macOS look too bright for comfort, you can reduce the screen's brightness by enabling Dark mode. As you can see in the top screen in Figure 20-1, Dark mode completely changes the appearance of windows, buttons, menus, and other interface elements from Light mode (shown in the bottom screen).

FIGURE 20-1: Three windows, the menu bar, and the Dock in Dark mode (top) and Light mode (bottom).

To choose Dark (or Light) mode, open the System Settings app, click Appearance in the sidebar, and then click Dark (or Light). Or click Auto to have macOS switch between the Light appearance and the Dark appearance based on the time of day.

TIP Try changing the accent and highlight colors in Dark mode; they look slightly different than in Light mode.

App Shopping Made Easy

Introduced in 2011, the Mac App Store is the largest catalog of Mac software in the world. Apple has made the App Store easy to navigate and use.

You'll find interesting new apps and recently updated apps in the Discover tab.

The Arcade tab is home to the Apple Arcade subscription service, which offers more than 200 games with no ads and no additional purchases for $5 a month. The best part is that one subscription gets you games on all your devices: iPhones, iPads, and even Apple TVs!

TIP You can also get access to Apple Arcade by taking out an Apple One subscription. Apple One offers various subscription plans that give you access to some or all of these six services: Apple Music, Apple TV+, Apple Arcade, iCloud+, Apple News+, and Apple Fitness+.

The Create tab is chock full of apps for video, audio, photo creation, editing, and more. The Work tab contains productivity apps galore. And in the Play tab, you'll discover lots of fun and games.

If you prefer to browse by specific categories, select the Categories tab and choose among nearly two dozen top-level categories, as shown in Figure 20-2.

When you click a category, you'll see two recommended apps at the top of the screen, followed by a pair of lists: Top Free and Top Paid. You can see only six apps at a time in each list, but when you hover your pointer over a section, Next and Previous icons appear, looking like giant greater-than (>) and less-than (<) symbols. Click the Next or Previous icon to browse further apps.

Finally, if any of your installed apps is in need of an update, you'll find them in the Updates tab.

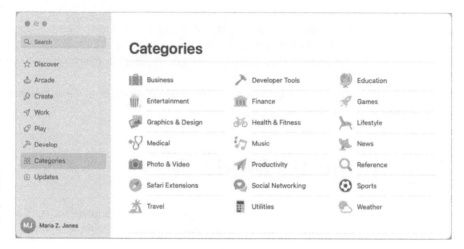

FIGURE 20-2:
The Categories
tab lets you drill
down into nearly
two dozen
categories.

Just about everything you learned in Chapter 17 about the iTunes Store could be said for the App Store. It works pretty much the same way, and it uses the same credit card you have on file at the iTunes Store.

TIP

If you see a little number on the App Store icon in your Dock, it means that some of your apps have updates available. Launch the App Store app and click the Updates tab to see the apps with updates awaiting them. Even if you don't see a little number on the App Store's Dock icon, it wouldn't hurt to launch the App Store every once in a while to check for updates manually, as the little number sometimes fails to appear on the icon.

Using Your iPhone as Your Mac's Camera or Scanner

Continuity Camera is among Ventura's coolest and most useful features. It lets you use your iPhone or iPad as a camera or scanner for your Mac.

Before you try it, here are the rules:

» Both devices (the Mac and the iPhone or iPad) must be logged into the same Apple ID and using two-factor authentication.

» Both devices must be connected to the same Wi-Fi network.

» Both devices must have Bluetooth enabled.

If you meet those criteria, you can use your iPhone or iPad as a camera or scanner and have the resulting photo or scan inserted into your document or saved to the Finder (almost) instantly.

To make the magic happen, just Control-click or right-click anywhere an image or scan can be used (Notes, Stickies, TextEdit or Pages documents, and Finder, to name a few).

Not every app or document supports Continuity Camera, but if it's available when you Control-click or right-click, the commands appear on the contextual menu. If only one device is available, you'll see a section such as the My iPhone section (the left screen in Figure 20-3). If two or more devices are available, you'll see the Insert from iPhone or iPad submenu (the right screen in Figure 20-3), from which you can choose the device you want to use.

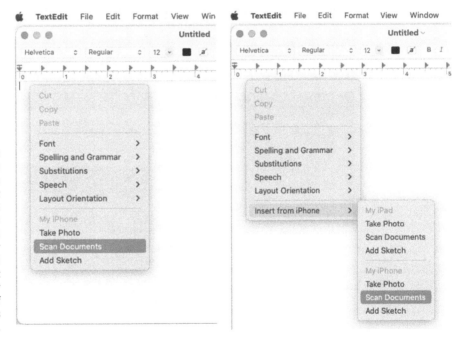

FIGURE 20-3:
If the app supports Continuity Camera, the contextual menu contains either a section for your iPhone or iPad (left) or the Insert from iPhone or iPad submenu (if multiple devices are available).

From the contextual menu or the submenu, choose Take Photo, Scan Documents, or Add Sketch, as appropriate.

If you choose Take Photo, the Camera app on your iPhone or iPad will launch automatically, and you'll see one of two things on your Mac. If you Control-clicked or right-clicked in a document, you'll see an overlay below the insertion point; if you Control-clicked or right-clicked in Finder, you'll see a dialog instead of an overlay.

Take the photo on your iPhone or iPad by tapping the Camera app's shutter-release button in the usual fashion. After you snap a shot, a preview appears, offering two options: Retake or Use Photo. Tap Retake if you're dissatisfied with the image and want to try again. When you get a shot you're happy with, tap Use Photo, and the shot appears in the document at the insertion point or in the Finder almost immediately.

Choosing Scan Documents is similar to taking a photo, with some minor differences. You'll still see an overlay or a dialog on your Mac, but this time, the overlay or dialog says Scan a Document rather than Take a Photo.

On your iPhone or iPad, however, the Camera app works differently. In the top-right corner is a button that toggles between Auto and Manual. In Auto mode, you move the camera up, down, and all around until the blue box contains the text you want to scan, as shown on the left side of Figure 20-4. When the Camera app thinks it's nailed the subject, it takes the shot.

Or if you tap Auto (which switches the camera to Manual mode), you tap the shutter-release button to capture text.

FIGURE 20-4:
Your iPhone or iPad captures the page automatically (left). Drag the circles to contain the text you want to scan (right).

After you've captured a page, a preview of it appears, but in addition to the two buttons at the bottom of the screen (Retake and Keep Scan), a box appears, with circles at each of its four corners, as shown on the right side of Figure 20-4. Drag the circles until the box contains all the text you want to scan and then tap Keep Scan.

After you tap Keep Scan, the camera reappears, with the message *Ready for Next Scan.* If you have additional pages to scan, continue capturing them as described. When you're finished, tap Save in the bottom-right corner.

Talking and Listening to Your Mac

Your primary methods of interacting with your Mac are typing, using the trackpad or mouse, and reading text. But there's another way you can commune with your faithful computer: voice.

Whether you know it or not, your Mac has a lot of speech savvy in its wheelhouse and can talk to you as well as listen. Believe it or not, it can type the words you speak and obey your spoken commands. All MacBooks and iMacs have microphones built in; if you have a Mac mini, a Mac Studio, or a Mac Pro, you'll need to add an external microphone.

Keyboard pane in System Settings: You talk, and your Mac types

Some users still don't realize that dictation is available in macOS at no extra cost (and has been for years). In this section, you find out how to harness its power.

First, make sure that Dictation is enabled. Choose System Settings⇨ Keyboard to display the Keyboard pane, go to the Dictation section, and set the Use Dictation switch to on (blue). (The switch has a long name, of which Use Dictation are the first two words.) If the Do You Want to Enable Dictation? dialog opens, click Enable.

TIP

Dictation requires an Internet connection unless you enable Voice Control (formerly known as Speech Recognition) in the Voice Control pane, which you reach via the Accessibility pane of System Settings. Otherwise, when you dictate text, what you say is sent to Apple's servers for conversion to text. If you enable Voice Control, you can use Dictation without an Internet connection after your Mac downloads the necessary files to your Mac. These files are pretty big — a 1.2GB download — but are well worth taking the time to download.

Other information, such as your contacts, may also be sent to Apple over the Internet to help your Mac understand what you're saying. If that fact makes you uncomfortable, you probably shouldn't use the Dictation feature without first enabling Voice Control.

After Dictation is enabled, with or without the Voice Control option, the feature couldn't be easier to use. First, click where you want your words to appear in a document, dialog, web form, or whatever. Then choose Edit ➪ Start Dictation, or press the Fn key twice in rapid succession.

If your keyboard doesn't have an Fn key, click the Shortcut pop-up menu in the Keyboard pane, and change the shortcut to one that works with your keyboard.

When you start Dictation, a little microphone icon appears. The white filling indicates the level (relative loudness) of your voice. Try to keep the white near the middle — not too high and not too low, as shown in Figure 20-5.

FIGURE 20-5:
Volume levels for dictation (left to right): too soft, just right, and too loud.

When you see the microphone icon, start speaking. After you dictate a few sentences, click Done, and let your Mac catch up. When the words appear, you can start Dictation again. Repeat as necessary.

Save your document after you speak a few sentences or paragraphs. If you don't, the words you dictated since your last Save will be lost if the app or your Mac crashes.

You can insert punctuation by speaking its name, such as "period" or "comma." You can also perform simple formatting by saying "new line" or "new paragraph" to add space between lines.

Here are a few more tips to help you get the best results when you dictate:

» **Speak in a normal voice at a moderate volume level.** Try to keep the white in the microphone icon about half-full (or half-empty, if you're a pessimist).

» **Avoid background noise.** If you expect to use dictation in a noisy environment or a room with a lot of ambient echo, use a headset microphone.

>> **Make sure that the microphone isn't obstructed.** Check your Mac's User Guide for the location of the Mac's built-in microphone (if it has one).

>> **Make sure that the input volume of an external microphone is sufficient.** If you're using an external microphone, and the white meter doesn't respond to your voice, choose System Settings ⇨ Sound, click the Input tab, and drag the Input Volume slider to the right until the meter shows a suitable response.

Commanding your Mac by voice

Voice Control enables your Mac to recognize and respond to human speech. The only thing you need to use it is a microphone, which a MacBook or iMac has; you need to add one to a Mac mini, Mac Studio, or Mac Pro.

Voice Control lets you issue verbal commands such as "Get my mail!" to your Mac and have it actually get your email. You can also create AppleScripts and Automator workflows (described later in this chapter), as well as Finder Quick Actions (see Chapter 5), and trigger them by voice.

If you've enabled Voice Control, you can use speech commands to instruct your Mac. To see a list of commands your Mac will understand if you speak them, choose System Settings ⇨ Accessibility, click the Voice Control button in the Accessibility pane, and then click the Commands button. A dialog appears, in which you can enable or disable the available dictation commands, as shown in Figure 20-6.

TIP

If you have a laptop or an iMac, you may get better results from just about any third-party microphone or (better still) a headset with a microphone. The microphone system built into your Mac is okay, but it's not great. To select a third-party microphone, first connect the microphone to your Mac. Then choose System Settings ⇨ Sound, and select the microphone from the list of sound input devices in the Input tab. Below the list is an Input Volume slider (not available with some third-party mikes) and a level meter. Adjust the Input Volume slider so that most of the dots in the Input Level meter darken (at least 11 out of the 15 dots) when you're speaking at a normal volume.

REMEMBER

You can also choose an external mike from the Microphone Source pop-up menu in the Dictation section of the Keyboard pane in System Settings. As before, use the Sound pane to adjust the microphone's input levels.

FIGURE 20-6:
The Dictation
Commands sheet
displaying some
things your Mac
will understand if
you say them
(properly).
Usually.

To give Voice Control a try, press Fn twice (or whatever shortcut you set earlier), and speak one of the items from the list of Voice Control commands, such as "Open TextEdit." If the command is recognized, it appears in text above the microphone icon, as shown in Figure 20-7.

FIGURE 20-7:
Open TextEdit
above the mike
icon means that
your command
was recognized.

Listening to your Mac read your screen

The camera pans back. A voice tells you what you've just seen. And suddenly, it all makes sense. Return with me now to those thrilling days of the off-camera narrator. . .. Wouldn't it be nice if your Mac had a narrator to provide a blow-by-blow account of what's happening on your screen?

Or perhaps your eyes are tired from a long day staring at the monitor, but you still have a lengthy document to read. Wouldn't it be sweet if you could sit back, close your eyes, and let your Mac read the document to you in a (somewhat) natural voice?

Both things are possible with macOS Ventura: the first scenario with VoiceOver and the second with Text to Speech.

VoiceOver

Ventura's VoiceOver technology is designed primarily for the visually impaired, but you might find it useful even if your vision is 20/20. VoiceOver not only reads what's on the screen to you, but also integrates with your keyboard so you can navigate around the screen until you *hear* the item you're looking for. When you're there, you can use Keyboard Access to select list items, select check boxes and radio buttons, move scroll bars and sliders, resize windows, and so on — all with a simple key press or two.

To check out VoiceOver, choose System Settings ⇨ Accessibility, go to the Vision section of the Accessibility pane, and then click VoiceOver. In the VoiceOver pane, set the VoiceOver switch to on (blue) to enable VoiceOver. Alternatively, press ⌘+Fn+F5 on Mac keyboards set to use dedicated hardware keys, or press ⌘+F5 on a keyboard that uses good old-fashioned function keys.

If the VoiceOver dialog opens, greeting you with a cheery Welcome to VoiceOver, select the Do Not Show This Message Again check box, and click the Use VoiceOver button.

While VoiceOver is on, your Mac talks you through what is on the screen. If you click the desktop, for example, your Mac might say something along the lines of "Application, Finder; Column View; selected folder, Desktop, contains eight items." It's quite slick. Here's another example: When you click a menu or an item on a menu, you hear its name spoken at once, and when you close a menu, you hear the words "Closing menu." You even hear the spoken feedback in dialogs such as Print, Open, and Save.

VoiceOver is kind of cool (talking alerts are fun), but having dialogs actually produce spoken text becomes annoying fast for most folks who aren't visually impaired. (Those who *are* visually impaired, however, rave about VoiceOver and say that it lets them do things they couldn't easily do in the past.) Check out VoiceOver anyway so that you'll know what your options are. You might like it and find times when you want your Mac to narrate the action onscreen for you.

As you'd imagine, you turn VoiceOver off in much the same way that you turned it on: Press ⌘+Fn+F5 or ⌘+F5 (whichever worked to turn on VoiceOver on your Mac), or navigate to the VoiceOver pane and set the VoiceOver switch to off (white).

Text to Speech

The second way your Mac can speak to you is via Text to Speech, which converts onscreen text to spoken words. If you used Text to Speech in earlier versions of macOS, you'll find that it sounds slightly less robotic these days; otherwise, it's mostly unchanged.

Why might you need Text to Speech? Sometimes, hearing is better than reading. After you write an important email or document, for example, you might have Text to Speech read it back so you make sure it sounds okay. You'll find that listening to what you've written makes you focus on the text in a different way from reading. (For one thing, you'll have a tough time skipping ahead while listening.)

Here's how to crank up Text to Speech:

1. **Choose System Settings ⇨ Accessibility to display the Accessibility pane of System Settings, and click Spoken Content to display the Spoken Content pane.**

2. **From the System Voice pop-up menu, choose the voice you want your Mac to use when it reads to you.**

3. **Click the Play Sample button to hear a sample of the voice you selected.**

4. **Use the Speaking Rate slider to speed up or slow down the voice.**

5. **Click the Play Sample button to hear the voice at its new speed.**

6. **(Optional) To make your Mac speak the text in alert boxes and dialogs, set the Speak Announcements switch to on (blue).**

   You might hear such alerts as "The application Microsoft Word has quit unexpectedly" or "Paper out or not loaded correctly."

7. **(Optional) To make your Mac speak text you've selected in a document, set the Speak Selection switch to on (blue).**

   The default keyboard shortcut for Speak Selection is Option+Esc, but you can assign any key combo you like by clicking the Info (i) button and typing a different keyboard shortcut.

8. **(Optional) To make your Mac describe whatever is below the pointer, set the Speak Items Under Pointer switch to on (blue).**

9. **(Optional) To make your Mac speak whatever you type, set the Speak Typing Feedback switch to on (blue).**

10. **(Optional) To explore additional options for the previous four items, click the appropriate Info (i) button.**

Now, to use Text to Speech to read text to you, copy the text to the Clipboard, launch any app that supports it (maybe TextEdit, the stunt app for this chapter), paste the text into the empty untitled document, click where you want your Mac to begin reading to you, and then choose Edit ⇨ Speech ⇨ Start Speaking. To make it stop, choose Edit ⇨ Speech ⇨ Stop Speaking.

Another great place where Text to Speech is available is the Safari web browser. The process works the same as in TextEdit, but you don't have to paste; just select the text you want to hear, and choose Edit ⇨ Speech ⇨ Start Speaking.

TIP

If you don't care for the sound of the default voice, choose a different one in the Spoken Content pane of System Settings. First, select Spoken Content in the list on the left side; then choose a new voice from the System Voice drop-down menu, or choose Manage Voices to download additional voices. There's a huge variation in the file size of the voices, from a couple of megabytes to nearly a gigabyte for a single voice, so pay attention to the download size if your Mac is strapped for space. The larger the file size, the better the voice will sound — but that doesn't mean you'll necessarily like the voice.

Automatic Automation

macOS Ventura offers a trio of technologies — AppleScript, Automator, and Shortcuts — that make it easy to automate repetitive actions on your Mac. You meet Shortcuts in Chapter 12; in this section, you meet AppleScript and Automator as well.

AppleScript is "programming for the rest of us." It can record and play back things that you do (if the app was written to allow the recording, as many apps are), such as opening an app or clicking a button. You can use AppleScript to record a script for a task that you often perform and then have your Mac perform that task for you again and again until the cows come home. You can write your own Apple-Scripts, use those that come with your Mac, or download still others from the web.

Automator is "programming without writing code." With Automator, you string together prefabricated activities (*actions*) to automate repetitive or scheduled tasks. How cool is that?

Automation isn't for everyone. Some users can't live without it; others could go their whole lives without automating anything. So the following sections are designed to help you figure out how much — or how little — you care about AppleScript and Automator.

Script Editor app: Write and edit AppleScripts

Describing AppleScript to a Mac beginner is a bit like three blind men describing an elephant. One man might describe it as the Mac's built-in automation tool. Another might describe it as an interesting but often-overlooked piece of enabling technology. The third might liken it to a digital recorder, recording and playing back your actions at the keyboard. A fourth (if there were a fourth in the story) would assure you that it looked like computer code written in a high-level language.

They would all be correct. AppleScript, a built-in Mac automation tool, is a little-known enabling technology that works like a recorder for apps that support AppleScript recording. And scripts do look like computer code, mostly because that's what they are.

If you're the kind of person who likes to automate as many things as possible, you might just love AppleScript, because it's a simple but powerful programming language you can use to create scripts that give instructions to macOS and the apps running on it. You could create an AppleScript that launches Mail, checks for new messages, and then quits Mail, for example. The script could even transfer your mail to a folder of your choice. Then there's Automator, which includes a whole lot of preprogrammed actions that make a task like the one just described even easier.

AppleScript can be a great time-and-effort enhancer. If you just spend the time and effort it takes to understand it, using AppleScript can save you far more time and effort down the road. Therein lies the rub. This stuff is far from simple; entire books have been written on the subject. So it's far beyond the purview of this book. Still, AppleScript is worth finding out about if you'd like to script repetitive actions for future use. To get you started, here are a few quick tips:

» Script Editor (in the Utilities folder in the Applications folder) is the app you use to create, edit, and view AppleScripts. You can write code in Script Editor, but you can also create many AppleScripts without knowing a thing about programming: Just record a series of actions you want to repeat, and use Script Editor to save what you recorded as a script. If you save your script as an app (by choosing Format ⇨ Application in the Save dialog), you can run that script by double-clicking its icon.

>> You can put frequently used AppleScripts on the Dock or on your desktop for easy access.

>> Many AppleScripts are designed for use on the toolbar of Finder windows; you can drag and drop items on them quickly and easily.

>> Scripts can enhance your use of many apps, including iTunes, iPhoto, and Finder, to name a few.

>> Apple provides a script-menu extra that you can install on your menu bar in the Script Editor's Settings window, along with several free scripts to automate common tasks (in the Scripts folder in the root-level Library, or choose Help ⇨ Open Example Scripts Folder in Script Editor).

>> If the concept of scripting intrigues you, explore the examples in the Scripts folder (in the root-level Library, or choose Help ⇨ Open Example Scripts in Script Edigtor). Rummage through this folder, and when you find a script that looks interesting, double-click it to launch the Script Editor utility, where you can examine it more closely.

Automator app: Automate almost anything

Automator does just what you'd expect: It enables you to automate many common tasks on your Mac. If it sounds a little like AppleScript to you, you're not mistaken; the two have a common goal. But Automator is much simpler to use than Apple-Script, albeit somewhat less flexible.

In AppleScript, for example, you can have *conditionals* ("if *this* is true, do *that*; otherwise, do something else"), but Automator is purely *sequential* ("take *this*, do *that*; then do the next thing; and then . . .").

The big difference is that conditionals allow AppleScripts to take actions involving *decision-making* and *iteration* ("while *this* is true, do *these* things"); Automator workflows can't make decisions or iterate.

The upsides to Automator are that you don't have to know anything about programming, and you don't have to type any arcane code. Instead, if you understand the process you want to automate, you can just drag and drop Automator's prefab actions into place and build a *workflow* (Automator's name for a series of actions).

REMEMBER

You do need to know one thing about programming (or computers), though: *Computers are stupid!* You read me right. Even a top-of-the-line Mac Pro is dumb as a post. Computers do only what you tell them to do, even though they can do it faster and more precisely than you can. But all computers run on the GIGO (Garbage In, Garbage Out) principle, so if your instructions are flawed, you're almost certain to get flawed results.

When you launch the Automator app, click the New Document button; the window and dialog shown in Figure 20-8 appear. Choose one of the starting points if you want Automator to assist you in constructing a new workflow, or choose Workflow to start building a workflow from scratch.

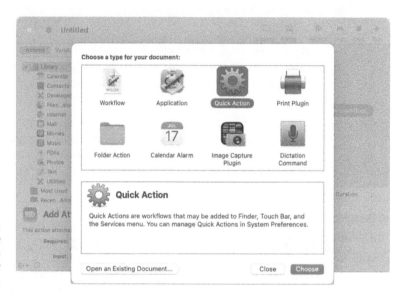

FIGURE 20-8:
Choose Workflow if you want to start a workflow from scratch.

This example uses Quick Action rather than Workflow; you'll see why in a second. When you select Quick Action and click the Choose button, the window shown in Figure 20-9 appears.

The Library pane on the far-left side contains all the apps Automator knows about that have Actions defined for them. Select an app in the top part of the Library window, and its related actions appear below it. When you select an action, the pane at the bottom of the Library window (Text to Audio File in Figure 20-9) explains what that Action does, what input it expects, and what result it produces. Just drag Actions from the Action list into the window on the right to build your workflow.

This particular Quick Action enables you to create an audio file from selected text so that you can listen to the text wherever you want, such as in the car or on a plane. You just select text in a source, such as a web page or a Microsoft Word document, and then run the Quick Action from the Services submenu on the application's menu. (Choose Word ⇨ Services after selecting text in Microsoft Word, for example.)

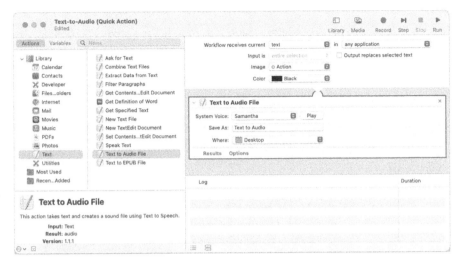

FIGURE 20-9:
This Automator
Quick Action
converts selected
text to an
audio file.

Automator is a useful addition to macOS; it's deep, powerful, and expandable, yet relatively easy to use and master. Do yourself a favor: Spend some time experimenting with ways Automator can save you time and keystrokes. You won't regret it.

TIP

For additional information about AppleScript, Automator, Services, and much more, visit www.macosxautomation.com.

A Few More Useful Goodies

Even more neat and useful technologies are built into Ventura. Here are another handful of apps and utilities that you may find useful.

Accessibility pane in System Settings: Make your Mac more accessible

If you've read the chapter to this point, you got a brief glimpse of the Accessibility pane in the section on commanding your Mac by voice. But this System Settings pane is designed mostly for users with disabilities and/or those who have difficulty handling the keyboard, mouse, or trackpad.

TIP

If you want to see the status of all Accessibility settings on the menu bar, choose System Settings ⇨ Control Center, go to the Accessibility Shortcuts section, and then set the Show in Menu Bar switch to on (blue). If you prefer to have the Accessibility Shortcuts in Control Center, set the Show in Control Center switch to on (blue) instead.

The Accessibility pane has four main sections — Vision, Hearing, Motor, and General — each of which contains multiple buttons that take you to further panes.

In the Vision section, click the Display button to show the Display pane, which provides settings for controlling the behavior of the screen display. In the Color Filters section of the Display pane, for example, you can choose Grayscale as your filter type, which will desaturate your screen into a grayscale display (so that it looks kind of like a black-and-white TV).

In the Display section of the Display tab, you can set the Invert Colors switch to on (blue) to reverse the colors you see onscreen — an interesting if only occasionally useful effect. After inverting the colors, you can go to the Invert Colors Mode row and choose between the Smart and Classic radio buttons. The main difference between the two is that Smart Invert Colors doesn't invert the colors of images and videos (because who would want those inverted?), whereas Classic Invert Colors figures "the heck with it" and inverts everything.

TIP

This setting is more useful: In the Pointer section of the Display pane, set the Shake Mouse Pointer to locate switch to on (blue). Then, when you lose the pointer, wiggle the mouse back and forth a couple of times, and the pointer momentarily grows much larger. If you'd like the pointer to be bigger all the time, drag the Pointer Size slider toward the Large end.

In the Vision section of the Accessibility pane, click Zoom to display the Zoom pane. This pane is where you can enable a terrific feature called *hardware zoom*, which lets you make things on your screen bigger by zooming in on them. To control hardware zoom with the keyboard, set the Use Keyboard Shortcuts to Zoom switch to on (blue). Then you can toggle hardware zoom on and off by pressing ⌘+Option+8, zoom in by pressing ⌘+Option+= (that's the equal sign), and zoom out by pressing ⌘+Option+– (that's the hyphen key). If your Mac uses a trackpad, set the Use Trackpad Gesture to Zoom switch to on (blue) to zoom in or out by double-tapping with three fingers and to change the zoom by double-tapping three fingers and then dragging. If you want to zoom by using a scroll gesture while holding down a modifier key, set the Use Scroll Gesture with Modifier Keys to Zoom switch to on (blue); then open the Modifier Key for Scroll Gesture pop-up menu, and choose the modifier key to use. Next, choose a style — Full Screen, Split Screen, or Picture-in-Picture — from the Zoom Style pop-up menu. Set the Hover Text switch to on (blue) to display a preview rectangle below the pointer. Finally, click the Advanced button and the Info (i) button on the Hover Text row for additional options and controls.

Try this feature even if you're not disabled or challenged in any way; it's actually great for everyone.

You've met some of the most useful Accessibility features, but there are a ton more that I don't have space to cover in this section. When you have a few minutes to spare, choose System Settings ⇨ Accessibility, and explore the other features in the Accessibility pane so that you'll know what help is available should you need it. For now, you might find the following features to be useful:

>> If you want the screen to flash whenever an alert sound occurs, click Audio in the Hearing section of the Accessibility pane and then set the switch titled Flash the Screen When an Alert Sound Occurs to on (blue).

>> To treat a *sequence* of modifier keys as a key combination, click Keyboard in the Motor section of the Accessibility pane and then set the Enable Sticky Keys switch to on (blue).

In other words, you don't have to simultaneously hold down ⌘ while pressing another key. With Sticky Keys enabled, for example, you can do a standard keyboard shortcut by pressing ⌘, releasing it, and then pressing the other key. If you enable Sticky Keys, click the Info (i) button to display the Info dialog, in which you can set switches to tell you (with a beep and/or an onscreen display) what modifier keys have been pressed.

TIP

As useful as Sticky Keys can be, they're really awkward in apps like Adobe Photoshop, Adobe Illustrator, and other apps that toggle a tool's state when you press a modifier key. If you're a big Photoshop user, you probably don't want Sticky Keys enabled.

>> To adjust the delay between a keypress and its activation, click Keyboard in the Motor section of the Accessibility pane and then set the Slow Keys switch to on (blue).

Battery pane and Energy Saver pane in System Settings: For energy conservation and sleep

The Battery pane (MacBooks) and Energy Saver (desktops) pane of the System Settings app are where you manage your Mac's energy-saving features.

All Macs are Energy Star–compliant, so the Battery pane and Energy Saver pane let you do things such as turn your Mac off at a specific time or after a specified idle period.

Battery pane (MacBooks only)

To get started, choose System Settings ⇨ Battery to open the Battery pane.

Next, click the button for the feature you want to configure, and work in the pane that appears. Click Usage History to see your battery's charge levels for the past 24 hours or past 10 days. Click Battery to control your MacBook's behavior when it's running on battery power (not plugged in); click Power Adapter to control its behavior when it *is* plugged in.

TIP

Turning off the display is handy if you want your MacBook to keep doing what it's doing but don't need to see its monitor.

To wake up your display, caress the trackpad with your finger, or press any key. Sometimes, the trackpad won't wake a sleeping MacBook, but a keystroke will.

Below the Turn Display Off After slider in the Battery pane and Power Adapter are switches for other battery-related settings, such as

>> **Slightly Dim the Display While on Battery Power** (Battery pane): The display dims slightly and uses less power when running on the battery.

>> **Optimize Video Streaming While on Battery Power** (Battery pane): This option reduces battery use while you're streaming video.

>> **Prevent Computer from Sleeping Automatically When the Display Is Off** (Power Adapter pane): This option prevents sleep when the lid is closed and the display is off.

>> **Wake for Network Access** (Power Adapter pane): Enable this option if you want your Mac to wake up automatically for network access.

>> **Low Power Mode** (Power Adapter and Battery panes): This option reduces energy use to increase battery life.

>> **Show Battery Status in the Menu Bar** (Battery pane): This option adds a little battery-status indicator icon and menu.

Finally, to start up, shut down, or put your Mac to sleep at a predetermined time, click the Schedule button, select the action you want to take, and specify the details for it.

Energy Saver pane in System Settings (desktops only)

To start, choose System Settings ⇨ Energy Saver. Below the Turn Display Off After slider are switches for its energy-related settings. Depending on the model of desktop Mac, you'll see some or all of the following settings, which are largely self-explanatory:

>> Prevent Computer from Sleeping Automatically When the Display Is Off

>> Put Hard Disks to Sleep When Possible

>> Wake for Network Access

>> Start Up Automatically After a Power Failure

>> Enable Power Nap

>> Prevent Computer from Sleeping Automatically When the Display Is Off

>> Wake for Network Access

Bluetooth pane in System Settings: Where Bluetooth lives

Bluetooth is wireless networking for low-bandwidth peripherals, including mice, keyboards, speakers, and headphones. All Ventura-capable Macs have Bluetooth built in, enabling you to blast music on Bluetooth speakers; input vocals via Bluetooth microphones; and connect keyboards, mice, and a plethora of other devices (preferably not all at the same time).

To manage your Mac's Bluetooth features, choose System Settings ⇨ Bluetooth to open the Bluetooth pane of the System Settings app.

Ink pane in System Settings: Visible to pen-input tablet users only

Ink is the macOS built-in handwriting-recognition engine. Sadly, it works only if a third-party drawing tablet with a stylus is connected. Even more sadly, "tablet" in this sense doesn't include your iPad (at least, not so far).

To write instead of type, enable Ink in this pane, and you'll be able to handwrite anywhere your Mac accepts typing with the keyboard.

To manage your Mac's Ink features, open the Ink pane by choosing System Settings ⇨ Ink.

The Ink pane appears only if you have one of the pen-input drawing tablets that Ink supports connected to your Mac. Most of the supported drawing tablets come from Wacom (https://www.wacom.com), with prices starting under $100 for a small wireless stylus and drawing tablet.

Automatic Login: Skip the login screen

If you dislike having to log in when you start up your Mac, you can set it to log in automatically with a specific account. Follow these steps:

1. **Choose System Settings ⇨ Users & Groups to open the Users & Groups pane of the System Settings app.**

2. **Open the Automatically Log In As pop-up menu, and choose the account you want to log in automatically.**

Automatic login is a security nightmare, because anyone who can power on your Mac can start using it under the account you've set to log in automatically. For security, you — and every other user of your Mac — should always log in manually.

Allow your Apple Watch to unlock your Mac

If you have an Apple Watch, you'll love this feature. Choose System Settings ⇨ Login Password to display the Login Password pane, go to the Apple Watch section, and then set the switch for your Apple Watch to on (blue). You can rock up to your Mac while wearing your unlocked Apple Watch, press a key or stroke the trackpad to wake the Mac, and be automatically logged into your user account without typing your password.

Boot Camp Assistant app: Run Windows on your Intel Mac . . . really

Boot Camp is macOS's built-in technology that allows you to run Microsoft Windows on Ventura-capable Macs with Intel processors. If your Mac meets the following requirements, you can run Windows on your Mac (if you so desire):

>> A Ventura-capable Mac (of course) with an Intel processor.

Boot Camp isn't available on Macs that have Apple processors. If you're not sure which processor your Mac has, choose ⇨ About This Mac, and look at the Chip readout. If it says something involving Apple and M, such as *Apple M1* or *Apple M2*, your Mac has an Apple processor and can't run Boot Camp. If the

Chip readout says something involving Intel, your Mac should be able to run Boot Camp.

>> A hard drive that isn't already partitioned.

>> (Optional) A printer (for printing the instructions). It's optional because you could just email them to yourself.

>> A full install copy of Windows 10 or Windows 11. (You *can* install older versions of Windows, such as Windows 8 or Window 8.1, but there's little point.)

REMEMBER

You really do need a *full retail* copy of Windows: one that was purchased in a retail box. If your copy of Windows came with your PC, you probably can't install it in Boot Camp.

To install Windows on your Mac, here are the basic steps:

1. **Launch the Boot Camp Assistant app, which is in your Utilities folder.**

   This step creates a partition on your hard drive for your Windows installation. *Note:* If your Mac has an Apple processor, Boot Camp doesn't appear in the Utilities folder.

2. **Install Windows on the new partition.**

   From now on, you can hold down Option during startup and choose to start up from either the macOS Ventura disk partition or the new Windows partition.

TIP

If running Windows on your Mac appeals to you, you may want to check out Parallels Desktop (around $80) or VirtualBox (free). Both apps allow you to run Windows — even older versions like XP and Vista — as well as Linux on your Intel Mac without partitioning your hard drive or restarting every time you want to use Windows. In fact, you can run Mac and Windows apps simultaneously with these products. If your Mac has an Apple processor, Parallels Desktop can run only the Windows 10 and Windows 11 versions for the ARM processors rather than the regular versions of Windows for Intel processors and AMD processors.

One last thing: Apple has a special Boot Camp support web page at `https://support.apple.com/guide/bootcamp-assistant/welcome/mac`.

AirPlay and AirPlay to Mac

AirPlay is the screen-mirroring feature that lets you stream what's on your Mac (or iPhone or iPad) screen to an Apple TV or a smart TV with built-in AirPlay. AirPlay also includes the AirPlay to Mac feature, which enables you to stream photos or videos from a Mac or Apple device to a Mac running macOS Monterey, macOS Ventura, or a later version.

The Mac running Ventura is also available as an AirPlay audio speaker, so you can stream music from another Mac (or iPhone or iPad) to a Ventura-equipped Mac as easily as you can stream to an Apple TV or smart TV with AirPlay. You just have to enable the AirPlay Receiver feature by choosing System Settings ⇨ General ⇨ Sharing and setting the AirPlay Receiver switch in the Sharing pane to on (blue). Then you can open the AirPlay Selector menu on another device, such as your iPhone, and choose your Mac as the AirPlay speaker on which to play audio.

To select a device to stream to — a Mac (running Ventura), an Apple TV, or a smart TV with Airplay — go to the Displays pane of System Settings, and choose the device from the Add Display (+) pop-up menu.

TIP

If you want to control screen mirroring from the menu bar, choose System Settings ⇨ Control Center to display the Control Center pane of the System Settings app. Open the Screen Mirroring pop-up menu, and choose Always Show in Menu Bar. Then you can choose an AirPlay receiver without visiting the Displays pane of System Settings.

Handoff

The Handoff feature lets you start working on a document, an email, or a message on any Apple device and pick up where you left off on another device. To enable it, choose System Settings ⇨ General, click the AirDrop & Handoff button in the General pane, and then set the switch titled Allow Handoff Between This Mac and Your iCloud Devices to on (blue).

Now make sure that you're signed into iCloud with the same Apple ID on your Mac and your iPhone or iPad and that Bluetooth is enabled on all devices.

Handoff works with Apple apps including Mail, Safari, Maps, Messages, Reminders, Calendar, Contacts, Pages, Numbers, and Keynote, as well as a handful of third-party apps. When another Handoff-enabled device is nearby and using one of these apps, you'll see an icon for it at the right end of the Dock, as shown in Figure 20-10. Clicking that icon (note the tiny phone on it) opens Messages on my Mac and displays the message or reply that's currently on my iPhone screen.

FIGURE 20-10:
My iPhone is nearby and using the Messages app.

Universal Control

Apple's cool Universal Control feature enables you to use your Mac's keyboard, mouse, or trackpad to control one or two nearby iPads or Macs. Universal Control is great for productivity, enabling you to work on your Mac and one or two additional devices without having to mess about with separate keyboards and pointing devices. You can even copy and paste material between the devices by using the Universal Clipboard feature.

As you'd imagine, you start by enabling Universal Control. I'll take it from the top.

Enabling and configuring Universal Control

On your Mac, follow these steps to enable and configure Universal Control:

1. **Choose System Settings ⇨ Displays to show the Displays pane of the System Settings app.**

2. **Click the Advanced button at the bottom of the pane to display the Advanced dialog (see Figure 20-11).**

3. **Set the switch titled Allow Your Pointer and Keyboard to Move Between Any Nearby Mac or iPad to on (blue).**

4. **Set the switch titled Push Through the Edge of a Display to Connect a Nearby Mac or iPad to on (blue).**

5. **(Optional) Set the switch titled Automatically Reconnect to Any Nearby Mac or iPad to on (blue).**

   Whether you'll want to enable this option depends on how you work. Having macOS reestablish the connection automatically can be great if you use the iPad or the other Mac consistently. If you use it only occasionally, though, having your Mac glomming onto it on sight like a lovestruck teenager can feel awkward.

6. **Click the Done button to close the Advanced dialog.**

Closing the Advanced dialog takes you back to the Displays pane of System Settings. Leave this pane open, because you're not finished there yet.

FIGURE 20-11:
Enable and
configure
Universal Control
in the Advanced
dialog for
Displays settings.

Connecting the iPad or Mac

Now fire up the iPad or the other Mac, if it's not already running, and connect it as follows.

1. **In the top-right corner of the Displays pane, click Add Display (+) to open the pop-up menu.**

2. **From the Mirror or Extend To list, choose the appropriate iPad or Mac.**

   The iPad or Mac appears at the top of the Displays pane, as you see in Figure 20-12.

3. **Click the Arrange button at the bottom of the pane to open the Arrange Displays dialog (see Figure 20-13).**

4. **Identify the display you want to move by holding the pointer over its thumbnail so that a screen tip appears.**

5. **Drag the display's to the appropriate position to indicate how the physical displays are placed.**

6. **When all the thumbnails are suitably positioned, click Done to close the Arrange Displays dialog.**

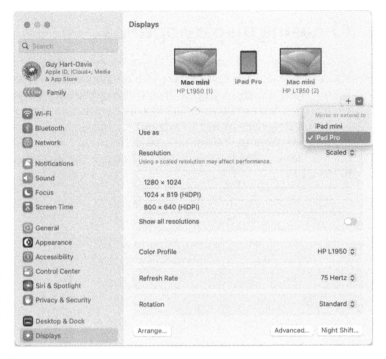

FIGURE 20-12:
In the Displays
pane, click + and
then choose the
iPad or Mac from
the Mirror or
Extend To list.

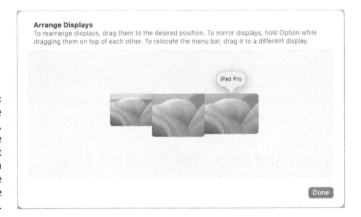

FIGURE 20-13:
In the Arrange
Displays dialog,
identify the
display you want
to move and then
drag it to the
appropriate
position.

At this point, you should be firing on all cylinders — or at least able to use all the displays you've connected. To move the pointer to the iPad or Mac, just push through the appropriate side of the display on your main Mac. When the pointer is on the display of the iPad or the secondary Mac, any keystrokes you type go to the active window on that display.

Choosing display options

By default, your Mac starts by using a connected iPad as a separate display, extending the desktop to it so that you have more desktop space. But you can also mirror your Mac's display to the iPad, which can be useful if you're giving a presentation, a demonstration, or the like. To switch to mirroring, click the Screen Mirroring icon (shown in the margin) on the menu bar and then choose the Mirror entry from the Mirror or Extend To list. In the example in Figure 20-14, the Mac has two displays connected, so you can choose which of them to mirror to the iPad.

FIGURE 20-14:
Use the Screen Mirroring menu on the menu bar to switch between using the iPad as a separate display and mirroring your Mac's display to it. This Mac has two displays connected, plus the iPad.

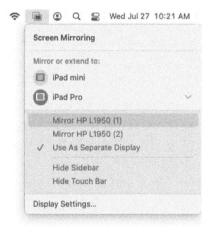

From the Screen Mirroring menu, you can also toggle the display of the Sidebar and the Touch Bar on the iPad's screen.

Disconnecting the iPad or Mac

When you finish using the iPad or Mac via Universal Control, disconnect it as follows:

1. **Click the Screen Mirroring icon (shown in the margin) on the menu bar to open the Screen Mirroring menu.**

2. **Click Display Settings to show the Displays pane of the System Settings app with the iPad's settings selected (see Figure 20-15).**

3. **Click the Disconnect button.**

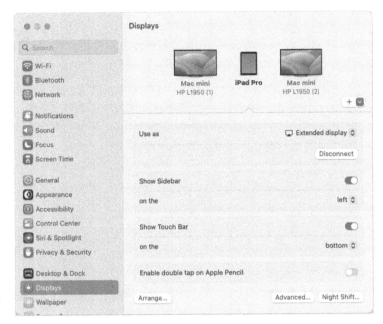

FIGURE 20-15:
Click Disconnect
in the Displays
pane of System
Settings to
disconnect
the iPad.

When you disconnect the iPad this way, macOS rounds up any of its windows that were on the iPad's display and returns them to the Mac's display.

Chapter **21**

Safety First: Backups and Other Security Issues

lthough Macs are generally reliable, someday your Mac's drive will die, whether it's a hard drive with spinning platters or a solid-state drive (SSD). The drive's death isn't an if; it's a when. *All* disks will die someday. And if you don't back up *your* drive (or at least back up any files that you can't afford to lose) before that day comes, chances are good that those files will be gone forever.

In other words, you absolutely, positively, without question *must back up* your files if you don't want to risk losing them. Just as you adopt the Shut Down command and make it a habit before turning off your Mac, you must remember to back up important files stored on your Mac to another disk or device — and back them up often.

How often is often? That depends on you. How much work can you afford to lose? If your answer is that losing everything you did yesterday would put you out of business, you need to back up hourly or perhaps even continuously. If you'd lose only a few unimportant documents if your Mac's drive died today, you probably can back up less frequently.

Following the comprehensive coverage of backup options, this chapter explains the possible threat to your data from viruses and other icky things, as well as how you can protect against them.

Finally, this chapter covers what you can do to keep other people from looking at your stuff.

Backing Up Is (Not) Hard to Do

You can back up your Mac's drive in basically three ways: the super-painless way with Ventura's excellent built-in Time Machine, the ugly way with the brute-force method, or the comprehensive way with specialized third-party backup and disk-cloning software. Read on to find out more about all three.

Backing up with Ventura's excellent Time Machine

Time Machine is an excellent backup system that has become better and more reliable since its introduction more than a decade ago. Time Machine is a complex technology built deep into macOS, but it manifests itself in the user interface as two parts: the Time Machine pane of the System Settings app (shown in Figure 21-1), which you use to configure the backup service, and the Time Machine app (shown in Figure 21-2), which you use to recover files from backup.

FIGURE 21-1:
The Time Machine pane of System Settings and the Time Machine menu on the menu bar.

FIGURE 21-2:
The Time
Machine app is
ready to restore
an image file in
Finder.

TIP

The easiest way to get to Time Machine is to add its menu to the menu bar. To do so, open System Settings, click Control Center in the sidebar, go to the Menu Bar Only section at the bottom of the Control Center pane, open the Time Machine pop-up menu, and choose Show in Menu Bar.

To use Time Machine to back up your data automatically, the first thing you need is another disk that's larger than your start-up disk. The disk can connect via USB 2, USB 3, USB 4, or Thunderbolt, and it can be your choice of hard drive or SSD.

To select a drive to use with Time Machine, choose System Settings ⇨ General ⇨ Time Machine. In the Time Machine pane in System Settings, click the Add Backup Disk button, select the drive you want to use for your backups, and then click the Set Up disk button.

Additional consideration

The only other consideration is this: If your Mac has other hard drives connected, you need to tell Time Machine which of them to back up and which not to back up. Click the Options button in the Time Machine pane to open the Options dialog, which includes the Exclude These Items from Backups list. To add a volume or folder to this exclusion list, click the little + icon, select the volume or folder, and click the Exclude button; to remove a volume from the list, select the volume and then click the – icon.

CHAPTER 21 **Safety First: Backups and Other Security Issues**   411

If your Mac is a laptop, the Options dialog also offers a check box to enable Time Machine backups when on battery power. This setting is disabled by default.

Time Machine runs approximately once per hour and creates the following backups:

>> Hourly backups for the past 24 hours

>> Daily backups for the past month

>> Weekly backups until your backup disk is full

When your backup disk gets nearly full, Time Machine intelligently deletes the oldest backups and replace them with the newest.

Buy the biggest drive you can afford to use as your backup disk. Otherwise, Time Machine will be deleting backups all the time rather than archiving them for future use.

You can also tell Time Machine to create a backup at any point you want. Simply click the Time Machine icon on the menu bar and then click Back Up Now.

What does Time Machine back up?

Time Machine backs up your entire hard drive the first time it runs and then backs up files and folders that have been modified since your last backup. That's what backup systems do. But Time Machine does more. It also backs up things such as contacts in your Contacts, pictures in your Photos library, events in your calendars, and emails in your Mail, not to mention its support of versions and locking. About the only thing Time Machine doesn't back up is the content of Home folders other than your own.

Those features make Time Machine unlike any other backup system.

How do I restore a file (or a contact, a photo, an event, and so on)?

To restore a file or any other information, follow these steps:

1. **Launch the app that contains the information you want to restore.**

   If you want to restore a file, that app is Finder, which (as you know) is always running; just open a Finder window to the folder that contains the file. But to restore a contact, a photo, an email message, or an event, for example, you need to launch Contacts, Photos, Mail, or Calendar, respectively.

2. **With the appropriate app running (or the appropriate Finder window open), launch the Time Machine app (refer to Figure 21-2).**

   If you chose Show in Menu Bar from the Time Machine pop-up menu in the Control Center pane in System Settings, you can click the Time Machine icon on the menu bar and then click Browse Time Machine Backups (refer to Figure 21-1).

   TIP

   It will be easier to restore a file in Finder if the folder that the file is in (or was in) is the *active* folder (that is, open and frontmost) when you launch the Time Machine app. Otherwise, you have to navigate to the appropriate folder before you can perform Step 3.

3. **Click one of the bars with dates near the bottom-right corner of the screen *or* click the big Forward or Back arrow on the right side of the Documents window in Figure 21-2 to choose a backup to restore.**

   TIP

4. **Select the file, folder, Contacts contact, Photos photo, email message, or Calendar event you want to restore.**

5. **Click the Restore button below the window.**

   If the file, folder, Contacts contact, Photos photo, email message, or Calendar event exists in the same location on your start-up disk, Time Machine politely asks what you want to do: Replace the original, keep the original, or keep them both.

   TIP

   You can search for files or folders in Time Machine by typing a word or phrase in the Search field of the active (frontmost) window.

Backing up by using the manual, brute-force method

If you think you're too cheap to buy a big hard drive, consider this: Amazon.com has numerous 4TB external USB 3 hard drives for less than $100. Prices keep dropping, so by the time you read this book, they may be even cheaper.

Face it — a backup disk is a lot cheaper than data recovery (which can run hundreds if not thousands of dollars). So bite the bullet, and buy the biggest backup disk you can justify.

If you're still not convinced, you should consider at least backing up important files manually. You accomplish this task by dragging said files a few at a time to another volume — usually, another hard drive or SSD, a Universal Serial Bus (USB) flash drive, or a burn-to optical medium such as a DVD-R or DVD-RW. (If you use an optical disc, don't forget to actually *burn the disc*; merely dragging those files onto the optical disc icon won't do the trick.) By using this method, you're making a copy of each file that you want to protect.

If doing a manual backup sounds pretty awful, you're right. It is. This method can take a long, long time; you can't really tell whether you've copied every file that needs to be backed up; and you can't really copy only the files that have been modified since your last backup. Few busy people find this method viable for long.

If you're careful to save files only in your Documents folder, you can probably get away with backing up only that folder. Or if you save files in other folders within your Home folder or have any files in your Movies, Music, Pictures, or Sites folders (which often contain files you didn't specifically save in those folders, such as your Photos app pictures and Music app songs), you should probably consider backing up your entire Home folder.

As you read in the following section, backing up your Home folder is even easier if you use special backup software.

Backing up by using commercial backup software

Another way to back up your files is to use a third-party backup app. Backup software automates the task of backing up, remembering what's on each backup disc (if your backup uses more than one disc), and backing up only files that have been modified since your last backup.

Furthermore, you can instruct your backup software to back up only a certain folder (Home or Documents) and to ignore the hundreds of megabytes of stuff that make up macOS, all of which you can easily reinstall from your Recovery disk or the Mac App Store.

Your first backup with commercial software might take anywhere from a few minutes to several hours and use one or more optical discs (CD-R, CD-RW, DVD-R, DVD-RW, magneto-optical disc) or nonoptical media (such as another hard drive or any kind of tape). Subsequent backups — *incremental backups,* in backup software parlance — should be much faster.

If you do incremental backups with optical discs, keep two things in mind. First, use DVD-R and DVD-RW discs rather than CD-R and CD-RW discs, because the latter's capacity is so low that you'll be swapping media in and out of the drive till kingdom come. Second, be sure to clearly label and number all the discs you use during that operation. Your backup software may prompt you with a message such as *Please insert backup disk 7.* If you haven't labeled your media clearly, you could have a problem figuring out which disc *is* disc 7 or which disc 7 belongs to that particular backup set.

One of the best things about good backup software is that you can set it up to automate your backups and perform them even if you forget. And although Time Machine is a step in the right direction and may be sufficient for your needs, power users may need a heavier-duty backup solution.

Why You Need Two Sets of Backups

You're a good soldier. You back up regularly. You think you're immune to file loss or damage.

Now picture yourself in the following scenario:

>> You leave the office one day for lunch. When you return, you discover that your office has been burglarized, struck by lightning, flooded, burned to the ground, or buried in earthquake rubble — take your pick.

>> Alas, although you did have a backup, the backup disk was right next to your Mac, which means that it was either stolen or destroyed along with your Mac and everything else.

This scenario is unlikely — but it *could* happen, and it does demonstrate why you need multiple backups. If you have several sets of backup disks and don't keep them all in the same room as your Mac, chances are pretty good that one of the sets will work even if the others are lost, stolen, or destroyed.

TIP

For true data security, consider a backup scheme such as this one: Create at least three sets of backups, and store at least one of them offsite. You might keep a full backup, which you update monthly, in a safe-deposit box at your bank. Next, use a cloud-based backup service such as Backblaze (www.backblaze.com) to create a second offsite backup that you can keep updated more frequently.

If you store all your files in the Documents folder or the desktop, you can store your Desktop and Documents folders in iCloud, which counts as another offsite backup (kinda). To do that, launch System Settings, click Apple ID, click the Options button next to iCloud Drive, and then enable the check box for Desktop & Documents Folders.

One last thing: Encrypt your Time Machine backups for security so that nobody unauthorized can use them. When setting up your backup disk, set the Encrypt Backup switch to on (blue), and enter a strong password to use for the encryption.

Nonbackup Security Concerns

Backing up your files is critical unless you don't mind losing all your data some-day. And although backing up is by far your most important security concern, several other things could imperil your data — things such as viruses or other types of malware, including worms, spyware, and intruder attacks. That's the bad news. The good news is that all those things are far more likely to affect Windows users than Mac users.

Even so, consider taking the following precautions.

About viruses and other malware

A computer *virus* is a nasty little piece of computer code that replicates and spreads from disk to disk. A virus could cause your Mac to misbehave; some viruses can destroy files or erase disks with no warning.

Malware (short for *malicious software*) is software that's hostile, intrusive, annoy-ing, or disruptive. Malware is often designed to gain unauthorized access to your computer or collect personal data (including passwords) without your knowledge, or both.

The difference between a virus and other types of malware is that malware doesn't spread by itself. It relies upon trickery, mimicry, and social engineering to induce unsuspecting users to open a malicious file or install a malicious app. So a virus is a type of malware, but not all malware is viral.

Almost all viruses are specific to a particular operating system. Mac viruses won't affect Windows users, Windows viruses won't affect Mac users, and so forth. And the vast majority of known viruses affect only Windows, mostly because it's a much larger, juicier, and more lucrative target than macOS.

The one real exception here is a "gift" from the wonderful world of Microsoft Office (Word and Excel, for example) users: the dreaded *macro viruses* that are spread with Word and Excel documents containing macros written in the Micro-soft VBA (Visual Basic for Applications) language. Microsoft has made the imple-mentation of VBA somewhat safer, but it's still wise to treat any incoming Microsoft Office file with caution.

Apple frequently releases security updates for macOS and Apple's apps to fend off specific threats that have been detected in the wild. To keep your Mac as safe as possible, you should allow macOS to apply security updates as soon as they become available. See the next section for details.

Although few truly viral Mac operating system threats have been spotted in the wild so far, most malware is spread via social engineering, which is easy to protect yourself against. Here's how:

>> On the General tab in the Settings window in Safari, deselect the Open "Safe" Files after Downloading check box.

>> If a suspicious alert or window appears on your screen while you're browsing the Internet, Force Quit your web browser (⇨ Force Quit or ⌘+Option+Esc) immediately.

>> If the macOS Installer launches for no apparent reason, *don't click Continue!* Don't install the software, and for heaven's sake, don't type your administrator password.

>> Don't run *any* installer — the kind built into macOS or the third-party kind — unless you're absolutely certain that it came from a trusted source.

>> Don't use credit or debit cards with unfamiliar vendors or nonsecure websites. (If you don't see *https* instead of *http* in the address bar of your browser, or if you don't see a little lock icon in the address field, the site may not be secure.)

>> Allow only apps from the App Store, not apps from other sources. This is safest, but if you want to install other browsers, such as Firefox and Google Chrome, you'll need to allow apps from identified developers as well, as these browsers aren't on the App Store. To control what you can install, choose System Settings ⇨ Privacy & Security, scroll down to the Security section of the Privacy & Security pane, and then select either the App Store option button or the App Store and Identified Developers option button, as appropriate, in the Allow Apps Downloaded From area.

REMEMBER

If you use disks that have ever been inserted into a computer you don't know and trust, you may need virus-detection software. If you download and use files from the Internet, you'll be well served by virus detection as well.

You don't have too much to worry about if

>> You download files only from commercial online services, such as CNET or MacUpdate, which are conscientious about malware.

>> You buy software only from the App Store.

>> You use only commercial software and never download files from websites with strange names.

You should definitely worry about malicious infection if

>> An unsavory friend told you about a website called PiratedIllegalStolenBootlegSoftware.com, and you actually visited it.

>> You swap disks or USB thumb drives with friends regularly.

>> You shuttle disks or USB thumb drives back and forth to other Macs.

>> You use your disks or USB thumb drives at public computers, photo-printing machines, or other computers that are likely to have been exposed to many disks.

>> You download files from various and sundry places on the Internet, even ones that don't sound as questionable as PiratedIllegalStolenBootlegSoftware.com.

>> You receive email with attachments (and open them). Note that you can receive malicious software in messages that look like they're from people you know and trust. This type of attack is called *spoofing,* and it's easy to accomplished, so think carefully before opening an attachment, and contact the sender if you have any doubt about the message's authenticity.

If you're at risk, do yourself a favor: Buy a commercial antivirus app. Or try a free malware scanner such as Malwarebytes, Bitdefender, or Avira. If you think you may be at risk, scan your drive with one of the free utilities before shelling out any cash. Get it if you need it; don't if you don't.

Install security updates — or more — automatically

By default, your Mac calls home to Apple once a day to look for any new or updated software. To keep your Mac as safe as possible, you should set it to install any new security updates automatically without consulting you. You may also want to install macOS updates or app updates from the App Store automatically.

To configure checking for updates, choose System Settings ⇨ General ⇨ Software Update. Opening the Software Update pane like this forces macOS to check for any new updates, so the information you see will be up to date. When the check is complete, click the Info button (the i-in-a-circle icon) on the right side of the Automatic Updates button to open the Automatic Updates dialog (see Figure 21-3). Then you can configure automatic updating by setting the following five switches:

>> **Check for Updates:** Set this switch to on (blue) to have macOS check for updates. There's really no reason not to do this.

- >> **Download New Updates When Available:** Set this switch to on (blue) to download updates automatically. Automatic downloading is usually helpful unless your Mac connects to metered networks, in which case you may prefer to download them manually when your Mac is connected to an all-you-can-eat network.

- >> **Install macOS Updates:** Set this switch to on (blue) to install all macOS system updates.

- >> **Install App Updates from the App Store:** Set this switch to on (blue) to install all app updates issued through the App Store.

- >> **Install Security Responses and System Files:** Set this switch to on (blue) to install security fixes and macOS system file updates. This category is the most important one for protecting your Mac, so install these updates automatically even if you prefer to install all others manually.

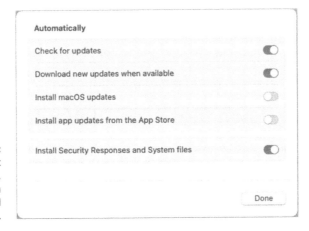

FIGURE 21-3:
In the Automatic Updates dialog, choose which updates to install automatically.

WARNING

Once in a blue moon, a software update has an unintended side effect: While fixing one problem, it introduces a different problem. If you're concerned that this situation might happen, set the Install macOS Updates switch and the Install App Updates from the App Store switch to off (white), and check an authoritative Mac tech site, such as Macworld (www.macworld.com) for headlines about faulty updates before you install any macOS updates or app updates.

Many third-party apps, including Microsoft Office and most Adobe products, use their own update-checking mechanism. Check to make sure that you have yours enabled. Many third-party apps offer a Check for Updates option on the Help (or other) menu or as a preference in their Preferences window or Settings window.

One last thing: If you see a little number on the App Store or System Settings icon in the Dock, you have that many updates waiting to be installed. Launch the Mac App Store and click the Updates tab, or launch System Settings, click the General icon in the sidebar, and then click the Software Update button.

Protecting Your Data from Prying Eyes

The last kind of security I look at in this chapter is protecting your files from other users on your local area network (LAN) and users who have physical access to your Mac. If you don't want anyone messing with your files, check out the security measures in the following sections.

Blocking or limiting connections

First, open the Sharing pane in System Settings by choosing ⌘ ⇨ System Settings ⇨ General ⇨ Sharing and then set each of the switches to off (white) unless you absolutely need to use those services. Disabling all the services in the Sharing pane helps prevent other people from accessing your Mac across the network.

Locking down files with FileVault

If you absolutely, positively never want anyone to be able to access the files in your Home folder without your permission, use FileVault. This app allows you to encrypt your entire disk and protect it with the latest government-approved encryption standard: Advanced Encryption Standard with 128-bit keys (AES-128).

When you turn on FileVault, you're asked to set a master password for the computer. After you do, you or any other administrator can use that master password if you forget your regular account login password.

WARNING

If you turn on FileVault and forget both your login password and your master password, you can't log in to your account — and your data is lost forever. Really. So don't forget these passwords, okay?

FileVault is useful primarily if you store sensitive information on your Mac. If you're logged out of your user account, and other people access to your Mac, there's no way for them to access your data. Period.

Because FileVault encrypts your entire hard drive, you may be prevented some carrying out some tasks that normally access your disk. For one thing, some backup apps (not Time Machine, of course) can choke if FileVault is enabled. Also, if you're not logged in to your user account, other users can't access your Shared folder(s).

REMEMBER

Because FileVault is always encrypting and decrypting files, it can slow older Macs a tiny bit when you add or save new files, and it can take extra time before it lets you log out, restart, or shut down. If your Mac is less than five years old, you'll probably notice little or no delay from enabling FileVault.

To turn on FileVault, follow these steps:

1. **Choose ➪ System Settings ➪ Privacy & Security to open the Privacy & Security pane in System Settings.**

2. **Scroll down to the Security section at the bottom of the pane, and click the Turn On button on the FileVault row.**

3. **Authenticate yourself with your password or Touch ID when challenged.**

   A dialog opens, giving you the choice between allowing your iCloud account to unlock your disk and reset your password, if needed, or creating a recovery key.

4. **Select the Allow My iCloud Account to Unlock My Disk option button or the Create a Recovery Key and Do Not Use My iCloud Account option button, as appropriate.**

5. **Click the Continue button, and follow the prompts.**

To turn off FileVault, mosey back to the Security section of the Privacy & Security pane in System Settings and then click the Turn Off button on the FileVault row.

Putting your Mac in Lockdown mode

NEW

Ventura includes a new feature called Lockdown mode that enables you to fire up an extreme level of protection against hacking and cracking threats. Lockdown mode is designed to protect your Mac against targeted attacks using custom malware or state-sponsored spyware.

REMEMBER

iOS 16 has a similar Lockdown mode. If you need to activate Lockdown mode on your Mac, activate it on your iPhone and iPad as well.

Lockdown mode is designed for the tiny minority of users who face these types of threats. You may need to use Lockdown mode if you're a human-rights activist, a crusading journalist, or a secret agent. If you're not exposed to such threats, Lockdown mode is likely to be overkill.

To keep your Mac safe, Lockdown mode must limit some of the functionality that Mac users enjoy. Here are examples of some (only some) of the limitations that Lockdown mode imposes:

>> Messages blocks incoming message attachments, including link previews.

>> FaceTime blocks calls and invitations from people who aren't in your Contacts list.

>> Safari's just-in-time compiler for the JavaScript programming language is disabled.

>> Photos hides shared photo albums and blocks shared album invitations.

>> macOS disables wired connections to external devices or accessories while the Mac's screen is locked.

>> macOS prevents you from configuring various sensitive settings, such as installing configuration profiles.

To put your Mac in Lockdown mode, choose ⬢⇨ System Settings⇨ Privacy & Security to open the Privacy & Security pane in System Settings, scroll down to the Security section at the bottom of the pane, and then click the Turn On button on the Lockdown Mode row.

Setting other options for security

macOS Ventura offers several other settings that can help keep your data safe. This section tells you where to find them and how to set them. To get started, choose ⬢⇨ System Settings to fire up the System Settings app. Then you can

>> **Change your password.** Click the Login Password category in the sidebar and then click the Change button in the Password area of the Login Password pane.

>> **Require a password to resume after sleep or a screen saver.** Click the Lock Screen category in the sidebar. Open the Require Password After Screen Saver Begins or Display Is Turned Off pop-up menu, and choose Immediately, After 5 Seconds, or After 1 Minute. (Don't use a longer time, because that makes your Mac less secure.)

TIP

In the Lock Screen pane, you'll also find the Show Message When Locked setting. If you want your Mac's screen to display a message when the Mac is locked, set the switch to on (blue), click the Set button, type the message in the Set a Message to Appear on the Lock Screen dialog, and then click OK. This option is popular but provides no security benefit.

>> **Limit app installation to apps from the App Store.** Click the Security & Privacy category in the sidebar, scroll down to the Securiy section of the Security & Privacy pane, and then select the appropriate option button in the Allow Apps Downloaded From area. You have two choices:

- *App Store:* This option allows you to run only apps you download from the Mac App Store. It's the safer and more restrictive setting.

- *App Store and Identified Developers:* Apple offers a Developer ID credential to certified members of the Mac Developers Program. Apple gives each developer a unique Developer ID, which allows macOS to verify that their app is not known malware and that it hasn't been tampered with. If an app doesn't have a Developer ID associated with it, macOS can let you know before you install it.

  This choice is probably best for most users. It allows third-party apps from Apple-vetted vendors, including Microsoft, Adobe, and thousands more. It's a lot less restrictive than the Mac App Store option and a lot safer than letting you download apps from anywhere.

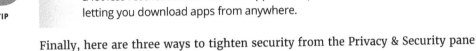

TIP

Finally, here are three ways to tighten security from the Privacy & Security pane in System Settings:

>> **Choose which apps can use Location Services.** Click Location Services to display the Location Services screen, and you'll see a list of apps that are allowed to use your computer's current location. Set the switch for each app to off (white) or on (blue), as needed.

>> **Limit access to your contacts, calendars, and reminders.** Click Contacts, Calendars, or Reminders in the Privacy list, and you'll see a list of the apps with access to their contents. Set the switch for each app to off (white) or on (blue), as needed.

>> **Prune the list of apps allow to control your Mac.** Click Accessibility in the Privacy list and then scrutinize the Allow the Apps Below to Control Your Computer list on the Accessibility screen. Set the switch for each app to off (white) or on (blue), as needed.

REMEMBER

Here are some ways to protect your data:

>> Use strong passwords.

>> Don't share your passwords.

>> Don't store passwords in insecure locations (such as on sticky notes on your monitor).

» Use a password manager (such as macOS's built-in Keychain Access or a third-party app like 1Password) to store your passwords securely.

» Don't log in to suspicious or insecure wireless networks.

» Don't visit suspicious websites or open suspicious emails.

» If you have any question about authenticity, just don't click!

Chapter **22**

Utility Chest

macOS Ventura comes with a plethora of useful utilities that make using your computer more pleasant or make you more productive when you use your computer or both. This chapter gives you a peek at a handful you're likely to use that are not covered elsewhere in this book.

REMEMBER

The first item, Calculator, is in your Applications folder (Go ⇨ Applications; keyboard shortcut ⌘+Shift+A). All other items in this chapter are in your Utilities folder (Go ⇨ Utilities; keyboard shortcut ⌘+Shift+U), which you'll find *inside* your Applications folder.

You don't need to remember which utility lives where, because you can run them all from Launchpad. Start typing the utility's name and then click the appropriate result. Or if you want to do things the hard way, open Launchpad and then click the Other folder to drill down to the icons for these utilities and some more esoteric ones.

Calculator

Need to do some quick math? The Calculator app gives you a simple calculator with all the basic number-crunching functions of a pocket calculator. To use it, you can either click the keys with the mouse or type numbers and operators (math symbols such as +, −, and =) using the number keys on your keyboard (or numeric keypad, if you have one). Calculator also offers a paper tape (Window⇔ Show Paper Tape) to track your computations — and, if you want, provide a printed record. It can even speak numbers aloud (Speech⇔ Speak Button Pressed and Speech⇔ Speak Result).

Check out Calculator in Figure 22-1.

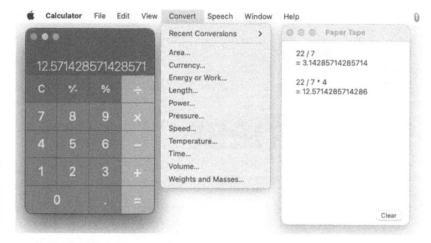

FIGURE 22-1:
Calculator (left),
Convert menu
(middle), and
Paper Tape
(right).

The Convert menu doesn't look particularly exciting, but it has one killer feature: live currency conversion. Type in the amount of the starting currency, such as 100; choose Convert⇔ Currency; specify the From currency, such as US Dollar, and the To currency, such as Japanese Yen; and then click the Convert button. Calculator grabs the current exchange rate off the Internet before returning the result. And if you need to perform more calculations of the same type, you can do so quickly from the Convert⇔ Recent Conversion submenu.

Beyond that, Calculator has three modes: Basic, Scientific, and Programmer. Basic is the default, and you access the other two modes as follows:

>> Pressing ⌘+2 (View ⇔ Scientific) turns the formerly anemic calculator into a powerful scientific calculator.

>> If you prefer Reverse Polish Notation (RPN), press ⌘+R or choose View ⇔ RPN Mode.

TECHNICAL
STUFF

>> Choosing View ⇔ Programmer (⌘+3) turns Calculator into the programmer's friend, letting you display your data in binary, octal, hexadecimal, ASCII, and Unicode. It also performs programming operations, such as shifts and byte swaps. (If you're a programmer, you know what all that means; if you aren't, it really doesn't matter.)

>> If you have a MacBook model with the Touch Bar control strip above the keyboard, you can customize the buttons that appear on the Touch Bar for Calculator. Choose View ⇨ Customize Touch Bar, and then work in the Customize Touch Bar dialog. This feature is great for putting the calculation operations you use most right at your fingertips.

One more thing: Spotlight (and Siri) can perform many basic math calculations and conversions faster than you can launch the Calculator app.

TIP

Activity Monitor

In Unix, the underlying operating system that powers macOS, apps and other things going on behind the scenes are called *processes.* Each app and the operating system itself can run several processes at the same time.

In Figure 22-2, you see 621 processes running, most of them behind the scenes. Note that when this screenshot was taken, the Mac had half a dozen or more apps running, including Finder, Safari, Messages, Photos, and Activity Monitor itself.

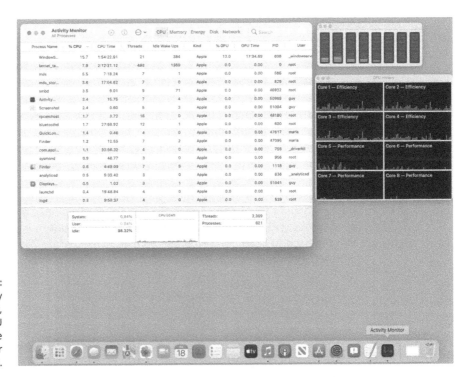

FIGURE 22-2:
The Activity Monitor window, two little CPU monitors, and the Activity Monitor Dock icon.

To display the two CPU monitor windows on the right side of the Activity Monitor window, as shown in Figure 22-2, choose Window⇨CPU Usage (⌘+2) and Window⇨CPU History (⌘+3).

You also select what appears on the Activity Monitor's Dock icon — CPU Usage (shown in Figure 22-2), CPU History, Network Usage, Disk Activity, or the Activity Monitor — by choosing View⇨Dock Icon. All but the Activity Monitor icon appear *live*, meaning that they update every few seconds to reflect the current state of affairs.

Note that you can't display CPU Usage or CPU History in a window and in the Dock icon at the same time. Those two items can be displayed on the Dock or a window, but not both.

To choose how often these updates occur, choose View⇨Update Frequency.

WARNING

Setting Activity Monitor to update more frequently causes it to use more CPU cycles, which can decrease overall performance slightly.

Finally, the bottom portion of the Activity Monitor window displays information for the active tab. Select the CPU, Memory, Energy, Disk, or Network tab at the top of the window, and the middle and bottom portions of the Activity Monitor window change to reflect that selection.

TECHNICAL
STUFF

Because all Macs that can run Ventura have at least a dual-core processor, you'll see at least two, and possibly four or more, CPUs displayed in Activity Monitor, one for each core.

Geeks and troubleshooters (and even you) can use Activity Monitor to identify what processes are running, which user owns the process, and how much CPU capacity and memory the process is using. You can even use this feature to quit or force-quit a process that you think might be causing problems for you.

WARNING

Messing around in Activity Monitor isn't a good idea for most users. If you're having problems with an app or with macOS, try quitting open apps, force-quitting apps (press ⌘+Option+Esc — the Mac three-finger salute), logging out and then logging back in again, or restarting your Mac before you start mucking around with killing processes.

Disk Utility

If you're having problems with your hard drive or need to make changes to it, Disk Utility is a good place to start. Start by clicking a disk or volume in the column on the left and then click one of the buttons on the toolbar as described in the following sections.

Volume +/−

The Volume + and Volume − buttons make it easier than ever to subdivide your hard or solid-state disk into virtual volumes, which look and act like separate disks but are volumes on a single disk.

If you think this sounds a lot like what we used to call *partitioning,* it is. But to understand the difference between a volume and a partition, you first have to understand the difference between APFS and HFS+ by reading the nearby sidebar.

Partition button

Speaking of partitions, you can use the Partition button to create disk *partitions* (multiple volumes on a single disk) on disks formatted as HFS+. macOS treats each partition as a separate disk. The Partition button is enabled only when an eligible item is selected in the column on the left.

Partitioning a drive lets you create multiple volumes. A *volume* is a storage space that (from the Mac's point of view) looks and acts just like a hard drive. A *partition* is simply a designated volume on a drive, separate from all other partitions (volumes). You can create any number of partitions, but it's a good idea to limit yourself to no more than a small handful.

By the same token, it's absolutely not necessary to use partitions unless you're running Boot Camp (see Chapter 20) on an Intel-powered Mac. Many users never partition a hard drive and get along just fine. If you do choose to partition, you probably should limit the number of partitions you create. An iMac with a 1TB drive will do just fine as shipped (with a single partition); there's no need to create more.

WARNING

Be careful here. Although some adjustments can be made to partitions without loss of data, not all adjustments can. Disk Utility will warn you if what you're about to do will permanently erase your data, so make sure you read all warnings that pop up. And, of course, you should always have a backup (see Chapter 21) before mucking with your disk.

APFS VERSUS HFS+

In the old days, the term *partitioning* described creating multiple virtual disks out of a single hard or solid-state drive. But with macOS High Sierra, Apple introduced a new file system called APFS (Apple File System). The old scheme (prior to High Sierra) is HFS+ (Hierarchical File System +). In other words, APFS is the modern replacement for HFS+, though HFS+ is still available in Disk Utility.

According to Apple, when you install macOS High Sierra, Mojave, Catalina, Big Sur, Monterey, or Ventura on a solid-state drive (SSD) or other all-flash storage device, the volume will *automatically* be converted to APFS. If, however, the drive is *not* solid-state or flash — a Fusion drive or a traditional hard disk — it will *not* be converted to APFS.

Disk Utility in Ventura can format most storage devices using either file system. If you need to reformat a device manually, consider these points made in a helpful Apple Support article:

- APFS requires macOS High Sierra or later. Earlier versions of the Mac operating system don't mount APFS-formatted volumes.

- APFS is optimized for SSDs and other all-flash storage devices.

- Disk Utility tries to detect the type of storage you're formatting and then shows the appropriate format in the Format menu. If it can't detect the type of storage, it defaults to Mac OS Extended (aka HFS+), which works with all versions of macOS.

To make a long story short, if you have to format an SSD, use APFS; for all other drive types, use HFS+.

To find out which format (file system) a device is currently using, Control-click or right-click the device in Finder, and choose Get Info from the contextual menu. In the Info window that opens, look at the Format readout in the General section. *Format: AFPS* means that the device is using AFPS, *Format: Mac OS Extended* means the device is using HFS+.

Although APFS will allow you to create partitions instead of volumes, volumes are almost always the better choice.

Finally, if you click the Partition button with an APFS disk selected in the sidebar, you'll see an explanation that suggests you might be happier with a volume than with a partition.

First Aid button

If you suspect that something's not quite right with your start-up disk (or any other disk connected to your Mac), try using Disk Utility's First Aid feature to verify and (if necessary) repair the disk. Select the ailing disk in the sidebar and then click the First Aid button on the Disk Utility toolbar. In the dialog that asks if you'd like to run First Aid on the selected disk, click the Run button.

If the disk you're trying to repair is your start-up disk, Disk Utility will warn you that it needs to temporarily lock the boot volume and that other apps will be unresponsive until the operation has completed, as shown in Figure 22-3. Go have a cup of coffee or something; the process takes 15–30 minutes for most disks.

FIGURE 22-3:
If you try to run First Aid on your start-up disk, you'll see this alert before you can continue.

When First Aid is finished, you'll get information about any problems that the software finds.

If First Aid doesn't find any problems, you can go on your merry way, secure in the knowledge that that disk is A-OK. If First Aid turns up a problem that it can't fix, it will advise you what to do next. In most cases, that advice is to boot from the Recovery disk (Macs with Intel processors: Hold down ⌘+R at startup; Macs with Apple processors: Press and hold down the power button until the Recovery Options screen appears, and then click Continue) and run First Aid again.

You can't use Disk Utility First Aid to fix a CD or DVD; neither can you use it to fix most disk image (DMG) files. These types of disks are read-only and can't be altered.

TIP

Erase button

Use Erase to format (erase) any disk except the current start-up disk.

WARNING

When you format a disk, you erase all information on it permanently. Formatting can't be undone — so unless you're *absolutely sure* this is what you want, don't do it. Unless you have no use for whatever's currently on the disk, make a complete backup of the disk before you format it. If the data is critical, you should have at least two (or even three) known-to-be-valid backup copies of that disk before you reformat.

After you click the Erase button, a dialog opens, prompting you to name the disk you're about to erase and specify the posterasure format in the drop-down Format menu.

REMEMBER

Use Mac OS Extended (Journaled) for rotational and hybrid disks. Use APFS for SSDs.

WARNING

Don't try any of the other options (case-sensitive, encrypted, and other variations) unless you know what you're doing and have a good reason. Formatting a disk using many of these options can cause Mac software to misbehave. Don't do it. Choose only Mac OS Extended (Journaled) or APFS — unless you're prepared to spend time troubleshooting when your Mac doesn't work as expected.

This warning applies only to bootable disks with macOS installed on them. If the disk isn't going to be used as a boot disk, you can format it any way you care to.

Mount/Unmount button

A drive can be connected but not available to your Mac. When you eject a hard drive or SSD, for example, it's still connected to the computer but doesn't appear in Finder. This drive is called an *unmounted disk*.

The Mount/Unmount button lets you dismount (eject) or mount a connected disk or partition on a disk. For reasons that should be obvious, you can't eject the disk from which your Mac booted.

Info button

Click the Info button to see myriad technical details about the selected disk, including its size, capacity, and free and used space. One last thing: You find out more about Disk Utility (mostly how to use it for troubleshooting) in Chapter 23.

Keychain Access

A *keychain* is a way to consolidate your passwords — your Mac login password, your email password, and passwords required by any websites. Keychain Access is the app you use to manage those passwords.

Here's how it works: You use a single password to unlock your keychain (which holds your various passwords), and then you don't have to remember all your other passwords. Your passwords are secure because only a user who has your keychain password can reach the other password-protected apps.

TIP

The Keychain Access utility is particularly cool if you have multiple email accounts and each one has a different password. Just add them all to your keychain, and you can get all your mail at the same time with one password.

macOS creates a special master keychain called the *login keychain* automatically for each user account on the Mac. macOS automatically unlocks the login keychain when you log into your account.

TIP

Here's how to add passwords to your login keychain:

>> **To add passwords for apps:** If the app supports the keychain, the first time you log in with your username and password, a dialog will ask whether you want to add this login to the keychain. Click Yes.

   How do you know which apps support the Keychain Access utility? You don't until you're prompted to save your password in a keychain in that Open dialog, connect window, or so forth. If an app supports Keychain Access, it offers a check box for it in the user ID/password dialog or window.

   If that doesn't happen the first time you provide your password, the app doesn't support macOS keychains and you're out of luck. You can add the account details manually (see the next bullet), but they won't be provided automatically when the app requests them — you'll have to open Keychain Access to look them up. The upside is that your passwords are secure as long as they're stored in a keychain.

TIP

   If you select the User Names and Passwords check box on the AutoFill tab of Safari's Settings window (Safari ➪ Settings or ⌘+, [comma]), you don't have to add sites, accounts, or passwords manually. Instead, the first time you visit a site that requires an account name and a password, Safari asks whether you'd like to save your password; then it saves the password.

>> **To add a website (or other) password to a keychain manually:** If your login credentials aren't being filled in automatically for a website, you can add them manually by using the Keychain Access app. Just choose File ➪ New

Password Item and type (or copy and paste) the URL of the page in the Keychain Item Name field of the dialog that appears. Then type your username in the Account Name field and your password in the Password field, as shown in Figure 22-4. (If you're adding a password for something other than a website, type a descriptive name in the Keychain Item Name field rather than a URL.)

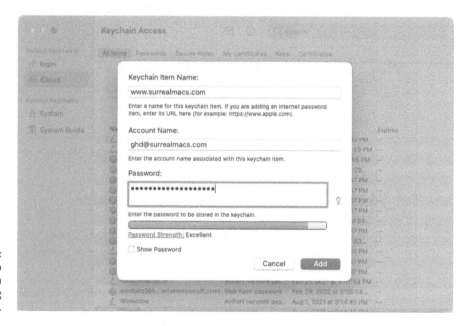

TIP

Click the little key to the right of the password field to use the Password Assistant window, which can help you select a high-quality password.

To use the new URL password, use Safari to open the URL. If the account name and password aren't filled in for you automatically, choose Edit ⇨ AutoFill Form (⌘+Shift+A), and they will be.

TIP

iCloud Keychain syncing is a great feature that makes keychains even better. Turn it on by choosing System Settings ⇨ Apple ID ⇨ iCloud and then setting the Keychain switch to on (blue). iCloud securely syncs your keychain passwords to (and from) all your Apple devices, including iPhones and iPads.

WARNING

Syncing your passwords makes them available on all your devices, so you must secure each device adequately to keep your passwords secure. If your iPhone has a weak passcode, take a minute to beef the passcode up to full strength. If you share your iPad with family members, cease and desist immediately.

Passwords System Preferences Pane

The Passwords pane in the System Settings app offers a user-friendly interface for managing your stored passwords.

To manage a password for a website, scroll the list in the main pane until you find the right website (or click in the Search box and search for it by name). When you locate the website, click the Info (i in a circle) icon to the right of the website's name to open a dialog for inspecting and changing the password. Click the Edit button to change the username or password for this site locally (on your Mac), or click Change Password on Website to launch Safari and change your password at its source.

To copy a password to the Clipboard, click the bullets (dots) in the password field and then click Copy Password. To paste the password, click in the password field and then choose Edit ⇨ Paste or press ⌘+V.

Finally, if you want your Mac to monitor and detect compromised passwords securely, click the Security Recommendations button at the top to display the Security Recommendations screen, and set the Detect Leaked Passwords switch to on (blue). Also on this screen, look at the list of recommendations for fixing problems with your passwords; click the Change Password on Website button to start making a change.

Migration Assistant

Migration Assistant is pretty much a one-trick pony, but that pony is a prize-winner. You use Migration Assistant to transfer your account and other user information from another Mac, another volume on the current Mac, or a Time Machine backup. You need to authenticate as an administrator to use it, but it's a pretty handy way to transfer an entire account without having to re-create your preferences and other settings. When you first installed Ventura (or when you booted your nice, new Ventura-based Mac for the first time), the setup utility asked you whether you wanted to transfer your information from another Mac. If you answered in the affirmative, it ran Migration Assistant.

TIP

Migration Assistant isn't just for new Ventura installs. You can launch Migration Assistant anytime to transfer all or some user accounts, apps, settings, and files from another Mac, PC, or Time Machine backup to this one. You can use it also after replacing a hard drive or reinstalling macOS. Last but not least, Migration Assistant can import user accounts, apps, settings, and files from Windows PCs as well as from Macs.

System Information

System Information is a little utility you can launch by clicking , holding down Option to make the System Information menu item replace the About This Mac menu item, and then clicking System Information. You can also launch System Information from Launchpad or by clicking the System Report button at the bottom of the General pane in System Settings.

System Information provides in-depth information about your Mac's hardware and software. If you're curious about arcane questions such as what processor your Mac has or what devices are stashed inside it or are connected to it, open System Information, and start digging. Click various items in the Contents list on the left side of the window, and information about the item appears on the right side of the window. System Information is read-only: The utility lets you view information but not change it, so you can't mangle your Mac's settings here. (For mangling settings, use the System Settings app — or Terminal, which you'll meet next.)

TIP

If you ever have occasion to call for technical support for your Mac, software, or peripherals, you're probably going to be asked to provide information from System Information.

Terminal

macOS is based on Unix. If you need proof — or if you want to operate your Mac as the Unix machine that it is — Terminal is the place to start.

Because Unix is a command-line-based operating system, you use Terminal to type your commands. You can issue commands that show a directory listing, copy and move files, search for filenames or contents, or establish or change passwords. In short, if you know what you're doing, you can do everything on the command line that you can do in macOS. For most folks, that's not a desirable alternative to the windows and icons of the Finder window. But rest assured that true geeks who are also Mac lovers get all misty-eyed about the combination of a command line *and* a graphical user interface.

WARNING

You can wreak havoc upon your poor operating system with Terminal. You can harm your macOS installation in many ways that just aren't possible using mere windows and icons and clicks. *Before you type a single command in Terminal, think seriously about what I just said.* And if you're not 100 percent certain about the command you just typed, don't even think about pressing Return.

IN THIS CHAPTER

» **Knowing what to do when your Mac won't boot**

» **Dealing with the prohibitory sign**

» **Recovering from start-up crashes**

» **Using the Optimize Storage feature**

Chapter **23**

Troubleshooting macOS

Macs have a great reputation for running well and just keeping on running well — and I hope that your Mac does just that. But even the best hardware and software can run into difficulties sometimes, so you should be prepared to troubleshoot your Mac and its operating system at some point.

When things go wrong with your Mac, turn to the advice in this chapter. It contains tried-and-tested tips and tricks that can help you resolve many common Mac issues without a trip to the repair shop — as long as your Mac's hardware isn't dead. If it *is* dead, turn to the Apple Store or the repair shop rather than this chapter.

Before I start, I need to explain two key terms. First, this chapter uses the term *hard disk* generically to refer to both hard disks (mechanical disks with spinning platters) and solid-state drives, or SSDs (electronic drives with no moving parts). Second, *booting* means using a particular disk or disk partition as the *start-up disk* — the disk from which your Mac starts (or tries to).

About Start-Up Disks and Booting

Although you usually see a stylish Apple logo when you turn on your computer, once in a blue moon, you may instead see a solid blue screen, a solid gray screen, a solid black screen, or something else entirely, as described in the next section.

Any of these screen types means that your Mac isn't starting up as it should. When this happens, it usually indicates that something bad has happened to your Mac or its start-up disk. Sometimes, a hardware component has bitten the dust; at other times, macOS itself has somehow been damaged.

Finding or creating a start-up disk

macOS Ventura is available only in the Mac App Store as a download. Because you can no longer purchase a bootable installer DVD, the macOS Installer automatically creates a bootable partition named Recovery HD when you install Ventura on a disk.

The Recovery HD partition can save your bacon (or vegetarian equivalent), but you'd be wise to also make a bootable recovery disk or a clone of your Mac start-up disk in case your Mac's hard disk dies and takes the Recovery HD partition with it. If you don't, you may wish you'd done so when your Mac starts acting wonky.

WARNING

Explaining how to create a bootable recovery disk or clone is beyond the purview of this book, but you'll find full details on the Internet. Start with this Apple Support Article: `https://support.apple.com/en-us/HT201372`. And bear in mind that you can't start your Mac from a Time Machine backup.

TIP

A great tool for creating a recovery disk is Carbon Copy Cloner (`https://bombich.com`), a $39.99 app that lets you create a clone of your boot disk with a minimum of fuss. Or you can try SuperDuper! (shareware from `www.shirt-pocket.com`); just add a hard disk as large as or larger than your boot disk, and you'll be good to go with either of these apps. Both Carbon Copy Cloner and SuperDuper! offer free trial versions that you can put through their paces.

They call it a prohibitory sign for a reason

When you turn on your Mac, the first thing it does (after running the hardware tests) is check for a start-up disk that has a viable copy of macOS on it. If your system doesn't find such a disk on your internal hard drive, it begins looking elsewhere — on a Thunderbolt or Universal Serial Bus (USB) disk, a thumb drive, or a DVD.

At this point, your Mac usually finds the (usually internal) hard drive, which contains the operating system, and the start-up process continues with the subtle Apple logo and all the rest. If your Mac can't find a suitable bootable disk, you encounter the dreaded prohibitory sign. Think of the prohibitory sign as your Mac's way of saying, "Please provide me a start-up disk."

REMEMBER

If you have more than one start-up disk attached to your Mac, as many users do, you can choose which one your Mac boots from in the Startup Disk pane in System Settings (choose System Settings ⇨ General ⇨ Startup Disk) or by pressing and holding down the Option key when you start up your Mac.

If you encounter any of the warning signs shown in Figure 23-1, go through the steps outlined later in this chapter. Try them in the order listed, starting with Step 1. Then, if one doesn't work, move on to the next.

Your computer restarted because of a problem. Press a key or wait a few seconds to continue starting up.

Votre ordinateur a redémarré en raison d'un problème. Pour poursuivre le redémarrage, appuyez sur une touche ou patientez quelques secondes.

El ordenador se ha reiniciado debido a un problema. Para continuar con el arranque, pulse cualquier tecla o espere unos segundos.

Ihr Computer wurde aufgrund eines Problems neu gestartet. Drücken Sie zum Fortfahren eine Taste oder warten Sie einige Sekunden.

問題が起きたためコンピュータを再起動しました。このまま起動する場合は、いずれかのキーを押すか、数秒間そのままお待ちください。

电脑因出现问题而重新启动。请按一下按键，或等几秒钟以继续启动。

FIGURE 23-1:
Any of these warnings means that it's trouble-shooting time.

Recovering with Recovery HD

If you see a prohibitory sign (top left in Figure 23-1), a spinning-beach ball-of-death (top right), or a kernel-panic alert (the text in other languages that appears below the other two images) that doesn't go away when you start your Mac, the first thing to do is attempt to repair hidden damage to your hard drive with Disk Utility's First Aid feature.

Step 1: Run First Aid

In most cases, the first logical troubleshooting step is to use the First Aid option in Disk Utility.

Every drive has several strangely named components, such as B-trees, extent files, catalog files, and other creatively named invisible files. They're all involved in managing the data on your drives. Disk Utility's First Aid feature checks all those files and repairs the damaged ones.

Because your Mac isn't able to finish the boot process, you'll need to boot from the Recovery partition to perform this repair. The steps for rebooting your Mac into Recovery mode are different depending on its processor type:

>> **Macs with Intel processors:** Restart while pressing ⌘+R, continuing to press them until you see the Apple logo appear. When it does, a window appears offering four buttons: Restore from Time Machine, Reinstall MacOS, Safari, and Disk Utility. Click Disk Utility to launch it.

The Recovery Mode boot process can take several minutes, during which time it may appear that nothing is happening. Be patient.

>> **Macs with Apple M processors:** Press and hold down the power button; continue to hold it down until the Options button appears midscreen, and then release it. Click the Options button, select a user and type their password, click Disk Utility, and then click Continue.

Now here's how to run First Aid using the Disk Utility app:

1. **Click the icon for your Mac's boot hard drive, to the left of the Disk Utility window.**

    Your boot drive is the one with macOS and your Home folder on it. It's normally called Macintosh HD unless you've renamed it.

2. **Click the First Aid button in the toolbar.**

    A dialog opens, asking whether you'd like to run First Aid on that disk.

3. **Click the Run button.**

    The Disk First Aid routine runs. It takes anywhere from a few minutes to an hour or more for First Aid to check and repair your disk and allow you to perform Step 6.

4. **(Optional) Click Show Details in the dialog if you want to see (mostly unintelligible) details.**

    When the routine is finished, the Done button is enabled.

    If First Aid finds damage that it can't fix, a commercial disk-recovery tool such as Prosoft's Drive Genius *may* be able to repair the damage.

5. **Click the Done button.**

6. **Quit Disk Utility.**

   Choose Disk Utility ⇨ Quit Disk Utility, press ⌘+Q, or click the red Close Window gumdrop button.

7. **Choose ⇨ Restart to exit Recovery mode and restart your Mac.**

WARNING

Make sure that you're running a current version of any disk utilities you try; older versions may not be compatible with macOS Ventura (or APFS) and could make things worse.

If everything checks out with First Aid, but you still get the prohibitory sign after you restart, proceed to the next section to try a dance called booting into Safe mode.

Step 2: Safe boot into Safe mode

Booting your Mac in Safe mode may help you resolve your start-up issue by not loading nonessential (and non-macOS) software at boot time. Again, the way you invoke Safe mode depends on your Mac's processor type:

>> **Macs with Intel processors:** Press and hold down the Shift key during startup.

>> **Macs with Apple M processors:** Shut Down your Mac, wait 10 seconds, and then press and hold the power button on your Mac until the Startup Options window appears. Select your start-up disk. Then press and hold down the Shift key, click Continue in Safe Mode, and release the Shift key.

If your Mac is set up so that you don't have to log in, keep pressing the Shift key during startup until Finder loads completely. If you do log in to your Mac, type your password as usual — but before clicking the Log In button, press the Shift key again and hold it down until Finder loads completely.

You'll know that you held the Shift key long enough if your Login Items don't load — assuming that you *have* Login Items. You can designate them in the Login Items pane in the System Settings app (choose System Settings ⇨ General ⇨ Login Items), but you may also find that some apps create them without consulting you.

TIP

To confirm that a Mac is in Safe mode, click to open the Apple menu, then hold down Option and click System Information. In the System Information window, click the Software heading in the sidebar on the left, and then verify that the Boot Mode readout in the right pane says Safe.

Booting in Safe mode does three things to help you with troubleshooting:

>> It forces a directory check of the start-up (boot) volume.

>> It loads only required kernel extensions (some of the items in /System/Library/ Extensions).

>> It runs only Apple-installed essential start-up items (some of the items in / Library/StartupItems and /System/Library/StartupItems). Note that the Startup Items in the Library folders are different from the Login Items in the Login pane in System Preferences. Startup Items run at boot time before the login window even appears; Login Items don't run until after you log into your user account.

Taken together, these changes often work around issues caused by software or directory damage on the start-up volume.

Some features don't work in Safe mode. Among them are DVD Player, capturing video (in iMovie or other video-editing software), and using FaceTime or certain audio input or output devices. Use Safe mode only when you need to troubleshoot a start-up issue, and reboot in normal mode as soon as possible.

Step 3: Zapping the PRAM/NVRAM

If your Mac has an Apple M processor, please ignore Step 3, which no longer applies to your Mac.

Sometimes, your Mac's parameter RAM (PRAM) or nonvolatile RAM (NVRAM) becomes scrambled and needs to be reset. Both of these small pieces of memory aren't erased or forgotten when you shut down your Mac. They keep track of things such as the following:

>> Time-zone setting

>> Startup-volume choice

>> Speaker volume

>> Any recent kernel-panic information

>> DVD region setting

To reset (a process often called *zapping*) your PRAM/NVRAM, restart your Mac and press ⌘+Option+P+R (that's four keys, so good luck; it's okay to use your nose) until your Mac restarts itself. It's kind of like a hiccup. You might see the spinning-disc pointer for a minute or two while your Mac thinks about it. Then the icon disappears, and your Mac chimes again (unless your Mac is one of the recent models, which, sadly, are chimeless) and restarts. Most power users believe that you should zap more than once, letting the Mac chime two, three, or even four times before releasing the keys and allowing the start-up process to proceed.

Now restart your Mac without holding down any keys. If the PRAM/NVRAM zap didn't fix your Mac, move on to "Step 4: Reinstalling macOS."

REMEMBER

Your chosen start-up disk, time zone, and sound volume may be reset to their default values when you zap your PRAM. So after zapping, open the System Settings app to reselect your usual start-up disk and time zone, and set the sound volume the way you like it if necessary.

Step 4: Reinstalling macOS

Reinstalling macOS is a second-to-last resort when your Mac won't boot correctly because it takes the longest and is the biggest hassle. Apple has a technical note on reinstallation at https://support.apple.com/en-us/HT204904.

Follow the instructions, taking care *not* to erase your disk before you reinstall macOS. As long as you don't erase the disk before you reinstall, you won't lose a drop of data. This procedure simply installs a fresh copy of Ventura; it doesn't affect your files, settings, or anything else.

Step 5: Things to try before taking your Mac in for repair

TIP

To get your Mac up and running again, you can try one of the following:

>> **Call the tech-support hotline.** Before you drag your Mac down to the shop, try calling 1-800-SOS-APPL, the Apple Tech Support hotline. The service representatives there may be able to suggest something else that you can try. If your Mac is still under warranty, it's even free.

>> **Ask a local user group for help.** Another thing you might consider is contacting your local Mac user group. You can find a group of Mac users near you by visiting Apple's User Group web pages at www.apple.com/ usergroups.

If neither suggestion works for you, and you're still seeing anything you shouldn't when you start up your Mac, you have big trouble. You could have any one of the following problems:

>> Your Mac's hard drive is dead.

>> Your Mac has some other type of hardware failure.

>> All your Mac's start-up disks are defective (unlikely).

The bottom line: If you still can't start up normally after trying all the cures explained in this chapter, you almost certainly need to have your Mac serviced by a qualified technician.

If Your Mac Crashes at Startup

Startup crashes are other bad things that can happen to your Mac. These crashes can be more of a hassle to resolve than prohibitory-sign problems, but they're rarely fatal.

You know that a *crash* has happened when you see a Quit Unexpectedly dialog, a frozen cursor, a frozen screen, or any other disabling event. A *start-up crash* happens when your system shows a crash symptom any time between the moment you flick the power key or switch (or restarting) and the moment you have full use of the desktop.

Try all the steps in the preceding sections *before* you panic. The easiest way to fix start-up crashes (in most cases) is to reinstall macOS from the Recovery partition. Again, Apple details this procedure online at `https://support.apple.com/en-us/HT204904`.

If you're still unsuccessful after that point, read "Step 5: Things to try before taking your Mac in for repair."

Managing Storage with the Storage Feature

macOS's Storage feature provides assistance if your start-up disk gets close to being full.

Here's why it's in the troubleshooting chapter, in case you're wondering: Your Mac will slow to a crawl as your start-up disk gets close to full. If your Mac's start-up disk is more than 90 percent filled, you'll begin to experience slowness and jerkiness. And as the drive approaches 100 percent fullness, things grow even slower and jerkier.

Managing Storage aims to help you out as your disk fills up by scanning for duplicates, old email attachments, and downloads so you can delete them or move them to the cloud. But you should read what follows even if your disk isn't approaching fullness right now, because Optimize Storage offers several options that may keep your disk from ever getting too full.

To check it out, choose ⇨ System Settings, click the General button to display the General pane, and then click the Storage button to display the Storage pane (see Figure 23-2). The Recommendations section provides suggestions, such as the following, for fixing your Mac's storage woes:

>> **Store in iCloud.** Store all your files in iCloud to save space, keeping only recently opened files on your Mac when storage space is needed.

WARNING

Storing files in iCloud could be convenient, but it's going to chew through your 5GB of free iCloud storage in no time. With additional iCloud storage currently selling for 99 cents a month (50GB), $3.99 a month (200GB), or $9.99 a month (2TB), it could be costly as well as convenient.

>> **Optimize storage.** Remove from your Mac movies and TV shows you've already watched.

>> **Erase Trash automatically.** Automatically empty files that have been in the Trash for 30 days.

>> **Recommendations for individual apps and categories.** This section lists categories, such as Applications and Documents, and individual apps, such as Mail and Messages, where you might be able to save some space. Click the Info icon (the i in a circle) to open a dialog that explains the possibilities for that category or app.

When your Mac's disk runs low on space, work your way through the recommendations on the Storage screen to make sure that the shortage never becomes critical.

FIGURE 23-2:
If your disk is
getting full, use
the Storage
recommenda-
tions to free
space.

6

The Part of Tens

Find ways to speed up a pokey Mac.

Get a list of awesome Mac websites worthy of your attention.

Chapter **24**

Ten Ways to Speed Up Your Mac Experience

This chapter is for speed demons only. At some time in their Mac lives, most users have wished that their machines would work faster — even if their Macs have multiple cores or processors. I can't help you make your Mac's processors any faster, but here's where I cover some ways to make your Mac at least *seem* faster. Better still, at least some of these tips won't cost you one red cent.

Use Those Keyboard Shortcuts

Keyboard shortcuts (see Table 24-1 for a nice little list of the most useful ones) can make navigating your Mac a much faster experience compared with constantly using the mouse, offering these benefits:

>> If you use keyboard shortcuts, your hands stay focused on the keyboard, reducing the amount of time that you remove your hand from the keyboard to fiddle with the mouse or trackpad.

>> If you memorize keyboard shortcuts with your head, your fingers will memorize them too.

>> The more keyboard shortcuts you use, the faster you can do what you're doing.

Using the keyboard shortcuts for commands you use often will save you a ton of effort and hours upon hours of time.

TIP

Make a list of keyboard shortcuts you want to memorize, and tape it to your monitor until your brain and fingers memorize them. Or photograph and print Table 24-1 and tape it to your monitor! Learn 'em once, and you'll save time with them forever!

TABLE 24-1   Great Keyboard Shortcuts

Keyboard Shortcut	Name	What It Does
⌘+O	Open	Opens the selected item.
⌘+. (period)	Cancel	Cancels the current operation in many apps, including Finder. The Esc key often does the same thing as Cancel.
⌘+P	Print	Brings up a dialog that enables you to print the active window's contents. (See Chapter 19 for info on printing.)
⌘+X	Cut	Cuts whatever you select and places it on the Clipboard. (Chapter 9 covers the Clipboard.)
⌘+C	Copy	Copies whatever you select and places it on the Clipboard.
⌘+V	Paste	Pastes the contents of the Clipboard at your cursor's location.
⌘+F	Find	Displays a Searching window or tab in Finder; displays a Find dialog in most other apps.
⌘+A	Select All	Selects the entire contents of the active window in many apps, including Finder.
⌘+Z	Undo	Undoes the last thing you did in many apps, including Finder.
⌘+Shift+Z	Redo	Redoes the last thing you undid in many apps, including Finder.
⌘+Shift+?	Help	Displays the Mac Help window in Finder; usually the shortcut to summon Help in other apps.
⌘+Q	Quit	Perhaps the most useful keyboard shortcut of all. Quits the current app (but not Finder because it's always running).
⌘+Shift+Q	Log Out	Logs out the current user. The login window appears onscreen until a user logs in.
⌘+Delete	Move to Trash	Moves the selected item to the Trash.
⌘+Shift+Delete	Empty Trash	Empties the Trash.

Improve Your Typing Skills

One way to make your Mac seem faster is to move your fingers faster. The quicker you finish a task, the quicker you're on to something else. Keyboard shortcuts are nifty tools, but improving your typing speed and accuracy *will* save you even more time. As a bonus, the more your typing skills improve, the less time you'll spend correcting errors. So you'll finish everything even faster!

TIP

The speed and accuracy that you gain have another bonus: When you're a touch typist, your fingers fly even faster on keyboard shortcuts, speeding them up even further.

The best and easiest way I know to improve your keyboarding skills is a typing training app for your Mac such as Ten Thumbs Typing Tutor ($25.99 at www. tenthumbstypingtutor.com), any of the myriad typing-instruction apps in the Mac App Store (search for *typing*), or a free typing-instruction website such as TypingTest (free at www.typingtest.com), which also offers free typing speed tests if you're curious.

TIP

While we're talking about keyboarding skills, make sure your keyboard is up to the job. If your Mac is a MacBook, you're likely stuck with the built-in keyboard while you're out and about; but when you dock your MacBook at home to use your external monitors (more on this shortly), you can connect most any keyboard you like — a 40 percent keyboard, a 60 percent keyboard, a full-size keyboard, an ergonomic keyboard, or even a split keyboard. The keyboard can be wired or wireless — whichever works better for you. If you have a desktop Mac, you can use your preferred keyboard all the time.

Use Text Replacements and Automatic Correction

No matter how fast and how accurately you type, you can enter text even faster by taking advantage of the Text Replacement feature built into macOS and similar automatic-correction features, such as the AutoCorrect feature in the Microsoft Office apps. With these features, you define each term you want to have replaced automatically, such as having *eavpsm* replaced with *Executive Assistant to the Vice-President of Sales & Marketing*. Then, when you type that term, the feature automatically replaces it with the replacement. You need never type your job title fully again.

To set up your terms in the Text Replacement feature, click System Settings on the Dock, click Keyboard in the sidebar in the System Settings window, click Text Replacements in the Keyboard pane, and then work in the dialog that opens.

Change Your Resolution

A setting that you can change to potentially improve your Mac's performance is the resolution of your monitor. Most modern monitors and video hardware can display multiple degrees of screen resolution. You change your monitor's display resolution in the Displays pane in System Settings. Click the Displays item in the sidebar, click the Scaled button for the display, and then select a resolution to try from the list that appears. You may need to set the Show All Resolutions switch to On to unearth the resolution that suits you.

Each LCD or LED screen has a "native resolution" specified by the number of pixels in its width and its height. The MacBook Air M2's LED screen, for example, is 2,560 pixels wide by 1,664 pixels high. macOS normally uses the native resolution, as it gives the best image in theory, because the pixels sent to the screen map exactly to the physical pixels in the screen. But that doesn't mean that the native resolution will suit you best. You see many more items on the screen at native resolution, but you can make everything bigger by switching to a lower resolution, or make everything smaller (and see more of it) at a higher resolution.

How will this speed up your Mac? Well, for one thing, if you can't discern icons on toolbars and other app components, using a lower resolution may enhance your work speed. Or if you can read more lines of smaller text comfortably at a higher resolution, that will save you time too.

REMEMBER

Choose a resolution based on what looks best and works best for you. If things on the screen are too big or too small at your current resolution, try a higher or lower resolution until you find one that feels just right.

Finally, click Accessibility in the sidebar to display the Accessibility pane, and then click Zoom in the Vision list to display the Zoom pane. Here, you can enable keyboard shortcuts to zoom in and out instantly, and Hover Text, a highly configurable mode that enlarges only what's under your pointer.

Buy a Faster Mac

Apple keeps putting out faster and faster Macs at lower and lower prices, and all current Macs now ship with at least 8GB of RAM. Although 4GB may be enough RAM to run macOS Ventura, if you like to keep more than one or two apps running all the time, it's not enough to run it at its best.

Check out the latest Macs with Apple's M processors — they're speedy and powerful. There are currently MacBook Air, MacBook Pro, iMac, and Mac mini models, plus the new Mac Studio, which delivers a huge amount of computing power in a small form factor. Alternatively, you might get a bargain on a used Intel-based Mac that's still faster than yours. eBay (https://www.ebay.com) has hundreds of used Macs up for auction at any given time.

TIP

Another excellent option is to visit the Apple website's refurbished and clearance section. You can frequently save hundreds of dollars by purchasing a slightly used Mac that has been refurbished to factory specifications by Apple. Another advantage to Apple refurbs is that they come with an Apple warranty. If you're on a tight budget, definitely check it out (www.apple.com/shop/refurbished).

Add RAM

Your Mac can never have too much RAM, and it will run better, smoother, and faster with at least 8GB of RAM. If you have an older Mac, you may be able to add RAM at a reasonable price. You can find instructions in your User Guide booklet or on the Apple Technical Support pages (https://support.apple.com/; search for *RAM upgrade* and your Mac model).

These days, most (or all) Macs are no longer user-upgradeable. These models are sometimes difficult to open, and Apple frowns upon users opening some models at all. Plus, many Macs have the RAM soldered to the motherboard or integrated with the processor, which means they can't ever be upgraded. If your Mac is upgradeable and you're uncomfortable with upgrading RAM yourself, opt for the services of an authorized, certified Mac cracker-opener.

TIP

The bottom line is that it's best to order your Mac with as much RAM as you can afford in the first place. It will cost you more up front, but it's worth it in the long run.

Add a Second Display

For almost as long as I've been using a Mac, I've used one with two or more displays. All Macs today support a second monitor, and many support a third and fourth monitor. I find four monitors great, but I have to admit I'm tempted by the Mac Pro, which supports a full dozen displays. In my opinion, screen real estate is among the biggest productivity enhancers you can add — right up there with typing faster.

Screen real estate is the holy grail when working in multiwindowed or multipaletted apps such as Photoshop, Final Cut Pro, and Logic Pro X. Multiple monitors are also great when you're working with two or more apps at the same time. With sufficient screen real estate, you can arrange all the windows and palettes for all apps in the way that's most expedient to the way you work.

You don't need an expensive 4K or 5K monitor, great though these can be. For a couple of hundred bucks, you can find a second display that will double your screen real estate. Or if you have an iPad of recent vintage, read the next section.

Use Your iPad as an Extra Display

The Sidecar feature allows you to use a late-model iPad as an extra screen for your late-model Mac. You'll find the official list of supported hardware and tips for using Sidecar at https://support.apple.com/en-us/HT210380. Or just connect your iPad to your Mac with a USB cable, open System Settings, and then click Displays in the sidebar. In the Displays pane, click the Add (+) pop-up menu to the right of the thumbnails for your current displays, and then click the iPad in the Mirror or Extend To list. Your iPad appears as a thumbnail along with your other displays, and you can click the thumbnail to display the controls for configuring the iPad's display settings.

If the iPad doesn't appear on the Mirror or Extend To list, make sure that the iPad and your Mac are both signed in to the same iCloud account.

When you've chosen settings for the iPad as a display, click the Arrange button at the bottom of the Displays pane to open the Arrange Displays dialog. Here, drag the thumbnails for the iPad and the other displays into an arrangement that reflects their physical positioning. Then you'll be able to move the pointer off a display and straight onto the iPad for easy navigation.

Upgrade to a Solid-State Drive (SSD)

The latest and greatest storage device to appear is the solid-state drive (SSD). It uses flash memory in place of a mechanical hard drive's spinning platters, which means, among other things, that it has no moving parts. Another benefit is that an SSD performs most operations at up to twice the speed of mechanical drives.

The bad news is that an SSD is more expensive — three or more times the price per gigabyte — than a mechanical hard drive or a hybrid drive with the same capacity. That said, most users report that it's the best money they ever spent on an upgrade. So if your Mac's hard drive dies, look to replace it with an SSD.

If your Mac is a model that requires pro skills and tools to open it, plus an oxyacetylene torch (okay, a soldering kit) to replace the drive, you can even use an external SSD as a temporary fix.

After switching to an SSD start-up drive — internal or external — your old Mac will feel almost new again.

Get More Storage

Your Mac will run slower and slower as its start-up disk gets fuller and fuller. If you can't afford to replace your start-up disk with a bigger SSD or purchase a bigger external SSD to use as a boot disk, another option is to get a big external hard disk (much less expensive per megabyte than an SSD) and move some of your data off your start-up disk and onto the external disk.

You can connect external hard disks (or SSDs) via USB or Thunderbolt. All Mac models that can run macOS Ventura have either USB 3 and Thunderbolt 2 or USB 4 and Thunderbolt 3. Usually, a single USB-C port provides both the USB and Thunderbolt connectivity.

To check which versions of USB and Thunderbolt your Mac has, follow these steps:

1. Click to open the Apple menu.

2. Press Option to display the System Information command in place of the About This Mac command.

3. Click System Information to open the System Information app.

4. In the sidebar, expand the Hardware category if it's collapsed.

5. Toward the bottom of the Hardware category, look at the Thunderbolt/USB4 item and the USB item.

TECHNICAL STUFF

Thunderbolt is faster than USB 3 and USB 4, but relatively few Thunderbolt devices are available, and most of them are more expensive than their USB 3 and USB 4 counterparts. This means a USB 3 or USB 4 device is usually a better choice than a Thunderbolt device. Unless the disk is preformatted for a PC and requires reformatting, there's nothing more you have to do!

Whether you get a USB device or a Thunderbolt device, you can usually just plug it in to your Mac's USB-C/Thunderbolt port and start using it. Depending on the cable the drive has, you may need a USB-C adapter, or a USB-C hub or dock, to make the connection.

Once you've connected your external disk, you can move data to it from your Mac's start-up disk. So copy the files or folders (your large files and folders are likely contained in your Pictures, Music, and Documents folders) to the new external disk; confirm that the files have been copied properly; make sure you have a backup, just in case; and then delete the files from your start-up disk.

Chapter **25**

Ten Great Websites for Mac Freaks

As much as I would like to believe that this book tells you everything you need to know about using your Mac, I know better. There's much more to discover about using your Mac, and new tools and products come out every day.

The best way to gather more information than you could ever possibly soak up about all things Mac is to hop onto the web. There, you can find news, *freeware* and *shareware* (try-before-you-buy software) to download, troubleshooting sites, tons of news and information about your new favorite OS, and lots of places to shop.

The sites in this chapter are the best, most chock-full-o'-stuff places on the web for Mac users. By the time you finish checking out these websites, you'll know so much about your Mac and macOS that you'll feel like your brain is in danger of exploding. On the other hand, you might just feel a whole lot smarter. Happy surfing!

Macworld

https://www.macworld.com

Although the print publication and exposition became extinct years ago, the Macworld site still describes itself as "your best source for all things Apple." And it's still true, more or less. Macworld is perhaps the best and most comprehensive source of product information for Apple products. It's especially strong for reviews of Mac, iPhone, and iPad products. When you want to know which inkjet printer or digital camera is the best in its price class, for example, Macworld can almost certainly offer guidance, feature comparison charts, and real-world test results. And you won't merely find product information here — you'll find it accompanied by expert opinions and professional editing and fact-checking.

TidBITS

https://tidbits.com

TidBITS is an online newsletter and website with the motto "Thoughtful, detailed coverage of everything Apple for 32 years." With some of the richest and most insightful writing on the web, TidBITS is another must-read for me. TidBITS publishes a new issue every Monday but also posts articles regularly throughout the week. You can subscribe to receive the email newsletter containing a handful of the top articles, or you can become a member to support the site.

The Mac Observer

https://www.macobserver.com

The Mac Observer gives you Apple news, views, reviews, and much more. TMO (as insiders refer to it) is known for insightful opinion pieces in addition to Apple news and product reviews.

iMore

https://www.imore.com

If you live the Apple lifestyle, iMore is your go-to website. With in-depth articles on all Apple products and operating systems, and tons of tips, hints, and tutorials as well, iMore is a great way to keep yourself informed and up to date.

AppleWorld.Today

```
https://www.appleworld.today
```

For the latest in Mac news, updated every single day, check out AppleWorld.Today, which arose from the ashes of The Unofficial Apple Weblog (TUAW) after its untimely demise. With a small staff of Apple newshounds, this site keeps you on the bleeding edge of Mac news — including software updates, virus alerts, and Apple happenings. It also offers extensive and unbiased reviews of many products soon after their release.

Wirecutter

```
https://www.nytimes.com/wirecutter/
```

Wirecutter is a great place to learn what others consider the best peripherals, tech tools, and toys. Now a *New York Times* company, Wirecutter has the resources to objectively evaluate many products and declare one of them the best.

Wirecutter covers a vast range of products, which it divides into categories ranging from Kitchen, Health & Fitness, and Baby & Kid through to Software & Apps, Cars, and Money. If you're after Mac-related information, Software & Apps, Electronics, and Office are good places to start.

Apple Support

```
https://support.apple.com/
```

Do you have a technical question about any version of macOS or any Apple product — including Ventura? March your question right over to the Apple Support page, where you can find searchable archives of tech notes, software update information, and documentation. The Support pages are especially useful if you need info about your old Mac; Apple archives all its info here. Choose among a preset list of topics or products, and type a keyword to research. You're rewarded with a list of helpful documents. Clicking any of these entries (they're all links) takes you right to the info you seek. The site even has tools that can help narrow your search.

The site also offers a section with user discussions of Apple-related topics. Although not officially sanctioned or monitored by Apple, this section is often the best place to gain insights, especially on slightly esoteric or obscure issues not covered in other sections of the site.

Other World Computing

https://eshop.macsales.com/

Other World Computing is the go-to place for Mac peripherals and upgrades, as if offers a great selection of RAM, hard drives, SSDs, optical drives, video cards, processor upgrades, cables, discs, and docks. If it enhances your Mac, Other World Computing probably has it at a reasonable price. And, if it's memory or internal storage, you'll usually get a comprehensive illustrated installation manual and (often) an installation video as well.

Because of its inexpensive and reliable delivery and a solid guarantee on every item it sells, you can't go wrong doing business with OWC.

Apple's Refurbished and Clearance Store

https://www.apple.com/shop/refurbished

I'm sure you've noticed that Apple products are rarely discounted. The price is about the same regardless of where you buy one of their devices. That's why whenever I need *any* Apple product, the first place I shop is the Apple Refurbished and Clearance page.

Apple refurbished products are like new, with the same one-year limited warranty as new devices. Refurbished iOS devices include a new battery and outer shell, and each device includes all appropriate accessories, cables, and operating system. Refurbished products are eligible for AppleCare and include free shipping (and returns). Savings are well worth having and can be up to 30 percent.

If you don't see a refurbished device with the specifications you're looking for, try again later (or tomorrow) because inventory is updated throughout the day. Better yet, you can use the Refurb Tracker website (`https://refurb-tracker.com`) to set a free alert for when the item you want becomes available.

Six Colors

`https://sixcolors.com`

Six Colors provides daily coverage of Apple, other technology companies, and the intersection of technology and culture. Its founder and editor-in-chief is Jason Snell, who was editor-in-chief of Macworld for more than a decade. Along with former Macworld writer and senior editor Dan Moren and a cast of stellar contributors, Six Colors provides timely analysis, insightful reviews, and expert commentary on all things Apple (and some things not).

Index

M

About the Author

Guy Hart-Davis is the author of more than 180 computer books, including *Teach Yourself VISUALLY iPhone 14*, *Teach Yourself VISUALLY MacBook Pro & MacBook Air*, and *Teach Yourself VISUALLY Google Workspace*.

Dedication

I dedicate this book to the memory of Robert M. Thomas, a great host, raconteur, author, and friend.

Author's Acknowledgments

My thanks go to the great team at Wiley, especially the following: Steve Hayes for asking me to update this book, Elizabeth Stilwell for arranging the contract, Thomas Hill for developing the book and managing the project, Keir Simpson for skilful copy editing, Dwight Spivey for brave efforts to keep the book on the technical straight and narrow, [layout] for laying out the book, and Debbye Butler for scrutinizing the pages and resolving problems.

Publisher's Acknowledgments

Executive Editor: Steve Hayes
Project Editor: Thomas Hill
Copy Editor: Keir Simpson
Technical Editor: Dwight Spivey

Sr. Editorial Assistant: Cherie Case
Proofreader: Debbye Butler
Production Editor: Mohammed Zafar Ali
Cover Image:
   © You Touch Pix of EuToch/Shutterstock

Take dummies with you everywhere you go!

Whether you are excited about e-books, want more from the web, must have your mobile apps, or are swept up in social media, dummies makes everything easier.

Find us online!

dummies.com

Leverage the power

Dummies is the global leader in the reference category and one of the most trusted and highly regarded brands in the world. No longer just focused on books, customers now have access to the dummies content they need in the format they want. Together we'll craft a solution that engages your customers, stands out from the competition, and helps you meet your goals.

Advertising & Sponsorships

Connect with an engaged audience on a powerful multimedia site, and position your message alongside expert how-to content. Dummies.com is a one-stop shop for free, online information and know-how curated by a team of experts.

- Targeted ads
- Video
- Email Marketing
- Microsites
- Sweepstakes sponsorship

20 MILLION PAGE VIEWS EVERY SINGLE MONTH

15 MILLION UNIQUE VISITORS PER MONTH

43% OF ALL VISITORS ACCESS THE SITE VIA THEIR MOBILE DEVICES

700,000 NEWSLETTER SUBSCRIPTIONS TO THE INBOXES OF *300,000* UNIQUE INDIVIDUALS EVERY WEEK

# of dummies

Custom Publishing

Reach a global audience in any language by creating a solution that will differentiate you from competitors, amplify your message, and encourage customers to make a buying decision.

- Apps
- Books
- eBooks
- Video
- Audio
- Webinars

Brand Licensing & Content

Leverage the strength of the world's most popular reference brand to reach new audiences and channels of distribution.

For more information, visit **dummies.com/biz**

PERSONAL ENRICHMENT

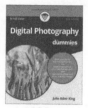

9781119187790	9781119179030	9781119293354	9781119293347	9781119310068	9781119235606
USA $26.00	USA $21.99	USA $24.99	USA $22.99	USA $22.99	USA $24.99
CAN $31.99	CAN $25.99	CAN $29.99	CAN $27.99	CAN $27.99	CAN $29.99
UK £19.99	UK £16.99	UK £17.99	UK £16.99	UK £16.99	UK £17.99

9781119251163	9781119235491	9781119279952	9781119283133	9781119287117	9781119130246
USA $24.99	USA $26.99	USA $24.99	USA $24.99	USA $24.99	USA $22.99
CAN $29.99	CAN $31.99	CAN $29.99	CAN $29.99	CAN $29.99	CAN $27.99
UK £17.99	UK £19.99	UK £17.99	UK £17.99	UK £16.99	UK £16.99

PROFESSIONAL DEVELOPMENT

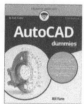

9781119311041	9781119255796	9781119293439	9781119281467	9781119280651	9781119251132	9781119310563
USA $24.99	USA $39.99	USA $26.99	USA $26.99	USA $29.99	USA $24.99	USA $34.00
CAN $29.99	CAN $47.99	CAN $31.99	CAN $31.99	CAN $35.99	CAN $29.99	CAN $41.99
UK £17.99	UK £27.99	UK £19.99	UK £19.99	UK £21.99	UK £17.99	UK £24.99

9781119181705	9781119263593	9781119257769	9781119293477	9781119265313	9781119239314	9781119293323
USA $29.99	USA $26.99	USA $29.99	USA $26.99	USA $24.99	USA $29.99	USA $29.99
CAN $35.99	CAN $31.99	CAN $35.99	CAN $31.99	CAN $29.99	CAN $35.99	CAN $35.99
UK £21.99	UK £19.99	UK £21.99	UK £19.99	UK £17.99	UK £21.99	UK £21.99